REGIONAL ECONOMIC INTEGRATION : A COMPARATIVE STUDY OF CENTRAL ASIAN AND SOUTH ASIAN REGIONS

REGIONAL ECONOMIC INTERGRATION
A Comparative of Central Asian and South Asian Regions

SAROJ RANI

PUBLICATIONS

KALPAZ PUBLICATIONS

DELHI-110052

Regional Economic Integration : A Comparative Study of Central Asian and South Asian Regions

Rs. 850

ISBN: 978-81-7835-731-7

Published in 2009 in India by
Kalpaz Publications
C-30, Satyawati Nagar,
Delhi-110052
E-mail: kalpaz@hotmail.com
Phone : 9212729499

Lasser Type Setting by: Rudra Computer Graphics, Delhi
Printed at : G. Print Process, Delhi

Dedicated
to
My Husband and Children

Contents

List of Tables

List of Figures

List of Maps

List of Boxes

Abbreviations

ADB	Asian Development Bank
ADO	Asian Development Outlook
AFTA	ASEAN Free Trade Area
AEC	ASEAN Economic Community
APEC	Asia-Pacific Economic Cooperation
ASEAN	Association of Southeast Asian Nations
BIMSTEC	Bay of Bengal Initiative for Multi-Sectoral Technical and Economic Cooperation
BTAs	Bilateral Trade Agreements
BTC	Baku- Tablisi Cyhen Pipeline
CAR	Central Asian Republics
CAC	Central Asian Community
CACO	Central Asian Cooperation Organisation
CAEU	Central Asian Economic Union
CAFTA	Central Asian Free Trade Area
CAREC	Central Asian Regional Economic Cooperation
CASAREM	Central Asia–South Asia Regional Electricity Market
CECA	Comprehensive Economic Cooperation Agreement
CEECs	Central and East European Countries
CEPA	Comprehensive Economic Partnership Agreement
CIS	Commonwealth of Independent States
CMEA	Council of Mutual Economic Assistance
CM	Common Market
COMESA	Common Market for Eastern & Southern Africa
CPC	Caspian Pipeline Consortium

CPSU	Communist Party of Soviet Union
CSATTF	Central and South Asian Transport and Trade Forum
CU	Custom Union
EBRD	European Bank for Reconstruction and Development
EC	European Commission
ECO	Economic Cooperation Organisation
EEA	European Economic Area
EU	European Union
FDI	Foreign Direct Investment
ESCAP	Economic and Social Commission for Asia and the Pacific
FTA	Free Trade Agreement
FSU	Former Soviet Union
GATT	General Agreement on Tariffs and Trade
GATS	General Agreement on Trade in Services
GCC	Greater Central Asian Countries
GDP	Gross Domestic Product
GMS	Greater Mekong Sub-Region
GPN	Global Production Networks
GSP	Generalized System of Preferences
GUUAM	Georgia, Uzbekistan, Ukraine, Azerbaijan and Moldova
ICT	Information and Communication Technology
IDSA	Indian Defence Strategical Analysis
IDB	Islamic Development Bank
ILFTA	Indo-Lanka Free Trade Area
IMF	International Monetary Fund
IMU	Islamic Movements of Uzbekistan
IOR-ARC	Indian Ocean Rim Associations for Regional Cooperation
IPR	Intellectual Property Rights
IT	Information Technology
LDCs	Least Developed Countries
MERCOSUR	Mercado Comn del Cono Sur (Southern come common Market)
MCWG	Multi-Country Working Group
MFN	Most Favored Nation

MOUs	Memorandum of Understanding
MW	Megga Watt
NAFTA	North American Free Trade Agreement
NGOs	Non Government Organisations
NTBs	Non Tariffs Barriers
OEC	Organisation for Economic Cooperation
OECD	Organization for Economic Cooperation and Development
OIC	Organization of Islamic Conference
QRs	Quantitative Restrictions
PRC	Peoples of Republic of China
PRGF	Poverty Reduction and Growth Facility
PTA	Preferential Trade Agreement
REER	Real Effective Exchange Rate
REI	Regional Economic Integration
RBI	Reserve Bank of India
ROO	Rules of Origin
RTA	Regional Trade Agreement
RTIA	Regional Trade Investment Agreement
SAARC	South Asia Association for Regional Cooperation
SACU	South Asian Customs Union
SAPTA	South Asian Preferential Trade Agreement
SAFTA	South Asian Free Trade Agreement
SAF	Structural Adjustment Facility
SALs	Sectoral Adjustment Loans
SCO	Shangai Cooperation Organisation
SCP	South Caucasus Pipeline
SES	Single Economic Space
SPECA	Special Program for Economies of Central Asia
SPS	Sanitary and Phyto-Sanitary Standards
TAPI	Turkmenistan, Afghanistan, Pakistan India Pipeline
TBT	Technical Barriers to Trade
TF	Trade Facilitation
TIFA	Trade Investment Framework Agreement
TRIPS	Trade Related Aspects of Intellectual Property Rights
UN	United Nations

UNCTAD	United Nation Commission for Trade and Development
UNDP	United Nations Development Program
UNESCAP	United Nations Economic and Social Commission for Asia and the Pacific
US	United States
VAT	Value Added Tax
WB	World Bank
WTO	World Trade Organization

Preface

The purpose of this study is to understand the problems faced by The Central Asian and South Asian Countries during their liberalization, and regional economic integration process. This book analyses and compares the regional economic integration in Central Asia and South Asia. The first Chapter broadly covers the global trends towards increasing regional economic integration. It mainly covers the theoretical aspects of the regional economic integration and will try to summarise the debate whether regional trade agreements are stumbling blocks or building blocks of global trade liberalisation. The Second Chapter covers the economic liberalisation policies of the Central Asian and South Asian regions. Broadly this presents cross-country analysis of economic policy regimes in both the regions in the last fifteen years. Specifically this chapter analyses the trade policies in both the regions. In the third Chapter this study describes and analyses all the regional/ bilateral and multilateral attempts towards regional integration in the Central Asian republics since 1992. It shows the significance, challenges and opportunities in regional economic co-operation in the Central Asian region. Fourth Chapter describes and analyses all the regional/ bilateral and multilateral attempts towards regional integration in the South Asian region particularly since the early 1980's. It shows the significance, challenges and opportunities in regional economic co-operation in the South Asian region. In the fifth Chapter, this study compares objectives, significance, progress and obstacles in the process of regional economic integration of both Central and South Asian regions. The Sixth Chapter deals with the possibilities/ obstacles of the expansion of South Asian economic co-operation to the Central Asian region. Importance of other countries like Iran and Afghanistan might also be discussed in this context. This book is on the doctorate thesis based topic "Regional Economic

Integration: A Comparative Study of Central Asian & South Asian Regions". In Conclusions, major findings of the this study are summarized. I wanted to acknowledge many persons who helped me while doing this study.

I owe my deep sense of gratitude to my respected supervisor, Dr. Tahir Asghar who rendered his constructive and valuable guidance throughout my work. However, any errors are solely mine.

I feel great privilege in expressing my profound sense of gratitude to Prof. Tulsi Ram Chairman Centre for Russian and Central Asian Studies (CRCAS) whose affectionate consideration of my difficulties, keen interest, constant support and encouragement were the main source of inspiration. His sincerity and co-operative nature helped me immensely to conduct the present study.

I wish to express my sincere thanks to Dr. Gulshan Sachdeva whose perspicacious comment and scholarly guidance helped me to complete my work. I thank to all my faculty members of the Centre for Russian and Central Asian Studies, who rendered invaluable help. I would like to thank the non-teaching staff of our Centre and library.

I also acknowledge the moral support of my husband Rahul Kumar and my children Gaurav and Saurabh who helped in this research work to be completed through their insistence that it be done and their patience while I did it. I express my heartfelt gratitude to my beloved parents. I wish to express my inestimable appreciation to my friends, Ritu Mathur, Kajal, Arti, Alka, Usha, Meena, Manisha, Sudhir and Laxmi for providing me a precious time whenever I need to share my pleasant and unpleasant moments while undergoing this process. Special thanks to Pushpa, my maid servant who kept me away from my domestic chores. I also acknowledge the support of the staffs of JNU Library and the staff of Exim Bank Library for helping me to get relevant materials. I express my gratitude adequately for Prof. S.K. Thorat. Prof. Ajay Patnaik, Prof. Anuradha Chenoy, Prof. Shashikant Jha, Prof. Manmohan Aggarwal, Dr. Nawal Paswan, Dr. Sanjay Panday, Dr. Preeti Dass and Mr. Som Nath Sharma and Dr. Namita, Sh. L.R. Balley, Editor Bheem Patrika, Jalandhar, for their encouragement.

15th August 2008 **Saroj Rani**

Abstract

Regional Economic Integration is a pervasive phenomenon shaping the global environment. A major element behind the growth of economic regionalism is the emergence of trade and investment agreements. Regional integration among developing countries is also part of a wider strategy to promote not only equitable growth but also increase competition, reduce private transaction costs, enable firms to exploit economies of scale, encourage inward foreign investment and facilitate macroeconomic policy coordination. Regional economic integration has been emerging in the world in various stages or forms. Normally the first stage is P*referential Tariff (trade) Arrangements*. This is a simple form of regional economic co-operation under which lower tariffs and non-tariff preferential treatments are provided to the commodities coming from member countries compared to non-member countries. Each country is allowed to have its own set of tariffs and non- tariffs against the third country imports. The second stage is F*ree Trade Area arrangements,* which normally means no tariff among the member countries. The third stage is called the C*ustom Union,* which involves common external tariff in addition to free trade arrangements. Next stage is C*ommon Market*, which adds free mobility of factors of production to custom union arrangements. The fifth stage is E*conomic Union* that goes beyond common market by harmonising economic policies of member countries. Finally, the stage of economic integration, a move towards complete unification of economic policies of member states as a consequence reduction of their independence in economic matters. The growth of regional economic blocs or Regional Trade Agreements (RTA) in the past decades has become a significant aspect of global economic relations.

The concept of regional trade arrangements was formed during the sixth session of United Nations General Assembly in June 1974. In fact, the genesis of regional trading blocs might be traced back to the establishment of New International Economic Order. The objective behind this was to encourage the trade among the developing countries (Bhatacharya, 2001). By definition, RTAs are agreements whereby members accord preferential treatment to one another in respect to trade barriers. RTAs vary in the level of integration among participating nation states.

A new strong wind of regionalization of trade and other economic relations has been blowing in the global economy since late the 1980s. As of July 2007, 380 RTA, have been notified to the GATT/WTO of these 300 RTAs were notified under Art. 24 of the GATT 1947 or GATT 1994; 22 under the Enabling Clauses; 58 under Art V of the GATS At the same date, 205 agreements were in force. (Sighted on dated 13th Sep 2008 at www.wto.org). It is believed that RTAs could serve as a stepping stone towards multilateral trade agreements. Among the important developments in recently concluded RTAs is that they are going beyond the tariff cutting exercises. Many of them also include services, investments, intellectual properties, technical barrier to trade, dispute settlement etc.

There has been a debate among scholars on issues like, whether RTAs are complementary to multilateral trading system or not. In addition, there is a huge literature in international economics and international political economy on the relationship between regional and global integration. Indeed, this debate spills over to a substantial degree into the policy domain where the virtues and vices of 'open' and 'closed' regionalism are debated The predecessor of WTO, GATT provided some exceptions to set up Regional Trade Agreements under the article 24 of WTO. The WTO has also set up a committee to monitor developments regarding RTAs. Under some circumstances, regional groupings are important to reduce tariffs and other barriers within the region. Still, they are hurdles in the way of multilateral trading system as they break the principle of equal treatment for all trading partners by setting up custom unions and free trade areas.

Are they building blocs or stumbling blocs to the multilateral trading system? Advocates of RTAs argue on the basis of gains from economies of scale, competition and attraction of FDI. The classical economists such as Ricardo, Adam Smith and modern economists like Herbler were also in favour of the free trade policy (Salvatore, 2001). The change of ideas and technology can increase the production capacity. UN officials on trade have been regularly discussing the merits of regional trade during the Trade and Development Board sessions. UNCTAD officials also meet annually in Geneva to review and examine global economic trends from a trade and development perspective. According to their former UNCTAD Secretary General Rubens Ricupero, regionalism is the only path available for many developing countries to integrate into world economy. He asserted that the best way to learn to compete is by competing, and initially competition should be among the neighbouring states. Carlo Trojan of the European Commission (EC) also believes that regionalism and multilateralism are complementary notions that reinforce each other as long as regionalism is open. Baldwin (1992), Either (1998) and Lawrence (1999) also argue that regionalism is much more as complementary to multilateralism.

Others who oppose argue that RTAs might pose threat to a balanced development of world trade through increased trade and investment diversion particularly if liberalisation on preferential basis is not accompanied by concurrent Most Favoured Nation (MFN). Many others like Bhagwati (1992), and Krueger (1995) etc., however, worry about the negative effects of growing RTAs. They argue that regional groupings are the main cause of the trade diversion. They feel that RTAs are a threat to the multilateral trading system. Those who favour, however, urge that if regional groupings are open towards the world market in the sense of keeping tariffs at a level that does not encourage trade diversion, it will rather increase the world's production efficiency and will be complementary to the multilateral system.

Overall, the successes of many regional groupings like the European Union (EU), North American Free Trade Area (NAFTA) and Association of South East Asian Nations (ASEAN) have compelled researchers to think that regionalism could prove very useful, it brings stability in the region and help the economies to grow faster. The result is that many developing countries are trying to form regional trade arrangements. Many negotiations are going on between neighbouring countries. Through regional co-operation, developing countries could explore an enormous potential and enhance trade among them. Following this global trend, the countries of Central Asia and South Asia are also undergoing the process of liberalisation and regionalisation of their economies.

Liberalisation and Regionalism in Central and South Asian Regions

Before studying the regional economic initiatives in Central and South Asian regions, and possibilities of their linkages, it is important to understand the present economic conditions of both the regions. South Asian region comprises seven countries, India, Nepal, Bhutan, Bangladesh, Pakistan, Sri Lanka and Maldives whereas Central Asian region that was formed after the disintegration of Former Soviet Union (FSU) in 1991 consists of five countries, Kazakhstan, Uzbekistan, Turkmenistan, Kyrgyzstan and Tajikistan. In 1991, Central Asian countries together covered about eighteen percent of land and seventeen percent of population of the FSU. At the time of independence the economic conditions of the region were not favorable for sustainable development strategy (Sapoor, 2000). Despite having rich endowment of mineral resources, these economies were characterized as low level of industrialization, large rural population, high population growth, authoritarian regimes, internal and external threats and ethnic problems and a relatively high degree of poverty. In an attempt to integrate them with the world economy, most of the countries in both the regions have engaged themselves with economic reforms and liberalisation of their trade and investment regimes. The economies of South Asian countries as well as of the these Central Asian countries have been undergoing deep economic transformation since mid eighties and nineties respectively. Since independence, these central Asian countries started witnessing transformation from command economy to market economy. The key measures of reforms have been macroeconomic stabilization, price and market liberalization, liberalization of exchange and trade system, privatization, establishing a competitive environment with few obstacles to market entry and exit. Speed and sequence of economic liberalisation varies in both the regions.

But the countries of this region have had different abilities to overcome the challenges of economic liberalization. The different transition paths can be seen within the spectrum of five Central Asian countries. The forms of the transformation vary in this region, which would be characterized as wide scale reforms (Kyrgyz republic and Kazakhstan), non-reforms (Turkmenistan) towards gradual partial reforms (Uzbekistan, Tajikistan). Overall, the success of market oriented reforms has been mixed, according to various indicators developed by multilateral institutions Kazakhstan and Kyrgyzstan have progressed faster. Tajikistan has also made some progress. The level of reforms is low in Turkmenistan and Uzbekistan. However, Kazakhstan, Kyrgyzstan and Tajikistan have made significant progress in external sector reforms, but Uzbekistan and Turkmenistan's low level of reforms in this sector has created some problems for regionalism.

South Asian economy on the other hand comprises traditional village farming, modern agriculture, handicrafts, wide range of modern industries, wide range of technological industries and large number of services. The region has been characterized as a region of large economic and social disparities. South Asia is a region of 1.4 billion people including forty percent of world's population living below poverty line (2004). The region has world's highest illiteracy rate at forty five percent. These economies are in the vicious circle of low- per capita income growth, high population growth and political instability. Despite that growth rate has remained positive in the region. This region is among one of the fastest growing region of the world with the five-percent average economic growth for the last one decade.

The South Asian economies are reorienting their policies according to the increasing role of globalization and privatization in the changing international economic scenario. Economic liberalization in South Asian region characterized as reform measures in the following areas: privatization of state enterprises, reduction of subsidies to the industries, liberalization of capital market and trade. Production trade and investment reforms implemented during the past two decades have provided new opportunities and generated faster economic growth. Trade liberalization has been an important aspect of economic reforms in late eighties and early nineties. Unlike the other transitional Asian countries, this region has generally avoided financial problems. Sufficient flow of Foreign Direct Investment in this region revived the confidence in economic perspective. Macroeconomic conditions in the region are fairly strong. But the progress among the seven South Asian countries varies. The common theme between two regions is that regional economic integration has become an integral part of their liberalizing economies.

Regional Economic initiatives in Both the Regions

The question of economic integration- at intra or inter regional level or at the global level, is an important issue for both the regions. Both the regions have an enormous amount of resources. Both the regions are suffering from an abundance of labor resources, and shortage of domestic savings or capital accumulation. Economic initiatives at the regional and supra-regional levels are required to exploit their resources. So the prospects of regions can not only be determined by the regional groupings but also by the degree to which successfully integrated into the world economy. Their richness in terms of natural resources, technology and labor resources have attracted the international community towards them.

The success of regional blocs like the EU, ASEAN and NAFTA in promoting trade among member nations and boosting their economic growth has influenced both the regions to go in for regional economic integration. Both the regions have taken many initiatives to form regional groupings within the regions as well as with the rest of the world. Many documents have signed and many regional summits held in both the regions. Although the Central Asian region is resource rich and offers considerable trade and investment opportunities, yet due to lack of effective transport routes and relative isolation made it difficult for all countries to access international markets immediately after the independence. So creating new transit and transport routes has become an important pre-condition for the promotion of trade and development (Bakhtior,

2001). Therefore, the need for regional co-operation is determined by geography, so lacking direct access to the sea, neither Kazakhstan nor Uzbekistan can expect to become major exports of hydrocarbons without close co-operation of their neighbors. Central Asia nevertheless remain closely bound to one another but their interdependence particularly pronounced in the critical network of energy and fuel transportation and communication force them to be Central Asia as a region. So far the Central Asian regional co-operation is concerned, four factors could potentially have an impact on the creation of real regional union that are military- strategic considerations, cultural religious ties economic and disposition of all important water resources. While keeping the limitations of this study in mind, this study analyses the economic ties in general and trade in particular.

Although Central Asian countries are important member of the Common Wealth Independent States (CIS), yet CIS has not implemented a custom union or Free Trade Area. Kazakhstan, Kyrgyzstan and Uzbekistan formed a Central Asian Union (CAU) considering economic integration among three countries in 1994. In 1995 they approved free trade among the three countries. In 1998, Tajikistan was also accepted as a member of CAU. Later, in 1998 it was renamed as Central Asian Community (CAC). CAC also granted observing member status to Georgia and Turkey. In 1998, CAC again renamed as Central Asian Economic Community (CAEC) and it has been transformed into Central Asian Co-operation Organizations (CACO) in 2001. Russia has become a member of this regional group in May 2004. The main objective of this co-operation has been to develop the economic infrastructure and transportation system within the region. In addition, Kazakhstan, Kyrgyzstan and Tajikistan with Russia and Belarus are enjoying the membership in Custom Union, which was formed in 1994, basically the main aim of this union was economic, social and financial policy co-ordination among the member countries. The other regional agreements like EEC (Eurasian Economic Community) and GUUAM Group, (Georgia, Uzbekistan Ukraine, Azerbaijan, Moldova Group) and Central Asian Region Economic Co-operation (CAREC), Economic Co-operation Organization (ECO) have been established with countries outside the region. The main purpose of these agreements is to promote regional cooperation and economic growth.

Though South Asia is geographically integrated region, the economic integration is still low despite a number of initiatives taken by the authorities. The idea of regional co-operation in South Asia was first mooted in 1980. The foreign Secretaries of the seven countries met for the first time in Colombo in 1981 to discuss about regional co-operation. Later, South Asian Association for Regional cooperation (SAARC) was established in 1985. The main objective behind this was to promote the welfare of the peoples of the member countries and improve their quality of life, accelerate economic growth, social progress, cultural development, peace and prosperity in the region. Although economic co-operation should be first priority to bring stability in the region, still SAARC has yet to emerge as a viable regional organization. Political instability and the souring relationship of Pakistan and India kept the region from coming together. Till 2002, intra South Asian trade was only five percent of their total trade volume, whereas intra-bloc trade recorded in EU, fifty five percent, NAFTA, fifty two percent and ASEAN twenty percent (Ahmed, 2002). Despite political problems, SAARC Preferential Trading Arrangement (SAPTA) was finalized in 1993 and came into existence in 1995. It was regarded as the first achievement of SAARC. The signing of agreement of South Asian Free Trade Area (SAFTA) in 2004 at Islamabad Summit has been regarded as another big success of the evolution of the SAARC. Achieving SAFTA by 2008, South Asian Custom Union (SACU) by 2015 and South Asian Economic Union (SAEU) in 2020 are the foreseeable prospects.

Some bilateral initiatives are in place between India and Sri Lanka, India and Nepal, India and Bhutan and others are under negotiations like between Pakistan and Sri Lanka and India and Bangladesh. South Asian sub-regional groups like, South Asian Growth Quadrangle was launched in 1997 among four countries (Bangladesh, Bhutan, Nepal and eleven contiguous eastern and north eastern states of India) BBIN quadrangle. Aiming at creating an enabling environment for rapid economic development and encourage co-operative projects in the Ganga- Brahmaputra-Meghna river basin. At the request of BBIN, Asian Development

Bank launched assistance for sub-regional co-operation under the South Asian Sub-Regional Economic Co-operation program in 2001. Countries of the South Asian region are also enjoying the membership of other groups like, Indian Ocean Rim Association for Regional Cooperation (IOR-ARC), Bangladesh- India- Myanmar-Sri Lanka-Thailand Economic Co-operation (BIMST-EC) etc. BIMSTEC has been renamed recently as Bay of Bengal Economic Community. Some of South Asian countries have also developed close relations with the ASEAN.

Major issues such as trade facilitation, investment, infrastructure, transit, hydroelectricity, natural gas exploitation, tourism, technology, water management have been discussed in regional co-operation since the negotiations started. Some common issues like lack of connectivity, geo-political issues, free movement of people and lack of information have also been discussed. Although some significant progress has been made in South Asia, regional cooperation has experienced several problems. First, the asymmetry between India and the rest of South Asian countries has been a major problem. Unlike other regional groupings, SAARC has not been able to solve this. Secondly, adversarial relationship between India and Pakistan has affected adversely SAARC functioning. Finally, despite all the talk of regional cooperation, South Asian countries lack even minimal understanding, on political and security issues.

Comparison of Regional Economic Initiatives in both the Regions

A comparative look at both the regions shows some similarities in their process of regionalism and globalization. Both the regions are somehow trying to create lost economic linkages. Multilateral institutions are trying to help both the regions in the areas of trade facilitation, transit, infrastructure etc. The difference in economic potential of the various Central and South Asian countries are enormous. As mentioned earlier, progress in South Asia is slow because of political problems between India and Pakistan. In Central Asia, Kazakhstan and Uzbekistan have competed for regional leadership. And Turkmenistan is least interested in regional economic integration. To link both the regions some initiatives are already underway. With the help of ADB in 2003, Pakistan, Afghanistan, Tajikistan and Uzbekistan signed an agreement called Central and South Asian Transport Trade Forum (CSATTF). The idea is to link north-south and east west trade and transport corridor-linking Central Asia with the Indian Ocean. Recently Iranian Foreign Minister also proposed the West Asian Economic Bloc comprising Iran, Pakistan India and Central Asian Region. This would enhance the regional connectivity. Afghanistan President also wants to join the SAARC. Pakistan and Afghanistan are already members of the Economic Co-Operation Organization (ECO). Other countries in the grouping are Azerbaijan, Iran Kazakhstan, Kyrgyz Republic, Tajikistan, Turkey, Turkmenistan and Uzbekistan. Both the regions need to look at each other and undertake measures for regional economic co-operation for mutual benefit. They have shown great potentialities of higher economic growth. Central Asian countries are source of energy (oil, natural gas etc.) which are highly demanded in the South Asian countries especially by India and Pakistan. India fulfills its energy requirement mainly through imports from West Asia. Central Asia can explore Indian demands. South Asia could be a supplier of basic commodities, services etc for the Central Asian countries. These links could be strengthened as many multilateral organizations are also trying to re-establish the old trade and other routes in Asia. The United Nations Asian Highway Project is already undergoing the process that will connect the South–East Asia with West Asia. Routes (rail, road, inter-modal) within the Asian Countries have been identified and agreements on the routes reached between the countries concerned. It has been revealed through the global experiences that improved transport integration leads to increased volume of trade at the regional as well as inter-regional trade. The potential constructive is enormous; trade and investment can increase exponentially. The efforts for cementing relationship with Afghanistan can provide a transit route for oil and gas pipeline from Central Asia. This land locked region can be much needed link with South Asian Region to make easy access to world market. This would allow member countries to effectively exploit their comparative advantages and competitiveness.

Central Asia Regional cooperation in Central Asia is necessary condition to break the land locked situation. While neighboring the world's largest and fastest-growing markets (PRC, India, and Russia), Central Asia's landlocked status means regional transport costs are a serious impediment to development. Cooperation in transport, trade, and transit will yield important benefits. Central Asian countries share vital resources, notably energy and water. Harnessing these resources in a sustainable manner and managing their shared use in support of agriculture, industry, and livelihoods require a high degree of regional cooperation and third party assistance. Regional trade agreements have been, and will likely remain, an important tool for trade liberalization. Most empirical studies find that trade creation dominates trade diversion. In practice several factors increase the benefits of RTAs including large and diverse membership, low external most-favored-nation tariffs, liberal rules of origin and trade facilitation measures.

There remains significant scope for trade liberalization in Central Asia. Regional and bilateral preference schemes can play a useful role in promoting regional trade, which remains underdeveloped in Central Asia. Closer regional cooperation through increased market integration needs to extend beyond trade. Regional transportation networks need to be developed to facilitate access to world markets. Kazakhstan, which accounts for a significant share of Central Asian transit trade, should bears a particular responsibility in this area. Certain aspects of the transit systems currently in place in the CARs impose constraints on cross-border movements of goods by rail and by road. These are, however, not crucial for cross-border movements of goods by rail, for which transport-related factors are a binding constraint. By contrast, inadequacies of the road transit systems impose a binding constraint on trade in Central Asia.

All countries in the region need to ensure that arbitrary restrictions and corruption do not interfere with the flow of goods and services. Moreover, a handful of primary commodities, such as crude oil, metals, and cotton fiber, continued to dominate the CARs' exports. Indeed, the rise in world prices for these commodities was a major factor that contributed to rapid growth of their exports. At the same time, participation of the CARs in GPNs and related international trade in manufactured products remained very limited. Furthermore, the CARs' exports and, to a lesser extent, imports remained concentrated in a small number of countries.

And reinforcing cooperation in the areas of water and energy will be crucial for the development of the region. Sound and sustained economic growth requires transparency and good governance. Experience, as well as recent research studies at the IMF, ADB and EBRD shows that transparency is correlated with better investment and growth performance. Otherwise countries that are rich in natural resources, studies have shown that some time rich resources proved to be a curse rather than a blessing.

Recent developments demonstrate that regional cooperation has not increased in Central Asia despite a number of factors favoring it. Insofar as the Central Asian states are retaining influence over trade and production, their actions do not for the most part conform with their many verbal commitments to regional cooperation. Financing for truly cooperative projects is small, and petty interferences at the border do occur. Recognizing that their trade performance depends not only on a countries own trade policy, transport sector, and transit systems but also on the trade policy, transport sector, and transit systems of neighboring countries, the CARs have actively to be pursued regional cooperation in these areas.

In particular, they have joined several regional organizations that involve or seek to reach a multilateral RTA. The two most promising regional institutions, the Intergovernmental Commission and the Central Asian Bank, are still finding their place and influence. Economic policy in these countries discourages mid-sized businesses that would most benefit from a free regional market. Political frictions among the states of the region and their preference for dealing with outsiders, perceived to be more capable and less dangerous, are responsible for the failure to put speech-making into practice. If regional cooperation is to increase, with all its benefits, it will require leadership from the inside or determined and patient assistance from the outside. This region has to face because of the lack of the diversification and the network of economic ties, the infrastructure for export specialization. To overcome from land locked status, this region continues to suffer from inadequate infrastructure, poor utilization of assets with weak managerial procedural, regularity and institutional system. There have been a number of regional cooperation initiatives aimed at removing the deficiencies of transport infrastructure and services and facilitating cross-border and transit traffic in the CARs and in neighboring countries. Notably, the CAREC member countries have recently agreed on the Regional Transport Sector Road Map, which formulates the strategic priorities for regional cooperation in the transport sector and addresses most of the deficiencies of rail and road transport in Central Asia. These agreements have, however, had a very limited effects on the custom transit in Central Asia due to many reasons. Some of them have not been entered into force, while those that have entered into force have not been fully implemented.

South Asia South Asia has recently witnessed some dynamism in economic growth. India is regarded as a major global player, especially in services. Pakistan achieved a growth rate of 8.4% in the last fiscal year and is on its way to becoming a significant global player. Recent growth performance is impressive also in Sri Lanka and Bangladesh. Regional cooperation in South Asia cannot be said to have evolved into a complete bloc in terms of 'regionalism and economic integration' due mainly to the prevalence of conflict over the desire of peace and stability. Given the historical legacy and contemporary reality of endemic conflicts and mistrust in the region, the fact that the formal cooperation process in the region has survived recurrent setbacks is testimony of resilience of the organization. The antagonistic nature of relations with large sets of outstanding issues, low levels of intra-SAARC trade and joint economic ventures, inadequate information and infrastructure facilities. Independent and largely uncoordinated economic policies pursued by each country of the region are all indicators of lack of 'region-ness' and indication a unwelcoming future for any type of sustainable economic integration.

However, South Asian countries are also fast reducing barriers to trade to the rest of the world under the auspices of the WTO, thereby opening themselves to trade with many other countries, Yet the trade within the region is very low as compare to other region. Low external tariffs can reduce the possibility of trade diversion, and non-restrictive rules of origin result in expanded trade possibilities. But compared to the successful South East Asian countries, South Asia has been unable as yet to integrate within the region as well as with the global economy in terms of its potential. The South Asian countries are keen to move towards a stronger regional groupings and bilateral trade arrangements. Though the signing of bilateral FTAs has resulted in a spaghetti bowl of FTAs, these can lead to benefits in terms of an increase in exports from the lesser-developed countries in the region, as well as an expansion in investment flows. India should take the lead in this regard and play the role of an anchor economy, especially for the successful implementation of SAFTA.

There is now a growing opinion that the process of economic integration in south Asia will remain held up unless there is a change in the mindset of the political establishment in these countries. There is an urgent need to redefine our strategy for the development of this region. Needless to say there is a need to put more emphasis on the security of the state and on human security in these countries. So in this context it is hard to over emphasize the need for closer economic ties among all the countries of South Asia as economic cooperation and economic integration has been observed to have played a positive role in providing political stability in many regions earlier suffering from political strive. European Union has set an example of stability and also proves the poor countries can also get the benefits of regional economic cooperation. The countries like German and France, which fought for many years, could cooperate by opening their boarders. This is an example of stability and progress. Moreover, under the impact of globalization and liberalization the states in South Asia have lost much of the space available to them earlier for the exercise of policy options and for making macroeconomic policy decisions. This has serious implications for ensuring peace, justice and sustainability of development in their own countries and for their ability to cooperate with each other. Therefore, a major task in the south Asian countries should cooperate with each other so that they could get the maximum benefits of this globalization process so that they could get better space in this world. The South Asian countries missed the tide that carried many of their East and Southeast Asian neighbors especially china to record rates of growth and poverty reduction during the 1960s and 1970s, but their later trade policy and other liberalizing reforms came in time to for them to benefit from the expansion of production and trade in the world economy. Now both the region should not miss the bus again. They should work collectively and help each other to overcome the challenges. The countries like Turkmenistan and Pakistan should realize that in this globalization era and interdependent on each other, it is difficult to survive. So for the betterment of living standrard of people they should cooperate with each other.

According to the latest researches by the International intellectual communities and the latest reports by multilateral, bilateral institutions and research scholars find that the Central Asian and South Asian regions continues to lag behind the other regional economic initiatives in the world. This is mainly due to unfinished reforms, especially in establishment of strong institutions to support market economy through the transparent, predictable and well-enforced rules and regulations.

1

Global Trends Towards Economic Regionalism

This book emphasises the significance of increasing regional trade agreements and other regional initiatives. The Main focus is to describe and analyse the existing as well as emerging regional economic initiatives in both Central Asia and South Asia regions. To understand and analyse why there is emerging trend of regional economic initiatives in both the regions, it is very important to know the global trends towards economic regionalism. The first chapter deals with the global trends towards increasing regionalism covering the theoretical aspects of regional economic integration. How has this concept of regional economic integration been developed over time? For what purpose integration is required among countries? What are the benefits of regional economic Integration? How the potential of any country can be tapped through multi-lateral regional level cooperation. What are the challenges it has to face while cooperating? In recent times this phenomenon of regionalism has been observed everywhere. Observing this trend the intellectual community and policy makers are interested to

MAP 1 : POLITICAL MAP OF SOUTH ASIAN AND CENTRAL ASIAN REGIONS

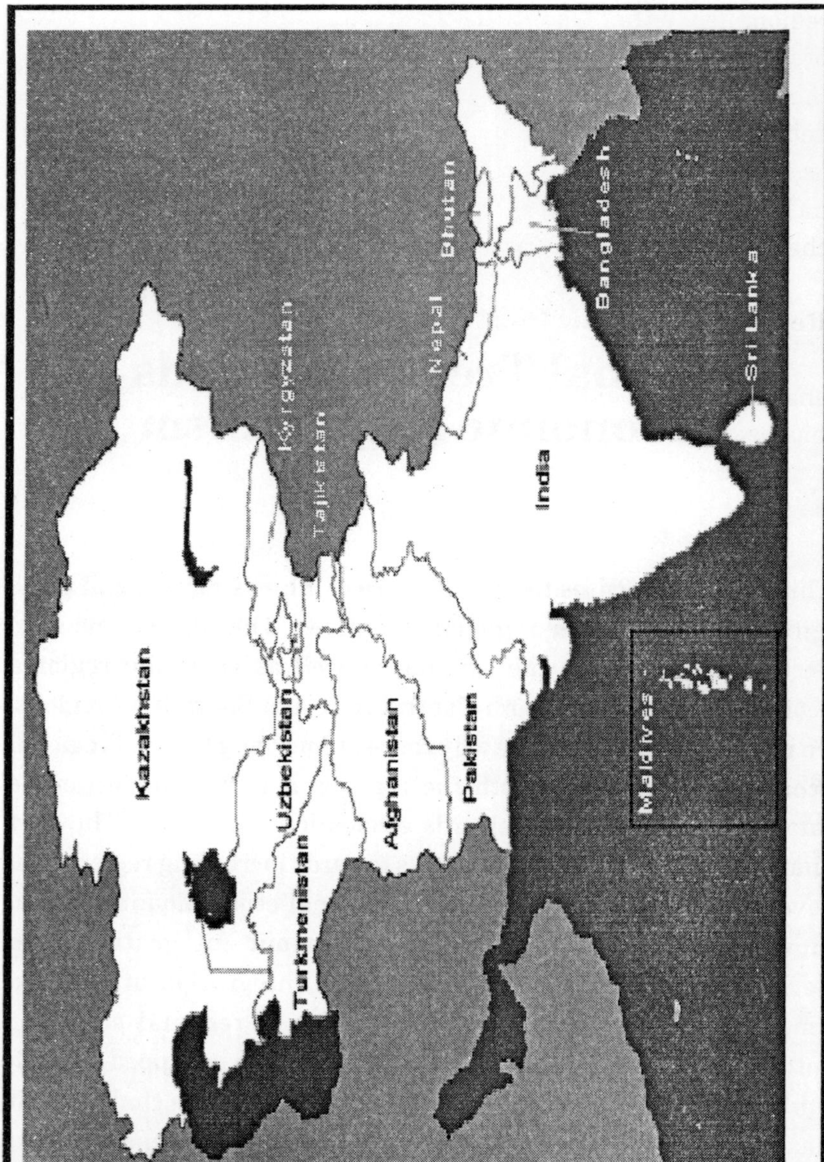

understand the benefits and challenges of integrating with each other. In the second part of this chapter the theories of renowned economists have been discussed. The third part of this chapter will broadly cover the global trends towards increasing regional economic integration. There has been a debate among scholars that through regionalism either trade is diverted or created. Do open economies prosper more than closed economies have also been analysed. In the fourth part of this chapter efforts are made to summarise the debate of 'whether regional trade agreements are stumbling blocks or building blocks of global trade liberalisation'. Open regionalism has been discussed in the last part of the chapter benefits and the challenges of Regional Economic Integration has been analysed.

Regional Economic Integration

Regional Economic Integration is a pervasive phenomenon shaping the global environment. The study of regional integration has been one of the major growths in the world Political Economy over the past few decades. The interaction between global and regional aspects of international phenomenon can be analyzed for transactions in goods services and finance. It has been observed and analyzed by think tank community that very often it is maintained that regionalism is way to manage globalization. According to the views of the analysts, the need for such arrangements among developing countries arose from the consequences of the import substituting industrialization strategies adopted by these countries. Under this strategy the goods were produced mainly for home markets, which was small in scale. The small scale of production meant that economies of scale could not be realized leading to high cost production, because of which these goods could not able to compete in the global market. Regional trading arrangements among developing countries were suggested as the way out of this dilemma. Larger production for regional market would enable the exploitation of economies of scale, lower costs of production and made the goods competitive in the world market[1]. (Agarwal, 2004). To enlarge market and lower the cost of production the countries felt the requirement of regional economic integration.

The Concept of Regional Economic Integration

Economic Integration is a term used to describe how different aspects between economies are integrated. It encompasses broader areas of political, economic and cultural links with nations joining together in a forum generally belong to one or several regions. Now the question arises that how region can be defined. Broadly region can be defined as a geographical proximity of countries, which facilitates cooperation among these countries As the economic integration increases, the barriers of trade diminish. As the trade and investment increase across borders, private actors demand elimination of costly barriers and provision of greater certainty in security of contracts and investments. They petition governments to create regional agreements that underpin liberalization of tariffs and non-tariffs barriers and harmonization of regulations. Lloyd defines economic integration in terms of law of one price, in a global market, common prices prevails everywhere with utility maximizing resources allocation.[2] (Richard,1997) *The Palgrave Dictionary of Economics* describes economic regionalism as "actions by governments to liberalise or facilitate trade on a regional basis, sometimes through free-trade areas or custom unions"[3]. (Palgrave Dictionary) Some scholars assess that co-operation would ease the barriers posed by the boarders among the countries and allow people to connect throughout the regions and beyond with trade and investment linked infrastructure and a free flow of ideas and knowledge.[4] (UNDP report, 2005) They think that the development of coherent regional economic and political spaces as an essential stepping stone towards an integrated global era. Moreover, regionalism is thought to be increasingly a natural phenomenon, because informal economic agents as businesses who become more international drive it. Trade is said to be greater in natural trade regions because the formation of such trade regions are influenced by geographical proximities, which reduces transaction costs and increases information flows.[5] (Krugman, 1993)

Theoretical Aspect of Economic Integration

The genes of economic integration originated from International economics. International economics deals with the economic interdependence among nations. Specifically it deals with international trade theory, international trade policy, balance of payments, foreign exchange markets and open economy macroeconomics. International economics has enjoyed long, continuous and rich development over two centuries with contributions from some of the world's most distinguished economists including Adam Smith, David Ricardo, John Stuart Mill, Alfred Marshall, John Maynerd Keyens, and Paul Samuelseon.[6](Salvatore, 2001). International trade generally improves social welfare and stimulates economic growth. Trade enables countries to specialize in line with their comparative advantages and achieve economies of scale that would not be possible without specialization. This improves the allocation of resources and social welfare, improves the quality of goods available to consumers, enhance competition and increases investment in both physical and human capital. In developing countries, trade also fosters economic growth and improves social welfare by helping them attract foreign direct investment (FDI) and acquire modern technologies available in developed countries through imports, FDI inflows, and participation in global production networks.[7](Srinivasan,1998).

Economic growth and improvements in social welfare in turn, reduce poverty in as much as they raise income and improve the welfare of the poor and increase resources available for social security, primary health care, education, water supply, and other basic services. Accordingly, openness to international trade is widely regarded as a necessary, even though not sufficient, condition for any country, particularly a small one to achieve sustainable economic development[8]. (Caminis, 2006) There are, however, few caveats to this general rule. First, participation in international trade has certain costs. Most notably, it makes a country vulnerable to fluctuations in world prices and possible projectionist measures by trading partners[9].

The classical source of gains from trade is that global free trade allows consumers and firms to purchase from the cheapest source of supply, hence ensuring that production is located according to comparative advantage. In contrast, trade barriers discriminate against foreign supply, inducing domestic import competing producers to expand even though they have higher costs than do imports. The concept of 'comparative advantage' underpins the economic logic of multilateral trade reform by dictating that under global free trade, production will be shifted to the most efficient producers. Regional Economic Integration can be categorised in the following forms.

Forms of Regional Economic Integration

Regional economic integration has been emerging in the world in various stages or forms. Normally the first stage is preferential tariff (trade) arrangements. This is a simple form of regional economic co-operation under which lower tariffs and non-tariff preferential treatments are provided to the commodities coming from member countries compared to non-member countries. Each country is allowed to have its own set of tariffs and non- tariffs against the third country imports. The second stage is free trade area arrangements, which normally means no tariff among the member countries. The third stage is called the custom union, which involves common external tariff in addition to Free Trade Arrangements. The fourth stage is common market which adds free mobility of factors of production to custom union arrangements. The fifth stage is economic union that goes beyond common market by harmonising economic policies of member countries. Finally, the stage of economic integration, a move towards complete unification of economic policies of member states as a consequence reduction of their independence in economic matters.

These Stages or Forms

Regional cooperation and integration may broadly be analysed and discussed in the areas economic links such as trade, transport, transit and investments, Natural resource links such as water, energy and environment, National security links such as terrorism, arms and drug trafficking and Islamic militancy and other important links include migration, education health natural disaster preparedness, gender and governance etc. But remaining within the scope of the study only key economic linkages such as trade, transport, transit and investments will be considered. Table 1.1 describes the all the forms of Regional Economic Integration.

Table 1.1

Regional Integration	*Definition*	*Some Examples*
Free Trade Area (FTA)	An area where tariffs and quotas are abolished for imports from area members, which, however, retain national tariffs and quotas against third countries	-In 1992 ASEAN countries launched the ASEAN Free Trade Area (AFTA) plan. On 1 January 2002 six out of ten ASEAN countries reduced internal tariffs on most goods to levels ranging between zero and five percent. The whole ASEAN area is scheduled to become a full-fledged free trade area in the coming years.- The USA, Canada, and Mexico are in the process of completing a North American FTA: many tariffs were eliminated already in 1994, with others being Phased out over a periods of 5 to 15 years
Customs union (CU)	A FTA setting up common tariffs and quotas for trade with non-members	-European Economic Community since 1968 - The MERCOSUR (Southern Common Argentina, Brazil, Uruguay, Paraguay) becoming a fully-CU by 2006.
Common Market (CM)	A CU abolishing non-tariff barriers to trade (product and services	-European Community since 1993 (establishment of the European Single Market). The CM was

(Contd.)

(Contd.. Table 1.1)

Regional Integration	*Definition*	*Some Examples*
	markets integration) as well as restrictions on factor movement (factor market integration)	already set up as an objective under the Treaty of Rome
Economic Union (EU)	A CM with a significant degree of Coordination of national economic policies and/or harmonization of relevant domestic laws	-European Union nowadays
Total Economic integration (TEI)	An EU with all relevant economic policies conducted at the supra -national level, possibly in compliance with the principle of subsidiarity. For this, supranational laws need to be in place.	- The euro area (i.e., 12 out of 15 countries of the European Union) can be currently classified Somewhere between an EUN and TEI. Supranational Authorities and rule making were established already with the Treaty of Rome in 1957, and subsequently enhanced.

Global Trends Towards Economic Regionalism

The growth of regional economic blocs or Regional Trade Agreements (RTA) in the past decades has become a significant aspect of global economic relations. The concept of regional trade arrangements was formed during the Sixth Session of United Nations General Assembly in June 1974.[10] (UNCTAD, 1976) In fact, the genesis of regional trading blocs might be traced back to the establishment of New International Economic Order. The objective behind this was to encourage trade among the developing countries.[11] (Bhatacharya, 2001). By definition, RTAs are agreements whereby members accord preferential treatment to one another in respect to trade barriers. Regionalism in trade and investment agreements has been on a steep rise since the early 1990s. The number of agreements under negotiation or under consideration is for all intents and purposes incalculable, changing on a weekly basis. Regional Trade Agreements (RTAs) have become in recent years a very prominent feature of the Multilateral Trading System (MTS). The surge in RTAs has continued unabated since the early 1990s. Some 368 RTAs have been notified to the GATT/WTO up to December 2006. At that same date, 215 agreements were in force. If we take into account RTAs which are in force but have not been notified, those signed but not yet in force, those currently being negotiated, and those in the proposal stage, we arrive at a figure of close to 400 RTAs which are scheduled to be implemented by 2010[12] This increasing trend towards regionalism posed challenges to both the economists, intellectuals and policy makers. It raised the fear that the world economy is disintegrating into the in-word looking trade blocs.[13] (Poon, 1995).

Regional trade agreements stimulate growth and investment, facilitate technology transfer and shift comparative advantages. Recent trade agreements have broadly been of two kinds, either a straightforward trade agreement or a trade agreement as part of a broader economic partnership agreement involving trade facilitation cooperation, labor and environmental cooperation along with a FTA. These agreements tackle issues relating to investment, government procurement, environment, competition policy, intellectual property rights. Some scholars have identified this recent phenomenon as the "second wave" of regionalism, the first wave having occurred in the 1960s and 1970s. There are some similarities and differences between the two waves. It has been noted that the first wave consists more of regional trade arrangements, but the second wave has led to a proliferation of bilateral trade agreements. As well, the first wave generated tariff reductions as the main objective of trade agreements but the recent wave of agreements between countries has included areas of economic cooperation beyond tariff reduction and many governments have adopted a multi-tracked approach to trade liberalization Effective regional integration will increase competition, reduce private transaction costs, and enable firms to exploit economies of scale, encourage stability and prosperity in the region. Countries have increasingly opted for free trade and investment relations with geographically proximate partners. Greater Regional Economic co-operation could provide a significant boost to the hopes for political and economic success [14] (UNDP report, 2005). The regional cooperation is recognized as a key policy issues not only in Asia or Europe but also in Middle East Africa and several other parts of the world. The degree of economic integration ranges from preferential trade arrangements (PTA) to free trade area (FTA), customs union (CU), common market (CM) and economic union (EU). Now the question that arises is, Do these regional agreements lead to trade creating impact or trade diverting impact on the global trade?

The modern analysis of Regional Integration Agreements can be drawn from the arguments of Viner (1950), Meade (1955), Gehrels (1956-57), Lipsey (1957) and Michaely (1965), who drew the distinction between the trade creating and trade diverting effects of regional integration.

Debate on Trade Creation and Trade Diversion

There are two schools of thought on trade creation and trade diversion impact of the regional agreements. Trade creation/ diversion terminology generated a substantial literature. Viner recognized that trade induced by a free trade area or a customs union was of two types, which he called trade creation and trade diversion. According to him the Trade creation is the substitution of a lower cost source of supply within the area for a more costly source in the importing country and is, therefore, beneficial to the member countries and the world as a whole. By contrast, trade diversion is the substitution of a more costly source of supply within the area for a less costly source outside the area. This led Viner to his famous prediction:

"...where the trade-diverting effect is predominant, one at least of the member countries is bound to be injured, the two combined will suffer a net injury, and there will be injury to the outside world and to the world at large."[15] (J Viner, 1950). Assuming that all economic resources are fully exploited before and after the formation of the custom union, this increases the welfare of the member countries because it leads to a greater specialization in production based on comparative advantages. A trade creating custom unions also increases the welfare of the non-members because some of the increase in its real income (due to greater specialization in production) spills over into increased from rest of the world.[16] (Salvatore, 2001)

Viner's contribution was to show that the answer is not necessarily that the gains from trade argument applies if all trade barriers are reduced, but that it does not apply to a partial and discriminatory reduction in barriers, as in a regional integration agreement. This is because discrimination between sources of supply is not eliminated, it is just shifted. If partner's countries production displaces higher cost domestic production then there will be creation of trade gains. But it is possible that the partner countries production may displace lower cost imports from the rest of the world, and this is welfare reducing trade diversion. The analysis of trade creation and trade diversion constitutes one of the analyses of the more general problem of 'second-best welfare economics'. The general principle of second best theory, of which the theory of custom unions is an example that has been examined here in conditions Custom Union, is more likely to lead trade creation and increase the welfare of the member countries. When a Custom Union is formed and trade barriers among member nations are eliminated, producers in each nation must become more efficient to meet the competition of other producers within the union, merge, or go out of business. The increased level of competition is also like to stimulate the development and utilization of new technology.[17] (Salvatore, 2001). The theory of Custom union is just an example of this general principle. From its somewhat vague beginning in the work of Viner, the theory of Second best was then fully developed by Meade in 1955 and generalized by Lipsey and Lanchaster in 1956.[18] (Salvatore, 2001) Within a few years of the publication of Viner's book, a number of writers demonstrated that some part or parts of Viner's predictions might not hold. In particular, a number of papers provided examples where the country, may gain when trade diversion occurs. The key publications were those of Meade (1955), Gehrels (1956-57), Lipsey (1957) and Michaely (1965).A custom union is more likely to lead to trade creation and increase the welfare under these conditions. First if the pre-union trade barriers of the member countries are higher, then there is a greater probability that the formation of custom union will create trade among the members rather than divert trade from non members. Second, custom union's the lower barriers on the trade with the rest of the world will make it trade diversion less costly. Thirdly, the greater is the number of countries forming the custom union and larger their size, greater probability that low cost producers are found within the union. Lastly, the more competitive rather than complementary are the economies of member nations, greater opportunities for specialization in production and trade creation with the formation of custom union.[19] (Salvatore, 2001)

The theories of economic integration based on the works of Lloyd and Richard have predicted two opposite outcomes, arguing that in short run, trade creation effects must outweigh trade diversion effects in order to achieve beneficial trade liberalization. However, apart from short run benefits, there are also the long run benefits such as greater technical efficiency due to greater competition, larger markets, higher consumer surpluses, and more foreign investment.[20] (Pomfret Richard,1997). Sapir (2004) stresses that integration is a gradual process. According to him there are five main considerations to ensure the success of a process of integration.

- Put in place clear and shared objectives.
- Proceed step by step with the right initial step.
- Define clear and feasible deliverables.
- Be mindful of derogation granted to members as they are not free from cost.
- Have a framework that allows partner to cope up with Shocks.[21] (Sapir,2004).

With the extraordinary and unprecedented level of activity post-Cancun regarding negotiations and explorations of future RTAs, it is imperative that trade economists have a clear view of the basic economics of RTAs. The predictions of trade theory, the way economic theorists have viewed discriminatory trade blocs has changed over time. At the time of the formation of the GATT in 1948, RTAs were viewed as a step towards free global trade. According to Mr. Augustin Carsten, the Deputy Managing Director of the international Monetary Fund,[22] (Augustin Carsten, 2005) new RTAs did not raise trade barriers *vis-à-vis* the rest of the World, they resulted in an overall lowering of trade barriers in the world economy and this was regarded as benign. Article XXIV is based on this view.

Despite the trend toward regionalization, many economists argue that regional integration can harm member countries if the evolving PTA does not pursue a policy of openness towards other countries. By restricting market access of more efficient producers from outside the PTA, they can lead to welfare losses at home and abroad. But economic theory also offers some broad insights for conditions under which PTAs are likely to be welfare enhancing. According to them the main conclusion of the analysis is that if the process is done carefully and rightly, PTAs can be stepping stones toward multilateral liberalization. Once formed, a PTA can be thought of as an entity participating in international trade just like individual countries constitute such entities. From international trade theory, it follows that the best trade policy for this larger entity towards the rest of the world is free trade. Thus, it is in a PTA's own interest to pursue multilateral trade liberalization.

Do open economies prosper more than closed economies?

Based on cross-country analysis for the 1970s and 1980s, primarily by Dollar (1992), Edwards (1992), Barro and Sala-i-Martin (1995), Sachs and Warner (1995), Wacziarg (1998), and Vamvakidis (1997 and 1998) have found that economies with low trade barriers grow faster[23]. (Athansios Vamvakidis,1999)

However, this is not a vigorous result. There are only very few empirical growth studies, and no theoretical ones, that address the issue of opening to the world economy versus opening to an

RTA. Participation in an RTA does not explain cross-country growth differences. Open economies grow faster while closed economies grow slower regardless of their participation in an RTA. Can we deduce that if an economy liberalizes it will grow faster? The answers in the existing literature to these questions are not satisfying and have often been criticized. One reason is that faster growth may be causing more trade and not the other way around. Another reason is that openness variables may be proxies for other country characteristics that have very little to do with trade. For example, most of the developing countries that have reduced trade barriers in recent decades have also implemented a variety of other policy reforms in fiscal and monetary policy, capital flows, financial regulation, and labor markets. Furthermore, most of the economies with high trade barriers are often also characterized by government intervention in internal competition and the financial sector, subsidy and tax programs favoring specific sectors in the economy, inefficient bureaucracy, inconsistent macroeconomic policies, and high inflation.

Therefore, policy implications for the impact of openness on growth based on cross-country analysis should be treated with caution. With this approach, many of the characteristics that differ across countries and are correlated with trade intervention do not influence the estimates. Comparing the growth performance of countries before and after trade liberalization can suggest what will happen when other countries follow similar policies in the future. Estimates of the impact of discriminatory, versus nondiscriminatory, liberalization on growth can lead to similar policy implications. This methodology can resolve the issue of whether a closed economy should liberalize to all countries or opt for a discriminatory approach via RTA.

Does Regional Trade Agreement a Stumbling block or a Building block ?

Are Regional Trade Agreement building blocs or stumbling blocs to the multilateral trading system? There are two basic schools of thought concerning the relationship between multilateral and regional trading arrangements. Professor Baldwin analyzed the ambiguity of regional trade liberalization, either this process can help or hinder multilateral negotiation efforts. Liberalization on a regional basis encompasses the positive effects linked to the removal of barriers to trade, but also accounts for the discriminatory components associated with the regional approach. The dual nature of regional liberalization has supported the two current opposite trends: regionalism viewed as a building block to multilateralism, as opposed to regionalism viewed as a stumbling block. The first trend stresses the discriminatory component, whereas the second emphasizes the liberalization component.[24] (Julie Mckay, 2005).

Regional Trade Agreements as a Stumbling block

Those who advocate total reliance on the multilateral process and against the regionalism express three main concerns. First they note that the regional agreements divert trade by creating preferential treatment for member country and non members. The critics do not like trade diversion, even if it is offset by the trade creating effects of the regional arrangements. The second concern of the critics is the attention diversion. They argue that countries may loose interest in multilateral system, when they will engage actively in regional initiatives. The third and the most important concern about regionalism is geopolitical impact. History provide evidences that in earlier years, regional trading arrangements and (more broadly economic blocks) had contributed to political and even military clashes among nations. They thought that extensive or intensive regional ties may lead to irritations and even conflicts that range beyond economics to broader spheres of international relations.[25] (Bhagwati and panagaraiya, 1996)

Many others like Bhagwati (1992,1995), (Bhagwati and Panagriya 1996) and Krueger (1995) etc., however, worry about the negative effects of growing RTAs. They argue threat to the multilateral trading system. According to them RTAs might pose threat to a balanced development of world trade through increased trade and investment diversion particularly if liberalisation on preferential basis is not accompanied by concurrent Most Favoured Nation (MFN).

Regional Trade Agreements as s Building block

Advocates of RTAs argue on the basis of gains from economies of scale, competition and attraction of FDI. The classical economists such as Ricardo, Adam Smith as well as modern economists like Herbler were also in favour of the free trade policy. The change of ideas and technology can increase the production capacity. UN officials on trade have been regularly discussing the merits of regional trade during the Trade and Development Board sessions.

UNCTAD officials also meet annually in Geneva to review and examine global economic trends from trade and development perspective. According to the former UNCTAD Secretary General Rubens Ricupero, "regionalism is the only path available for many developing countries to integrate into world economy". He asserted that the best way to learn to compete is by competing, and initially competition should be among the neighbouring states. Carlo Trojan of the European Commission (EC) also believes that regionalism and multilateralism are complementary notions that reinforce each other as long as regionalism is open. Baldwin (1992), Either (1998) and Lawrence (1999) also argue that regionalism is much more complementary to multilateralism. Those who favour, however, urge that if regional groupings are open towards the world market in the sense of keeping tariffs at a level that do not encourage trade diversion, it will increase the world's production efficiency and will be complementary to the multilateral system.[26] The statement made by Director General of WTO has also proved that the regional trade agreements are not the stumbling block to the global trade.

"This decision will help break the current logjam in the WTO on regional trade agreements. This is an important step towards ensuring that regional trade agreements become building blocks, not stumbling blocks to world trade. It is important to note as well that this breakthrough comes at a critical juncture in our broader Doha round negotiations. Hopefully this decision is a good omen for much needed progress in other areas of the talks, such as agriculture and industrial goods trade, where agreement is urgently needed."[27] (Pascal Lamy, 2006)

Those who favour, however, recommend that if regional groupings are open towards the world market in the sense of keeping tariffs at a level that does not encourage trade diversion, it will rather increase the world's production efficiency and will be complementary to the multilateral system. The present study tends to agree with argument that while cooperating with your regional partner it becomes easier to negotiate at the world level. European Union is the best example of economic integration as well as open regionalism, because it was started with the cooperation of six countries. Now twenty six countries are the member of it and many are negotiating to become a member of this regional grouping, A rising share of international trade is occurring within the regions.

However, since 1990s open regionalism is the debatable topic in the history of trade and this concept is prevalent in various parts of the world. Open regionalism represents an effort to resolve one of the central problems of the contemporary trade policy: how to achieve compatibility between the explosion of regional trading arrangements around the world and global trading systems embodied in World Trading Organisation. The concept seeks to ensure that regional agreements will in practice be building blocs for further global liberalisation rather than stumbling blocs that deter such progress.[28] (Bergston, 1997)

The new regionalism since mid 1980's has challenged traditional custom union theory. The New Trade Theory is based on the models of imperfect competition.[29] The new regionalism has not been developed as a coherent set of ideas, but there are numbers of common themes. It downplays the significance of trade diversion in which tariffs have become less important than non-tariffs barrier to trade. It also draws on the new trade theories, which integrated scale economics trade diversion costs, and emphasizing the scale based pro-compressive benefits of integration. The new regionalism has a more positive vision of discriminatory trading arrangements than traditional customs union theory does. Deeper in integration involving institutional integration may be more feasible among neighboring countries sharing political and eco-preferences. Open regionalism represents an efforts to resolve one of the central problems of contemporary trade policy that how to achieve compatibility between the explosion of regional trading arrangements and the global trading system.

Open Regionalism

There are some definitions of open regionalism[30] (Garnaut,1994) which are important to understand and implement simultaneously as well as independently. These are as follows:

Open Membership: The first proposed definition of open regionalism is the open membership in the regional arrangements. Any country that indicates a credible willingness to accept the rules of the institution would be invited to join. The trade liberalising effect of the group would expand to an increasing number of countries. This approach would, of course, convert regional arrangements into something much broader than at some point give up its regional character. Such an evolution would ultimately evolve into a global institution[31]

Unconditional MFN: The open regionalism concept is unconditional Most- Favoured–Nation (MFN) treatment. This strategy relies on the economic self interest in liberalisation. It concerns itself with the behaviour of trading pattern. It would prevent the need to work out preferential rules of origin and detail plans to qualify as a free trade area under the Article 24 of the WTO.[32] (Bergstern, 1997)

Global Liberalisation: This definition of Open Regionalism would be for any region's members to simply continue reducing there barriers on a global basis while pursuing there regional goals. This option could indeed be deployed to achieve the broadest possible definition of open regionalism- simultaneous achievement of free trade in the region and the world.

Trade Facilitation: Liberalisation of such barriers specially focus on tariffs and traditional barriers would force the member countries to decide to trade with non members. An alternate approach is trade facilitation through non tariffs and non boarders reforms[33] Trade Facilitation can be described as the improvement in the efficiency of the processes associated with trading goods across the national boarders.

It has been defined that, "Simplification and standardisation of procedures and associated information flows required to move goods internationally from seller to buyer and to pass payments in other direction[34]" (UNESCAP, 2006). According to their views that trade facilitation makes easier to comply with trade registration, documentation and custom requirements. Moreover, it facilitates international transport of goods and trade financing process.

Under this approach trade could be enhanced by custom harmonisation and mutual recognition of standards. With cooperation, they could enforce national competition policies and deregulate of key domestic markets. All the member countries willing to participate effectively in regional as well as in global economy would get more benefits from trade and investment flows through trade facilitation. Governments would adopt the policies and plans to reduce non physical bottlenecks in international trade and transport through strengthening national trade and transport facilitation committee. It has observed that countries that have made facilitation an easy process, those are able to get maximum benefit by cutting the cost at low level. The regions can set up the institutions, which can work public and private partnership in support of Trade Facilitation. They can reduce the number of documents and procedures. Regional priorities for trade and transport facilitation would make easy formalisation of the operation and facilitation of imports and exports and transit arrangements.

Benefits and Challenges of Regional economic integration

Regional integration among developing countries is part of a wider strategy to promote equitable growth. A regionally coherent liberalization strategy will reduce and smooth the cost of adjustment to an economy in the face of globalization, both for the private and the public sector[35]. As the past decades has witnessed the revival of regionalism in the global trading systems. The question arises here why are such blocs emerging? Why do countries feel that they are able to negotiate more at regional than at a global level?. The high adjustment cost of unilateral liberalization has been a cause of policy reversal in a number of developing economies. Based on the above principles, the EU supports realistic regional economic integration initiatives among developing countries that are consistent with national economic reform programs. This support usually comprises these interrelated areas such as capacity building (including technical assistance, training and research) on the subject of regional economic integration at the level of regional institutions and national governments. Assistance to the private sector to facilitate restructuring in the larger regional and world market is also to make it more competitive. This also includes improvements in the financial sector and support to governments committed to implement regional integration to help them cope with net transitional effects on budgetary resources (balance of payments or budgetary support, complementary to national economic adjustment support).

Why did the countries started to look towards their neighbors for co-operation? Why has WTO been loosing its significance to some extent? There are some inherent problems within the framework of GATT/WTO that lead countries to turn to their neighbors. Krugman listed the following reasons:[36] (Baldwin, 1997)

First, the large number of participants in multilateral trade negotiations reduces the costs of non-cooperation (a key consideration in co-operative game theory) and fosters greater rigidity in negotiations.

Second, contemporary trade barriers are more varied, more complex and less transparent than the tariffs and quotas considered in early GATT rounds.

Third, Socio-political-economic differences between Asian economies (China and Japan in particular) makes it much easier for the regional level and get away with non compliance. So the countries are reluctant to bargain on an unconditional Most Favored Nations (MFN). Economists generally agree that the trade barriers are detrimental and decrease the economic efficiency. This makes multilateral bargaining harder and renders monitoring of any eventual agreements more problematic.

Overall, the successes of many regional groupings like the European Union (EU), North American Free Trade Area (NAFTA) and Association of Southeast Asian Nations (ASEAN) have compelled researchers to think that regionalism could be proved very useful, it brings stability in the region and help the economies to grow faster. For example France and Germany borders were unstable for many decades. After the liberalising and becoming EU member they are move to free anywhere and there is stability between France and Germany. This has proved that the formation of regional integration has been greatly successful in bringing historically hostile countries together. While observing EU Model many developing countries are trying to form regional trade arrangements. Many negotiations are going on between neighbouring countries. Through regional co-operation, developing countries could explore an enormous potential and enhance trade among them. The tussle between India and Pakistan in South Asian Region can be diluted or resolved by economic cooperation and should think in the welfare of the people. Central Asia can also take lessons from European Union and integrate among each other for the welfare of the people and utilise all their resources efficiently. A challenge of removal of mistrust among the countries in both the regions can be solved by economic cooperation.

Deep Integration and Shallow integration

According to the functional existence there are two types of regionalism, deep integration and shallow integration.[37] The EU's single market programme and Maastricht Treaty are archetypical deep integration agreements.[38] European Union is a good example of deep integration. US- Canada FTA, US-Israel FTA, NAFTA and MERCOSUR are the example of shallow integration.

European integration started much earlier and has gone much deeper than North American integration. International treaties among the 'original six' members like Belgium, France, West Germany, Italy, Luxembourg and the Netherlands were signed in 1951. The desire among the Western Powers, especially the USA was to strengthen Western Europe politically and economically[39]. By using the door of Art. 24 in GATT, Economic Community passed in 1957with US approval.[40] USA helped the economic unification of Europe as a part of needed to restore the western Europe to prosperity, strengthening it against the Soviet Menance.[41] (Bhagwati, 1999) The European Community (EC) completed its CU in 1968. A separate group of West European nations formed the European Free Trade Area (EFTA), which is an FTA for industrial goods that was completed in 1968. The EEC and all EFTA signed bilateral FTAs in 1974, implicitly forming a duty-free zone for industrial goods covering most of West Europe. The membership of the EC was enlarged in 1972. Initially responsible for regulation of specific sectors of the economy (coal, steel, agriculture), over a time European institutions have been entrusted with responsibilities over an increasing range of tasks. The EC's 1986 Single European Act promised to establish the 'Single Market' by removing all intra-EC barriers to the moment of goods, services and people and capital by 1992. The Single

European Act also centralized economic decision making on matters concerning the Single Market and doubled EC funds available for intra-regional transfers. The 1992 European Economic Area (EEA) agreement extended EC92 to the EFTA with the exception of food trade. EEA members account for about half of world trade and a third of world GDP. The EC has recently, or soon will, sign agreements with 10 Central and Eastern European countries (CEECs). These 'Europe Agreements' are FTA in industrial goods (with longer phase out of barriers for certain 'sensitive' sectors). They include evolutionary clauses leading to deeper integration including eventual EC membership. At the end of Twentieth Century, European institutions included monetary policy, the protection of human rights, and coordination in foreign policy and military security, thus encroaching on what many regard as the core of state sovereignty[42].

In principle, the member states can not restrict imports of the EU goods or services at their borders. All boarder measures including antidumping and countervailing duties are excluded. They can not restrict Intra-EU capital and labor movements or inhibit establishment of firms from the EU-Nations. Member states can not freely choose their state aid policy, competition policy or indirect taxation (VAT) rates. All these restrictions are supervised by the Supra national European commission and can be enforced by the supranational European Court of Justice. European Union is the best example of the Deep integration.

Regional cooperation in East Asia, unlike the European Union (EU) or the North American Free Trade Agreement (NAFTA), has been slow in forming institutional frameworks despite a proliferation for dialogue and are considered as shallow integration. Regional integration in East Asia is well advanced and unique in character. The process of trade and financial (mainly FDI) regional integration has developed significantly since the early 1990s, and shown standard indicators of economic interdependence, the levels of which are comparable to those recorded in Europe. Another specific feature of East Asia's economic integration has been the predominance of intra-industry, rather than inter-industry, cross-border trade flows. This reflects the development of vertical production sharing networks within the region, as large corporate has been exploiting significant disparities in economic development and comparative advantages across countries in East Asia.[43]

ASEAN 's regional economic integration was hampered by such factors as competition and rivalry between Japan and China, dissatisfaction and suspicion among some about U.S. regional leadership. Moreover, East Asia's economic fate is highly dependent on the U.S. market. Despite the recession in US market, the result may be both improved economic conditions and strengthen up security as well. Second, structural reform and revitalization of Asian economies are becoming urgent against the backdrop of a deepening global recession, which became more severe after Sept. 11. East Asia must reduce its dependence on exports outside the region and base its economic growth more firmly on domestic or regional demand in order to stabilize the global, as well as the regional, economy. This requires external policy initiatives in addition to solving domestic problems such as deregulation or clearing up bad debt. To stimulate regional demand, the elimination of barriers to cross-border movement of corporate resources will be critical, thereby integrating long-fragmented regional markets and, in turn, enhancing the profitability of business activities to serve regional demand.

Furthermore, the speed of change in the business environment is too rapid for the World Trade Organization or other multilateral organizations to keep pace. Rather, regional efforts will offer a critical complement to enhance the stability of the global system. Quietly, but steadily, momentum for East Asian regional economic integration is gaining ground. just as it helped realize European reconciliation and integration after World War II. Asia is different from Europe in its diversity and geopolitical challenges. But stronger economic relations and integration have proven to be a welcome and promising path to stability. It is an enterprise well worth pursuing further.

In the line with European Union's growing role in economic and social regulations , West Europe has come to acquire greater weight in international affairs for the EU. By observing the success of EU and ASEAN, a new strong wind of regionalization of trade and other economic relations has been blowing in the global economy since late the 1980s. It is believed that RTAs could serve as a stepping stone towards multilateral trade agreements. Among the important developments in recently concluded RTAs is that they are going beyond the tariff cutting exercises. Many of them also include services, investments, intellectual properties, technical barrier to trade, dispute settlement etc. *Following the above trend, This book put emphasis on present situations of the Central Asian's integration as well as South Asian's integration..*

Successful regional cooperation will be a crucial element in the future peace and prosperity of Central Asia and South Asia, according to recent Asian Development Bank (ADB) surveys of the sub-regions. ADB's experience across Asia shows that rapid, sustained, and pro-poor economic growth is the most effective tool in the fight against poverty. In Central Asia, achieving such growth will require expanded export activity, stronger private enterprise, and an increase in investment in areas currently excluded from economic gains, according to ADB's Regional Cooperation Strategy and Program for Central Asia.

Regional cooperation offers the fastest and most effective way to put the building blocks of sustainable growth in place," says M.E. Tusneem, Director General of ADB's East and Central Asia Department.

"To expand growth and reduce poverty, Central Asian nations need to create efficient transport infrastructure, rehabilitate energy networks, restore and improve irrigation systems, and enable seamless transit across the region to external markets. Success in each of these areas will require close cooperation," M.E. Tusneem says.[44]

However, there are still procedural delays, reserved industries where foreign investors are not allowed to invest and ceilings in many industries/sectors in each of these countries. Accelerating the economic reform process and making their economies politically stable and free from internal conflict would go a long way toward making South Asia and Central Asia an attractive destination for FDI. The basic indicators, including infrastructure, show that all Central Asian and south Asian countries lack adequate infrastructure facilities and governance. Thus, more effective public investment on economic and social infrastructure, along with stable economic policies to create an enabling environment, would attract more foreign direct investment. Other significant factors that contribute to growth are exports, gross domestic capital formation and infrastructure. Therefore both the regions need to improve their domestic investment, exports and infrastructure facilities, along with more foreign investment, to achieve higher growth.

The Association of South East Asian Nations (ASEAN), European Union (EU), North American Free Trade Area (NAFTA) are few examples of such integration. the kind of overwhelming geopolitical challenge that helped postwar Europe to join together.

Following these role models, the countries of Central Asia and South Asia are also undergoing the process of liberalisation and regionalisation of their economies. The quest of economic integration however, remained inhibited by the colonial heritage of these countries. Whether economic interests will drive South Asian and Central Asian region toward greater cooperation and durable peace? If so, what is the potential for the growth of regional economic integration within the regions as well as with each others?. This study will look into detail in the following chapters.

South Asian region comprises seven countries, India, Nepal, Bhutan, Bangladesh, Pakistan, Sri Lanka and Maldives whereas Central Asian region that was formed after the disintegration of Former Soviet Union (FSU) in 1991 consists of five countries, Kazakhstan, Uzbekistan, Turkmenistan, Kyrgyzstan and Tajikistan.

Regional integration among developing countries is also part of a wider strategy to promote not only equitable growth but also increase competition, reduce private transaction costs, enable firms to exploit economies of scale, encourage inward foreign investment and facilitate macroeconomic policy coordination.

The question of economic integration- at intra or inter regional level or at the global level, is an important issue for both the regions. Both the regions have an enormous amount of resources and have an abundance of skilled labor resources, but are suffering from shortage of domestic savings or capital accumulation. Economic initiatives at the regional and supra-regional levels are required to exploit their resources. So the prospects of regions can not only be determined by only the regional groupings but also by the degree to which they successfully integrated into the world economy. Their richness in terms of natural resources, technology and labor resources have attracted the international community towards them.

All five Central Asian states are landlocked and distant from world markets that depended heavily on an intricate Soviet system of trade routes and energy pipelines for essential input supplies and exports. Mineral, and fuel resources of the region, though, made it a potentially attractive outlet for foreign investors. Following a long period of isolation and catering to the needs of the Soviet Union, these countries faced the tough challenge of how to exploit more effectively their natural resources to improve living standards. Another tough challenge was how to introduce the systemic changes' needed to achieve a market framework and to integrate their economies with the rest of the world.

Till the late 1960s, most of the developing economies, including those of East Asia, adopted closed macroeconomic policies with import substitution industrialization policies, under which self-reliance and indigenous efforts were encouraged. At the same time, a dominant role was assigned to the state in the development process. These import substitution strategies, coupled with the large public sectors, resulted in rent seeking activities and uncompetitive production processes therefore, export-led industrialization and liberalization was advocated to make the production process efficient and competitive. Following the export-oriented growth argument (Bhagawati and Srinivasan, 1975 and Kruger, 1975)[45], and the success of East Asian countries with higher exports and economic growth during the period from the early seventies to mid nineties, most of the South Asian countries started opening up their economies from the early eighties. The South Asian economies are currently enjoying the benefits of economic reforms, particularly reforms related to trade and investment. These countries undertook reform processes and opened up their economies after having experienced sluggish growth rates throughout the seventies and eighties. The economies of South Asian countries as well as of the Central Asian countries

---

Footnote : As history proves that the spread of trade and commerce was the single most important reason for changing the mode of production of the feudalism to capitalism, and also in history after 1991 collapse of socialism trade also played important role to give rise to capitalism, so trade plays an important role in systemic changes. (E.K. Hunt, 2004), p. 11.

have been undergoing deep economic transformation since mid eighties and nineties respectively. Speed and sequence of economic liberalisation varies in both the regions. So before studying the regional economic initiatives in Central and South Asian regions, and possibilities of their linkages, it is important to understand the present economic conditions of both the regions. In an attempt to integrate them with the world economy, most of the countries in both the regions have engaged themselves with economic reforms and liberalisation of their trade and investment regimes.

In the next chapter, the economic reforms and macroeconomic performance Central Asian countries in South Asian countries during last two decades will be briefly explained and analyzed.

Table 1.2
Some Important Regional Trade Agreements of the World

AFTA	ASEAN Free Trade Area	Brunei Darussalam Cambodia Indonesia Laos Malaysia Myanmar Philippines Singapore Thailand Vietnam
ASEAN	Association of South East Asian Nations	Brunei Darussalam Cambodia Indonesia Laos Malaysia Myanmar Philippines Singapore Thailand Vietnam
BAFTA	Baltic Free-Trade Area	Estonia Latvia Lithuania
BANGKOK	Bangkok Agreement	Bangladesh China India Republic of Korea Laos Sri Lanka
CAN	Andean Community	Bolivia Colombia Ecuador Peru Venezuela

(Contd.)

(Contd. Table 1.2)

CARICOM	Caribbean Community Common Market	Antigua & Barbuda and Bahamas Barbados Belize Dominica Grenada Guyana Haiti Jamaica Monserrat Trinidad & Tobago St. Kitts & Nevis St. Lucia St. Vincent & the Grenadines Surinam
CACM	Central American Common Market	Rica El Salvador Costa Guatemala Honduras Nicaragua
CEFTA	Central European Free Trade Agreement	Bulgaria Croatia Romania
CEMAC	Economic and Monetary Community of Central Africa	Cameroon Central African Republic Chad Congo Equatorial Guinea Gabon
CER	Closer Trade Relations Trade Agreement	Australia New Zealand
CIS	Commonwealth of Independent States	Azerbaijan Armenia Belarus Georgia Moldova Kazakhstan Russian Federation Ukraine Uzbekistan Tajikistan Kyrgyz Republic
COMESA	Common Market for Eastern and Southern Africa	Angola Burundi Comoros Democratic Republic of Congo Djibouti Egypt Eritrea Ethiopia Kenya Madagascar Malawi Mauritius Namibia Rwanda Seychelles Sudan Swaziland Uganda Zambia Zimbabwe

(Contd.)

(Contd. Table 1.2)

EAC	East African Cooperation	Kenya Tanzania Uganda
EAEC	Eurasian Economic CommunityKyrgyz	Belarus Kazakhstan Republic Russian Federation Tajikistan
EC	European Communities	Austria Belgium Cyprus Czech Republic Denmark Estonia Finland France Germany Greece Hungary Ireland Italy Latvia Lithuania Luxembourg Malta Netherlands Poland Portugal Slovak Republic Slovenia Spain Sweden United Kingdom
ECO	Economic Cooperation Organization	Afghanistan Azerbaijan Iran Kazakhstan Kyrgyz Republic Pakistan Tajikistan Turkey Turkmenistan Uzbekistan
EEA	European Economic Area	EC Iceland Liechtenstein Norway
EFTA	European Free Trade Association	Iceland Liechtenstein Norway Switzerland
GCC	Gulf Cooperation Council	Bahrain Kuwait Oman Qatar Saudi Arabia United Arab Emirates
GSTP	General System of Trade Preferences among Developing Countries	Algeria Argentina Bangladesh Benin Bolivia Brazil Cameroon Chile Colombia Cuba Democratic People's Republic of Korea Ecuador Egypt Ghana Guinea Guyana India Indonesia Islamic Republic

(Contd.)

(Contd. Table 1.2)

		of Iran Iraq Libya Malaysia Mexico Morocco Mozambique Myanmar Nicaragua Nigeria Pakistan Peru Philippines Republic of Korea Romania Singapore Sri Lanka Sudan Thailand Trinidad and Tobago Tunisia United Republic of Tanzania Venezuela Vietnam Yugoslavia Zimbabwe
LAIA	Latin American Integration Association	Argentina Bolivia Brazil Chile Colombia Cuba Ecuador Mexico Paraguay Peru Uruguay Venezuela
MERCOSUR	Southern Common Market	Argentina Brazil Paraguay Uruguay
MSG	Melanesian Spearhead Group	Fiji Papua New Guinea Solomon Islands Vanuatu
NAFTA	North American Free Trade Agreement	Canada Mexico United States
OCT	Overseas Countries and Territories	Greenland New Caledonia French Polynesia French Southern and Antarctic Territories Wallis and Futuna Islands Mayotte Saint Pierre and Miquelon Aruba Netherlands Antilles Anguilla Cayman Islands Falkland Islands South Georgia and South Sandwich Islands

(Contd.)

(Contd. Table 1.2)

		Montserrat Pitcairn Saint Helena Ascension Island Tristan da Cunha Turks and Caicos Islands British Antarctic Territory British Indian Ocean Territory British Virgin Islands
PATCRA	Agreement on Trade and Commercial Relations between the Government of Australia and the Govern -ment of Papua New Guinea	Australia, Papua New Guinea
PTN	Protocol relating to Trade Negotiations among Develo -ping Countries	Bangladesh Brazil Chile Egypt Israel Mexico Pakistan Paraguay Peru Philippines Republic of Korea Romania Tunisia Turkey Uruguay Yugoslavia
SADC	Southern African Development Community	Angola Botswana Lesotho Malawi Mauritius Mozambique Namibia South Africa Swaziland Tanzania Zambia Zimbabwe
SAPTA	South Asian Preferential Trade Arrangement	Bangladesh Bhutan India Maldives Nepal Pakistan Sri Lanka
SPARTECA	South Pacific Regional Trade and Economic Cooperation Agreement	Australia New Zealand Cook Islands Fiji Kiribati Marshall Islands Micronesia Nauru Niue

(Contd.)

(Contd. Table 1.2)

		Papua New Guinea Solomon Islands Tonga Tuvalu Vanuatu Western Samoa
TRIPARTITE	Tripartite Agreement	Egypt India Yugoslavia
UEMOA WAEMU	West African Economic and Monetary Union	Benin Burkina Faso Côte d'Ivoire Guinea Bissau Mali Niger Senegal Togo

Source:www.wto.org/english/traptop_e/region_e/region_e.htm

Post War Chronology of Regionalism

Following is the chronology of the growth of regionalism in the postwar trading system and its acceleration in recent years.

Table 1.3

1947	GATT agreed to by 23 countries, and with Article XXIV which allows formation of customs unions free trade areas under certain conditions.
1957	Treaty of Rome establishes the European Economic Community, a customs union between Belgium, Luxembourg, France, the Netherlands, Germany, and Italy. Treaty in force January 1, 1958.
1959	Stockholm Convention establishes the European Free Trade Association (EFTA) in effect July 1,1960. Members include Austria, Denmark, Norway, Portugal, Sweden, Switzerland, and the United Kingdom.
1960	Montevideo Treaty establishes Latin American Free Trade Association (LAFTA) comprising Brazil, Chile, Peru, Uruguay, Argentina, Mexico, and Paraguay.
	Central American Common Market (CACM) formed; includes Costa Rica, El Salvador, Guatemala, Honduras, and Nicaragua.
1963	Convention between the E.E.C and former French, Belgian, and Italian colonies in Africa gives these countries preferential access to the E.C and sets up the European Development Fund.

(Contd.)

(Contd. Table 1.3)

1965	Canada and the U.S sign Automobile Products Trade Agreement.
1973	European Community enlarged to include Britain, Ireland and Denmark.
1978	ASEAN formed. Includes Indonesia, Malaysia, Philippines, Singapore, and Thailand.
1981	Greece joins the European Community.
1983	Australia and New Zealand form Closer Economic Relationship to provide for a free trade agreement.
1984	U.S. implements Caribbean Basin Economic Recovery Act to extend duty-free treatments to 21 beneficiary countries to be eliminated.
1985	U.S.-Israel Free Trade Area Agreement enters into force. Over a 10-years periods, all tariffs between the two countries to be eliminated.
	Iran, Pakistan and Turkey created a Economic Cooperation organization.(ECO)
1986	Portugal and Spain join the European Community. Single European Act signed to provide for full European integration in 1992.
1989	Canada-U.S. Free Trade Agreement enters into force. Under agreement, by 1998 all items should be traded duty-free between the two countries.
1990	E.C. and EFTA undertake discussion on a European Economic Area to provide for freer movement of goods, services, capital, and people between the two associations.
	United States announces "Enterprise for the Americas" Initiative to explore a hemispheric-wide free trade zone between countries of North, Central, and South America.
1991	U.S., Mexico, and Canada enter discussions on a North America free trade area, leading eventually to the signing of NAFTA.
	Andean Pact members (Bolivia, Columbia, Ecuador, Peru and Venezuela) sign accord to implement free trade zone by the end of 1995.
	Treaty of Asuncion signed between Brazil, Argentina, Uruguay and Paraguay to form Mercosur (the South American Common

(Contd.)

(Contd. Table 1.3)

	Market). Aim is to create a duty free common market by the end of 1994.
	Chile and Mexico sign Free Trade Accord. All non tariff barriers to be eliminated. Common tariff of 10 percent to apply to 95% of trade as of January 1992.
	Turkey and EFTA to eliminate duties on import of industrial goods (excluding textiles and processed farm products.EC and EFTA finalize EEA to go into effect in 1993. ASEAN Free Trade Agreement formed. Group agreed to 15 year time period in which to create single ASEAN Market.
	EFTA sign trade cooperation accords with Bulgaria, Romania and three Baltic States.
	EC signs association accords with Poland, Hungary and Czechoslovakia Agreement to result in free trade within 10 years.
	Belarus, Russia and Ukraine established the Commonwealth of Independent states (CIS).
1992	El Salvador, Guatemala, and Honduras agree to from a free trade zone. The countries agree to allow unrestricted movement of most goods and capital, and work toward establishing uniform tariffs on imports.
	NAFTA (U.S.-Mexico-Canada) negotiations concluded. Agreement provides for the elimination of tariffs in stages over a period of no more than 15 years, and in 10 years in some cases, including a phase-out of tariffs on textiles and apparel. Side agreements later negotiated on labor and environment. The agreement goes into effect January 1, 1994.
	Implementation of European Economic Area (EEA) (due to go into effect January 1, 1993) delayed when Switzerland voted against joining.Poland, Hungary, Slovakia, and the Czech Republic establish a regional trade zone. Aim is to gradually eliminate tariffs over next 17 years and become more compatiblewith the E.C. and EFTA.
	In 1992 ECO was enlarged with the addition of Afghanistan, Azerbaijan, Kazakhstan, Kyrgyzstan, Tajikistan, Turkmenistan and Uzbekistan.

(Contd.)

(Contd. Table 1.3)

1993	Hungry and EFTA conclude a free trade agreement. Extends free trade in a range of goods, including processed agriculture goods, industrial goods, and fish. Bulgaria and EFTA conclude free trade agreement. Extends free trade in inindustrial goods, processed farm goods and fish products. Chile and Venezuela sign a free agreement, import tariffs expected to illuminate on 90 percent of the products by 1997. Chile and Bolivia sign a bilateral agreement to reduce tariffs. South Asian Preferential Trading Agreement established with aim of forming a common market between Bangladesh, Bhutan, India, Maldives, Nepal, Pakistan, and Sri Lanka Nicaragua, Honduras, El Salvador, and Guatemala reach an agreement to liberalize trade. Barriers to trade in textiles, shoes, and leather goods will be reduced. Groups of Three (Mexico, Venezuela, and Colombia) sign a free trade agreement to go into effect June 1994. Agreement covered market access, rules of origin, investment, government procurement, and intellectual property. Chile and Colombia sign a free trade agreement. Most non tariff barriers eliminated and tariffs reduced. Guatemala, Honduras, El Salvador, Nicaragua, Costa Rica, and Panama sign an Agreement toward freer trade and integration. Turkey and the European community negotiate leading to a customs union between Turkey and the E.C. by 1995. By 1993 all the former Soviet Republics (members like, Armenia, AzerbAijan, Georgia, Kazakhstan, Kyrgyzstan, The Republic of Maldova, Russia, Tajikistan, Turkmenistan, Ukraine and Uzbekistan) except the Baltic States had joined CIS.
1994	EEA comes into effect, creating a free trade area between the European Union (Community) and the EFTA countries of Austria, Finland, Norway, Sweden, and Iceland.Sweden, Finland, Austria, and Norway negotiate full membership in the European Union. Mexico and Costa Rica conclude a free trade agreement to go into effect January 1995. Tariffs and most nontariff barriers to

(Contd.)

(Contd. Table 1.3)

	be eliminated. Provisions included on national treatment for investment, intellectual property rights, labor mobility, and dispute settlement.
	MERCOSUR members reach a compromise agreement on a common a tariff structure allowing customs unions to become effective January 1995.
	APEC (Asia-Pacific Economic Cooperation) members agreed to accelerate liberalization of trade and investment measures within the group. Members will begin liberalizing tariff and other barriers in 2000, and developed country members will achieve an open market by 2010. The developing will have until 2020 to complete their liberalisation. APEÇ consists of Australia, Brunai, Derussalam, Canada, Chile, Hong Kong, Indonesia, Japan, Malaysia, Mexico, New Zealand, Papua New Guinea, Peoples Republic of China, Philippines, Singapore, South Korea, Taiwan, Thailand, and the United States.
	Chile was formally invited to begin negotiations to join NAFTA.
	At the Summit of the Americas held the Miami (December 9-11) the 34 countries located in North Central, South American and the Caribbean Jointly agreed to negotiate a Free Trade Area of Americas by the year 2005.
	Central Asian Economic Union (CAEU) was formed by Kazakhstan, Kyrgyzstanand Uzbekistan.
1995	The EU and Turkey agreed on the custom union accord. Tarriffs will be eliminated and a common tariffs establish on products from outside the custom union. Some EU agriculture restrictions will still apply to Turkish exports. The Custom Union goes into effect January 1,1996.
	Chile began negotiating with the members of NAFTA: Mexico, Canada and United States.
	Estonia, Lithuania and Latvia signed association agreements with the European Union. The agreements provide trade and cooperation deals and possible future EU membership.
	Vietnam joined the association of South east Asian Nations and was given longer implementation periods to fulfill ASEAN liberalization timetables.

(Contd.)

(Contd. Table 1.3)

1996	Chile and Bolivia became associate members of MERCOUSUR. Shanghai Five group created by China, Kazakhstan, Kyrgyzstan, Russia and Tajikstan.
1998	Cyprus, the Czech Republic, Estonia, Hungry, Poland, and Slovenia began negotiations to become members of the European Union.Talks to form the Free Trade Area (FTAA) among the 34 democractics countries of North and South America by 2005 started.
	The Special Programme for the Economies of Central Asia (SPECA) was established by the presidents of Kazakhstan, Kyrgyzstan, Tajikstan and Uzbekistan. Turkmenistan also joined in the same year.
	Tajikistan became a member of CAEU and CAEU was renamed as Central Asian Economic Cooperation (CREC).
1999	Bulgaria, Latvia, Lithuania, Malta, Romania, Slovakia and Turkey started negotiated to become members of the European
2001	The Shanghai Cooperation Organisation was established in Schanghai, China with the addition of Uzbekistan.
2002	Azerbaijan has become a member of SPECA.
	CAEC was again renamed as CACO. Central Asian Cooperation Organization (CACO).
2004	Russia joined CACO.
	SAFTA has been signed in Islamabad among SAARC countries.
2005	Iran and Pakistan applied for the membership of SCO. Turkmenistan declared its attention to reduce its participation in the CIS.

Source compiled from : J. Whalley and C. Hamilton , The Trading System The Uruguay Round (Washington DC: Institute for International Economics, 1996), pp. 169-174. Domnick Salvatore, and upgraded till 2005.

References

1. Manmohan Agarwal, (2004) " Regional trading Arrangements in the Era of Globalization: An Indian Perspective" in *International Studies*, vol. 41, no. 4, p. 412.
2. Pomfret Richard, (1997), *The Economics of Regional Trading Arrangements,* Oxford University Press, New York., p. 174.

3. The Palgrave Dictionary of Economics.
4. UNDP, (2005) " Bringing Down Barriers: Regional Cooperation for Human Development and Human Security" in *Central Asian Human Development Repor*, Regional bureau for Europe and the CIS, Slovak Republic., p. 1.
5. P. Krugman,(1993), "Regionalism verses Multilateralism", in J. De Melo and A. Panagariya, eds, *New Dimensions in Regional Integration*, Cambridge University Press, Cambridge, pp. (58-79). p. 73.
6. Dominick Salvatore, *International economics*, New York: John Wily & Sons, 2001.p-8.
7. Theoretically, the impact of trade on social welfare is always positive in the absence of market failures and policy-induced distortions, but may or may not be negative in the presence of market failures or policy-induced distortions (see, for example, Bhagwati, Panagariya, and Srinivasan [1998]). Likewise, there are theoretical models in which the impact of trade on economic growth is positive and models in which it is negative. Empirically, a large body of evidence suggests that trade stimulate economic growth, although there are several conceptual and technical difficulties in establishing a link between trade and growth. See Berg and Kruger (2003) and Winters (2004) for a survey of the recent empirical literature on the relationship between trade and economic growth.
8. Asimina Caminis (2006), Integrating poor countries into the world trading system, economic issues no.37, www.imf.org/pub. p. 2.
9. Participation in global production networks (GPNs) requires participation in international trade. It also increases the gains from trade for developing countries by enabling them to specialize in the labor-intensive stages of manufacturing processes (which, overall, might be technology or capital intensive) and helping them gain better access to markets in developed countries, attract foreign direct investment (FDI), acquire modern technologies, boost manufactured exports, and climb the value-added ladder.

   At the same time, participation in GPNs poses certain risks for developing countries. See ADB (2003) for a more detailed discussion of opportunities and challenges GPNs represent for developing countries.
10. United Nations Trade and Development reports,1976.

11. S.K.Bhatacharya, "Regional Trading Arrangements among SAARC Countries: Do they Increase India's Imports? in *South Asia Economic Journal,* Vol. 2, No. 2, 2001 p. 283.
12. www.wto.org/english/traptop_e/region_e/region_ehtm. sighted on 28th July 2007 www.wto.org.
13. J.Poon, (1995), "Global Regionalization Tendencies: spatial structure and Linkages" South East Asian Studies working paper, National University of Singapore, Singapore., pp. 5-7.
14. Central Asia Human Development Report (2005), op.cit., pp, 13.
15. Viner.J (1950)., *The custom union issue*, Carnegie Endowment press, New York., p. 44.
16. Dominick Salvatore, op. cit, p. 329.
17. *Ibid*, p. 334.
18. *Ibid*, p. 333.
19. *Ibid*, p. 333.
20. Pomfret Richard, op. cit, p. 174.
21. G-20 workshop, 22-24 September, 2004 by Prof Sapir in session II, on process of regional integration a desirable sequencing or a "Menu Approach".
22. The Making Regional Economic Integration Work
Speech by Mr. Agustín Carstens Deputy Managing Director of the International Monetary Fund At the 20th Annual General Meeting and Conference of the Pakistan Society of Development Economists Islamabad, Pakistan, January 12, 2005. www.imf.org.
23. Athansios Vamvakidis, (1999), IMF Staff Papers vol. 46. no. 1 p. 43.
24. Julie Mckay, at all.ed., *Regional Economic Integration in the global Framework,* G-20 Workshop, 23-24 September,2004,Germany: European central Bank, 2005. p. 113.
25. Bhagwati, Panagriya, (1996), "Preferential Trade Areas and Multilateralism: Strangers, Freiends or Foes?"in *The Economics of Preferential Trade Agreements*, ed, AEI Press, Washington DC., pp. 1-78.
26. Julie Mckay, at all , ed, *Regional Economic Integration in the global Framework* op. cit. p. 116.
27. Director-General Pascal Lamy, welcomes WTO agreement on regional trade agreements at www.wto.org/english/traptop_e/region_e/region_ehtm., visited on 10th July 2006.
28. C.Fred Bergsten, "Open Regionalism",*The World Economy*, Vol.20,No. 5,1997.p.545.

29. Imperfect competition or imperfectmarket, themarket comprises a large numbers of independentlyacting firms and buyers.the product offered by the competing firms are differentiated from each others, free market entry and exit.
30. R. Garnaut, "Open Regionalism: Its Analitic Basis And Relevance to the International system" *Journal of Asian Economics*, Vol. 5, No. 2, summer 1994, pp. 273-90.
31. Created in 1951, by the Treaty of Paris. The members were- Belgium, France, West Germany, Italy, Luxembourg and the Netherlands. The UK was invited but declined.
32. Bergstern, "Open Regionalism", op.cit. p. 553.
33. Lawerance,(1996) *Regionalism, Multilaterism and Deep Integration,* Washington: Booking Institution,1996.p. 179.
34. by Munakata Naoko (pac News letter, # 46 vol. November 16, 2001)
35. P. Krugman,(1993),"Regionalism verses Multilateralism", op.cit., p. 73.
36. Richard, E. Baldwin, "the Causes of Regionalism", *The Economic Journal*, 1997, p. 867.
37. *Ibid*, p. 868.
38. John Baylis and Steve Smith (2006), *The Globalisation of TheWorld Politics, Oxford University Press* New Delhi. p. 582.
39. Bhagwati, Jagdish., (1999), *A Stream of Windows,* Oxford University Press, New Delhi., p. 280.
40. *Ibid*, p. 282.
41. John Baylis and Steve Smith, op.cit, p. 582.
42. (USSFTA, the ASEAN FTA (AFTA), 2 the Republic of Korea-Chile FTA, the JSEPA, the ASEAN- 1 Information taken from the WTO web site as of October 12, 2004. http://www.wto.org/english/tratop_e/region_e/region_e.htm, and from WTO (2003a)).
43. M.E.Tusneem, A speech by Director General of ADB's East and Central Asia Department at www.adb.org.
44. Bhagwati, J and TN Srinivasan, (1975) *Foreign Trade.*
45. *Regimes and Economic Development*, Macmillian, New Delhi.

2

Economic Liberalization in Central and South Asian Region

This chapter will discuss and analyse the economic liberalisation process in general and Central Asian and South Asian region's Trade liberalisation in particular. Broadly, this will present a cross-country analysis of economic policy regimes in both regions in the last two decades and will assess the transformation phase of both the regions. Brief history and some similarities of the regions will be discussed. It will also discuss the challenges and compare the transition from one system to another system. The transition processes from market economy to planned economy or from planned economy to market economy involves a complex process of institutional, structural and behavioral changes. How these regions proceed towards new system, gradually or through shock therapy, will be assessed in this chapter. To know the developments of economic liberalisation in both the regions, it is important to understand the process of transformation. Transformation took place in all the areas such as fiscal adjustments, stabilisation, structural reforms and external sectors reforms. While understanding all reforms, this chapter will concentrate only on external sector reforms of the economies of both the regions. How these regions dealt with the price liberalisation and trade liberalisation will be discussed. How these regions have been competing with the international prices and trying to integrate with world will also be analysed in this chapter.

Brief History and Similarities of the Regions

The Central Asia region mainly consists of the five Central Asian republics - Kazakhstan, Kyrgyz Republic, Tajikistan, Turkmenistan, and Uzbekistan, which is the home of 50.25 million people. South Asia, consists of Bangladesh, Bhutan, India, Maldives, Nepal, Pakistan and Sri Lanka, which has population of about 1.5 billion people (in 2001).These regions have high man power and natural resources, which are essential for human life and advancement. They have man power, hydel power, mineral wealth and natural resources. But these regions are suffering from lack of knowledge and will power. Political stability is another requirement for economic and industrial recovery. These countries have labor resources in abundance. They are prone to the high pace of the demographic growth. Acute shortage of domestic savings and capital accumulation is another critical challenge they are facing.

Both the regions were under the colonialism. Russian Empire ruled Central Asia and British Empire ruled the South Asia. With the rise of the Soviet Union, Central Asia became integrated to the Soviet Command Economy, but remained geographically and economically distant from the Soviet Empire, It was largely cut off from rest of the world, including its immediate neighbors and historic trade partners (Afghanistan, Iran,and South Asia Subcontinent)[1] (Central Asia Human Development Report, 2005.) Practically all the South Asian and Central Asian countries have introduced economic reforms and have undertaken liberalization measures which are aimed at integrating their economies with the global economy. The progress of regional cooperation will enlarge mutual interest within the regions as well as with each other. In the long run, it will help in solving the development problems of the regions and will also create an environment for friendship. Both the regions are undergoing the liberalization process, speed and sequence varies in the countries of both the regions. While going through the liberalization process these regions face many challenges which will be discussed and analyzed in this chapter, It's very important to understand the brief history about these regions before proceeding towards analysis of economic liberalization policies.

Brief History of Central Asia.

This region is located in the center of the Eurasian continent. It is bordered on the north by the Russian Federation, on the south by Iran and Afghanistan, and on the east by the Xinjiang Uygur Autonomous Region of the People's Republic of China (PRC). Azerbaijan, a member of the Caucasus, lies on the western side of the region near Turkmenistan. To know the perspective of Central Asian people, one can not understand the recent changes in the economy of Central Asia without knowing its historical background. Historically Central Asian economic developments can be divided into three main periods: pre-Revolutionary period, Soviet Period and Post Soviet period.

The level of economic development was extremely low during the pre revolutionary tsarist era (as part of the Russian Empire until1917). This period witnessed the establishment of the forts and creations of new cities and settlements, commercial routes, educational institutions, postal systems and railroads. New agricultural crops like cotton, potatoes, sugar beets etc. were introduced at this time. Most of Central Asia was incorporated into the Russian Empire in the 1860s and 1870s, and was subsequently developed as a supplier of cotton to mills in Russia[2](Richard,2003). In the Soviet era the Central Asian republics were open economies, supplying raw materials (cotton, oil, gas and minerals) to the rest of the USSR, but quite distanced from the global economy.

During this period Central Asia lacked access to sea and was separated from the main trade routes. But during the Soviet period, the military and economic requirement of the USSR gave some importance to this region. These include the development of agriculture as well as considerable achievements in the fields of culture, science, education and public health[3](Rumer, 2003). During this period industrialization enveloped the entire Soviet Russia. Kazakhstan and Uzbekistan offer instructive examples of the most industrially developed countries in Central Asia. The inward-oriented trade patterns within the centrally planned Soviet economy were reinforced by transport, pipeline, and other communications facilities. The railways and pipelines led to Russia, and most air services and international phone lines passed through a Moscow hub[4]. (Richard, 2003)

The modernization and industrialization had been uneven and was not guided by a long term strategy. The burden of the whole Soviet Union fell on Uzbekistan and Kazakhstan. Central Asian Countries are geographically land locked and resource rich countries. At the time of independence the economic conditions of the region were not favorable for sustainable development strategy. There was also a loss of subsidies for budgets, enterprises and households which was earlier paid directly or indirectly through social payments. There was also a loss of administrative structure and skilled labors.[5]

Kazakhstan stretches from the Chinese border to the Caspian Sea and is bounded by Russia, Uzbekistan and Kyrgyzstan. Ethnically this country diverse whose population includes over hundred nationalities, about 60% population live in urban areas. Kazakhstan has half of the Former Soviet Unions total deposits of the resources like copper, lead and zinc. Other minerals like, coal tungsten, oil, nickel, chromium, molybdenum, manganese are also available in Kazakhstan. It has the second largest oil field in the world in Kasagan and sits on an estimated 3 billion tones of oil and 2 trillion tones of gas. In agriculture grains, sugar beet, potatoes vegetables, meat, milk, eggs and cotton are the main crops in Kazakhstan. It has been noted for its sheep which yields high quality of wool. It is also popular for its industries as iron ore, sulphuric acid, agricultural machinery, ferroconcrete, knitwear, footwear, hosiery.

Kyrgyzstan is situated on the Tien-shan Mountains. It has China, Kazakhstan, Uzbekistan and Tajikistan as neighbors. It has been famous for its livestock breeding, grain, cotton, potatoes. Vegetable fruits, meat milk, eggs, wool tobacco are the products obtained here, Bee keeping is well developed Main industries are sugar, food, cotton, wool, tanning, flourmills, tobaccos, timber, textiles, engineering, metallurgy, oil and mining.

Tajikistan is boarded by Uzbekistan, Kirghizia, China, and Afghanistan. Farming horticulture and cattle breeding are the main occupations. Products like grain, potatoes, vegetables, fruit, grapes, meat, milk, eggs, wool and cotton are available here. Tajikistan is rich in resources like brown coal, lead, zinc, oil uranium, radium and arsenic. Some industries like mining, engineering, food textiles, clothing, silk, bricks, ferroconcrete, knitwear and footwear are set up in this country.

Turkmenistan is bounded by the Caspian Sea on the west. Its neighbors are Uzbekistan, Iran and Afghanistan. Maize, grapes, fruits and vegetables, cotton are the main agricultural products. Natural resources like ozocerite, oil coal, sulphur, salt magnesium and extensive oil and gas reserves give Turkmenistan an edge over the other Central Asian Countries. Food textiles, chemical, cement agricultural implements, ferroconcrete, footwear, knitwear are the main industrial set up in this country. Uzbekistan is bordered by Kazakhstan, Kyrgyzstan, Tajikistan, Afghanistan and Turkmenistan.

Uzbekistan has an excellent record in agriculture. Intensive farming, based on artificial irrigation is practiced here. It is the chief cotton growing area in the former Soviet Union and third in the world. Crops like cotton, grain, potatoes, vegetables, grapes, fruits and berries are the main products of this county. This country is rich in resources like oil, coal, copper ozocerite building materials. Agricultural machinery, cement textiles paper ferroconcrete are the main industries available here. All the five countries of Central Asia have started liberalizing their economies since the onset of independence in 1991.

Brief History of South Asia

South Asian economy encompasses traditional village farming, modern agriculture, handicrafts a wide range of modern and traditional industries and a multitude of support services. South Asian region is blessed with exceptional diversities of natural and manmade resources such as land forms and climate regimes ranging from sea level to the highest mountains and deep gorges; hottest plains to snow clad mountains; wettest to driest places; dissected green valley to coral islands. Thousands of rivers with immense hydroelectric potentials, mineral resources such as Coal, iron, natural gas etc. are available in this region. This region is also blessed with extensive diversity of forest resources including extensive variety of animals, herbs and timber[6].(Kumar,2003)

South Asia, emerging from colonialism after the Second World War, was also primarily agrarian in the late 1940s. South Asia has also inherited from the colonial period common institutional and legal infrastructures and a common physical infrastructure of roads, railways and inland waterways. Mostly they developed the port areas to export things from South Asia. These got disrupted and disconnected at places, because of prolonged neglect, disuse and even deliberate destruction during periods of conflict. These can be restored without much cost. South Asia has a market consisting of 1.3 billion consumers with rising incomes. And lastly, over the last two decades, there has been a convergence of the macroeconomic policies of these countries and also diversification of their economies along similar lines[7].

The major economies of South Asia grew slowly at first, but began to pick up momentum in the mid-1980s and may now be in the early phases of sustainable high growth, There are some signs in India, Sri Lanka and Bangladesh that their economies may be moving again toward the higher growth rates after 1990s.

India Indian economy is not only becoming stronger, more competitive globally and increasingly resistance to absorb external shocks and also seems confidently poised for higher rate of growth in a stable environment. Minerals resources like coal and lignite, bauxite, chromites, copper, gold, iron ore, lead-zinc, manganese, nickel, Tungsten, Barytes, Diamonds, Dolomite, fire clay, fluorspar, gypsum, Graphite, Limestone, Mica, Magnesite etc. are found in India. Economic reforms started in the early eighties, but a comprehensive liberalization and privatization process started in July 1991 in the backdrop of the balance of payment crisis and foreign exchange liquidity crisis faced by the economy. Since then, there have been attempts to integrate the Indian economy with the rest of the world in a variety of ways, i.e., the removal of quantitative restrictions, reducing tariffs and exchange rate flexibility. India launched its second-generation reforms in 2002, with a focus on reducing the fiscal deficit, improving infrastructure, reforming labor laws and energizing the states to participate actively in stepping up the pace of reforms. India raised its FDI limits in many important sectors including telecommunication, banking and insurance and civil aviation.

Pakistan is primarily an agricultural economy. Wheat is the main subsistence crop, fruits and livestock are important in north. Pakistan is not yet self-sufficient in food production. Its diverse mineral resources are yet to be fully developed, but low grade coal and iron ore, chromites gypsym and limestone are being mined. Deposits of natural gas and oil are potentially large. Pakistan exports wool and cotton textiles and leather goods and has a growing industrial base. Though several reform measures were carried out prior to 2001, formally the economic reforms program had its genesis in the year 2001 when Pakistan signed a three year arrangement with IMF under the Poverty Reduction and Growth Facility (PRGF) program. Since its approval, seven program reviews have been completed successfully and discussions for the eighth review have been scheduled for April 2006. The key to restoring growth has been the authorities' determined implementation of sound financial policies and structural reforms including tax reform, financial sector reform, investment policies including FDI policy, and enterprise reform. These policies have reduced distortions and increased efficiency, and also lifted uncertainty about the future course of economic policies.

Bangladesh is surrounded by India, Myanmar and Bay of Bangal. A republic of South Asia, Bangladesh was formerly East Pakistan. East Pakistan became an independent entity named Bangladesh on 16 Dec 1971. Most people live in rural areas and make their living from agriculture. Major reforms were implemented as a part of structural adjustment policies under the auspices of the World Bank and the IMF in the 1980s and early 1990s. The efforts started with World Bank Structural and Sectoral Adjustment loans (SALs and SECLs) in 1980. IMF introduced a three-year Structural Adjustment Facility (SAF) in 1986 under which major reform initiatives were undertaken in areas such as agricultural policy, trade and industrial policy, along with privatization and public enterprise reforms, fiscal policy reform and financial sector reform. Moreover, the implementation of these reforms gained momentum during the 1990s.

Bhutan economy is largely subsistence economy. People are engaged in subsistence farming; and barter is practiced. The transition to market economy has changed social life. Large deposits of lime stone, graphite, lead, copper, slate coal, talc, gypsum, beryl, mica, pyrites and tufa have been found. Chief crops are rice millet, wheat, barley, maize, cardamom, potatoes, oranges etc. Extensive and valuable forests abound livestock includes cattle, Yaks, pigs, sheep and goats and poultry, food industry and cement industries are the main industries.

Nepal is among the poorest and least developed countries in the world with nearly half of its population living below the poverty line. Agriculture is the main stay of the economy, providing a livelihood for over 80% of the and accounting for 41% of GDP[8] (ADB,2006).Textiles and carpet production is accounted for major foreign exchange earnings. Industry contributes about 22% of Nepal's GDP. Tourism is the second largest industry. In line with changes in the development aid strategy of donors, Nepal embarked upon a new economic policy regime in the mid 1980s. It has carried out various components of economic reform policies including fiscal, trade and FDI policies during the last decade. Quantitative restrictions on imports have been fully removed. Customs duties have been rationalized and substantially reduced. Reforms have also been executed on the foreign exchange front. However, political instability has stopped the reform process and the ambitions of the business community

Sri Lanka has liberalized economic policies in early eighties. In 1977, Sri Lanka became the first among all the South Asian economies to open up its economy to the outside world, and even to this day it remains one of the most outward oriented economies in the region. The economic reforms, from their inception, marked a sharp shift from a relatively closed economy prioritizing import-substitution policies to a liberalized market and an export-oriented economy. Some of the major reforms were carried out in the areas of: (i) liberalization of trade policy and exchange rate system; (ii) export promotion and incentives to investment, and (iii) the rationalization of public expenditure.

Maldives became independent in 1965, the land is in the south fed by the Niger and Senegal rivers supports the chief cash crops of peanuts and cotton subsistence crops of rice, millets, maize. Exports include fish from Niger and livestock. Extensive minerals resources are largely untapped.

All the seven countries started liberalizing their economies at different points in time in tandem with the global trend and the requirement of both the regions, these countries have also adopted liberal economic policies, which will be discussed in detail in later in this chapter.

Economic Transformation

An important aspect to look into is why do societies establish or create one or the other type of economic system? In economic terms, the economists try to explain this aspect by what they call the law of scarcity at any given point of time, there are insufficient goods and services to satisfy all human wants of the society. The societies tried to choose a system, which would work efficiently and exploit the resources in a best manner possible. It is convenient to classify economic systems into three types, Command economy, market economy and mixed economy. A different way of dealing with universal problem of scarcity, adopted by many ancient as well as contemporary societies, is by command economy. Where a central authority decides what goods will be produced, allocate human and physical resources at will in their production and determine distributive shares of the society[9]. In a market system, all economic activities consists of engaging in exchanges, that is buying and selling factors of production and goods and services through the network of market places.[10] Mixed economy is one in which some economic activities are decided by the command economy and some activities by the market economy.

About one third of the world population rejected market economy and launched an experiment constructing socialistic economic system during 1917 and 1950, which was based on the ideology of Marxism and Leninism. This system is known as the command economic system. This system was adopted by the Former Soviet Union and Mongolia and after World War II in Central and Eastern Europe, Baltic States, China, North Korea and Vietnam.[11] History has shown many phases of successes and failures on the journey, whether it is from market economy to command economy or from command economy to market economy.

Transition was never easy, whether it's from market economy to planned economy or from planned economy to market economy. In establishing a socialistic system, massive efforts were made to centrally control production of goods and allocate all resources through state planning. Now its failure has set in motion just as a radical transformation, as the transition economies change course, seeking to rebuild markets and reintegrate themselves into the world markets[12](World Bank Report, 1996). This transition process from planned economy to market economy involves a complex process of institutional structural and behavioral changes.[13](Martha, De Melo, 1999) Since independence, Central Asian countries started witnessing transformation from command economy to market economy[14] (Kornoi, 2001).

Transformation of Command Economy to Market Economy

Transformation of a command economy to a market economy was also a big challenge for these regions[15] (Kornoi, 2001), because both the systems are contradictory to each other. Capitalism has been defined as an economic system in which productive assets are privately owned as goods are produced with hired labor for sale in the market to earn profit whereas in command economy most assets are publicly owned. This short definition describes the essence of these systems.[16] (Gregory Grossman, 1967) Through the Fig. 2.1, One could easily understand that how these systems are distinguished from each other.

These regions had to face an enormous challenge of liberalizing, privatizing and globalizing their respective economies. The key measures of reforms were macroeconomic stabilization, price and market liberalization, liberalization of exchange and trade system, privatization, establishing a competitive environment with few obstacles to market entry and exit and redefining the role of the state. It is important to state that the success of transition process depends not only upon the appropriate economic policies but also an availability of supporting political and legal economic institutions. The objective of stabilization is to reduce inflation either by reducing fiscal deficit or tightening monetary policy. Structural reforms on the contrary contribute to the growth in the long term, they aim at restructuring commercialization, privatization of state enterprises and enforcing on them financial discipline, External sector reform aim at diversifying trade, liberalizing prices and capital inflows[17]. (Gurgen, 1999) The table 2.1 describes elements of transition in detail.

The component of transition was generally classified having four major dimensions. Micro economics of transition, in which the focus was on creating market price signals through privatization. In macroeconomic of transition, the focus was on creating financial

Fig. 2.1

Model of the Socialist and Capitalist Systems

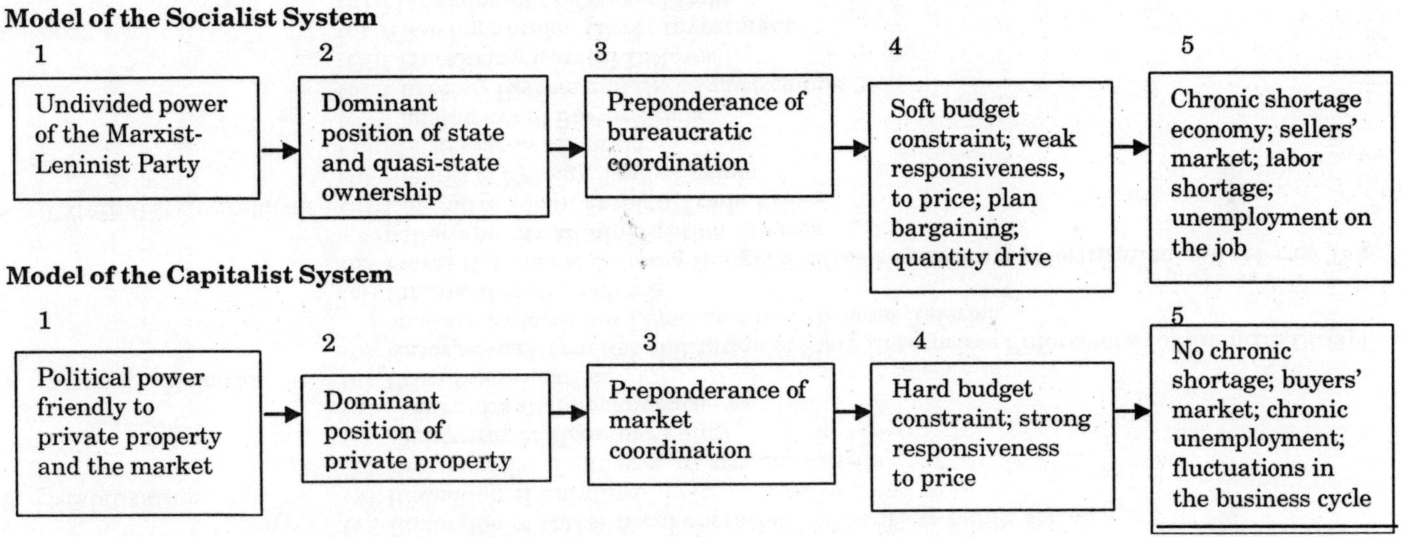

Source: Janos Kornai, (2001) "What the change of System From Socialism to Capitalism Does and Does not Mean", Journal of Economic Perspectives, Vol. 14, No. 1.

Table 2.1
Elements of Transition

1.	Fiscal Adjustment	(a). ReduceFiscal Imbalances without recourse to Inflation Tax
		(b) Reduction of government payment arrears
		(c) Reduction of Quasi-fiscal operations by banks to public sector.
2.	Stabilization	(a). Reduction of inflation
		(b). Reducing fiscal and cement account deficits
		(c). Tightening of Monetary Policy
		(d). Central Bank independence
3.	Structure Reforms	(a). Price liberalization
		(b). Enterprise reform Rehabilitation of State Enterprises Enforcement of financial Discipline on state Enterprises Legal and Institutional Reforms
		(c) Financial sector reforms
		(d) Fiscal Reforms Reforming Budget Process Expenditure prioritization and reforms Tax policy and tax administration reforms
4.	External sector reforms	(a) Liberalization of Foreign Trade Prices
		(b) Reform of Foreign Trade System
		(c) Market Diversification
		(d) Phasing out of Barter Trade
		(e) Currency Reform and Exchange Regimes
		(f) Liberalizing Capital Inflows
		(g) Allowing Foreign Direct Investment
		(h) Management of External Debt.

Table 2.2
Shock Therapy Vs Gradualism

	Shock Therapy	*Gradual Approach*
1. Change	Quick elimination of state ownership of new firms.	Emphasis on natural selection. Free entry and exist
2. Privatization	Very quick e.g. voucher privatization	Commercialization and Corporatization may precede privatization, which is gradual e.g. Employee. Management buyout, ESOPs.
3. Target	Intended end point	Shaped by requirements of present needs
4. Institutional Knowledge	Institutions have no value in the end state. Hence rapid destruction	Old institutions are built on past knowledge,this should be processed during reform. Hence gradual replacement
5. Reversibility ırreversibility	Logic of end point target requires	Policies are judged by performance reversible
6. Liberalization economics	Requires this as a first step to market building	Slow liberalization accompanied by institutional
7. Stabilization	Based on rigid monetarist polices. Quick disinflation	Exchange rate as an indicator for stabilization. No emphasis on quick disinflation.

Source: 1. Janos Kornai, "Ten Years After the Road to a Free Economy: The Authors Self-Evaluation", *Annual World Bank Conference on Development Economics 2000,* World Bank, 2001, pp. 53-54.

2. P. Murrel, "Evolutionary and Radical Approaches to Economic Reform", *Economic of Planning,* 25, 1992, p. 81.

3. Joesph E. Stiglitz, "Wither Reform? Ten Years of the Transitioin", *Annual World Bank Conference on Development Economics 1999*, World Bank, 2000, pp. 46-47.

4. Emine Gurgen, et.al., "Economic Reforms in Kazakhstan; Kyrgyz Republic, Tajiksitan, Turkmenistan and Uzbekistan", *IMF Occasional Paper, 183*, (Washington D.C., IMF, 1999).

system, financial infrastructure and developing new role of state. It also includes new roles for International trade and finance, trading arrangements, movements to convertible currency. In addition to it also included provision of safety nets. In addition to other reforms the external sector reforms plays crucial role in the economic growth of any country. The question arises that how these reforms took place, gradually of by big bang policy?

Transformation Through Gradual Process or by Shock Therapy

Some transition economies adopted the "big bang or shock therapy" policy changes and some adopted the gradual policy changes. Shock therapy means very radical structural reforms, whereas gradual means slow change. The first is to launch a rapid, all their program, undertaking as many as reforms as possible. The second is to change by way of partial and phased reforms. Table 2.2 explains all the reforms that under the big bang process, how quickly these reforms have been taken and under the gradual process how gradually these reforms implemented in a country's economy?

From the out set of transition, economists have been remarkably divided on the best strategy. There was never much doubt about what had to be done but the question was always, how these economies should proceed. Should they adopt gradual reform approach or they adopt the policy of shock therapy, whereas gradualism means a slow change and shock therapy means a rapid change of all policies.[18] (Naray, 2001). While understanding all the economic policies, this study put emphasis on the external sector reforms owing to its limitations.

Trade as Generator of Growth

Trade is an important generator of growth through attracting investors, who would be willing to explore resources from smaller markets to larger markets. The type of exports and imports classifies international transactions, which can be sorted out into two major categories: Current account transactions and capital account transactions. First include merchandise trade, services and investments and second include sale and purchase of financial assets-stocks, bond and other financial assets. Trade means buying and selling of commodities within a nation or among the nations. Prof Jagdish Bhagwati elucidated free trade policy, "as absence of tariffs, quotas, exchange restrictions, taxes and subsidies on production factors used and consumption.[19] (Jhinghan, 2001). Liberalization of the foreign trade regime, including elimination of export controls and taxes, and substitution of low-to-moderate import duties for import quotas and high import tariffs and current account convertibility. Liberal economic policies could provide a comfortable environment to the investors. Those investors would help to explore resources from smaller markets to larger markets.

The developing countries had protectionist policies towards the rest of the world, of course, protectionist policies are harmful to developing countries, their own trade barriers also retard their development by creating disincentives to export. From an economics perspective, quotas are thought to be less economically efficient than tariffs which in turn are less economically efficient than free trade economic analysis. This has been explained in this diagram that how quotas impact on trade, see fig. 2.2.

An import quota works by reducing amount of foreign goods a country may import. In a competitive market, the equilibrium point which determines the price and quantity produced of a good is where the demand curve and the domestic supply curve intersect. In the case of a purely domestic market, this point is at P* and Q* (see Fig. 2.2). When international trade is introduced into the market, this equilibrium may change. Let us assume that the price of a certain good is less when imported from abroad than when produced domestically. We will also assume that the world economy can supply more goods at that price than could ever be consumed by the domestic economy. In this case, the international supply curve is a horizontal line at P2, which is the price of that imported good. In this case, the equilibrium price lowers to P2, and the equilibrium quantity produced increases from Q* to Q4. Domestic producers will actually produce less (Q1), while the balance (the difference between Q1 and Q4) will be supplied by imports.

When free international trade is introduced, consumers benefit significantly. In a purely domestic market, the consumer surplus is represented by the area A. With free international trade, this surplus increases to include B, C, D, E, F, G, H, and I because they only

Fig.2.2

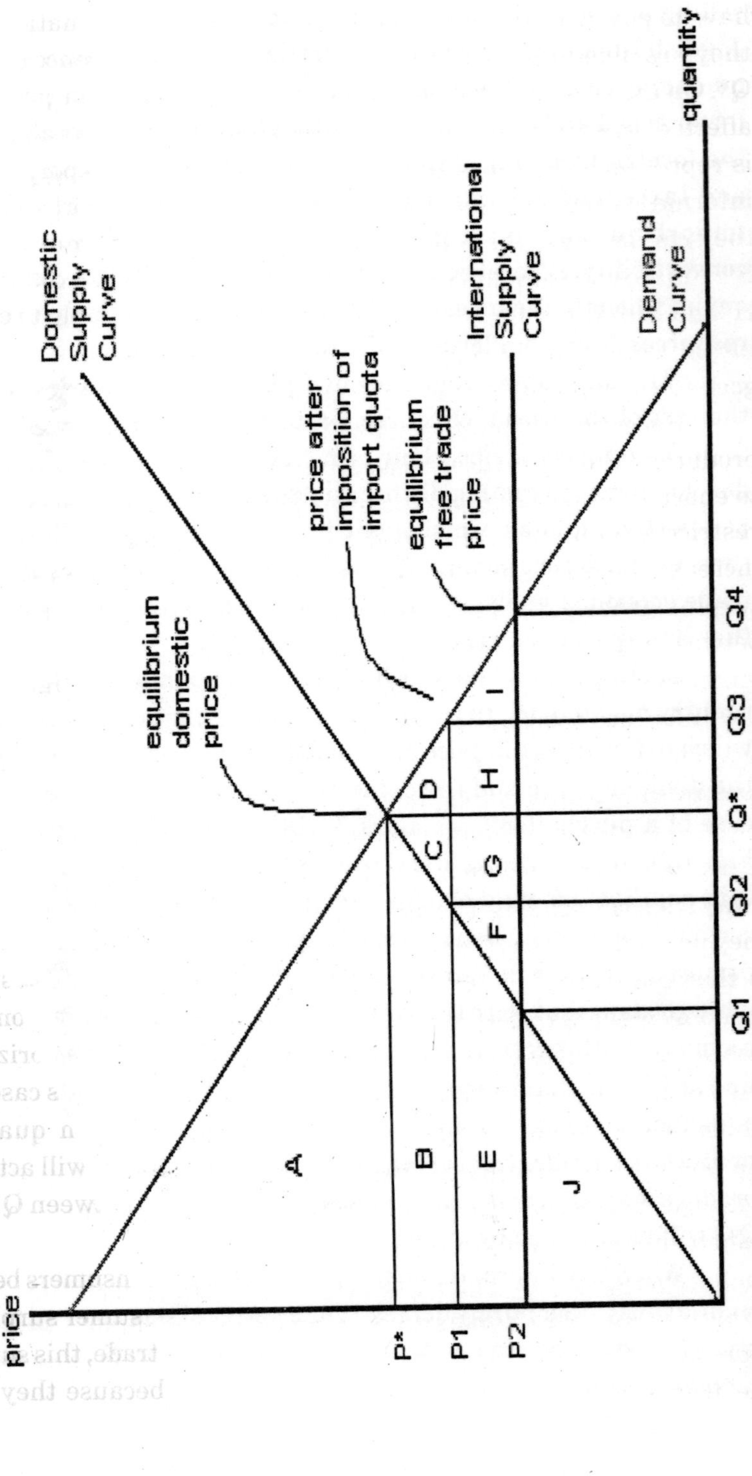
price
quantity
Domestic Supply Curve
International Supply Curve
Demand Curve
equilibrium domestic price
price after imposition of import quota
equilibrium free trade price
P*
P1
P2
Q1
Q2
Q*
Q3
Q4
A
B
C
D
E
F
G
H
I
J

have to pay price P2 for the good instead of the higher price P*, and they are able to purchase the quantity Q4 instead of the quantity Q*. On the other hand, domestic producers of the good are adversely affected. In a purely domestic market, the domestic producer surplus is represented by areas B, E, and J. With the introduction of free international trade, they lose areas B and E to consumers because they can only get the price P2 for their goods instead of the price P*. Finally, the economy on the whole benefits by areas C, D, F, G, H, and I, as these are areas of surplus that did not exist before the introduction of free trade. As is evident, all of the economic benefit goes to consumers.

Because of the adverse effects of free trade on domestic producers, those producers may attempt to petition the government to enact an import quota. When this happens, the government will restrict the quantity of a good that can be imported in order to increase the price and allow producers to recover some of their lost surplus. If the government restricts total imports to the difference between Q2 and Q3, three things will happen First, producers will increase output from Q1 to Q2. Second, imports will decline from the difference between Q1 and Q4 to the difference between Q2 and Q3. Third, the price will rise to reflect the new total quantity consumed, which is now Q3.

The effect of an import quota on domestic producers is to allow them to recover the producer surplus in area E, which they take away from consumers. The effect on international producers is that they now obtain areas G and H as a surplus. The effect on consumers is that they lose E, F, G, H, and I. The effect on the total world economy is that areas F and I are lost in what is called a deadweight loss. F represents consumer surplus which is lost by goods consumed but not at a surplus to producers. I represents consumer surplus which is lost as these goods are not consumed at all. The effect on the domestic economy is that E is gained, but F, G, H, and I are lost. The following figure summarizes the effect on the various stakeholders of an import quota. To summarize, free international trade represents the highest net benefit for consumers, the world economy, and the domestic economy. Purely domestic trade represents the least beneficial situation for domestic consumers, the world economy, and the domestic economy, but the most beneficial situation for domestic producers. An import quota is the most beneficial to foreign producers and somewhat beneficial to domestic producers, but is somewhat harmful overall to consumers, the world economy, and the domestic economy.

Other issues that deserve consideration are whether the international producers which obtain the quota rights are the most efficient producers or not. If they are not, this represents an additional deadweight loss to the world economy and a reduced benefit to those producers. Tariffs are generally seen as a more advantageous way to protect domestic producers without creating as much damage to the world economy as a whole.

Economic theory and empirical studies suggest that import protection works as any government intervention in the price setting process-it distorts resource allocation and consumption decisions and is therefore generally welfare reducing. Tariffs raise the domestic price of imported goods and shelter domestic producers from international competition. Thus, import-substitution industries are helped while exporters and producers of non tradable are hindered. Therefore, protectionism affects the distribution of income as it always benefits some firms or sectors at the expense of the rest of society. Governments usually overestimate their ability to choose the right industry to protect and, over-time, are heavily influenced by special-interest politics rather than a consideration of national costs and benefits.

Since the break of the Former Soviet Union in 1991 the five Central Asian countries have been trying to move from previous autarchic dependencies towards greater openness in foreign economic relations. They are trying to integrate regionally as well as globally. The aim of this was to overcome the major weaknesses of the prior system so that appropriate strategies have been made for better understanding with the regions and the rest of the world. South Asian Countries have started liberalizing their economic policies early eighties and nineties. In some countries the reform process had started earlier than 1990s. Sri Lanka began its reform in 1977. However the economic liberalization in Bangladesh and Pakistan, as in India gathered momentum only in the early 1990s. Central Asian countries started liberalizing their economies in 1990s since independence. These countries are going under the process of economic transformation. Liberalization has taken place in all sectors but this study will discuss and analyze the external sector reforms in Central Asia and South Asia in detail. The countries of these regions have had different abilities to overcome the challenges of economic liberalization. Initially these economies had to suffer a lot, because there was no single blue print of reforms available to countries in transition process, which involves institutional structural as well as behavioral changes.[21] (Martha, De, Melo)

Economic Transformation in Central Asia

After Independence, Central Asian economies have gone through the systemic transformation a command economy to market economy. How can the government of Central Asian countries approach the array of reforms required in this transition phase? The command economy from which the Central Asian States emerged had already been partly dismantled under perestroika, particularly with respect to foreign trade.[22] Despite having rich endowment of mineral resources, such as oil (Kazakhstan), natural gas (Turkmenistan and Uzbekistan, precious metal such as gold and tungsten (Kazakhstan, Uzbekistan, Kyrgyz republic) and thermal potential in (Kyrgyz Republic and Tajikstan), this region was one of the poorest and least developed in the FSU. Despite having full potential, these economies were characterized as low level of industrialization, large rural population, high population growth, authoritarian regime, internal and external threat and opposition of ethnic religious origin, a relatively high degree of poverty than in the former Soviet Union. These countries have succeeded in achieving macroeconomic stabilization and implementing market reforms. In these countries, including Kazakhstan, prudent fiscal and monetary policies have sharply reduced inflation. The past decade of transition has shown a deep crisis in the first half of the decade, with the most extreme case of Tajikistan, which was devastated by full scale civil war. During the large part Post independencee decade the countries had to face high domestic inflation. High inflation caused disruption of investment pattern, changing consumer behavior, barter trade flourished and increased import bill. Main focus on the oil and gas sector and the other sectors have remained non-competitive. But some of them are rapidly recovering to achieve economic stability[23]. (Gidadhubli, 1997) They have established legal framework for introducing economic reforms and looking forwards to policies to be implemented. Currently these economies are involved in the simultaneous tasks of state building, development and socio-political and economic restructuring, institutional building[24]. (Kolkodo, 1999) Some scholars described these reforms in a different way as Aslam and Banerji argued that there is stagnation in reform indicator related with the absence of the institutional reforms in the state.[25] (Aslam and Benerjee) EIlman called these 'mutant economies' inefficient states even mafia-dominated markets.[26] (Ellman, 2000). From elements of transition process as shown in figure 2 one can easily understand how difficult the transition process is. The economic conditions of the former Soviet Central Asian countries were not favorable for sustainable development strategy[27] (Spoor, 2000). Similarities in the economic situation: despite considerable differences in details, none of the Central Asian economies had a higher level of competition, and all the states find themselves at approximately the same stage of development. Moreover, these economies are looking for partners, who would exploit their natural resources and facilitate their entry into the global economy. The ultimate objective was to restore growth and improve the living condition of their populations. Even after independence, the Central Asian countries are finding difficult to put these resources into full exploitation. There is greater need to deal with the initial conditions of the Post soviet Central Asia. These were connected with historical, cultural, social demographic, geopolitical background. There were common features that originated from the Centrally Planned economy prevailed in the former Soviet Central Asia. It's very important to understand the transition process of these economies.

The model of development has been very important for this region's economic thought. Central Asian countries could take an example from the Chinese economic model how to gradually introduce reforms and successfully overcome all the challenges. The Chinese experience is shown in Box (a) However, these countries need not necessarily limit to study the Chinese model but other models also so as to adopt the best measures and policies offered by the various models.

How Gradually China follows a Policy of Socialistic Economic Development

Box (A)

China followed a policy of socialist economic development based primarily on the centrally directed allocation of resources through administrative means. By the late1970s, this approach was increasingly recognized as being untenable and unsustainable, and an overhaul of the economic system was initiated. China's approach to economic reform has been gradual and incremental, without any detailed "blueprint" guiding the process. This incremental approach is best depicted in a metaphor attributed to Deng Xiaoping as "crossing the river by feeling the stones under the feet" and is still applicable to many of the reforms being carried out by China today. The following features have characterized this incremental approach, First, reforms tend to be undertaken first on experimental basis in some localities before they are applied to the whole country. This minimizes disruptions to the economy, allows deficient policies to be modified based on experience, and provides time to build the necessary institutions for full implementation. Second, another strategy frequently employed has been the use of intermediate mechanisms to smooth the transition to a market-oriented economy. One example of this is the setting up of Special Economic Zones in the early 1980s as a way of gradually introducing foreign capital and technology. Finally, the Chinese leadership has consistently tried to preserve the socialist character of the economy while introducing market-oriented reforms. For example, even though policies have been conducive to the rapid growth of the non-state sector, state enterprise reform has been gradual with no signs of a mass privatization strategy for large and medium-sized enterprises as pursued by other transition economies.

In late 1980s and early 1990s, The development model debates were quite intensive during the first years of the post-Soviet development of Central Asia, partly because the Central Asian governments had attempted to start a new round of economic reforms. Actually, the followers of technocratic, Central Asian leaders had been trained in, and had experience of the Soviet command economy only and they had vague idea about market driven economies as well as deregulation of the state system. Kazakhstan's leaders turned out to be admirers of the so-called East Asian economic miracle especially in South Korean and Japan. It was widely believed in Kazakhstan that it was possible to replicate the Korean economic miracle. Moreover, their first comprehensive perspectives strategy was rapid development in independent Kazakhstan. Kyrgyzstan's leaders also devoted themselves to the South Korean and Japanese economic models. What they called the Korean Model of economic development and decided to explore the opportunities for joint co-operation in developing Kyrgyzstan impressed Kyrgyz officials who visited South Korea in 1990. Uzbekistan's own road of renovation and progress has been always supplemented by a call to learn from the Chinese experience of gradual reforms. However, outside the country one of the most intensive discussions on Uzbekistan's model of development centered on the Turkish secular model and the Iranian theological model, because of the strong traditions of Islam in Uzbekistan. Thus, demonstrating the country's dedication to the modern and secular model of development was one of the most important tasks for Uzbekistan's foreign policy-makers.

This model should have been attractive and acceptable to all people in the multicultural and multinational society in Central Asia. Central Asian Countries, especially in Kazakhstan and Kyrgyzstan, the ruling elite had to handle carefully nationalistic ideas in order to pacify the mood of their ethnic minorities[28]. Also this model should have been powerful enough to meet the challenge of rising nationalistic and democratic expectations in society. Reference to Chinese and other Asian model of development has given the Central Asian Country's elites a rare opportunity to advocate preservation of strong state institutions, capable of promoting political and economic reforms. References to the experiences of China, South Korea and others helped the elite to justify their decision to maintain the regulatory role of the state, at least in the medium-term, and to delay radical economic changes. In 1991-1992, the Central Asian countries only partially accepted the Russian concept of shock therapy, price liberalization and relaxation of state institutions' activities in economic affairs. However, very soon Turkmenistan and Uzbekistan chose their own way of development and endorsement of the Chinese way of gradual reforms justified their return to strict government control and to gradual economic changes. Kazakhstan initially followed the shock therapy approach. However, later on its government made serious corrections and revived some level of state intervention and control. Only Kyrgyzstan, which managed to overcome initial temptations to delay reforms, consistently carried out the recommendations of the World Bank and IMF and implemented shock therapy.

The forms of the transformation vary in this region, which would be characterized as wide scale reforms (Kyrgyz republic and Kazakhstan), non-reforms (Turkmenistan) towards gradual partial reforms (Uzbekistan, Tajikistan). Overall, the success of market oriented reforms has been mixed, according to various indicators developed by multilateral institutions Kazakhstan and Kyrgyzstan have progressed faster. Tajikistan has also made some progress. The level of reforms is low in Turkmenistan and Uzbekistan. However, Kazakhstan, Kyrgyzstan and Tajikistan have made significant progress in external sector reforms, but Uzbekistan and Turkmenistan's low level of reforms in this sector has created some problems for regionalism. Table 2.3 shows the key indicators and the reform status of Central Asian Countries. Table 2.4 explains that how these economies focused on economic policy and how much they successful in implementing these policies.

Mixed response has been seen in these countries since independence. The countries of the Former Soviet Union had much more trade with each other than with the out side world before independence. The dependence of these countries on trade with each other was significantly high. So Central Asian countries were part of a strongly integrated economy domestically, within the FSU, and rather closed externally.[29] (Bakhtior, 2001). The disruption of administrative command system and the state monopoly of trade especially Council of Mutual Economic Assistance (CMEA), without the emergence of new market based mechanism. So with the other economic policies Central Asia also liberalizes their trade policies.

Table 2.3
Key indicators and Reform Status of Central Asian Countries

Country	*GDP Per Capita, 2004 (in US dollars)*	*Population, 2004 (in million)*	*Share of World*		*Geography*	*Reform Status*
			Oil	*Gas*		
Oil Exporters						
Kazakhstan	2,723.9	15.0	3.3	1.7	Landlocked	Active
Turkmenistan	1,250.7	6.2	0.042	1.6	Landlocked	No reforms
Non-oil Exporters						
Kyrgyz Republic	432.4	5.1			Landlocked	Active
Tajikistan	323.1	6.7			Landlocked	Active
Uzbekistan	461.2	26.0	0.05*	1.0	Double Land locked	Partially active

Source: ADB key indicator 2005, World Bank, World Development indicator,2006.

Table 2.4

Overall Principle Measures of economic policies since 1992-2005.

Policy Type	*Focus of Policy*	*Results*
Type I	Macroeconomic-inflation, monetary and fiscal policies, and exchange rate Policy Microeconomic-labor market and wages, social safety nets, price liberalization (exceptions for energy, staple food, and housing) and removal of subsidies	These reforms did not achieve the anticipated increase In productivity in the CARs. One reason was that governments were unable to quickly create revenue flows to finance even recurrent expenditures, particularly those tied to state-owned enterprises (SOEs).
	Banking and State-owned Enterprises-reduced subsidies, privatization, and bank liberalization.	As a result, there was a hesitation to replace inefficient SOEs with more efficient pivate enterprises, as removing subsidies frequently led to the failure of these SOEs. Banking reforms were successful in allowing entry although state Banks, which retained their influence in many CARs. Social benefit systems were inadequate given limited resources. This overall situation did not improve until the Late 1990s.

(Contd.)

(Contd. Table 2.4)

Policy Type	*Focus of Policy*	*Results*
Type II	Primarily legal policies: Developing legal and regulatory Frameworks for industry and finance Privatization of medium- and large- scale enterprises-sale of assets to employees or independent parties Restructuring the labor market-wage determination, Unemployment compensation, and retirement benefits	Withstanding pressures from special interest groups was the main obstacle governments faced in trying to to attract build a level playing field attractive to foreign investors. In the oil exporting CARs, for example, these policies proved successful in providing a reliable environment foreign direct investment. For non-oil exporters, these reforms were less successful. Privatization did not bring expected benefits and special interest groups were able to influence policy.

(Contd.)

(Contd. Table 2.4)

Policy Type	*Focus of Policy*	*Results*
Type III	Regional cooperation-within the CARs using various initiatives such as trade facilitation, transport, and energy policy dialogue and cooperation. Develop industrial competitiveness policies- to foster diversification away from natural resources and other raw material production into manufacturing.	These policies were slow to develop, particularly in the first half of the 1990s when the CARs were more concerned with developing national identities and earning revenue through customs taxation. Recent developments, however, suggest a greater willingness to lower tariffs and cooperate on both transport and energy policies. To Foster economic diversification, Kazakhstan introduced an innovative industrial development strategy in 2003, which contains elements of an industrial competitiveness policy agenda such as fostering industrial clusters. Azerbaijan is also assessing its industrial competitiveness and may Follow suit.

Source: Malcom Dowling and Ganeshan Wignaraja, Central Asia after fifteen years of transition: Growth, regional cooperation and Policy choices in ADB working paper series on Regional Economic Integration no.3 at www.aric.adb.org. p.3.

Trade Liberalization Policies in Central Asia

There is no doubt that foreign trade has been playing an important role in Central Asian Region. This region is highly economic dependence on external trade as comparable to other CIS countries. As a result these economies are also extremely vulnerable to external shocks. It has higher ratios of exports and imports in their GDP. The main challenges for these countries involve strengthening the capacity of broad, market based institutions, those which are more specifically more trade related, such as the financial sector, customs and trade, which would facilitate them to integrate into the World Trading System. Studies shows that effective integration includes country's own economic policies specially trade policies and institutions, and of coarse their trading partner, which affect market access and the terms of trade.[30] (Michlopus, 1999). Progress towards trade liberalization has varied across the Central Asian region. Since independence External economic reforms occurred in five areas: trade liberalization, reform of trade system, from previous autarchic dependencies towards greater openness in foreign economic relations, market diversification, phasing out of barter trade and currency reforms.[31] The major trade policy issue facing the global economy was the challenge of regionalism.[32]Although during the Soviet period Central Asia acted as a singular unit but the economic condition of countries differ substantially at the time of disintegration.

Kazakhstan and Kyrgyzstan have been liberalizing their trade policy more or less steadily since their independence. Tajikistan liberalized its trade policy regime fairly rapidly after the end of civil war 1997. Turkmenistan has undertaken little trade liberalization. Uzbekistan liberalized its trade policy regime in 1990. But this has been partly reversed later on. The present status of these countries trade policy range varies from a very liberal in Kyrgyzstan and Tajikistan to fairly liberal in Kazakhstan to quiet restrictive in Turkmenistan and Uzbekistan.

Price liberalization

The key trade development was the collapse of the Council of Mutual Economic Assistance (CMEA). Trade among the Soviet-bloc economies was planned and organized under the auspices of the

CMEA, but in the International market buyer and sellers come from different countries to exchange goods and services. Prices play an important role. After dismantling of CMEA, first steps were taken towards price liberalization. All new states of Central Asia practically faced the consequences of almost full price liberalization. In October1994, the government of Kazakhstan abolished almost all subsidies, keeping only few utility prices under control. Uzbekistan adopted a more gradual approach. Price control was largely phased out during 1992-1995. In Turkmenistan most prices have been kept under state control. In Tajikistan reforms were started in 1992 but interrupted by civil war and were resumed only after peace reconciliation in mid 1997[33].(Bakhtior, 2001, p,60.) The Uzbekistan tried to moderate the impact of full liberalization of prices and to complement the introduction of market mechanism with the traditional tools of economic governance had lower inflation at the initial stage 1992-1994. It suffered less negative effects compared with the radical reformers. Kyrgyzstan and Kazakhstan had also lower levels of non weighted average inflation within this stage of transition compared to other transition countries. It has been observed that the liberalization of prices without efficient financial institutions, which could provide fast, low cost and risk free money transactions even under high inflation certainly led to a barter trade. Price differentials emerged in Central Asian markets, due to different regulatory regime countries are not able to trade cross boarders. Turkmenistan and Uzbekistan are the countries with the regulated price , where trade potential has been converted into a shuttle trade[34]. The Central Asian Countries could considerably expand trade and diversify exports by reducing policy-related and institutional barriers to trade. They could cooperate with each other and their neighboring countries in improving their transport links with the rest of the world. For this they need to be open by reducing their tariffs etc.

Tariffs, Non-tariffs, Subsidies, and Quota

The Central Asian Countries had very similar trade policy regimes before their independence. But since independence, their regimes have diverged significantly. These countries were closely related to the former Soviet countries. Tariffs on imports create a bias against exports by raising the domestic price of imports relative to exports, or equivalently, by lowering the domestic price of exports relative to imports. Thus, import tariffs are equivalent to a tax on exports. Import tariffs also create a disincentive to export by increasing the cost of imported intermediate inputs used by export industries. For a given price of exports, a tariff on imported intermediate inputs effectively acts as a "cost penalty" on the production of exports. Duty drawbacks and similar schemes are designed to eliminate the bias against exports, but they can be difficult to administer. Empirical research has shown that the size of the export tax arising from import tariffs can be substantial. Tokarick, (2006) studied 26 low-income countries and found that, on average, import tariffs in these countries were equivalent to about a 12½ percent tax on their exports and 4 of these countries had export-tax equivalents between 26 and 34 percent.[35] These estimates do not take into account the disincentives that arise from other types of import barriers, namely nontariff barriers (NTBs), In economics, a subsidy is a kind of financial government assistance, such as a grant, tax break, or trade barrier, in order to encourage the production or purchase of a good. The term *subsidy* may also refer to assistance granted by others, such as individuals or non-government institutions, although this is more commonly described as charity.

Non-Tariff Barriers to Trade

These are restrictions to imports but are not in the usual form of a tariff. They are criticized as a means to evade free trade rules such as those of the WTO, the EU or NAFTA that restrict tariffs. Most common examples are antidumping measures and countervailing duties, which, although they are called "non-tariff" barriers, have the effect of tariffs but are only imposed under certain conditions. Their use has risen sharply after the WTO rules led to a very significant reduction in tariff use.

Non-tariff barriers may also be in the form of manufacturing or production requirements of goods, such as how an animal is caught or a plant is grown, with an import ban imposed on products that don't meet the requirements. Examples are the European

Union restrictions on genetically modified organisms or beef treated with growth hormones.

Some non-tariff trade barriers are expressly permitted in very limited circumstances, when they are deemed necessary to protect health, safety, or sanitation, or to protect depletable natural resources.

Non-tariff barriers to trade can be: State subsidies, procurement, trading, ownership. National regulations on health, safety, employment. Product classification. Quota shares.

Foreign Exchange: controls and multiplicity. Over elaborate or inadequate infrastructure.

'Buy national' policy. Intellectual property laws (patents and copyrights). Bribery and corruption. Unfair customs procedures. restrictive licences import bans seasonal import regimes so the actual bias against exports from all types of import barriers is likely larger. Developing countries typically have many "informal barriers" to trade as well, such as high levels of port and internal transportation charges that make it even more difficult for these countries to expand their exports Reducing import tariffs, therefore, is an export-promotion strategy that countries can implement, regardless of whether their trading partners reduce their tariffs. Countries should be careful, however, as to how they design tariff reductions. In order to maximize the benefits, research shows that countries should reduce higher tariffs by more than lower ones and not exempt sectors from reductions. Critics say quotas often lead to corruption (bribes to get a quota allocation), smuggling (circumventing a quota), and higher prices for consumers.

In Kazakhstan, In the starting of 1992 the government began to apply tariffs and other measures to regulate foreign trade. The first law adopted by the Kazakhstani Parliament included status on tariffs principal of foreign trade, and inducement for foreign investment. In 1995 Kazakhstan reduced the list of goods subject to export quotas to minimum five items. The state policy had several negative characteristics: changes in exports and imports duties were frequent. The level of duties were high: excuse tax imposedon imported goods. In 1993, the new currency was established, which

Table No.2.5

Tariff Rates of Central Asian Countries

Central Asian Countries				
	1996		2004	
Kazakhstan	Simple mean tariffs	Weighted mean tariffs	Simple mean tariffs	Weighted mean tariffs
	10.0	8.4		
	1995		2003	
Kyrgyzstan	Simple mean tariffs	Weighted mean tariffs	Simple mean tariffs	Weighted mean tariffs
	0.0	0.0	4.3	4.3
			2002	
Tajikstan	Simple mean tariffs	Weighted mean tariffs	Simple mean tariffs	Weighted mean tariffs
			8.0	7.1
	1998		2002	
Turkmenistan	Simple mean tariffs	Weighted mean tariffs	Simple mean tariffs	Weighted mean tariffs
	0.0		5.3	2.9
	2001			
Uzbekistan	Simple mean tariffs	Weighted mean tariffs		
	10.6	5.9		

Source: World Development Indecators2005.p 339&340

has enabled the country to conduct an independence economic policy. Kazakhstan has a rather complex tariffs schedule (with 10 advoleram and seven specific tariifs rates and somegoods subject to both) but a relatively low non weighted average rate. Excise taxes are imposed on both imported and domestically produced alcohol beverages and tobacco products. Kazakhstan also levies exports taxes on limited number of goods when they are exported to the countries that are not members of EEC. Kazakhstan also apply quantitave restrictions, such as prohibition , quotas and licenses to the trade goods Tariff rates are fairly low and uniform in Kyrgyzstan and Tajikistan. In Turkmenistan the tariffs ranging from 10 percent to 100 percent are applied to 94 commodities when they are imported by legal entities, imports by individual in amount upto $500 (as of August 2005) are exempted from tariffs[36]. All countries apply quantitative restriction, such as prohibitions, quotas and license, to trade in goods that have implications for national security public health and the environment. Turkmenistan and Uzbekistan restrict imports of certain products to protect domestic producers of these products. They also prohibit exports of some food products to ensure their availability in the domestic market at relatively low prices. The Table 2.5 assesses the simple mean tariffs and weighted mean tariffs in all the Central Asian countries. A major problem in all these countries is that changes in tariffs schedule have been frequent and unpredictable.

Despite having formal tariffs low, there are many other policy instrument that Central Asian Countries use, often in a discretionary and non transparent manner, to regulate trade. Lowering and rationalizing the non tariff trade barriers as well as making those more transparent and less discretionary should be major goal for regional cooperation.

3.3 Currency convertibility

The establishment of new currencies for the Central Asian governments at the moment of independence there were overwhelming advantages in the continued use of the Soviet rouble. The largest CIS economy outside Russia, Ukraine, broke away in 1992, but for the others a single rouble area was seen as a benefit to the maintenance (or restoration) of trade and payments relations within it; the newly-created central banks had no experience of monetary management, although the quarterly construction of 'the cash plan' by Union-Republican Ministries of Finance afforded a certain statistical expertise and network; and the EU's Maastricht Agreement was perceived as a model for the inheritance of a common currency which should not needlessly be dismantled. In pursuit of those expectations a group within the CIS - Armenia, Belarus, Kazakstan, Kyrgyzstan, Russia and Uzbekistan - meeting in Bishkek in October 1992 prepared for an Interstate Bank of the CIS, as had been delineated by a CIS Heads of State meeting in Tashkent the previous May.

The Central Asian Countries have been divided into two groups with regard to their exchange rate policies. . The unexpected collapse of the rouble zone in 1993 put the CARs' leaders in a difficult position and urged them to adopt radical steps towards currency reforms. Kazakhstan and Kyrgyzstan following the concept of radical 'shock therapy'accepted the conditions of Article VIII of the IMF charter rather fast on March 29, 1995 and July 16, 1996 respectively.[37] However new currencies like Tenge, Som and Somoni were introduced in Kazakhsytan, Kyrgyzstan and Tajikistan. Yet it took two years in Kyrgyzstan and three years in Kazakhstan for the introduction of national currencies.

Exchange Rate policy

Following the introduction of domestic currencies the Central Asian States maintained the complex multiple exchange rate systems, complimented by the legislation that required exporters to repatriate export earning and surrender a portion to either the govt or central Bank. The ensuring multiple currency practices imposed an implicit tax or exports or subsidizing imports which benefited from a more appreciated exchange rate. Multiple exchange rate practices also contributed to foreign exchange shortages by encouraging undervaluation of exports and diverting proceeds away from official channels of conversion. This promoted the rationing of foreign exchange by central Bank, which in turn fueled a parallel market activity. The Channeling of economic activity to the informal sector added to the tax collection problems and left some transactions entirely out side the tax base. One could say that multiple exchange rate arrangements lacked transperancy, distorted resource allocation and eroded budgetary tax revenue. [38] (Emine Gurgen, 1999. p. 42.) The exchange rate regime in today's international and monetary and financial system and the system unfavorable Foreign exchange and payment regulation in some Central Asian Countries creates additional hurdles. The Central banks used the foreign exchange obtained from exporters to purchase domestic currency at a more depreciated rate its always not transferred to the govt. More recently most of the Central Asian States have moved towards more flexible, unified and market oriented exchange rate regimes.

All the Central Asian states have chosen similar exchange rates regimes based on managed and floating systems of exchange auctions since the moment of their own currency introduction. These countries have been divided into two groups with regards to their exchange rate policies[39]. (Bakhtior, 2001,). The first group of countries such as Kazakhstan and Kyrgyzstan following the concept of radical shock therapy reforms accepted Artcle VIII status in IMF in 1996[40] have eliminated multiple currency practices.(Emine Gurgen, 1999.) Tajikstan unified its exchange rate and abolished surrender requirements in April 1998. In second group of countries like Turkmenistan, restricted access to foreign exchange constitutes a major obstacle to imports while the requirement that certain categories of exporters surrender part of their foreign exchange earnings. Uzbekistan continues to maintain multiple exchange rates and surrender requirements.

Box (b)

Main Definitions used in the Analysis of Trade Taxes

Harmonized System: An International classification developed by the World customs Organization, which is arranged in six digit codes allowing all participating countries to classify traded goods on a common basis. Beyond the six digit level, countries are free to introduced national distinctions for tariffs and many other purposes.

(Contd)

(Contd Box (b))

Tariffs : Custom duties on merchandise imports levied either on an ad-valorem basis (percentage of value) or on a specific basis . Tariff give price advantage to similar locally produced goods and raised revenues for the government.

Ad-Valorem Tariff- An import duty with a tariff rate charged as the percentage of the price.

Specific Tariffs- An import duty with a tariff rate charged as affixed amount per quantity.

Compound Tariffs - A combination of advalorem and specific tariffs.

Mixed Tariffs- A choice between advalorem and specific tariff depending on the conditions attached.

Tariff binding- Commitment not to increase a rate of duty beyond an agreed level . Once a rate of duty is bound, it may not be raised without compensating the affected Parties.

Tariff peaks- Reltively high tariffs, usually on sensitive products. Tariffs of 15% and above are generally recognized as international tariffs peaks. Tariffs at least three times than the members overall simple average are recognized as domestic peaks.

Duty Drawbacks- providing rebates to exporters for the tariff duty paid on imported intermediate inputs.

Most Favored Nation- Most favored nation treatment(GATT ArticleI , GATT Article II, and TRIPSArticle IV), the principle of not discriminating between one's trading partner.

Source; WTO, WTO/ Glossary- A Guide to-" WTO Speak" in www.wto.org.

Import Taxes in Central Asian countries

Governments have different arguments in favor of various tariff or other tax measures to control imports. The rationale behind levying them includes the need to (i) protect some domestic sectors; (ii) raise additional revenue; (iii) reduce imports due to balance of payments problem; and (iv) use tariffs as bargaining tool in negotiations with trading partners. However, import tariffs and other import protection measures have significant negative effects on the economy.

Assessing the level of import tariff protection is further complicated by the complex tariff system in place in Central Asian

Table no. 2.6
Exchange rate of Central Asian Countries

Kazakhstan	Tenge per SDR: End of the period			Tenge per US$: end of the year			Tenge Per US$: Average of the year		
	1999	2002	2005	1999	2002	2005	1999	2002	2005
Official rate	189.6	210.1	191.4	138.2	154.6	133.9	119.5	153.2	132.8
Kyrgyzstan	Som per SDR: End of the period			Som per US$: end of the year			Som Per US$: Average of the year		
	1999	2002	2005	1999	2002	2005	1999	2002	2005
Official rate	62.3	62.6	59.0	45.4	46.	41.3	39	46.9	41
Tajikistan	Somoni per SDR: End of the period			Somoni per US$: end of the year			Somoni Per US$: Average of the year		
	1999	2002	2005	1999	2002	2005	1999	2002	2005
Official rate	1.9	4.0	4.5	1.4	3	3.1	1.2	2.7	3.1

countries. Many CAREC countries have shifted their tariffs to the ad valorem methodology under the WTO Harmonized System of classification of trade goods. At the same time, combined and mixed tariffs are still widespread in these countries. Kazakhstan, the Kyrgyz Republic, Tajikistan and Uzbekistan apply specific tariffs expressed in EUR, U.S. dollars, or national currency to a volume of some imports expressed in a specific unit (liter, ton, units, etc). Some countries (e.g., Kazakhstan and Uzbekistan) use compound tariffs for some goods applying specific tariffs simultaneously with ad valorem tariffs. Therefore, assessing the overall level of tariffs is complicated by the need to convert these specific and combined tariffs to ad valorem for comparability.

Export Taxes The rational behind taxing exports is broadly to raise revenue in case of exploitation of natural resources, to support domestic industry by ensuring lower prices on raw material inputs, substitute for income tax and compensate for the costs of the customs procedures.

Trade Taxes are very complex and difficult to enforce in some Central Asian countries. Import tariffs are relatively low in all Central Asian Countries but the trade taxes regimes are very complex.

Economic Liberalization in South Asia

It is evident that the five south Asian countries, i.e., India, Pakistan, Bangladesh, Sri Lanka and Nepal, have been consistently following economic reform policies emphasizing the market economy and integrating their economies with the rest of the world. Bangladesh, Sri Lanka and Nepal also had higher GDP growth rates in the nineties than the eighties. While the higher growth in India during 1991-2002 was accompanied by substantial growth in the service sector and a marginal improvement of the agricultural sector, the growth in Bangladesh, Sri Lanka and Nepal was supported by both higher industrial and service sector growth. But, GDP growth rate in Pakistan slowed down substantially during the nineties compared to the eighties due to internal conflict, political instability, social insecurity, and the interrupted business climate. Per capita income growth also slowed down in Pakistan during the nineties, whereas it improved in India, Bangladesh, Sri Lanka and Nepal. Other important macro indicators like gross domestic savings and gross domestic capital formation improved in all these countries except Pakistan. Following economic reforms, particularly trade reforms in these countries during the nineties, export and import growth has substantially improved. Further, India, Bangladesh, Sri Lanka and Nepal have improved considerably on the external sector front such as the current account balance, capital account, foreign exchange reserves and overall improvement in balance of payments during the post-reform period. There has also been an improvement in most of the macro indicators except the fiscal deficit, both on the domestic and external sector front. Indeed, the South Asian region has been one of the fastest growing regions in the world in recent years. The above analysis suggests that with the exception of Pakistan, the South Asian countries have registered higher export growth during the nineties than the eighties[41]. (Pravakar Sahoo, 2006) Though Pakistan failed to accelerate its exports growth in the 1990s, it has managed to maintain a constant rise of exports in absolute value. The region has world's highest illiteracy rate at forty five percent. These economies are in the vicious circle of low-per capita income growth, high population growth and political instability. Despite that growth rate has remained positive in the region. South Asia GDP growth rate was 7.0 percent in 2003 and remained 7.1 percent in 2004[42]. This region is among one of the fastest growing region of the world with the five percent average economic growth for the last one decade. Almost all the South Asian countries have discarded the import substitution policy as a failed strategy. Orientation towards economic liberalization and greater reliance on the private sector development is now deeply rooted in almost all these countries[43]. (ADB, 2004) To make it more convenient for the private sector all the governments of South Asian countries started liberalizing their trade policies.

Trade liberalization policies in South Asia

During the last decade, South Asia's five largest countries - India, Pakistan, Sri Lanka, Bangladesh and Nepal - have been implementing trade policy reforms, gradually moving their economies away from protectionism toward greater trade openness and global economic integration. Sri Lanka had started liberalization process in the late 1970s and the four mainland countries began to follow the liberalizing course in the late 1980s and early 1990s. All the other countries in the region have initiated major policy reforms with respect to the external sector. Trade liberalization in India moved ahead in a major way with the removal of most remaining Quantitative Restrictions, but it stalled and went backwards in some other respects. However, the liberalizing momentum resumed with large cuts in industrial tariffs between 2002 and February 2004. In Bangladesh, the mid-1990s some aspects of trade policy reform continued, although more slowly, but in other respects import policies steadily became more selective and protective until this trend was reversed to some extent in Bangladesh's 2004-05 budget. Pakistan's comprehensive liberalization of its trade policies since 1996-97 including its agricultural trade policies, and Sri Lanka's potential to resume 1ong-deferred reform as prospects improve of ending its civil war - contribute to a regional picture of very mixed achievement but widely shared opportunity. The South Asian countries missed the tide that carried many of their East and Southeast Asian neighbors to record the rates of growth and poverty reduction during the 1960s and 1970s, but their later trade policy and other liberalizing reforms came in time to for them to benefit from the expansion of production and trade in the world economy during the 1990s. They have now an opportunity to undertake a reform in which they could further lower their barriers against trade-by general developing standards still very high in Indian and Bangladesh and further strengthen their economies' performance through international commerce and competition.

Each country faces differing opportunities to exploit and resistances to overcome. Because many of their circumstances and choices are similar, however, this book seeks to assess their situations collectively as well as separately. There have been significant reform measures with respect to the domestic sectors of the economy like the industrial de-licensing to do away with entry barriers, reforms in agricultural prices, removal of subsidies and fiscal consolidation. The early years of the new millennium witnessed further initiatives to consolidate the efforts made during the last decade.

Tariffs, Non-Tariffs, Subsidies, and Quota

The 1990 witnessed comprehensive reform process in All the South Asian Countries. With the exception of Sri Lanka which began opening trade and capital flow in 1977.All countries initiated major policies related to external sector including reduction of tariffs and quantitative reductions and removing regulations on foreign investments.[44] (SA annual report, 2004)

India, trade liberalization that started during 1991-92 continued for about five years during the 1990s, but lost momentum in some key respects between 1997 and 2001. Under outside pressures which originated in the Uruguay Round, the large number of QRs that India retained to protect consumer good producers were phased out during this period. On the other hand, many industrial import tariffs rose, antidumping became a major activity, specific duties were imposed to protect the textile and garment industry, local content arrangements were used in the auto industry, and towards the end of the period especially, tariffs protecting major agricultural products and agro-industries were substantially increased. Import weighted tariffs in India has fallen from 87 percent in 1990-91 to 20.3 percent in 1997-1998. The maximum tariff during this period was 35 percent because for few products it exceeds this limit.[45](Srinivasan, 2001)

Substantial tariff reform resumed, however, with the reduction of the general maximum customs duty from 35 percent to 30 percent in the 2002-03 budget, to 25 percent in the 2003-04 budget, and to 20 percent on January 8, 2004, when another protective import tax (the Special Additional Duty) was also abolished. But agriculture was excluded from this new liberalizing initiative: state trading import monopolies are being maintained over the major foodgrains, and agricultural tariffs have been going up even as the average level of industrial tariffs has been declining. India's unweighted average agricultural tariff in February 2004 (including tariffs on processed foods) are more than the other developed and developing countries.

Pakistan, trade liberalization which started in the 1980s continued slowly but without serious interruptions until 1996-97. A new, comprehensive trade liberalization program commenced in that year and continued until 2002-03, when the general maximum customs duty was reduced to 25%. Actual protection rates are a bit higher then customs duties, however, owing to differences in the incidence of an income withholding tax which is applied to imports and domestic transactions. No major changes to tariffs were made in the 2003-04 budget, and there are no officially announced plans for further reductions in industrial tariffs. On the other hand, the government has largely completed an ambitious and politically sensitive program of comprehensive liberalization of the trade and other policies that affect its agricultural sector. This contrasts with India, Bangladesh and Sri Lanka, where there are strong protectionist elements in agricultural policies. One factor influencing trade policy liberalization in Pakistan is the recognition of the large volumes of illegal imports via Afghanistan and from India that high protection has encouraged

Bangladesh has a very large export-oriented garment industry established in the 1980s. However, many of the manufacturing industries supplying the domestic market are still heavily protected: tariffs (including the effects of protective import taxes on top of customs duties) of 50 to over 100 percent are common. In Bangladesh maximum tariff rates has been slashed from 300percent in 1992-1993 to 37.5 percent in 1999-2000. customs duties were reduced, but these reductions were offset by the use of a variety of other protective import taxes. By 2000-01 these tariffs accounted for more than one-third of customs collections from protective import taxes. Bangladesh has also progressively eliminated the QRs on imports and reduced the number of banned items. Only 2 percent of the items are subject to QRs. The products that are either banned or restricted account for only 11.7 percent of tariff lines during this period.[46] The 2002-03 budget reduced the basic maximum customs duty and abolished one of the tariffs, and there was a further reduction in the basic maximum customs duty in the 2003-04 budget, but increases in the other tariffs more than offset this reduction. In early 2004, as measured by its average unweighted protective import taxes. The average tariffs on capital good, intermediate goods and consumer goods are very low. But Bangladesh was the most protected of the South Asian economies, with especially high tariffs and other taxes in agriculture. However, the extent to which these measures actually enable local firms to increase their prices is uncertain, owing to the large volumes of illegal imports, especially from India. The illegal imports include conventional smuggling across the border that by-passes customs posts, but a larger volume is generally considered to be "official" smuggling which comes through both the port and land customs posts, involving under-invoicing and other without declarations, despite the opeations of pre-shipment inspection organizations.

Sri Lanka's trade and its industrial sector are dominated by its export-oriented garment industry and Its textile sector. Despite the addition of a surcharge to customs duties, industrial tariffs are low, and in 1997 all textile tariffs were abolished and since then the textile industry has been operating under free trade conditions, both in supplying garment exporters and the domestic market. However, there is significant protection of some manufacturing industries, and also considerable intervention and protection of some major agricultural import substitution crops, especially rice, potatoes, onions and chilies. Sri Lanka's early trade liberalization and the appreciation of its currency in relation to the Indian Rupee led to a large and growing trade deficit with India, and in the hope of correcting this deficit, Sri Lanka entered into a free trade agreement with India which became operative in March 2000. Although Sri Lankan exports to India have increased quite rapidly since then, up to 2002-03 they were still very small, and the bilateral trade deficit with India had increased substantially. Sri Lanka provides incentives to the exporters including easy financing, unrestricted and duty free excess to imported inputs, and official assistance in identifying export markets. In addition to these incentives companies that export 90 percent of their output and use advanced technology in manufacturing are allowed to tax exemption on profits and dividends for five years.[47]

Nepal has generally low, but some moderate and a few high industrial tariffs. Agricultural trade is quite open with low tariffs. India-Nepal Treaty of Trade 1951 were renewed in Feb 2002. Nepal gives generally rather small preferences to imports from India, but most of its exports to India are duty free, although subject to quite restrictive rules of origin and other barriers. Comprehensive FTA with Pakistan, so far has been granted duhes and fee excess to export of tea to pakistan. Of the very substantial illegal trade with India, some of which bypasses customs posts, a large portion is under-invoiced, misclassified, or otherwise unrecorded at customs. Because Nepal's tariffs are generally much lower than India's, India is highly sensitive to Nepal's trade policies and periodically imposes special tariffs or other restrictions. This happened in early 2002 when India imposed tariff rate quotas on Nepalese exports to India of vegetable ghee (hydrogenated palm oil) and copper wire and rods and imposed anti-dumping duties on acyclic yarns. These measures caused considerable disruption in Nepal. In 2002, in order to finance the conflict with the Maoist guerilla movement, the Nepalese government added a security tax to its customs tariffs but not to domestic transactions, thereby increasing tariff protection for local industries. At least while the conflict continues, it seems unlikely that Nepal will reduce tariffs or otherwise liberalize its trade policies. FTA with Sri Lanka talks moving slowly.

Bhutan About 80 percent of Bhutan's merchandise trade is with India, approximately three quarters of its imports and 95 percent of its exports. In addition, its hydro-electricity exports, which are the principal driving force in its economy, are entirely to India. India's dominance in Bhutan's trade is a natural outcome of its location, but is reinforced by a free trade agreement under which Bhutan's exports are exempt from Indian tariffs, and Bhutanese imports from India are exempt from Bhutan's import licensing and from tariffs. For a tiny economy, some of Bhutan's tariffs are rather high, and protection is further increased by a sales tax which is applied to imports but not to the production of local import substitution firms. These arrangements appear to be economically inefficient in some ways, by diverting imports from third countries to higher cost suppliers in India, and by providing excessive protection to local import substitution production. On the other hand, the FTA may benefit some Bhutanese exporters by giving them duty free access to protected markets in India.

Maldives' Foreign exchange earnings in the Maldives are predominantly from tourism and fish exports. Customs duties on imports provide about two-thirds of government tax revenue, as there are no other indirect taxes. For a very small economy, tariffs are quite high, averaging about 21 percent, and even though there is no local production of most imported goods, they have the potential to shelter pockets of high cost local production and to distort resource allocation away from economically more efficient activities, especially export related activities. In the past a number of imported products were subject to QRs, but most of these were removed quite recently in 1998. However, as of December 2002, import quotas, most of which were allocated to a parastatal (the State Trading Organization), were still being used to regulate imports of rice, sugar and wheat flour. About a fifth of Maldives trade (mainly imports) is with South Asia, about 13 percent with Sri Lanka and 8 percent with India: trade with Pakistan, Bangladesh, Nepal and Bhutan is zero or negligible.

Exchange Rate policy

One broader area of notable advance which has facilitated trade policy reforms, in the region, is the move towards more market-based exchange-rate regimes. India, Pakistan, and Sri Lanka now maintain floating exchange rates; Bangladesh, which had a moderately flexible exchange rate system after 1991, floated its currency as of May 2003. Maldives's currency is pegged to the US dollar, and periodically devalued. Nepal's and Bhutan's currencies are pegged to the Indian rupee. Floating or flexibly managed exchange rates have been important supports for the trade liberalizations that have occurred in the region, by offsetting or partially offsetting the effects of Quantitative Restrictions removal and tariff cuts on import competition for domestic industries, and by increasing the domestic currency prices received by export industries. Because of their fixed exchange rates with the Indian Rupee, for Nepal and Bhutan, these effects have been partial and indirect and have not affected their trade with India. More generally, unlike the other South Asian countries, they are not able to use the exchange rate as a means of adjusting to terms-of-trade and more general macro-economic changes. The massive devaluation of the Indian Rupee between 1985 and 1992 (in real terms almost 150% as measured by its Real Effective Exchange Rate index or REER) facilitated India's initial slow trade liberalization during the late 1980s, and made its much more sweeping post 1991 import liberalization program on the whole quite painless[48]. Because Nepal's currency is tied to the Indian Rupee, the same Indian devaluation also supported the major liberalization of Nepal's import policies that was implemented in the early 1990s. Pakistan's REER was devalued at a steady rate between the mid-1980s and 1992, stabilized at or slightly below this level until mid 1998, and then was devalued rather sharply until late 2001, after which it strengthened somewhat. The continuing real devaluation trend was in part a consequence of, but has also facilitated, trade liberalization, especially the new program that commenced in 1997. Bangladesh's REER has been remarkably stable for over 20 years. The strength o f the Taka is in part due to the rapid growth of ready-made garment exports and increasing remittances from Bangladesh workers outside the country. Together, these more than offset aid inflows which declined relative to GDP, and were sufficient to balance whatever increases in imports resulted from the trade liberalization measures that were implemented during the late 1980s and early 1990s. An important reason for the relative stability of the Sri Lankan Rupee has been the rapid and sustained expansion of garment exports and tourism receipts. In Sri Lanka as in the other South Asian countries, in recent years flexibly managed or floating exchange rates have replaced the periodic official use of multiple exchange rates in the past, and largely eliminated black market premier, both of which used to be a source of distortions and rent ceiling behavior that complicated the administration of import and export policies.

The Indian devaluation up to 1992 was more than sufficient to sustain the pre-announced tariff reduction program that continued into the 1990s, and from 1992 to the present India's REER index has remained at about the same level, reflecting nominal exchange rate changes that have approximately offset but not exceeded India's inflation rate relative to the inflation rates of its principal trading partner countries. However the initial devaluations were much larger than the devaluations that occurred in Pakistan, Bangladesh and Sri Lanka, with the result that the Indian Rupee became much cheaper relative to their currencies in real terms. This has helped spur Indian regional exports, both recorded exports and unrecorded informal exports, especially to Bangladesh and Sri Lanka, while its more difficult for these countries to export to India. This expansion of Indian exports to the region represents a correction of many earlier years during which exports which would otherwise have occurred were constrained by import barriers in the other South Asian countries, and by the substantial overvaluation of the Indian Rupee, which was in turn a consequence of its own highly restrictive import policies The resulting bilateral trade deficits and increased competition for domestic industries have affected regional trade policies, with resistance to the expansion of tariff preferences for India in Bangladesh, and by contrast a Sri Lankan initiative which culminated in 2000 in a free trade agreement with India. In Sri Lanka, the free trade agreement was perceived as having relatively low trade diversion costs on the import side owing to Sri Lanka's generally low tariffs, and substantial potential benefits on the export side, provided India was willing to offer tariff exemptions for products which Sri Lankan exporters can supply and which are still subject to high MFN tariffs in India. In Bangladesh, on the other hand, tariffs and therefore the probable trade diversion costs of preferential Indian imports are high, as would be the competitive impact on local industries, while there i s much pessimism about the prospects of Bangladesh exporters succeeding in the Indian market, even with duty free access.

Following the Asian financial crisis of 1997, the exchange rates of a number of the East and South East Asian countries, including South Korea, Indonesia, Thailand, and Malaysia were sharply devalued in real terms in relation to the South Asian currencies. This increased competition for South Asian exports and slowed down their growth, and at the same time sharpened import competition. With the notable exception of Pakistan, this increase in import competition was an important factor in the slowing of the general momentum of import liberalization in the South Asia region, and its reversal in some respects in India and Bangladesh between 1997 and 2002. The resumption of trade liberalization in India and Sri Lanka during 2002, in part reflected improvements in their balance

Table 2.7
Exchange Rates of South Asia

India	Rupees per SDR: End of the period			Rupees per US$: end of the year			Rupees Per US$: Average of the year		
	1999	2002	2005	1999	2002	2005	1999	2002	2005
Market rate	59.6	65.2	64.1	43.4	48.0	45.6	43.0	48.6	44.1
Bangladesh	Taka per SDR: End of the period			Taka per US$: end of the year			Taka Per US$: Average of the year		
	1999	2002	2005	1999	2002	2005	1999	2002	2005
Market rate	69.9	78.7	94.6	51.0	57.9	66.2	49.0	57.8	64.3
Pakistan	Rupees per SDR: End of the period			Rupees per US$: end of the year			Rupees Per US$: Average of the year		
	1999	2002	2005	1999	2002	2005	1999	2002	2005
Market Rate	71.0	79.5	85.5	51.7	58.5	59.8	49.5	59.7	59.5

of payments situations, which in turn are linked to a pick-up in the growth of manufactured exports, in India the rapid expansion of software exports, and increased capital inflows. Consequently, in contrast to the earlier trade liberalizations, real exchange rates have so far not weakened significantly and in the case of India have strengthened to some extent. As a result, the effects of reforms such as tariff reductions on import competing activities are presently not being cushioned by exchange rate devaluation, which in turn has meant that they are politically more difficult to manage, with pressures to make exceptions for firms or industries which are able to lobby effectively, or to obtain special treatment in various ways e.g. through tariff increases, tariff reductions for intermediate inputs., anti-dumping in India, or through the proper implementation of these policies. This table 2.7 shows that how Rupees float at the market rate with the US $.

Central Asian and South Asian countries integration into the world economy

The major Challenges facing the Central Asian Countries concern transportation of oil and energy resources to the world markets. Before Independence of these countries, transportation of these resources was carried by pipeline through Russia. Russia has imposed strict quota on the passage of oil through Russian pipelines. Land locked location and harsh condition make to and from central Asia more expensive. Undoubtedly the economic leader was Kazakhstan, contributing almost half the region's GDP in 1991. Uzbekistan was enjoying one-third of the regional GDP, and the remaining portion was split almost evenly among the other three republics.The scale of the Central Asian economies was not sufficient. Central Asia was responsible for 0.4 percent of the world GDP in 1991, but comprised 0.97 percent of the world population. Kazakhstan is the regional leader in natural resources and minerals. Its raw material base includes the widest range of minerals in the region fuel, ores, non-metallics and is already mining a relatively high volume of minerals at the present time. The mineral base of other Central Asian states includes gas and gold in Uzbekistan, gas in Turkmenistan, and uranium in Kyrgyzstan and Tajikistan.

Central Asia was the least urbanized region in the former Soviet Union. According to the 1989 Census, the level of urbanization fluctuated in these countries from 31 percent in Tajikistan to 57 percent in Kazakhstan. These figures are partly misleading, since a significant portion of the nominal cities are really large villages and regional centers in which the environment, culture and way of life are far from urban. However, the level of urbanization of the native populations of these regions is actually lower than the official figures. The percentage of city-dwellers among Russians fluctuates from 70 percent in Kyrgyzstan and 77 percent in Kazakhstan, to nearly 100 percent in Tajikistan, Uzbekistan and Turkmenistan, and the percentage of city-dwellers among the indigenous population's range from 20.5 percent to 38.5 percent.

SAARC economic integration process is often viewed with skepticism and perceived as one perpetuating the asymmetries further in a number of key countries such as Bangladesh and Pakistan but sometimes also in Nepal and even Sri Lanka. These apprehensions have affected the pace of regional economic integration in South Asia. Therefore, there is need for a better understanding among the people of the region about the gains from the regional economic integration and opportunity cost of non-cooperation. Against that background, the proposed project will quantify the gains from regional economic integration for the region and for each of the participant country. This will be accompanied by identification of other benefits of regional economic integration such as its potential in facilitating intra-regional FDI flows and building supply capabilities and the pros and cons of regional versus bilateral approaches. The study will also provide a way forward to the region for optimizing the gains from regional economic integration.

The South Asian economies are reorienting their policies according to the increasing role of globalization and privatization in the changing international economic scenario. Production trade and investment reforms implemented during the past two decades have provided new opportunities and generated faster economic growth. Trade liberalization has been an important aspect of economic reforms in late eighties and early nineties. Unlike the other transitional Asian countries, this region has generally avoided financial problems. Sufficient flow of Foreign Direct Investment in

Table 2.8 Import Policies Principle Measures of Trade Policy Since Liberalization

	India	*Bangladesh*	*Nepal*	*Pakistan*	*Srilanka*
Policy objectives	Maximising the benefits from expanding global market opportunities	Reduction of tariffs Elimination of quantitative restrictions on imports	Enhancing contribution of trade sector to the national economy by promoting international trade.	Rationalisation of the tariff structure Reduction of non-tariff barriers Simplification of import procedures.	Tariff reductions Harmonisation of Tariff structure Tariffication of Quantitative Reductions
Tariffs	Peak tariff rates 35% four non-zero tariff rates: 5% 15% 25% &35%. Import weighted average tariff rate: 1997-8:20.3% 1990-1:87%	Customs duty rates range (1997): 7.5%-45% 1999-2004: four Maximum tariff reduced from 300 to 37.5%.	Unweighted average tariff rate: 1981-2: 15.4% 1994-5: 8.2% Basic tariffs Rates 5%,10%, 20%, 30% and 80%.	Maximum tariffs: 1986-7: 225% 1994-5:70% 1999-2000:35% four tariff slabs: 10%, 15% 25%, 35%.	Three pronged tariff structure Tariff rates: 10%, 20% and 35%.

(Contd.)

(Contd. Table 2.8)

	India	*Bangladesh*	*Nepal*	*Pakistan*	*Srilanka*
Import Licencing	Licencing requirements dismantled for about a third of consumer goods 340 items have been removed from negative list.		A few Quantitative restricted products are subject to import licencing.	Restricted list has been abolished Licencing requirements for outside the negative list have been removed.	Licencing required only for some agricultural products A few items requiring licence for health or religious reasion
Banned items	As of April 1998 import of 58 items were completely prohibited 2714 items were on the restricted list and 168 importable canalized.	11.7% items subjects to import ban on restrictions	QRs removed on a wide range of products.	As of 1999, only, 28 items banned for religious health and security and reasons	Import of reserved items restricted to government or state corporation

(Contd.)

(Contd: Table 2.8)

	India	*Bangladesh*	*Nepal*	*Pakistan*	*Srilanka*
Quantitative restrictions	QRs on 714 tariffs lines have been removed	QRs have been progressively removed. At 8- digit HS level only 2% of items are subject to Quantitative restrictions.	QRs removed on a wide range of products Products subjects to QRs firearms wireless transmitters and precious metals and Jewellary.	In 1999, only 32 products on negative list.	

this region revived the confidence in economic perspective. Macroeconomic conditions in the region are fairly strong. But the progress among the seven South Asian countries varies. The common theme between two regions is that regional economic integration has become an integral part of their liberalizing economies.

South Asia is full of rivers mountains and large glaciers ands an abundance of sunshine which can be harnessed to produce power for life and industry. The economies in South Asia continue to prosperous. Regional Gross domestic products in this region update at 6.8% for 2005 and 6.6% in 2006 or it might be slightly better than that. Factor behind this is that India and Pakistan are running very successfully. The region as a whole is getting benefit from its further integration into an expanding global economy. Both the economies are raising consumer spending, generally accommodating monetary policies and continuing market liberalization policies that faster business activities and investment[49].

References

1. UNDP, (2005) "Bringing Down Barriers: Regional Cooperation for Human Development and Human Security" in *Central Asian Human Development Report*, Regional bureau for Europe and the CIS, Slovak Republic., p. 20.
2. Richard Pomfret, (2003), "Central Asia Since 1991: The Experience of new Independent states" paper presented in OECD seminar on 19th Feb. 2003. p. 3.
3. Boris Rumer, (2003), Central Asia in Transition: Dilemmas of Political and Economic Development Aakar Books, New Delhi. p. 58.
4. Richard Pomfret, 2003, "Central Asia Since 1991: The Experience of new Independent states" op. cit., p. 4.
5. Sachdeva, (2006), "India's attitude towards China's growing influence in Central Asia", in *China and Eurasian Forum quartly* Volume 4 No. 3, 2006., p. 23-34.
6. Kishore Kumar Guru -Gharana, (2003) "Macro economic modeling of South Asian Economies with Intra-SAARC Trade Link" A report submitted to South Asian Network of Economic institutes.

7. Muchkund Dubey, 2007, " SAARC and South Asian Integration" in *Economic Political Weekly*. 7th April, 2007 pp. 12-38.
8. www.adb.org country analysis sighted on 25th Dec. 2006.
9. Kalman Goldberg, (2000), *An Introduction to the Market Sustem,* M E Sharpe, New York, p. 35.
10. *Ibid*, p. 36
11. "Understanding Transition" in *World Development Report 1996,* Washington DC: World Bank, 1996. p. 1.
12. The World Bank, The World Bank Report, 1996, *From Plan to Market,* Oxford University Press, New York.
13. Martha, De Melo, Martha De Melo, Cavdet Denier and Alan Gelb, "Pattern of Transition from plan to market" *The World Economic Review,* Vol. 10, No. 3. p. 397.
14. Janos Kornai, "What the change of System From Socialism to Capitalism Does and Does not Mean", Journal of Economic Perspectives, Vol. 14, No. 1.
15. *Ibid.*
16. Gregory Grossman,(1967), *The economic Systems,* Printice-hall press, New Jersey., pp. 33-36.
17. Emine Gurgen, et al., ' Economic Reforms in Kazakhstan, Kyrgyz Republic, Tajikstan, Turkmenistan and Uzbekistan" Occassional paper no. 183, Washington DC: IMF, 1999.
18. Peter Narray,2001, p,75. Charles Wyploz,1999 p,323, Chenoy, p, 191. 2001. Janos Kornai, 2000, p. 53-54., P. murrel, 1992 p. 81., Stiglitz, 2000, pp. 46-47., EmineGurgen, et.all, 1999. p. 183.
19. M.L, Jhinghan, International Economics, New Delhi: New offset, 2001, p, 191.
20. http://en.wikipedia.org/wiki/image, effect of_import_quotas.
21. Martha De Melo, Cavdet Denier and Alan Gelb, "Pattern of Transition from plan to market" *The World Economic Review,* Vol. 10, No. 3. pp. 397-424.
22. Economic Survey of Europe, (1997) " The Central Asian Economies", 1991-1996, UN publications, Washington DC., p. 200.
23. R.G. Gidadhubli, "India'a Economic ties with the Central Asian States- Need for more Productive Engagement", paper presented on India-Central Asia conference, 16-18 December at New Delhi p. 2.

24. Gregorz, W.Kolkodo,(1999), "Ten Years of Post Socialistic Transition: The lessons for policy reforms", in Policy Research Working Paper No. 2095. The World Bank, Washington DC.
25. Asad Aslam and Arup Banerji, "Uzbekistan and Kazakhstan: A Tale of Two Transition Path". See on www.imf.org.
26. Ellman, M."The Socialistic Costs and Consequences of the Transformation Process", 2000, see on the website ww.unese.org.
27. Max, Sapoor, (2000) " Central Asian Transition: Dual Economies and Growth and equality", see on website, www Iss.nl/cest rad.
28. Ethinicity; broadly explaines the collection of individuals united by ties of culture and or hereditary, who are conciuos of forming a sub group within the society.
29. Islamov, Bakhtior, A., (2001), *The Central Asian States Ten Years After: How to overcome Traps of Development, Transformation and Globalization?* Maruzen Co., Ltd., Tokyo., p. 167.
30. Constastine Michlopous, (1999)" The integration of low income CIS members in the World Trading System", see on the website, www.worldbank.org.
31. Gulshan Sachdeva, (2003) "Understanding Central Asian Economic Models" in Joshi, Nirmala, ed, *Central Asia : The Great Game Replayed* New Century Publication, New Delhi, p. 218 and Jimmy McHugh and Emine Gurgen, (1999) "External Sector Policies", IMF Occasional Paper No.183. p. 35. Bakhtior A., Islamov, "The Central Asian States ten Year after: How To Overcome Traps of development, Transformation and Globalization", Tokyo: Maruzen Com. Ltd, 2001, p. 185.
32. Pomfret Richard, "The Uzbek Model of Economic Development,1991-99" in Economies of Transition, Vol. 8 , No.3 pp. 733-748
33. Islamov, Bakhtior, A (2001), *The Central Asian States Ten Years After: How to overcome Traps of Development, Transformation and Globalization.*, op. cit p. 60.
34. UNDP, (2005), Central Asia Human Development Report , op.cit., p. 53.
35. Tokarick,Stephen,(2006), "Does Import Protection Discourage Exports?" IMF Working Paper 06/20, Washington DC: International Monetary Fund.
36. UNDP, *Central Asia Human Development Report* op.cit. p. 55.
37. Islamov, Bakhtior, A (2001), *The Central Asian States Ten Years After: How to overcome Traps of Development, Transformation and Globalization.*, op.cit., p. 193.

38. Emine Gurgen, et all (1999), "Economic Reforms in Kazakhstan, Kyrgyz Republic, Tajikistan, Turkmenistan and Uzbekistan" op.cit., p. 42.
39. Islamov, Bakhtior, A (2001), *The Central Asian States Ten Years After: How to overcome Traps of Development, Transformation and Globalization.*, op. cit., p. 193.
40. Emine Gurgen,et all (1999), "Economic Reforms in Kazakhstan, Kyrgyz Republic, Tajikistan, Turkmenistan and Uzbekistan" op.cit., p. 42.
41. South Asia Annual Report, 2004.
42. World Economic Outlook, (2005), The World Bank, Washington DC. p. 33.
43. Asian Development Bank Report, (2004), ADB, Manilla., p. 32.
44. South Asian Annual Report, (2004), RIS, p. 13.
45. Srinivasan, T.N., ed, (2002) *Trade Finance and Investment in South Asia,* Social Science Press, New Delhi., p. 243.
46. *Ibid.*, p. 242.
47. *Ibid.*, p. 246.
48. South Asian Trade Policies, (2004) World Bank Document, The World Bank, Washington DC. Vol. 1. p. 4.
49. (Asian Development Outlook , 2005, p. 21.)

3

Regional Economic Integration in Central Asia

The chapter will describe and analyse all the regional, bilateral and multilateral attempts towards regional integration in the Central Asian republics since 1992. In this chapter the potential within the region has been quantitatively analysed. That will show the significance, challenges and opportunities in regional economic co-operation in the Central Asian region.

Regional Economic Integration in Central Asia

The newly independent republics of Central Asia have had to implement strategies for economic development since becoming independent of the Soviet Union in 1991. The question, however, was how to strengthen cooperation in economic sphere within the region as well as with other neighboring countries, without sacrificing their new found sovereignty and independence.

The central legacy of the Soviet period was that this region was considered as a single economic zone. Integration was forced on them. After the Collapse of USSR, these countries want to protect their independence. Soviet practice imposed from the 1920's until 1991 did in some ways develop intra-regional cooperation. Central Asia was treated as a single economic subdivision within the "unified economic complex of the USSR." Major plants and

Map 2: Political Map of Central Asia

industries were subordinate to all-Union ministries, their production plans determined from Moscow. Only minor activities were under dual (Union-republic) or republican control, which might have allowed a more regional focus. In Kyrgyzstan, for example, over a third of enterprises were administered directly from the center. All-Union ministries habitually took little notice of regional authorities and their needs. New investments of any size had to be approved in the five-year or one-year plans set forth by the Communist Party of Soviet Union (CPSU). For the most part, then, Central Asian production was run from Moscow for the benefit of the Union, as determined by CPSU authorities. Moscow decided the trade amounts and direction for the Central Asian republics; the USSR Ministry of Foreign Trade and internal supply agencies made these deals on behalf of all the 15 constituent republics, mostly to assure priority industries adequate supplies. The system resulted in exceptionally high levels of intra-Union trade—88.2% for Kazakstan's trade turnover, 89.6% for Kyrgyzstan, Tajikstan 83%, Turkmenistan 90.8% and 89% for Uzbekistan in 1991.[1] Moscow's policy was hardly one-sided exploitation for the benefit of Russia. Rather, the Party hierarchy took a long-run view of the benefits for the entire Soviet Union, assuming as they did that it would last indefinitely.

Integration of the Central Asian economies into the Soviet system during Soviet Period, even their inclusion in a common administrative region did not, however, create sufficient infrastructure to facilitate their trade with each other. Little had been spent to integrate the national republics within themselves or with each other. For example, Kyrgyzstan lacked direct rail connection from its capital, Bishkek (then called Frunze) its second largest city (Osh) or to its nearest neighboring city, Almaty, (then called Alma-Ata). Kazakhstan's metallurgical and energy base was linked primarily northwards, towards the Russian Republic. Gas pipelines had different pressures, complicating inter-republican supply. The tourist industry was run from Moscow, flights and hotels were booked by tourist from the Russian capital. Hence, local officials in this important industry, like manufacturers, had little direct contact with foreign decision makers. Through regional cooperation they wanted to integrate. Although the Central Asian region is resource rich and offers considerable trade and investment opportunities, yet due to lack of effective transport routes and relative isolation made it difficult for all countries to access international markets immediately after the independence. So creating new transit and transport routes has become an important pre-condition for the promotion of trade and development.[2] (Islamov, 2001)

Central Asian's geopolitical and economical situations induce them to closely bound to one another. So their interdependence particularly pronounced in the critical network of energy and fuel transportation and communication force them to be Central Asia as a region. The need for regional co-operation is determined by geography, so lacking direct access to the sea, neither Kazakhstan nor Uzbekistan can expect to become major exports of hydrocarbons without close co-operation of their neighbours.[3]

It is important to distinguish regional cooperation from regional integration. Regional cooperation refers to policy measures jointly undertaken by a group of countries typically located within a geographic area, to achieve a higher level of welfare. The regional initiatives are projected to facilitate or enhance economic integration. Regional integration, on the other hand, is in effect an integration of economies within a geographic region. It may be market-driven integration, or policy-induced integration to action among countries within a region to integrate their economies that is one that results from regional cooperation. Regional integration can vary in intensity. Full economic integration occurs when goods, services, and factors of production can flow freely and financial markets are unified among countries within a region.

There is also a difference between regionalization and regionalism, thus the need to distinguish regionalization from regionalism. Regionalization is market-driven integration, inspired by unilateral reforms in individual economies within a particular region. In the area of trade and investment, for instance, a favorable trade and investment regime combined with other factors, such as geographical proximity and social and cultural factors may encourage multinational enterprises (MNEs) to establish factories in different countries within a region for specialized production of specific components of finished goods. This process gives rise to regional production networks characterized by increased international specialization, interdependence, and integration. Regionalism, on the other hand, refers to formal economic cooperation and economic arrangements of a group of countries aimed at facilitating or enhancing regional integration. For instance, a group of countries enter into a regional trade agreement (RTA) to facilitate economic integration.

In the base of regionalism there is an understanding that only through cooperation and partnership with neighbors each separate country will be able to provide its national interests at maximum. Among the regions trade and integration in the modern world economy, there is a need to mark out the following:

- Technological cultural and social changes that would led to decrease the distances between the countries.
- Reduction and or full abolition of government limitation of inter country operation
- Geographic closeness, as economic integration between neighbors is more economically efficient than between those situated far from each other.

It has been realized that in this era of globalization, regionalism as a process will get further strengthen continuing to cover first of all, the economic sphere, it will start manifesting itself more actively in politics.[4](Primbetove, 2004) So relying on regions would become a necessary condition for their survival and adequacy to the world political economy. Thus regions will grow more and more into the international community. So regionalism will become an important factor for the world economy.

"No country in the world today not even Turkmenistan can operate a closed market. This is the reality of globalization. Resources like air and water simply can not be controlled individually. We have to depend upon each another for technological advances. Other countries domestic policies penetrate our boarders and have an impact on our own economy whether we like it or not"[5] (W. Andersen, 2003)

Motivation and Objectives of Economic Cooperation in Central Asia

The main objective of this co-operation has been to develop the economic infrastructure and transportation system within the region. The Central Asian Cooperation Organizations along with economic benefits create communicative ground for a dialogue, confidence building measures and development of good neighborly relations. The main purpose of these agreements is to promote regional cooperation and economic growth. Regional cooperation can become an important factor in the maintenance of peace and security in the region, which are necessary for stable economic growth.[6] (Chanachev, 2004)

It is wildly believed that the Central Asian countries can increase the gains from participation in international trade through regional cooperation and liberalizing their trade policy, transport, and customs transit. They need to promote trade and closely integrate into the international trading system to achieve sustainable economic development. Central Asia's potential is enormous and immense, but it remained choked with complications not able to get benefits economically, geographically and politically. The leaders of the Central Asian countries are actually aware of the need to revive the areas deeply rooted traditions of economic interaction. For the past decade it has been observed that the leaders of Central Asian are keen to establish regional integration as they have signed many bilateral and multilateral agreements within the region. According to these agreements the states are obliged to provide mutual support to each other, on issues related to threats to independence, conflicts cross boundary crime and illegal migration. They are also interested in cooperating on issues such as creating common transport, energy infrastructures and conducting coordinated policy in the sphere of border and custom controls. Events of the last few years confirm that the states need to interact for the purpose of maintaining stability and geographical balance in the region.

Regional cooperation in trade policy can help them to do so. Trade liberalization under regional trade agreements (RTAs) can help the CACs liberalize trade policy at relatively low costs, reduce the risks of protectionist measures by trading partners, create new trade, and improve social welfare. Trade integration is one of the main area of regional concern for Central Asia if it is to achieve competitiveness and integration with the world economy. Since all these countries are land locked, they depend on each other and their neighbors for access to market. For example, liberalization of trade policy by a CAC and its nonadjacent trading partner will boost their bilateral trade as well as their regional trade. If these countries facilitate the movements of transport equipment and goods through connecting countries by the rail road etc, they would be able to access to the world market. It would be beneficial for all the countries. Due to deficiencies of transport infrastructure or restrictive transit systems in these countries, the neighboring countries will do little to closely integrate a CAR into the international trading system if its trade policy remains restrictive. If combined, however, regional cooperation in trade policy, transport, and customs transit can make a major contribution to the expansion of trade and economic development in the CACs. Trade policy was discussed .in detail in the second chapter. Taking into account the importance of regional cooperation in trade policy, transport, and customs transit for the CAR, it attempts to quantify costs of the lack of cooperation and potential benefits of improved regional cooperation. The Asian Development Bank is committed to helping these nations create a better future for their people and the region.[7] This is evidenced by the experience of the Kyrgyz Republic, which significantly liberalized its trade policy in the first half of the 1990s and gained better access to markets in many nonadjacent countries through its accession to the World Trade Organization in 1998, but was not able to expand its trade with those countries considerably due to poor transport links with non-former Soviet Union countries and difficulties with transit of goods and transport equipment through neighboring countries.

The integration of Central Asia into world economy directly depends on how quickly and how successfully the leading transnational corporations are able to find ways to solve the problems. The salient geographic characteristic of the region is its remoteness. The countries in the region including the other participating countries are all landlocked. Uzbekistan is a double landlocked country.

According to United Nations Development Program Report, "Bringing Down Barriers: Regional Cooperation for Human Development and Human Security," the five Central Asian republics could as much as double their incomes over the next 10 years by strengthening regional economic cooperation Most of the targets are to be reached over a period of 25 years from 1990.[8] (UNDP Report, 2005), There has been recent progress towards regional cooperation, but this report has also highlighted that the barriers created by borders negatively affect peoples' lives. The report contends that increased cooperation among the Central Asian republics, with a common political and economic history, these countries are geographically contiguous. They have been linked for centuries by strong ethnic and cultural and linguist ties.[9] (UNDP Report, 2005). This shows that how much bondage is present among them. Moreover, it is important to note that the contemporary boundaries of the countries were set in Soviet days without regard to any geographic economic or ethnic features that might naturally separate them. The cost of non-cooperation is continued deterioration in income distribution, social services and general living conditions, and possibly a descent into the vicious cycle of economic crisis and corrupt governance that often leads to social unrest. International communities, politicians, researchers and business community have identified the immense potential economic and human benefits of regional cooperation for Central Asia and its neighbors. Improved trade, transport and transit, and better water and energy management on a region-wide basis would bring the biggest gains. But cooperation among members are essential to deal with natural disasters, drug trafficking and epidemics.

Work toward more efficient pricing and effective management of infrastructure at the national level as well as international level could be solved by cooperation only. Establish a regional Water-Energy? Consortium to manage the abundant regional water and energy resources for greater efficiency, human development and regional stability. Work together to address the risks from potentially catastrophic environmental hot-spots, strengthen the regional, national and civil society environmental organizations. There is a need to strengthen regional networks of governments, academic and civil society organizations in the areas of health, education and culture. Clarify the mandates and strengthen the capacity of regional institutions. Regional cooperation is essential, but must go hand-in-hand with domestic reform. "Progress on the problems facing Central Asia, including a poor investment climate, threats from natural disasters, health epidemics and terrorism, is hindered by corruption, poor administrative capacity and lack of accountability."[10] (UNDP Report, 2005)

Benefits and the Status of Economic Cooperation

Benefits of regional trading are difficult to quantify because existing data reflects barter trade instead of economic pricing. In qualitative terms, the main opportunities and potentials are: (i) lower unit energy service costs for the whole region and several alternative sources (gas, electricity, oil); (ii) less investment needed for expansion of electricity generation because reserve requirements will be less (rather than one large station, a number of stations can provide same reserve Mega Watt with a lower probability of failure); (iii) maximum use of existing hydropower capacity to strengthen environmental sustainability; (iv) increased exports of gas and oil from the region; (v) a well-established energy-trading framework and a competitive market would attract new investors, increase efficiency of current operations, and allow combined investment projects across national borders to capture economies of scale; (vi) sharing knowledge and development of the knowledge pool on energy efficiency; (vii) capacity building of regional technical research institutes; (viii) expanded access to new markets in Europe, South Asia, Russia and Turkey;[11] The energy demand of SA if growing day by day. Central Asia can get maximum benefits from SA by accessing towards SA. (Richard, 2006) They called for stronger coordination and cooperation to meet challenges ahead, and reaffirmed their commitment to working together toward the shared vision of sustained economic growth and poverty reduction. Research studies, delegations, expertise, intellectual communities from all over the world observed and shared the vision that regional economic cooperation is a strategic means to reducing poverty, and achieving stability and prosperity in Central Asia, particularly in the wake of the 11 September events, and emphasized that for regional economic cooperation to be effective, viable and sustainable, it must be based on mutual understanding, trust and consensus, and yield mutual benefits. Economic cooperation is particularly important to Central Asia, as the countries in the region have a shared history and face common development challenges, including location disadvantage, small domestic markets, and the shared use of resources such as energy and water. Economic cooperation complements and supports national development strategies.

UNDP Administrator Kemal Dervis said that integration of the economies of the five Central Asian republics is an uphill task. Regional economic integration is the key to human development in the Central Asian countries (Khan, 2006) The transit route for oil and gas exports from the region still is monopolized by Russia and alternative routes through Afghanistan, China and Iran have yet to be developed. Central Asia's land locked location required economic integration with other countries.[13] (Khan, 2006) Lowering trade barriers and trade facilitation will help them to expand and boost economic growth and employment. According to some estimates, slashing trade cost by 50% would increase GDP by 20% in Kazakhstan and 55% in Kyrgyzstan over 10 years. The poor will benefit most from the facilitation of trade.[14]

High transport costs and long and unpredictable transit times undermine competitiveness of exports of landlocked countries in world markets, make their imports more expensive and limit their participation in international trade. Landlocked countries find it particularly difficult to export time-sensitive products, such as perishable goods, to compete with coastal countries in manufactured export activities, where imported inputs account for a large proportion of the value of output and profit margins are small, In turn, small volumes of trade make it more difficult for landlocked countries to exploit economies of scale in transport and reduce transport costs. Many developing landlocked countries are, therefore, trapped in the vicious cycle of small trade volumes keeping transport costs high and high transport costs constraining trade, economic growth, and development. Regional cooperation in transport and customs transit can help landlocked countries break this vicious cycle and overcome the disadvantage of their location. Moreover, liberalization of trade policy and regional cooperation in transport and customs transit are closely interlinked for landlocked countries [16].(UNDP Report, 2005)

Fig.3.1 How Regional Cooperation in Trade Policy, Transport, and Custom Transit can contribute to Economic development in Landlocked Countries[15]

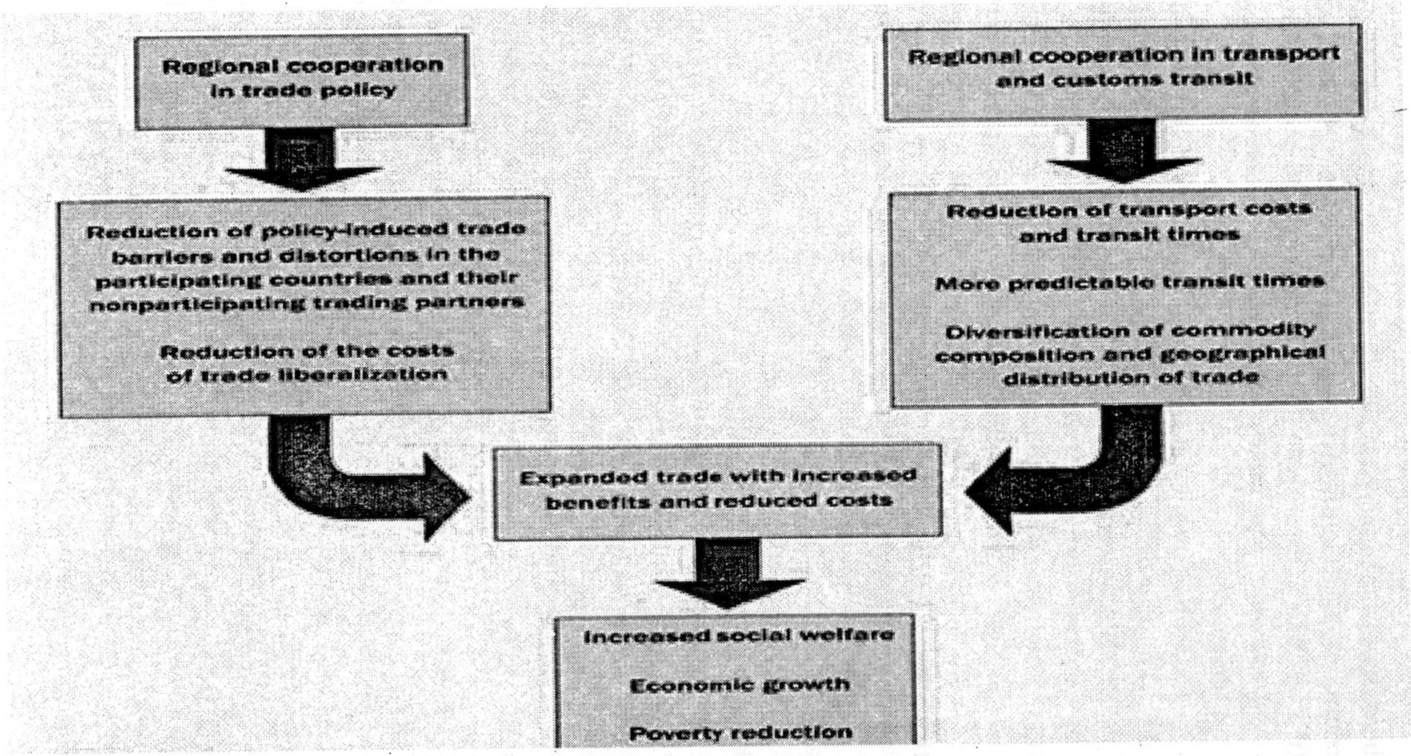

So far the Central Asian regional co-operation is concerned, benefits of stronger economic integration among Central Asian countries can be summarized as follows:

(i) The integration would provide a sufficiently large market for reaching an efficient scale of output and greater specialization by pooling markets through the removal of remaining barriers to trade.

(ii) The countries can substantially reduce the transport and transit costs because of geographical come within reach of one another.

(iii) Capital goods produced within the region may be more compatible to the factor endowment of member states than those imported from developed countries.

(iv) The increasing competition among the member states would result in technical efficiency in existing industries as marginal firms might be forced to reduce their costs.

(v) Economic Cooperation among members states would encourage them to pursue harmonious liberalization polices, resulting in the maximum realization of supposed benefits. The eliminated artificial barriers to trade within the free trade area may help meeting out the price and exchange ratios among members. In trade relations of members with non-members, domestic competition may result in improved terms of trade. Members will also have enhanced bargaining position.

(vi) Stronger regional co-operation may also pave the way for regional banks with joint ventures which might be influential in promoting regional investment in large projects, could expand toward South Asian markets.

(vii) As economic ties grow stronger and countries become committed to common economic goals, political problems may recede in their complexity[17]. (Richard, 2006). When economic benefits gain significance, friendly environment may be created for resolving political problems.

(viii) As the economic ties grow stronger there is a possibility of transparency and the information about each other and possibility of more connectivity.

These advantages for stronger integration are discussed by many distinguish authors in their articles or books.[18] Since independence various meetings were held with regard to economic integration. One of the first regional initiatives of the post-Soviet period was establishment of the Commonwealth of Independent States (CIS), formed in 1991 by Boris Yeltsin and 11 other heads of former Soviet states (excluding the three Baltic states of Latvia, Lithuania, and Estonia). This institution, however, has shown little vitality in the military, political, or economic areas. Early efforts to preserve economic unity were destined to fail. Divisive reactions were only to be expected during 1991-93 with the collapse of the Russian economy and currency. Various protective measures were taken everywhere at that time to prevent the flow of necessary food, energy, materials, and consumer goods to higher price areas. By 1993 the common ruble zone collapsed as Moscow could no longer prevent the former republics from expanding their ruble credits and contributing to the zone.s hyperinflation. A number of decisions on joint structural reconstruction of economies were made.

During 1992 the five countries held regular negotiations and agreed to establish Central Asian Common. In early 1993, concrete discussions were held for creating a Central Asian Economic Co-operative Area in February 1995. These countries have been most active among the Islamic countries in pursuing new opportunities in Central Asian region and making efforts on building close ethnic, linguistic and cultural ties to the region.[19] The five Central Asian Countries are homogeneous. There boundaries are the product of a drive by the Russian state in the nineteenth century. As a result state boarders blindly traverse ethnic enclaves, turning Central Asia into a patchwork quilt rent by complex disputes (ethnic, regional, and tribal) over land water and natural resources.[20] (Rumer, 2003) These states are now divided into separate countries after three generations of Soviet Rule, they have come to see themselves as Kazakhs,Uzbeks, Kyrgyz, Taziks and Turkmen. Turkey and Iran wants to re-establish or redefine long-standing ties based on ethnicity, language culture, and religion.

Dervis, who said that Central Asia's bid to become linked to the world economy is complicated because of the different needs of each country. He said that a general development policy framework for the region will not work[21]. (Andersen, 2003)

"Integration in the region develops on the bilateral basis the agreement on allied relations (between Kazakhstan an Kyrgyzstan signed in Dec 2003 provides for a complex of measure economic integration, creation of common customs and Transport areas. Among 112 bilateral agreement and contracts signed between Kazakhstan and Kyrgyzstan over the fall of trade relations. Kazakhstan demonstrates its readiness to participate in construction of energy objects in Kyrgyzstan.[22] (Chanachev, 2004) Slow process shows the poor implementation of the agreements and contact signed by countries. One of the priorities in cooperation between Uzbekistan and Kyrgyzstan is interaction in the transport sphere, including realization of transport communication, which could unite Central Asia with Russian European and the world markets. For example reconsruction of the Tashkent-Andizhan-osh-Sarytash-Irkshtam motor highway.

Despite the apparent conflict with other commitments, both Kyrgyzstan and Kazakstan have been enthusiastic proponents of the Central Asian Free Trade Area (CAFTA). Their presidents signed agreements in 1993 and 1996 to allow completely tariff-free trade among the three countries, only to find Uzbekistan, which had acceded formally, holding out for restrictions in important categories. Since 1996 the inconvertibility of the Uzbek Som has prevented much expansion of mid-level trade between Uzbekistan and its near neighbors. As of mid-1999 the three presidents have again postponed hard decisions on creating any single economic zone, but Uzbekistan has promised to return to convertibility during the year 2000. Meanwhile, continual petty disputes have occurred among the Central Asian neighbour's over non-payment of bills for fuel, transit fees, and water. Openness across regional borders would increase competition; it would also tend to reduce petty government interference in the market.

The Status of Economic Cooperation in Central Asia

Although Central Asian countries are important member of the Common Wealth Independent States (CIS), yet CIS has not implemented a custom union or Free Trade Area. Kazakhstan, Kyrgyzstan and Uzbekistan formed a Central Asian Union (CAU) considering economic integration among three countries in 1994.

In 1995 they approved free trade among the three countries. In 1998, Tajikistan was also accepted as a member of CAU. Later, in 1998 it was renamed as Central Asian Community (CAC). Russia has become a member of this regional group in May 2004. CAC also granted observing status to Georgia and Turkey. In 1998, CAC again renamed as Central Asian Economic Community (CAEC) and in 2001 it has been transformed into Central Asian Co-operation Organizations (CACO)

In addition, Kazakhstan, Kyrgyzstan and Tajikistan with Russia and Belarus are enjoying the membership in Custom Union, which was formed in 1994, basically the main aim of this union was economic, social and financial policy co-ordination among the member countries. The other regional agreements like EEC (Eurasian Economic Community) and GUUAM Group, (Georgia, Uzbekistan Ukraine, Azerbaijan, Moldova Group) and Central Asian Region Economic Co-operation (CAREC), Economic Co-operation Organization (ECO) have been established with countries outside the region. The main purpose of these agreements is to promote regional cooperation and economic growth.

Kazakhstan is keen in economic integration of Central Asia and establishment of dynamic market in the regions of Caspian sea and black sea. It will also focus on implementing economic projects in Central Asian countries.which may be carried out with the help of international financial institutions. He put stress on Kazakh's goal to form a business friendly climate environment in Central Asia, which will enable Kazakh and other companies to freely make investment in neighboring countries and remove red tape and protectionist barriers in the movement of goods capital and labors.[23]

It has been observed and analyzed by many scholars that political reintegration is inconceivable without the creation of corresponding economic ties. Since disintegration of Central Asian countries, the leaders of these countries have been talking about the cooperation among each other. President of Kyrgyz Republic A. Akayev during signing the agreement on the establishment of the Organisation of Central Asian Cooperation in 2002 said that the new model of regional cooperation would allow the countries to participate in the international labor division system efficiently with rapid formation of Free trade areas and would promote rational use of water and energy resources.[24] (Chanachev, 2004)

ADB started its Central Asia Regional Economic Cooperation (CAREC) Program in 1997, with early efforts focused on raising awareness of the importance of cooperation. In November 2003,a second Ministerial Conference was held, with delegates from each of the seven participating countries: Azerbaijan, People 's Republic of China, Kazakhstan, Kyrgyz Republic, Mongolia, Tajikistan, and Uzbekistan. Turkmenistan is expected to become more active in the future. Notable is that since 2003, the CAREC program has developed into a joint platform for multilateral institutions (namely, EBRD, IMF, ISDB, UNDP, WB and ADB as secretariat) in support of regional cooperation in the region. The CAREC Program now targets three main areas for development: energy and water, trade, and transport. The program has received strong support. Five regional loan projects amounting to $224.1 million have been approved since it started. In 2000, ADB approved a $57 million loan and $1.2 million in technical assistance grants, and organized an additional $25.8 million in co financing for the Almaty- Bishkek Regional Road Rehabilitation Project. The project is upgrading the badly deteriorated road, built in the Soviet era and modernizing border control policies and facilities. As the first stage of a regional assistance program to promote regional energy cooperation, a loan project amounting to $90 million was approved in 2002 to provide for the modernization of regional power transmission in Tajikistan and Uzbekistan. Due to the fluctuation in policies the intra- regional trade has been influenced since independence.

So the countries need to coordinate their macro policies like taking into account budget deficits and ways to finance them, fluctuations in the rate of exchange for nations.[25] (Rumer, 2003). We can say that many programs have been launched by the multilateral institutions. Even though the integration processing very low. This is because of the poor implementation of the programs.

Intra-regional Trade among Central Asian Countries (5*5)

There are some internal and external factors which are affecting the Central Asian Region trade. Their inherited economic structures, import demand for western consumer goods was very high, keeping reasonable trade with traditional partners and to enlarge trade with the rest of the world. There is no doubt that share of trade within CIS countries have declined in the region. The share of trade with non-CIS countries has been growing faster.

Many countries in Central Asia show a high concentration of export commodities and markets. This makes them more vulnerable to fluctuations in commodity prices and to developments in specific markets, as experienced during the crises in Russia and Turkey, all the Central Asian countries has to face the problem.

Table 3.1
Main Commodity of Export and Import of Central Asia

Country	*Main items of Exports(%)*	
	1995	*2001*
Kazakhstan	Oil (16.7), Steel products (14.5), copper (10.5)	Oil (50.6), Steel products (9.8), copper (7.1)
Kyrgyzstan	Non-Ferrous Metallurgy (15.3), Electricity (10), Machines (10.9)	Non-Ferrous Metallurgy (51.7), Electricity (9.8), Machines (12)
Tajikstan	Aluminium (56), Cotton Fibre (27.7), Electricity (5.2)	Aluminium (61), Cotton Fibre (11), Electricity (12)
Turkmenistan	Gas (65), Oil/oil product (8.5) Cotton Fibre (16.5)	Gas (65), Oil/oil product (8.5) Cotton Fibre (16.5)
Uzbekistan	Cotton (51.3), Gold (12.8), Energy (0)	Cotton (24.4), Gold (28.3), Energy (11.8)

The commodity structure of Central Asian exports is mainly comprise mineral resources and agricultural raw materials. Central Asian Region is main exporter of oil, steel products and copper (Kazakhstan) main products are non- ferrous metallurgy, electric energy and machine building (Kyrgyz), Aluminum, cotton fiber and electricity products (Tajikstan), Gas, oil and oil products and cotton fiber (Turkmenistan) and cotton, gold and energy (Uzbekistan). (see table 3.1) Promoting diversification will require high quality investment by both the public and the private sectors to develop new sources of growth. Promoting the development of small and

Table 3.2
Intra-Regional Trade of Goods

From \ To	*Kazakhstan*	*Kyrgyz Republic*	*Tajikistan*	*Uzbekistan*
Kazakhstan		Petroleum, coal, wheat, nonferrous metals, chemicals and plastics, machinery	Wheat, flour, petroleum products, tractors	Gasoline, wheat, clothing, chemicals, rubber, copper, wool, meat
Kyrgyz Republic	Electricity, antimony, sulfur, tobacco, ores and scrap, textiles		Asbestos and cement, flour, natural gas	Electricity, meat and milk, coal, ores and scrap, wool, cloth, sugar, medicines
Tajikistan	Aluminum, ore, ethanol, fruit	Electricity, ethanol, ore		Electricity, aluminum, rail services
Uzbekistan	Natural gas, electricity, cotton, consumer goods	Natural gas, fertilizer, fuel oil, gasoline	Petroleum products, fertilizer, cement, fabric	

medium-sized enterprises, which regularly account for the bulk of job creation, benefits particularly from a level playing field and transparent and well-enforced rules. Table 3.2 Shows the Trade matrix of Commodities To and From within the four countries of the region.

As a whole Central Asian countries succeeded in diversifying export markets. Fig. 3.5 shows that Central Asia's trade within the region has been contracting. Despite signing many agreements for regional cooperation, trade within the region remains 5% in

Table 3.3

Foreign Trade of Central Asian Countries
(in million US$)

Group	*1999 Exports*	*1999 Imports*	*1999 Total Trade*	*2004 Exports*	*2004 Imports*	*2004 Total Trade*
CARs	740.5	792.8	1533.3	1067.4	1260	2327.4
Rest of CIS	2148.8	2333.4	4482.2	4709.8	7750	12460
EU-15	2399.3	1915.4	4314.7	7401	3747.4	11148
East Asia	685.6	923.6	1609.2	2378.7	2225.8	4604.5
South Asia	58	67.3	125.3	349	131	480
		1726.4	5636.2	10103	3375.1	13479
Total						
		9941.9				
		7758.9	17701	26009	18489	44499

Fig. 3.2

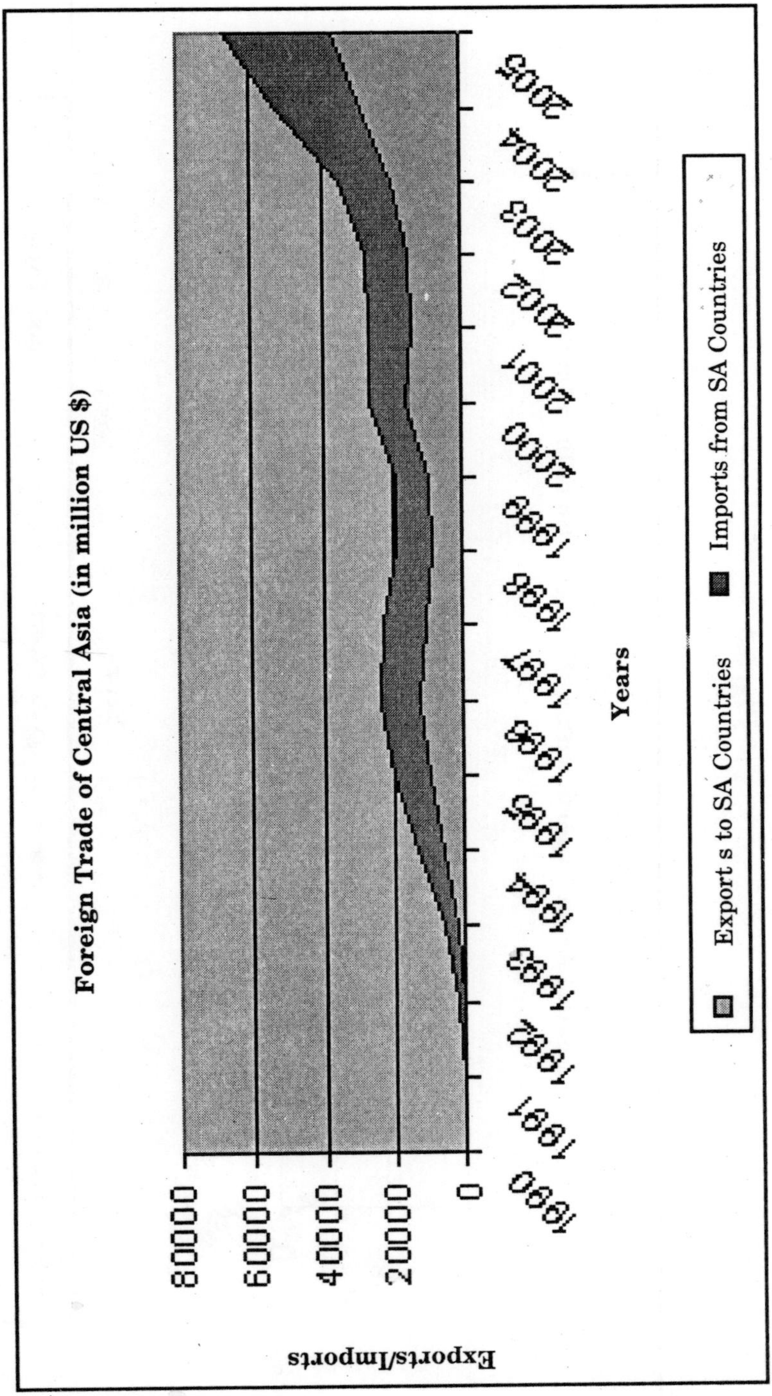
Foreign Trade of Central Asia (in million US $)
Exports/Imports
800000
600000
400000
200000
0
1990
1991
1992
1993
1994
1995
1996
1997
1998
1999
2000
2001
2002
2003
2004
2005
Years
Export s to SA Countries
Imports from SA Countries

Fig. 3.3

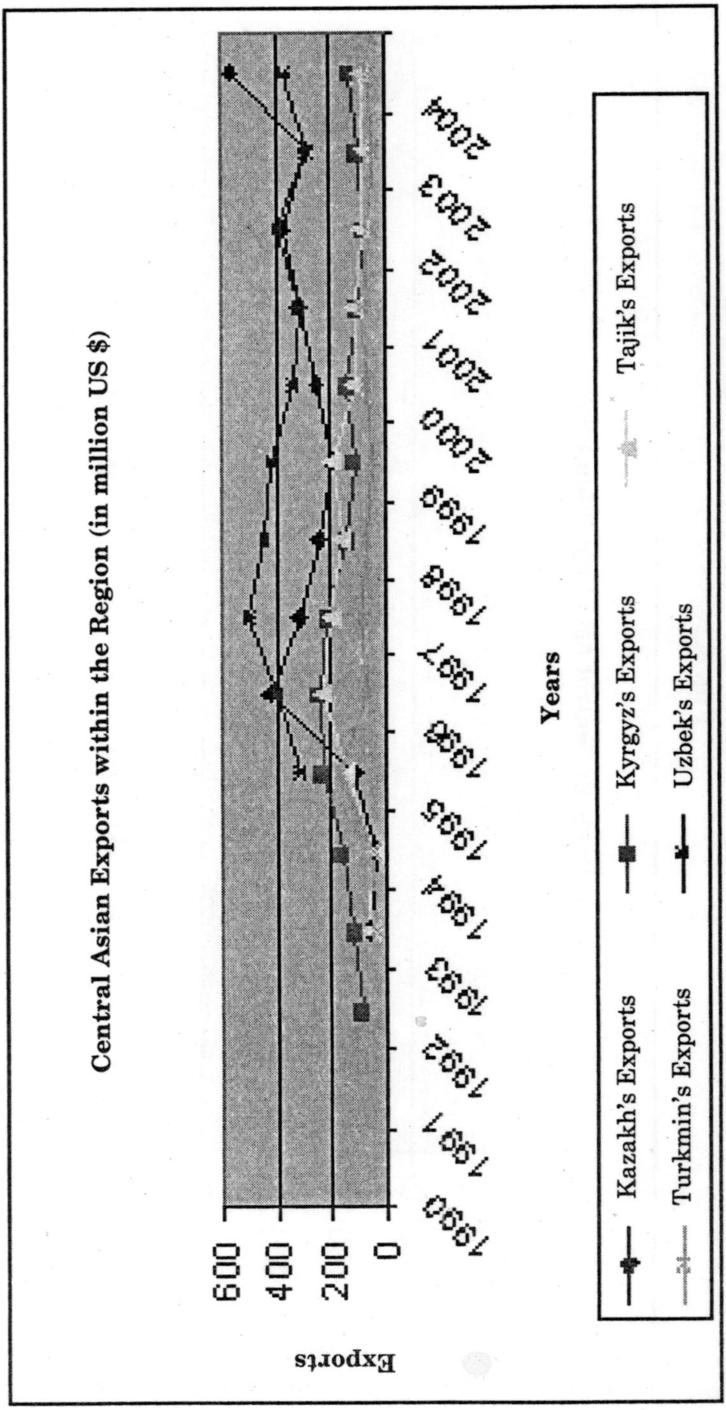
Central Asian Exports within the Region (in million US $)
Exports
600
400
200
0
1990
1991
1992
1993
1994
1995
1996
1997
1998
1999
2000
2001
2002
2003
2004
Years
Kazakh's Exports
Kyrgyz's Exports
Tajik's Exports
Turkmin's Exports
Uzbek's Exports

Fig. 3.4

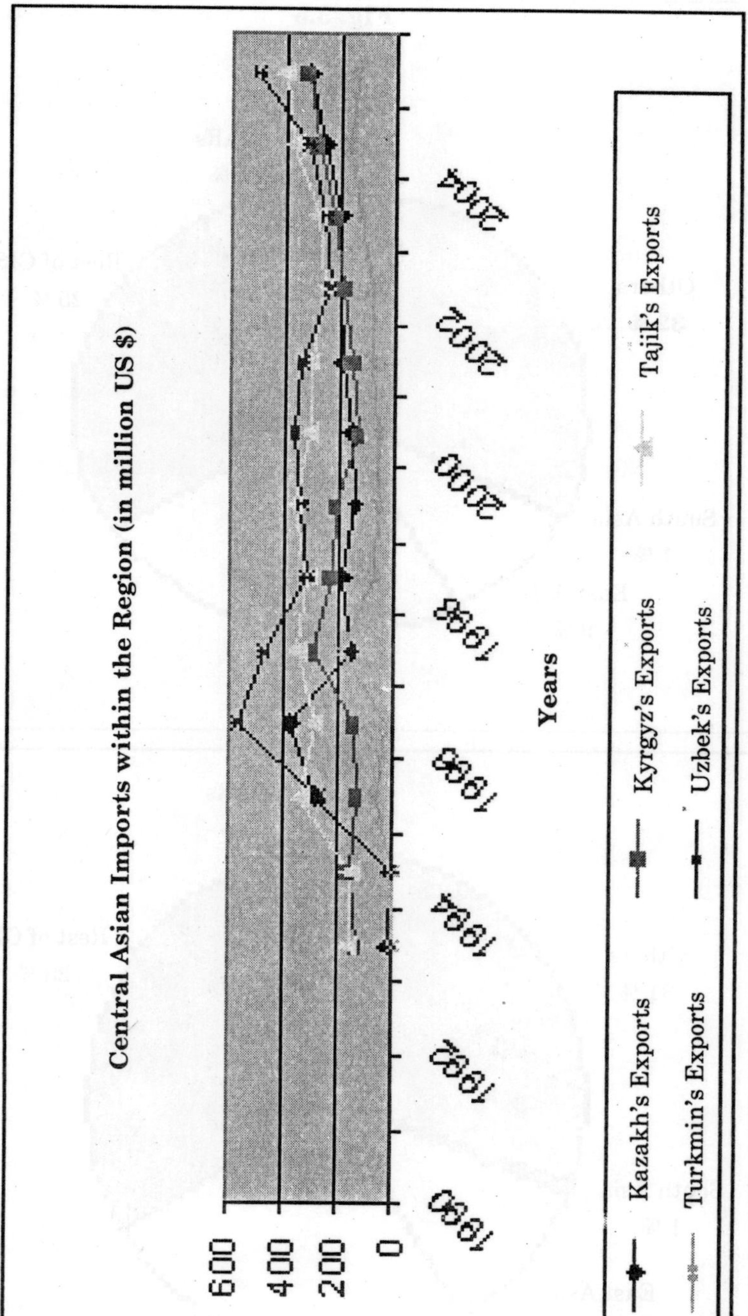
Central Asian Imports within the Region (in million US $)
Imports
600
400
200
0
1990
1992
1994
1996
1998
2000
2002
2004
Years
Kazakh's Exports
Kyrgyz's Exports
Tajik's Exports
Turkmin's Exports
Uzbek's Exports

Fig. 3.5

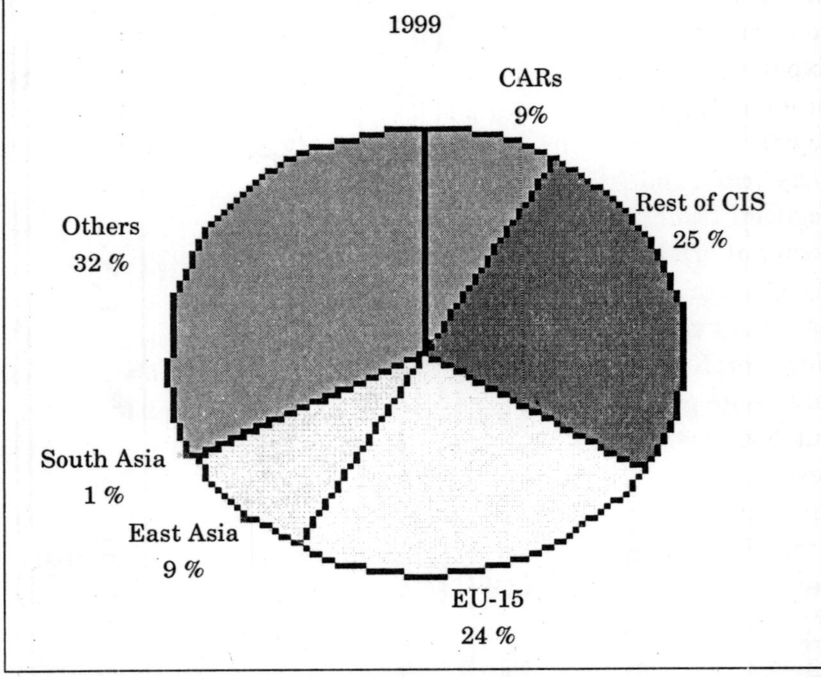
1999
CARs
9%
Rest of CIS
25 %
Others
32 %
South Asia
1 %
East Asia
9 %
EU-15
24 %

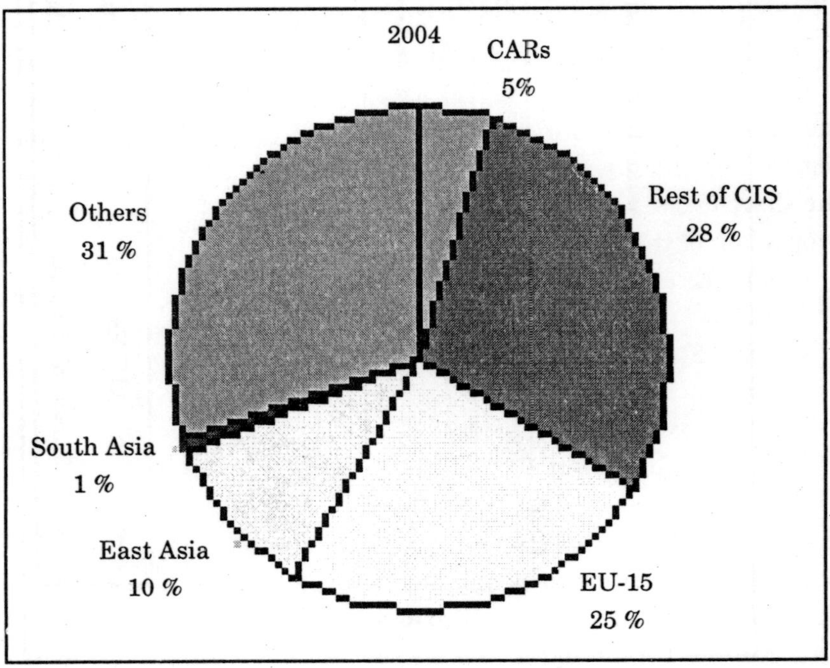
2004
CARs
5%
Rest of CIS
28 %
Others
31 %
South Asia
1 %
East Asia
10 %
EU-15
25 %

2004 and it was 9% in 1999. This shows that the trade has been increasing at a faster rate with the rest of the world. The individual countries experience varies. The Uzbekistan and Turkmenistan experienced dramatic shift of trade flows. Progress was less pronounced in Kazakhstan and Kyrgyzstan, where as Tajikistan registered a rising share of trade with the tradition partners. Uzbekistan and Turkmenistan were the main cause of drop in intra-regional trade. The dependency of individual countries on intra-regional trade varies considerably. Most dependent of all is Kyrgyzstan and Tajikstan. Uzbekistan, but especially Kazakhstan and Turkmenistan depend far less on intra-regional trade.[26] However, Kazakhstan, Turkmenistan and Uzbekistan, nonetheless make high priority objective to development of intraregional trade, but Kyrgyzstan and Tajikstan have no realistic alternative to development of intra-regional trade. Through the trade intensity this can be analyzed that how these two countries are more dependent on the intraregional trade, where as other three countries gradually diversifying their trade to the world and they have been decreasing their share within the regions for mid 1990s.

Trade Intensity Index :

In an attempt to explore the potential of intra-Central Asian trade expansion, This study has computed trade intensities for individual country with other Central Asian Countries as a whole region. This index was first used by K. Kojima [27] (1964). It measures the share of one country's trade with other country (or region) as a proportion of the latter's share of world.

The **Export Intensity Index** (EII) is defined as :

xij = {(Xij)/(Xi)/(Mj)/(Mw-Mi)} ..... **[1]**

where :

xij = EII of trade (Exports) of country Kazakhstan (i) with other Central Asian Countries (j)

Xij = Exports of Kazakhstan i to trading partner Other Central Asian Countries (j)

Xi = Total exports of Kazakhstan (i)

Mj = Total imports of other Central Asian Countries (j)

Mw = Total world imports

Mi = Total imports of Kazakhstan (i)

Note; Here i is for Kazakhstan and j for Central Asian region, in the same way other countries trade intensity has been calculated (eg. Kyrgyz with the whole region).

It is defined for Kazakhstan **i**'s exports to other Central Asian Countries j as the share of its exports going to **j** (Xij/Xi) relative to the share of **j**'s import to (Mj) in world imports net of i's import (Mw-Mi). The equality of these two terms would lead to the value of this Kazakhstan **i**'s export in the same proportion as Kazakhstan **i**'s share in total (net) world imports. Value of this index which is greater than unity would imply over-representation of other Central Asian Countries **j** in country **i**'s exports, while a value less than unity would imply under representation.

Similarly, **Import Intensity Index** (III) can be defined as:

mij = {(Mij)/(Mi)/(Xj)/(Xw-Xi)} .... **[2]**

where :

mij	=	EII of trade (Imports) of country **i** with country **(j)**
Mij	=	Imports of country **i** to trading partner **(j)**
Mi	=	Total Imports of country **(i)**
Xj	=	Total Exports of country **(j)**
Xw	=	Total world Exports
Xi	=	Total Exports of country **(i)**

Similarly, it is defined for county **i**'s imports from country j as the share of **i**'s imports coming from **j** (Mij/Mj) relative to the share of **j**'s exports (Xj) in world exports net of i's exports **(Xw-Xi)**. When these two terms are equal, this would imply that country i accounts for the proportion of country **j**'s exports identical to country **j**'s importance in total (net) world exports. If this index is numerically greater than unity this would imply over-representation of country **j** in the country **i**'s imports; on the other hand, if a value of less than unity of this index would imply under-representation.

When they were a part of the FSU, the CARs traded extensively with other FSU countries but little with the rest of the world. Moreover, their trade with other FSU countries was directed by central planners and conducted at administered prices. It therefore contributed little to improving social welfare and fostering sustainable economic growth in the CARs and other FSU countries. Following the breakup of the FSU in 1991, the CARs embarked on

Table 3.4

Share of merchandise trade with the Former Soviet Unions,1988-2004(%)

Country	*1988*	*1996*			*2004*		
	Total Trade	*Exports*	*Imports*	*Total Trade*	*Exports*	*Imports*	*Total Trade*
Kazakhstan	86	57	70	63	21	49	32
Kyrgyzstan	87	78	63	69	40	62	52
Tajikistan	86	45	58	51	24	72	53
Turkmenistan	89	-	31	-	42	49	45
Uzbekistan	86	21	32	27	32	41	36

Source: UNDP report, 2005. p. 52.

transition from a centrally planned to a market-based economy. As part of this process, they started introducing market-based principles in trade with FSU countries and opening up to trade with non-FSU countries. Their trade levels declined sharply in the early 1990s, reflecting the breakdown of trade links and payment mechanisms among the FSU countries and difficulties in engaging in trade with non-FSU countries. Since then, the CARs have made considerable progress in expanding market-based trade with both FSU and non-FSU countries and integrating into the global economy. From the above table it can be analyzed that the percentage trade of Central Asian countries decreased with the FSU countries. In 1988, 1996 and 2004, the total trade of central Asian countries with other FSU countries was 86.8% , 52.5% and 43.6% respectively. The shares for individual countries in these years can be seen in detail in the table 3.4 This table shows that actual trade between the CARs and other CIS-countries was, in most cases, above its potential. The comparisons of actual and potential bilateral trade among a large group of countries made by the International Trade Center suggest that Kazakhstan, Kyrgyz Republic, Tajikistan, and Uzbekistan "overtrade" with the Russian Federation but "under-trade" with most developed countries in North America, East Asia, and Western Europe as well as many emerging markets in South Asia and South East Asia.[28] Since independence, It's an opportunity to look forward to other neighbouring markets

One reason could be the payment mechanism. Due to the break down of trade links and payments mechanism (collapse of CMEA), trade levels declined sharply in Central Asia in the early 1990s. Central Asia tried to establish trade with non- soviet countries and set up new trade links and payment mechanism with the former Soviet countries on market principles. Valuation problems in barter trade have presented serious problems. The over valuation of barter trade has distorted balance of payments statistics. In order to resolve payment difficulties the Central Asian countries tried to resolve the barter trade. The Available information suggests that particularly in Turkmenistan where large quantities of gas is exported through such arrangements. Soviet-era trade therein was sub-optimal, particularly if high costs of

Table 3.5
Central Asian Trade Intensity with the Region

Years		*1993*	*1994*	*1995*	*1996*	*1997*	*1998*
Kazakhstan	Ex- Intensity	65.280	6.220	14.256	30.401	24.814	24.454
	% share of World	6.36	1.04	2.79	6.68	5.01	4.28
	Im-Intesity	16.543	2.042	30.345	39.199	18.165	22.926
	% share of World	1.15	0.30	5.78	8.78	3.77	4.05
Years		1993	1994	1995	1996	1997	1998
Kyrgyzstan	Ex- Intensity	366.042	235.671	157.493	208.426	195.269	232.831
	% share of World	35.63	39.50	30.85	45.75	39.41	40.75
	Im-Intesity	89.004	30.800	364.630	210.327	109.640	119.322
	% share of World	6.21	4.47	69.39	47.04	22.71	21.05
Years		1993	1994	1995	1996	1997	1998

(Contd)

(Contd Table 8.5)

Years		*1999*	*2000*	*2001*	*2002*	*2003*	*2004*	*2005*
Kazakhstan	Ex- Intensity	21.572	16.632	18.086	15.386	10.472	10.971	8.631
	% share of World	3.32	2.55	3.43	2.80	2.03	2.69	2.40
	Im-Intesity	21.754	11.138	12.305	12.577	9.073		4.391
	% share of World	3.80	2.77	2.98	2.99	2.39	1.75	1.57
Years		1999	2000	2001	2002	2003	2004	2005
Kyrgyzstan	Ex- Intensity	147.373	173.078	105.206	88.375	85.462	70.287	69.883
	% share of World	22.69	26.53	19.96	16.08	16.52	17.21	19.44
	Im-Intesity	131.570	101.452	172.037	141.272	107.485	61.120	39.931
	% share of World	22.95	25.23	41.59	33.56	28.27	19.33	14.24
Years		1999	2000	2001	2002	2003	2004	2005

(Contd)

(Contd Table 8.5)

Years		*1993*	*1994*	*1995*	*1996*	*1997*	*1998*
Tajikstan	Ex- Intensity	258.305	52.139	25.218	85.202	143.773	192.705
	% share of World	25.14	8.74	4.94	18.70	29.02	33.72
	Im-Intesity	425.863	196.434	219.270	190.068	218.230	251.972
	% share of World	29.70	28.52	41.73	42.51	45.20	44.44
Years		1993	1994	1995	1996	1997	1998
Turkmenistan	Ex- Intensity	217.326	21.273	9.769	43.052	45.521	76.119
	% share of World	21.15	3.57	1.91	9.45	9.19	13.32
	Im-Intesity	11.540	1.780	25.035	10.213	73.130	41.662
	% share of World	0.80	0.26	4.77	2.28	15.15	7.35
Years		1993	1994	1995	1996	1997	1998
Uzbekistan	Ex- Intensity	217.326	21.273	7.477	54.822	66.307	122.396
	% share of World	21.15	3.57	1.47	12.04	13.39	21.43
	Im-Intesity	11.540	1.780	50.208	53.107	49.986	61.705
	% share of World	0.80	0.26	9.56	11.88	10.36	10.89

(Contd)

(Contd Table 8.5)

Years		*1999*	*2000*	*2001*	*2002*	*2003*	*2004*	*2005*
Tajikstan	Ex- Intensity	178.445	92.333	82.590	66.357	51.066	37.084	35.244
	% share of World	27.47	14.16	15.67	12.08	9.87	9.08	9.80
	Im-Intesity	315.587	182.476	186.724	151.772	124.429	99.563	83.488
	% share of World	55.05	45.37	45.15	36.06	32.73	31.49	29.77
Years		1999	2000	2001	2002	2003	2004	2005
Turkmenistan	Ex- Intensity	21.339	16.401	17.532	9.758	6.297	5.467	4.561
	% share of World	3.29	2.51	3.33	1.78	1.22	1.34	1.27
	Im-Intesity	27.147	14.399	15.902	16.025	19.533	19.641	14.773
	% share of World	4.74	3.58	3.85	3.81	5.14	6.21	5.27
Years		1999	2000	2001	2002	2003	2004	2005
Uzbekistan	Ex- Intensitv	135.369	99.613	80.646	136.554	73.086	58.257	40.580
	% share of World	20.85	15.28	15.30	24.86	14.13	14.27	11.29
	Im-Intesity	76.231	69.505	59.328	47.666	38.824	31.274	38.962
	% share of World	13.30	17.29	14.35	11.33	10.21	9.89	13.90

transport are taken into account. Newly built capacity could mean lower costs because of economies of scale. Even if less than optimal, considerable intra-regional trade in the area is already based on different factor endowments. The trade intensity among all the countries was very high in the initial years. But it has been observed that recently the trade has been diversified to the other countries. In the initial years the share of world trade was high within the region but gradually it has slowed down. Initially these countries adopted the Russian Ruble as domestic currency. However the lack of convertibility of ruble proved problematic and segmented system of payment developed, trade being conducted in ruble as well as hard currency. During the session of 1993-1995, these countries introduced their own currencies.[29] New currencies failed to strengthen inter state payment system. Countries were more interested to get the hard currency. So trade diverted to other regions and they started demanding hard currency within the region.

During the period 1993-2005, the data shows that in value terms, the trade increases within the region. It approximately exceeds from 100 million dollar to 900 million dollars. This could happen due to increase in oil and energy prices in the world market. It shows fluctuating trend during the initial years. Later on trade stabilized and shows increasing gradually. Kazakhstan is relying on exploitation of its vast natural wealth. The central Asian countries mutual trade has played an important economic role. It has been observed that since independence the trade among majority of them was higher in 1992-1996. In January 1994 the CAU was formed by Kazakhstan, Kyrgyzstan and Uzbekistan and its provision was to free movements of goods, capital and labor. But when Russia and Belarus joined this custom Union posed the problem of trade diversion from the region also. After that the trade within the region has decreased in percentage in all the countries specially Kazakhstan's trade share of world's trade decreased from 8.38% in 1996 to 1.2% in 2005. Following sharp fluctuations in the late 1990s caused by swings in world commodity prices and the 1998 Russian financial crisis, levels of trade rose considerably in Kazakhstan in 2000–2005 (see fig 3.6) Kazakhstan, exports grew at an impressive more than 200% approximately, boosted by an increase in the volume of oil exports and a rise in world oil prices. Imports soared by more than 250%, driven by an increase in imports of capital goods for oil sector development. Despite increase in volume of trade the percentage share of the world has been decreased in the region. One can see many fluctuation in these years. The trade intensity within the region is also fluctuating. Since independence the disruption of administrative command system without the emergence of new market based mechanism, the terms of trade become worse in Kazakhstan, there were outstanding non payments problems. Kazakhstan has started liberalizing trade policy more steadly since early 1990s. After that there has been seen little improvements within the region but after the Russian financial crisis the share of trade as compared to world was only 1to 2 %. Only. The impact of Russian crisis was more substantial in Kazakhstan the trend towards reduction was further reinforced. Kazakhstan the share of crude oil in Kazakhstan's exports rose to 56.8% in 2004 from 39.3% in 1999. It is estimated that 102 percentage points of the 242% increase in Kazakhstan's exports were due to the rise in world prices for crude oil; This is especially true of Kazakhstan imports of which are dominated by capital goods for oil sector development Kazakhstan exports Petroleum, coal, wheat, nonferrous metals, chemicals and plastics, machinery to Kyrgyzstan, Wheat, flour, petroleum products, tractors to Tajikistan and Gasoline, wheat, clothing, chemicals, rubber, copper, wool, meat to Uzbekistan. only land locked countries like Central Asia need good transport infrastructure, high quality transport services and easy secure transit across boarders and through neighboring countries to integrate into the world. A reduction in transport and transit cost will have little positive impact if trade policy remains restrictive[30] (UNDP report,2005p.50.)

The Kyrgyz Republic has an especially low Kyrgyz and Tajikistan are open economies but benefits from them are very limited by the restrictions imposed by their neighboring countries Uzbekistan and Kazakhstan. This country is more dependent on the other countries of the region, despite that the fig 3.7 shows that it has less trade within the region in volume terms as compared to other countries. Trade intensity of Kyrgyzstan and Tajikistan is higher than the other countries of the region(see table3.5). This

Fig. 3.6 Kazakhstan VS other Central Asian Countries (1*4)

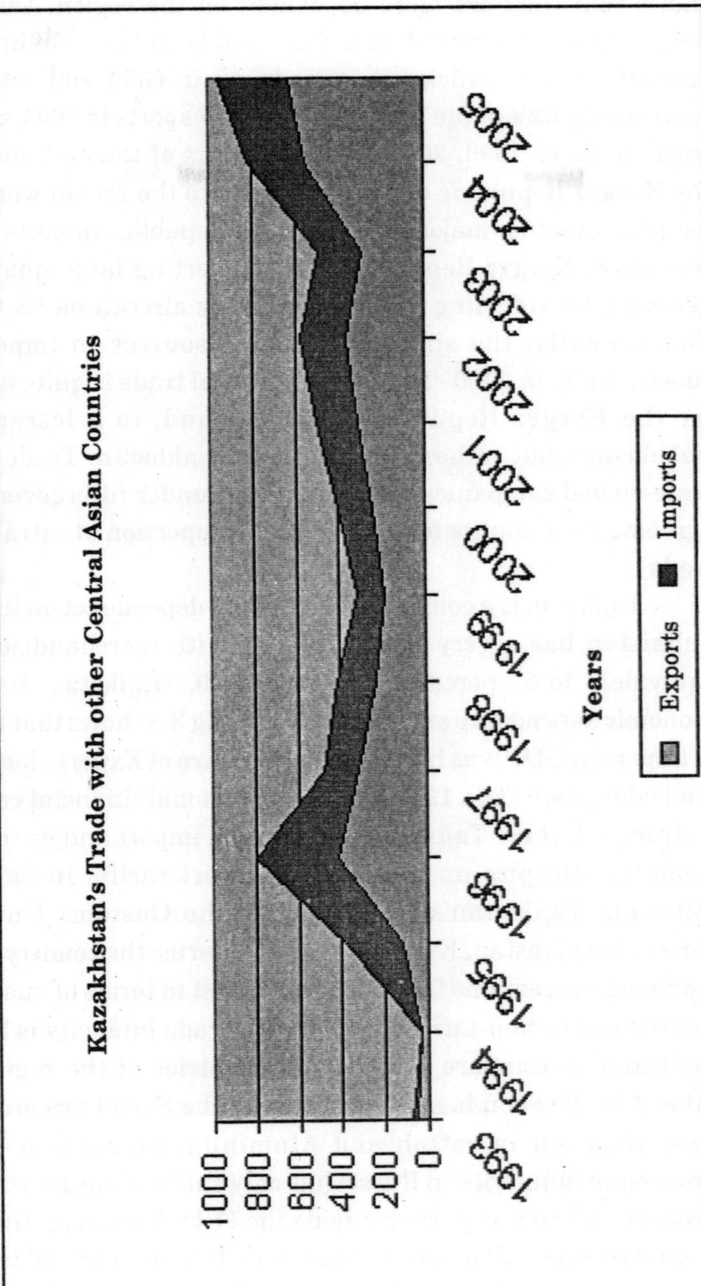

shows that they are more dependent on the region. During this period these economies had to face sizable and persistent external current account deficits as it is shown in Gold and cotton fiber comprised 46.2% of the Kyrgyz Republic's exports in 2004, compared with 45.4% in 1999. 20 percentage points of the 58% increase in the Kyrgyz Republic's exports were due to the rise in world prices for gold; . Another major item in Kyrgyz Republic's imports is energy resources. Kyrgyz Republic started importing large quantities of kerosene for refueling of foreign military aircraft on its territory. Consequently, the share of energy resources in imports rose substantially in 2000–2004. Intra-regional trade is quite important for the Kyrgyz Republic, Tajikistan and, to a lesser extent, Uzbekistan, but rather insignificant Kazakhstan. Trade between state-owned companies often conducted under intergovernmental agreements accounts for a significant proportion of intra-regional trade

Tajikstan is a country which is more dependenet on the region. Tajikistan has a very open economy, with merchandise exports equivalent to 63 percent of GDP in 1999. Tajikstan has strong economic dependence on external trade. Fig 3.8 shows that the share of import in GDP was higher than the share of Exports had chronic trade deficits.[31] The 1998 global and regional financial crisis had a strong effect on Tajikstan's export and import and on overall on economy. Despite an increase in import tariffs in early 1999 following Tajikistan's inclusion into the Customs Union with Russia, Kazakhstan, Kyrgyzstan, and Belarus, the country's foreign trade regime remains fairly liberal, at least in terms of quantitative restrictions or non-tariff barriers. The Trade intensity is higher in Tajikstan as compare to the other countries of the regions.(see table 3.5) The emphasis placed during the Soviet era on extreme specialization in cotton and Aluminum production to serve processing industries in Russia has only shifted in as much as these products are now exported outside the FSU. Therefore, the foreign trade structure that has evolved over fifteen years of transition renders the country highly dependent on conditions in the world commodity markets or its main exports and imports. The concentration of two-thirds of Tajikistan's exports in two

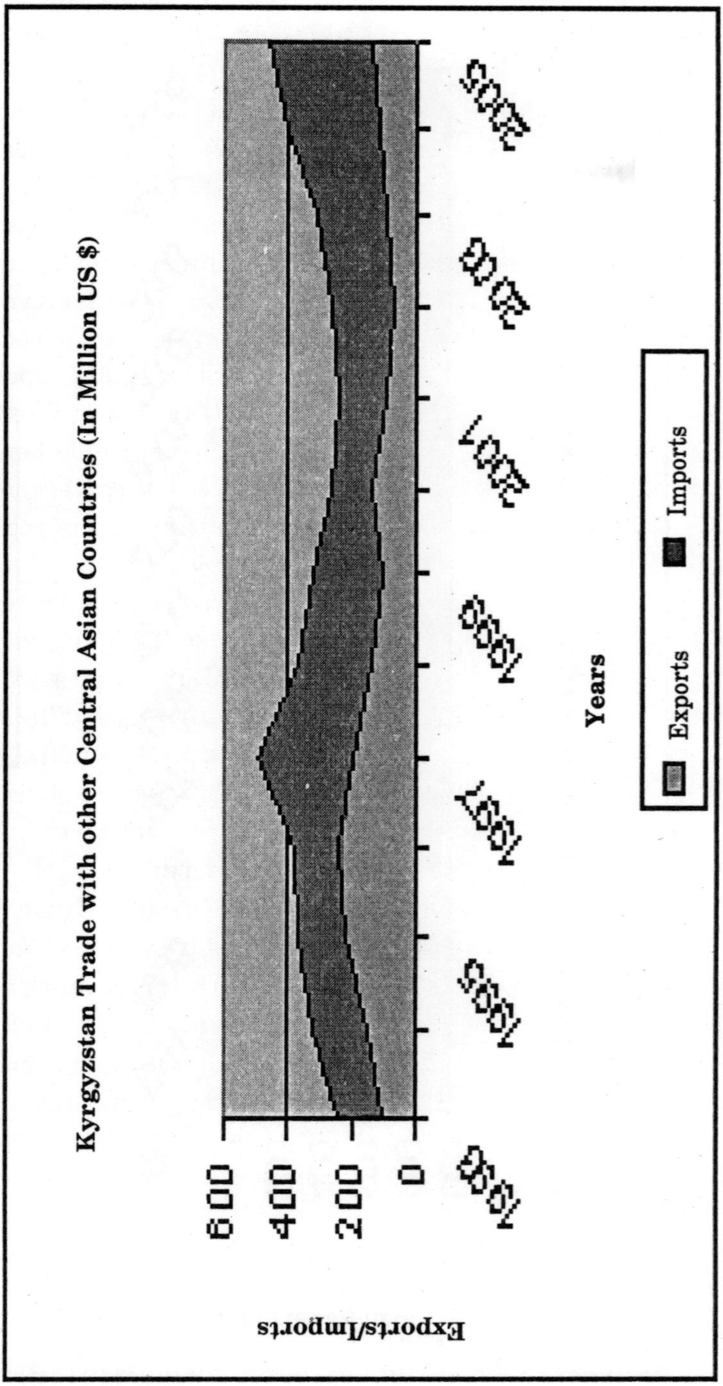

Fig. 3.7 Kyrgyz Republic VS other Central Asian Countries (1*4)

Fig. 3.8 Tajikistan vs other Central Asian Countries (1*4)

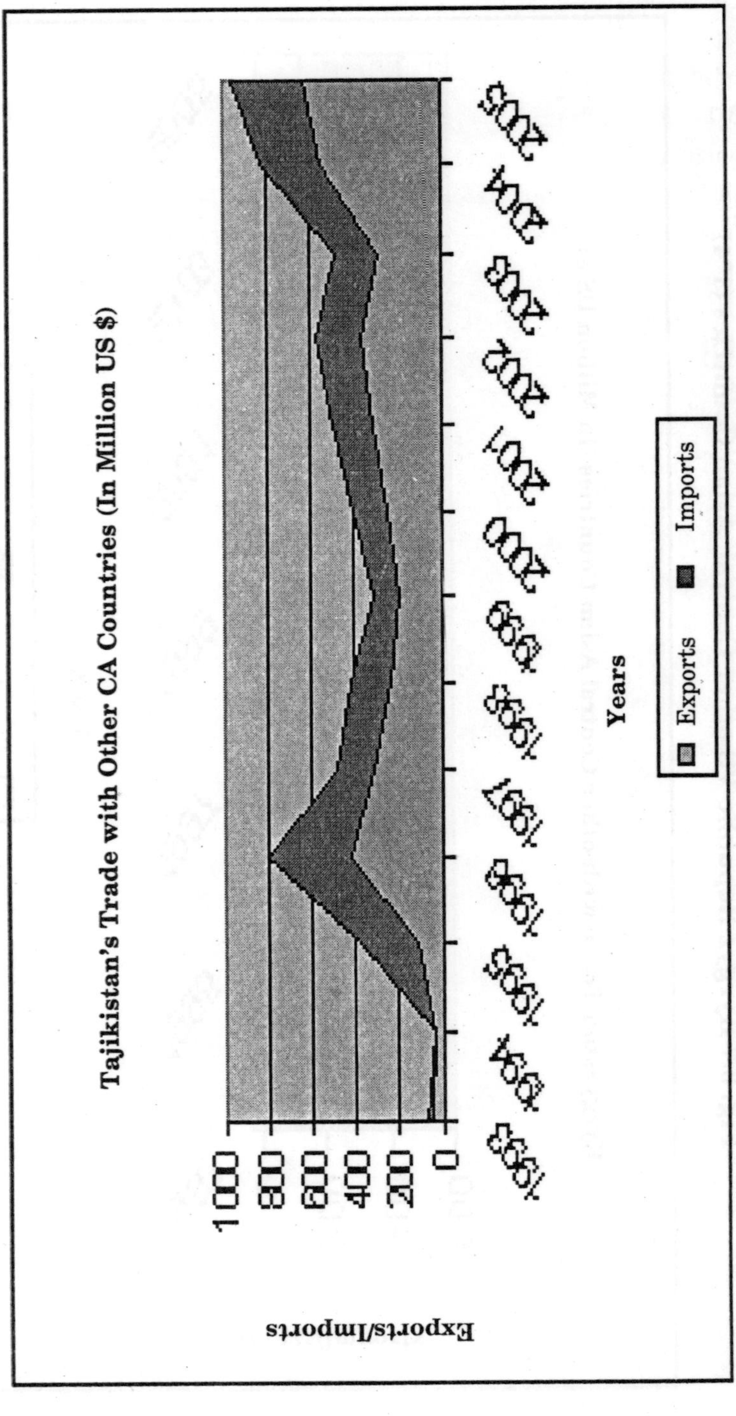

commodities-aluminum and cotton fiber-has led to substantial fluctuations in foreign exchange earnings from year to year because of changes in the world prices of these commodities(see the table 3.1). Export and import price fluctuations have occasionally offset each other. The trade deficits in effect replaced the subsidies the republic received as a part of the Soviet Union. The rising debt problem required a reduction of deficits by cutting non-essential imports and increasing export earnings. Despite the introduction of flexible exchange rate policies in 1996 that adjusted in line with inflation, current account deficits remained high. Following the Russian crisis and real devaluation of the Tajik ruble, the country's foreign trade deficit declined. Trade policies range is very liberal in Tajikstan.

Valuation problems in barter trade have presented serious problems. The over valuation of barter trade has distorted balance of payments statistics. In order to resolve payment difficulties the Central Asian countries tried to resolve the barter trade. The available information suggests that particularly in Turkmenistan where large quantity of gas is exported through such arrangements. Trade data by type of payment indicate that in 1996, 24% of Turkmenistan 's export were paid in cash, 54% in barter goods and construction services and the reminder was accounted by the accumulation of arrears[32]. Due to the restrictive policies of the Turkmenistan the fluctuations can be seen in the fig 3.9 from the years 1993-1999. Turkmenistan unified its exchange rate in April 1998. Although it continued to restrict access to foreign exchange and sustain surrendered requirements. It has been observed that after 1999 the trade intensity with in the region has become low and the %age share of the world also decreased(see table 3.5). One reason would be that the central Asian region had taken step to discourage the barter trade. Turkmenistan had some success in reducing the barter component on non gas exports. For example Cotton. Oil and oil derivatives have been increasingly on a cash basis since 1996.Trade share within the region also reduced. In 1993 it was 21% of total export to the world, and decreased to 9.19% and 1.27% in 1997 and 2005 respectively. The volume of trade has

Fig. 3.9 Turkmenistan vs other Central Asian Countries (1*4)

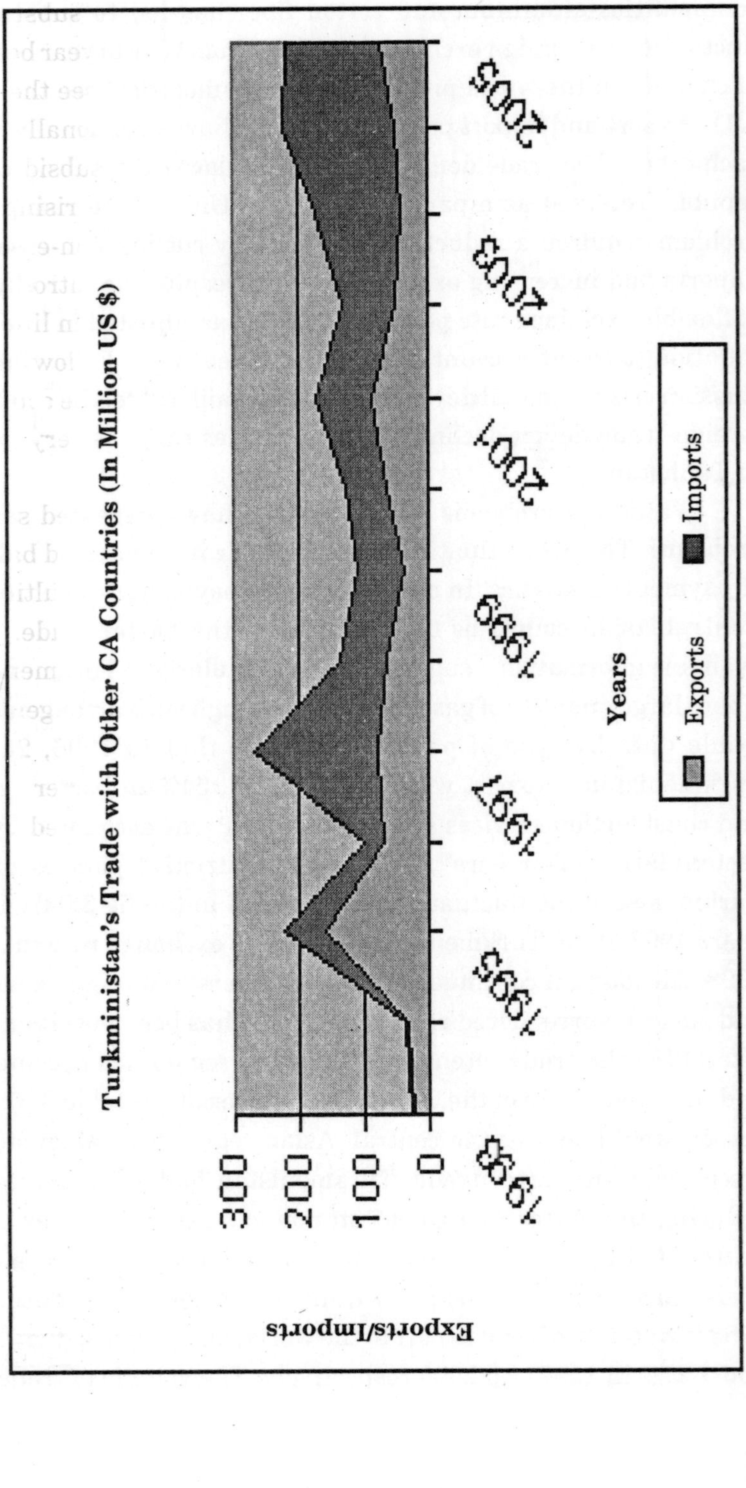

Fig. 3.10 Uzbekistan vs other Central Asian Countries (1*4)

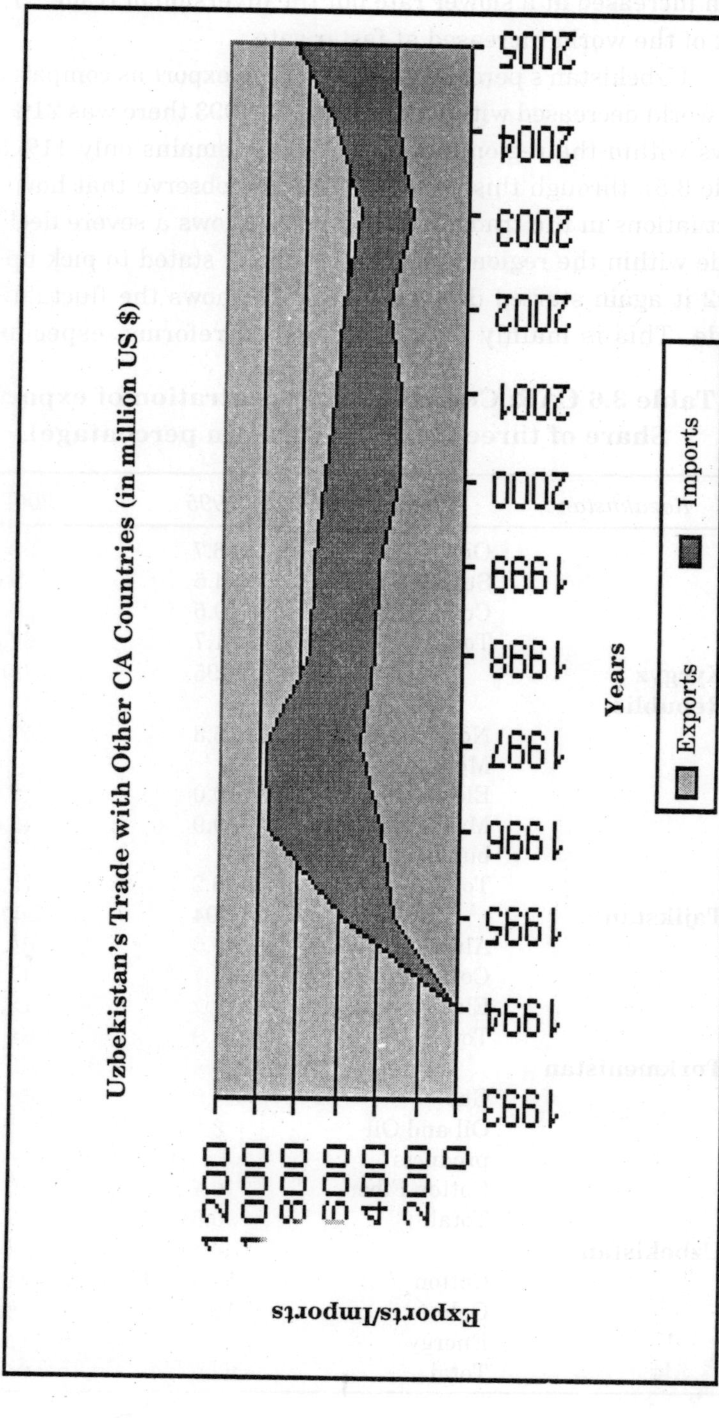

been increased at a slower rate but the diversion of trade with the rest of the world increased at faster rate.

Uzbekistan's percentage share of the export as compared a to the world decreased within the region. In 1993 there was 21% trade flows within the region and in 2005 this remains only 11%.9 (see table 3.5). through this table this can also observe that how much fluctuations in the trade in 1994-1995 it shows a severe decline in trade within the region and than gradually stated to pick up after 2002 it again started dropping. Fig 3.10 shows the fluctuation in trade. This is mainly due to unfinished reforms, especially in

Table 3.6 CAR: Commodity concentration of exports, Share of three main products (in percentage).

Kazakhstan	*Products*	*1995*	*2002*
	Oil	16.7	50.6
	Steel product	14.5	9.8
	Copper	10.5	7.1
	Total	41.7	67.5
Kyrgyz Republic		1995	2002
	Non- Ferrous Metallurgy	15.3	51.7
	Electric Energy	10.0	9.8
	Machine building	10.9	12.0
	Total	36.2	73.5
Tajikstan		1994	2001
	Aluminum	56.0	61.0
	Cotton Fiber	27.7	11.0
	Electric energy	5.2	12.0
	Total	88.9	84.0
Turkmenistan		1994	2002
	Gas	65.6	58.0
	Oil and Oil products	8.5	14.0
	Cotton Fiber	16.7	6.0
	Total	90.9	78.0
Uzbekistan		1994	2001
	Cotton	51.3	24.4
	Gold	12.8	28.3
	Energy	0.0	11.8
	Total	64.0	64.5

Fig. 3.11 Commodity composition of Central Asian Countries

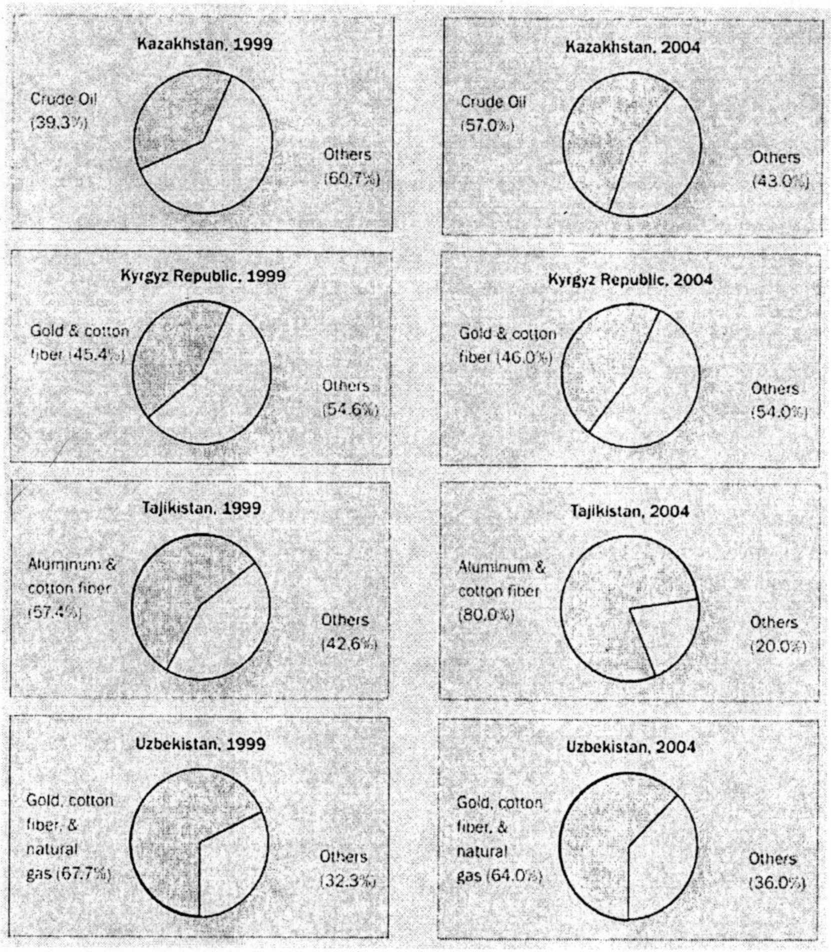

establishment of strong institutions to support market economy through the transparent, predictable and well-enforced rules and regulations. In Uzbekistan, growth suffered from heavy restrictions on external and domestic trade, and a drop in non-traditional exports and foreign direct investment due to the very difficult business environment.[33]

As of early 2000 no Central Asian country has recovered the level of GDP it had achieved in 1989, though Uzbekistan is close. Besides exploiting natural resources for export, renewed growth in Central Asia will depend in some greater part on local manufacturing for local needs. But efficient production requires a minimum assured output to achieve reasonably low costs. For example, assembly of automobiles or farm machinery is subject to economies of scale that cannot be fully exploited at the scale of Kyrgyzstan, or even Uzbekistan. Similarly for electronics goods and probably consumer appliances, formerly provided by Russian factories to Central Asia. VCR's, digitally controlled machine tools, automatic production lines, computer equipment, microwaves, and similar products were once produced in Kyrgyzstan for the large, if unselective, Soviet market. That trade has ceased altogether. Revival of civilian machine-building would make sense in Central Asia only with access to nearby markets. In view of accumulated technical skills in all these countries, the potential for development is considerable if trade outlets can be assured.

Many otherwise well-informed sources have erred in stating that Central Asian states have no natural complementarily Kyrgyzstan supplies electricity, hides and wool, and non-ferrous ores to its neighbors. Kazakstan is a supplier of coal, chemicals and fertilizers, as well as non-ferrous minerals. Uzbekistan supplies natural gas and cotton. All these rely on specific factor endowments. The Fig 3.11 shows that there trade share of main commodities have been increasing. Furthermore, the complementarities that exist could be enhanced by regional cooperation in manufacturing investment. After all, intra-industry trade is the fastest growing type of trade among advanced countries around the world. A free trade area in Central Asia would constitute a much larger market than any of the isolated countries. An economic union allowing free movement of factors of production as well as goods would be even better. Foreign investors would be attracted by the prospect of operating in this larger market. While the market for Coca-Cola, snickers candy, cigarettes, and personal communications already seems to be large enough in each of these countries—and monopoly privileges or exclusive franchises actually increase the profitability of exclusive access. The market seems too small and fragile for big ticket items with substantial after-sale service.

To assure efficiency and progressiveness, industrial structures in Central Asia area must have several competing manufacturers in each product market. As shown by the experience of Japan, Western Europe, and the United States, it is mainly competition that spurs innovation, cost-reduction, and management efficiency. Insulated as they are to some extent by the natural barrier of distance, needed competition must come in large part from within the Central Asian region. Without salt-water ports within easy reach, Central Asia must create a large enough arena to accommodate workably competitive industries that can survive and thrive without budgetary subsidies. But ensuring competition by fostering small- and medium-sized enterprises is a neglected aspect of economic reform in all these countries. Even in free-market Kyrgyzstan, enterprises with more than 500 employees still produce more than half of all industrial output. Only social functions have been spun off. There has been little done for establishing a market structures to increase competition. The governments have preferred to regulate monopolies with stifling price controls rather than encourage free entry from domestic and nearby foreign sources.

The poor condition of Central Asia's extensive transport network and high barriers to transit double the costs and time required for trade within the countries and to major markets abroad. Corruption hampers trade and investment According to one survey, more than 30 per cent of firms make bribes frequently. "Around 3.3 per cent of annual firm revenue is soaked up by unofficial payments (almost twice the eight post-communist EU states)[34]," (UNDP, 2005) The halving of tariffs, transport and transit costs a prime area for improved regional cooperation would increase real GDP in 2015 by about 20 per cent in Kazakhstan and by 55 per cent in Kyrgyzstan, and allow increased consumption and employment, especially among the poor. Many studies by expertise recommends that the governments of Central Asia pursue multilateral trade liberalization with WTO membership, and that they use bilateral and regional trade agreements to ease trade and transit by improving customs, visa and border management. Governments should avoid costly transport investments in detours around borders, liberalize air traffic, reduce interference with shuttle traders and improve the investment climate at home. Regional organizations need a clear mandate for improving regional transport networks and transit. The two sub-regions have joined together in an effort to connect landlocked Central Asia and seaports in South Asia via Afghanistan. Based on this partnership, we can envisage Afghanistan as a regional hub, and a critical link between the South and Central Asian markets[35]

This has noted that there are political and institutional obstacles to regional cooperation in Central Asia. Not all political and economic interests benefit from cooperation and, even where there is interest in cooperation at the top, implementation may be blocked by those who would lose. Corruption, poor administrative capacity and lack of accountability hinder reforms. More participation by communities would help by giving voice to those who suffer from poor borders. Comprehensive, region-wide cooperation may not occur in Central Asia for some time, due to political and institutional constraints, but progress on many selected issues is possible and desirable. The neighbors and international partners of Central should work together toward their strong, shared interest in a stable, prosperous and cohesive Central Asia region. Differing interests among partners and fragmented support have choked effective international support. neighbors and international partners must find common ground in their support for political and economic progress.

The capital of Xinjiang, Urumqi, is farther from a seaport than any other large city in the world. International trade in the region thus involves shipment of goods over long distances through neighboring countries. The terrain of the region ranges from 154 meters below sea level, the second lowest point on earth, in Turpan basin to mountain peaks as high as 7,400 in Kyrgyz Republic and Tajikistan. The region is generally mountaineous. The Kyrgyz Republic is predominantly mountaineous and dominated by the Tien Shan range. Into this mountain range run the dry grass of Kazakhstan. Ninety percent of Tajikistan is mountaineous, largely covered by Trans-Alay range in the north and the Pamirs in the southeast. Travels on the mountains and borders are limited to only a few corridors and passes. Within Central Asia lies one of the most inhospitable deserts in the world, the Takliman desert. There are little natural resources in the area including vegetation and wildlife. Local people call it "the Land of Death" or the "the Land of the Irrevocable Death." Turkmenistan is 80 percent desert, which is part of the great Garagum desert. The region's terrain is generally harsh and poses substantial barriers to transportation and communication. The climate in the region is generally dry. Weather varies from arid to semi-arid in desert and steppe areas, respectively. The region usually has hot summers and mild to cold winters. The agricultural center of the region, the fertile Ferghana valley, is shared by Kyrgyz Republic, Tajikistan, and Uzbekistan. Also, high and almost impassable mountains separate the Osh region of the Kyrgyz Republic and the Leninabad region of Tajikistan from their respective capitals. Land transportation means created during the Soviet period including highways and railroads defy the national boundaries in the region. An example of this is the major highway between Tashkent and Samarkand in Uzbekistan that passes through Kazakhstan. Azerbaijan and Turkmenistan border the Caspian Sea while Kazakhstan includes the southern portion of the Aral Sea with a 420 km shoreline. Farming is the region's main industry. It occurs in line with the climactic and natural conditions of the area. For most of the Central Asian republics, cotton is one of their main products. These countries, including Krygyz Republic, Tajikistan, Turkmenistan, and Uzbekistan are some of the top world's producers of cotton. Livestock and grain industries are important for a number of the Central Asian republics. Also the primary manufacturing industry for several of these republics is well developed. As a whole, the Central Asia region has abundant supply of mineral resources that include petroleum, natural gas, and rare metals. Kazakhstan and Turkmenistan including Azerbaijan are the three main oil and gas exporters in the region and nearby countries. (see table 3.6)

The Central Asia has become a member of many regional, subregional and multilateral institutions or organisation since independence.

4) Other Regional subregional and multilateral economic initiatives of Central Asia

During the first month of independence theses states aimed an intensive search for new ties Muslim countries. In May 1992, they held a summit in Ashgabat in the capital of the Turkmenistan. Central Asian region joined the organization for economic co-operation (OECO) which has previously consisted of the Muslim States of Iran, Turkey and Pakistan. Selected regional organisations, Initiatives and programmes in Central Asia.

Table 3.7

	CACO	*CAREC*	*CIS*	*ECO*	*EEC*	*SCO*	*SES*	*SPECA*
Kazakhstan	X	X	X	X	X	X	X	X
Kyrgyzstan	X	X	X	X	X	X		X
Tajikstan	X	X	X	X	X	X		X
Turkmenistan			X	X		X		X
Uzbekistan	X	X	X	X		X		X

- CACO -The Central Asian Cooperation Organisation
- CAREC)-The Central Asia Regional Economic Co-operation Intitiatives
- CIS -The Commonwealth of Independent States
- ECO-The Economic Cooperation Organization
- EEC or EURASEC -The Eurasian Economic Community
- SCO -The Shangai Cooperation Organization
- SES -The Single Economic Space
- SPECA -The Special Programme for the Economies of Central Asia .

Challenges of Regional Economic Integration

The main challenges such as huge currency devaluation after independence, low tariff levels, poor collection, lack of financial and management control, absence of a credible regulatory framework, poor dispute resolution, and lack of rule of contractual law are common challenges the region faces. The regional cooperation strategy is about overcoming challenges to cooperation rules, regulations, attitudes, investments and political will that is forcing inefficient decisions on the energy sector at the cost of overall economic growth. Trade in power and natural gas is constrained by the following policy issues: (i) national tariffs for electricity and district heat are still lower than economic costs, which require

Table 3.8

Regional Initiatives	*Year of formation*	*Members*	*Observers*	*Objectives*
CACO	1994	Kazakhstan, Kyrgyzstan,Russia, Tajikstan, and Uzbekistan	Afganistan, Georgia, Turkeyand Ukraine	-Increasing regional Cooperation -Fighting regional crime -Create unified economic space -Harmonise customs and boarder policies. -Expand water and environmental cooperation -aim to expand cooperation in politics, economic transport energy, infrastructure, water and energy resources, agriculture trade and science technology culture tourism, above all to maintain regional stability.
CAREC	1997 by ABD	Azerbaijan, China, Kazakhstan, Kyrgyzstan, Magnolia, Tajikistan and Uzbekistan		-Promote economic growth raise living standard by emerging eco cooperation in the region. -Focus on financing the infrastructural projects -Improve policies for promoting cross boarder activities in areas of transport, energy. - trade policy to improve trade facilitation especially customs operations

(Contd)

(Contd Table 3.8)

Regional Initiatives	*Year of formation*	*Members*	*Observers*	*Objectives*
CIS	1993	Armenia, Azerbaijan, Belarus, Georgia, Kazakhstan		-aim at serving for future development -strengthening the relationship of friendship, good neighborhood, inter ethnic harmony, trust, mutual understanding and mutually cooperation among members
ECO	1985	Afghanistan, Azerbaijan Azerbaijan, Iran, Kazakhstan, Kyrgyzstan, Pakistan, Tajikistan, Turkey, Turkmenistan and Uzbekistan.		-to obtain sustainable development of member states, - removal of trade barriers to promote of intra-regional trade, and gradual integration of the economies of the member states with the world economy. -to develop transport and communication infrastructure
The Eurasian Economic Community (EEC or EURASEC)	1994	Belarus, Kazakhstan, Kyrgyzstan, Russia and Tajikstan	The republic of Moldavia and Ukraine	establishment of common market for labour and capital , free intra copmmunity trade and trade policy harmonization . to develop an agreement among Iran/Kazakstan Russia and Tajikstan to rehabilitate hydro-electric power plants in Tajikstan

(Contd)

(Contd Table 3.8)

Regional Initiatives	*Year of formation*	*Members*	*Observers*	*Objectives*
The Shangahi Cooperation Organization (SCO)	2001	China, Kazakhstan, Kyrgyzstan, Russia, Tajikstan and Uzbekistan	India, Iran, Mongolia, And Pakistan	to strengthen mutual trust, friendship and good –neighborliness between the member states to encourage effective cooperation between them in the political, trade and economic , scientific and technical , cultural , educational , energy , transport , environmental and other spheres , and to undertake joint efforts for the maintenance of peace ,security and stability in the region
The Single Economic Space (SES)	2003	Belarus,Kazakhstan,Russia and Ukriane		to create a single economic space,preceded initially by a free trade zone and then a customs union. .Russia also has promoted the idea of a single currency , and advocated decreasing tariff and customs barriers.
The Special Programme for the Economies of Central Asia (SPECA)	1998	Afghanistan, Azerbaijan, Kazakhstan, Kyrgyzstan, Tajikstan, Turkmenistanand Uzbekistan		to support the central Asian states in developing their cooperation creating incentives for economic development and integration into the economies of Europe and Asia.

continued government subsidies and obstruct the establishment of competitive electricity and gas markets; (ii) barter trade in power decreases transparency, reduces allocative efficiency, and promotes corruption; and (iii) revenue stream over the long-term cannot be projected under existing. Kazakhstan the private banking sector with major investments in the Kyrgyz Republic and the Russian Federation is leading the way. The efforts to develop Almaty as a regional financial center is praiseworthy but activities need to be carefully thought out. Priority needs to be given not only to the development of laws and regulatory procedures but also, more importantly, to upgrading that city's aging physical infrastructure. Sustainable and balanced development of the Caspian region represents a major challenge as past significant investment has not translated into efficient utilization of the labor force in the region[36] (ADO, 2007, p.106) Many developed countries of Europe including US have been attracted to the Central Asian region for exploiting natural resources. Particularly Kazakhstan, due to its rich resource base and its sound record on structural reforms and commitment to safe guarding macroeconomic stability attract many investors. Total cumulative investment 1993-2000 was over \$10000m. Major business partners companies operating there, are USA, Canada China, Germany Japan South Korea Switzerland and the UK.

Given these common challenges, transport, energy and trade facilitation are the priority areas for economic cooperation in Central Asia. It has been considered that human resource development to be an important aspect of the three priority areas. The key to this approach is to focus on concrete projects that bring tangible benefits. These benefits would help build confidence and promote trust, which would in turn lay the foundation for achieving longer term strategic objectives. Central Asia should stay focused on addressing the long term challenges identified above, and continue to play a key role in mobilizing resources for financing investment and other projects. This represents a new phase of cooperation between the countries will provide an opportunity to enhance coordination with all development partners for effective support to economic cooperation.

The legacies of the Soviet period are not favorable to regional cooperation. State trading is an obstacle to the kind of decentralized commerce that would naturally flow across borders in the area. Most trade in energy (gas, petroleum, electricity) is state-to state, but when the customer fails to pay, as often happens, there is no alternative but to shut off supplies, provoking a minor diplomatic crisis and sometimes revenge. The same applies to trade in water, essential to Uzbekistan's irrigated agriculture and also important in Kazakstan and Turkmenistan. The Syr Darya, Amur Darya, and several smaller rivers flow from Kyrgyzstan and Tajikistan to irrigate much of the arable land of Uzbekistan and Turkmenistan before dribbling into the much-reduced Aral Sea. When the downstream states refuse to help Kyrgyzstan maintain the dams on the Naryn headwaters, the Kyrgyz have the option of releasing water at their own convenience, not during the hot growing season. Despite repeated proclamations of intent, agreements to promote intra-regional trade by preferential tariffs have yet to be executed fully. Actually, because of low tariff schedules and inability to collect whatever tariffs exist over their long borders, tariffs are relatively insignificant as barriers to trade among the Central Asian countries. Tariffs and specific trade taxes are reasonable by GATT standards, and bribes and other unofficial payments are often in place of tariffs, not in addition. Moreover, there are still substantial non-tariff obstacles to trade. It is indirect impediments to trade which disadvantage commerce, such as poor roads, hijacking, and unofficial police stops. With all the problems, informal trade among the Central Asian countries appears to be working reasonably well, although the use of shuttle-traders and street and bazaar methods is very labor-intensive. Such trading methods probably would not be efficient were these Central Asian republics able fully to employ their labor force in agriculture, manufacturing, and higher value services.(As things stand now, trade represents a viable employment for older women, young men, and others displaced by the sharp dislocations of the 1990's. However, intra-regional trade is not advancing as much as trade with the "far-abroad" (non-CIS), at least according to official estimates.[37] (UNDP, Human resource Development Report, 2005. p. 53). But Foundation of joint ventures and enterprises has had a great importance for the development of regional economic cooperation. Till 2003, 53, Kazakh- Kyrgyz and 91 kazakh- Uzbek enterprises operate in Kazakhstan. 295 Kyrgyz-Kazakh and 71 Kyrgyz- Uzbek in Kyrgyzstan. In Uzbekistan, 22 Uzbek- Kazakh and 12 Uzbek-Kyrgyz joint enterprises in different branches of national economy[38]. It can be seen that as more and more joint business among each other are established, there is enormous potential for cooperation in these countries. They are certainly facing major problems, as and if these problems are overcome they can be a integrated into a single region thereby facilitating integration with the world.

Key Challenges

- **Different economic reform model** : One of the basic challenges is that these countries are pursuing different development strategies in their countries. From the very beginning Kazakhstan opened up its economy and undertook drastic reforms as a means to stimulate its economy. Uzbekistan adopted partial reforms and continue to carry on the state management techniques of the former Soviet Union[39]. (Richard, 2006) Turkmenistan has adopted the mixed policies, initially Government gave low priorities to economic reforms. Kyrgyzstan mean while able to get a membership from the WTO but due to less cooperation from neighbouring countries are not able to get maximum benefits. Tajikstan is a very small economy and more dependent on other countries of the region. It has no alternate rather than integrating with the region.[40]
- **Different political regime :** The authoritarian natures of the Central Asian Regimes also affect the regional integration process because of their tendency to impose control over society. Thus boarders are tend to be tightly controlled and information restricted.
- **Differ in terms of size :** geographic, demographic, natural resources endowment, social, enviornmental conditions.
- **Lack of Communication:** Due to lack of information and regulations it restricted the cross boarder trade and cooperation. Data also proves that the percentage of trade among the region decrease over the past years. At the policy

level, the timing of structural and policy reforms envisaged in the outlook could be delayed. These reforms include regional cooperation arrangements in the oil and natural gas sector that would increase revenue and reduce transit taxes as well as general regional cooperation measures to deal with trade and transit bottlenecks and could increase efficiency.

- **Insecurity, threat to independence:** Terrorism is a continuing potential threat to the region, particularly where ethnic tensions could surface. More generally, political instability and poor governance pose considerable risks to the CARs' outlook. There seem to be increasing pressure for democratization in some CARs. Particularly relevant in this vein is the prospect of prolonged political and economic uncertainty in the Kyrgyz.
- **Political will to resolve these issues:** Republic following the sudden change of government, escalating tensions in Uzbekistan in the aftermath of the Andijan events, instability in Kazakhstan in the run up to the presidential election, and a possible resumption of civil strife in Tajikistan. The economic impact of these uncertain political developments is hard to forecast. Moderate political instability would have a relatively modest economic impact Severe political instability, however, would further dampen the growth projections and raise poverty compared to the levels envisaged in scenario.
- **Fergana Valley has been most severly affected by the Zig saw puzzle like coarse of the new boaders** Another observation provided by the ADB is that " most of the regional initiatives been used to ensure the political stability rather than promoting economic cooperation. As a result of these challenges actual progress of regional cooperation is slow"[41]

(5) Opportunities and Potential in Regional Economic Cooperation

Resource rich Central Asia, unique minerals in mountain area, and human potential are the strategically promising directions of economic cooperation. A joint development of these resources will provide an opportunity to form regional markets of factor of production and growth of export potential of this region[42] (Komilove, 2003) Ethnic, linguistic, ideological-Islamic identities exist in the states of Central Asia which interact with the state-centric nationalism. These identities have cultivated interaction and connections with their ethnic brethren or the people with similar political-ideological orientations in the neighboring states. However, these identities and their transnational interaction have not so far threatened the state-centric nation and state-building processes in these states. These identities have not been politicized to the extent that could endanger the existing political order and stability. This does not mean that the political situation will stay like this forever. There is enough potential for trouble between the socio-cultural identities and the state-centric identity as the Central Asian states pursue the state- and nation-building processes. Central Asia is just at the earliest stage of initiating several institutions that have the legal standing and potential to further this cooperation. The Prime Ministers of the Central Asian states meet regularly to negotiate and agree on drafts dealing with such issues as railroad and transit rates, immigration, tax integration, customs inspections, joint investment projects, and so forth. The Intergovernmental Council-Executive Committee, a small organ headquartered in Bishkek, coordinates their regular intergovernmental meetings and prepares materials for adoption by unanimous consent of the members. In the mid-1990's Uzbekistan, Kazakstan, and Kyrgyzstan also created the Central Asian Bank for Cooperation and Development, with offices in Bishkek and Almaty. This small bank has financed some modest projects ($500,000 up to $5 million) in the three member states. The CABRD has received grants from some foreign governments and multinational banks for its work and has correspondent relationships with several important overseas and regional banks. A small staff at the Bank helps firms from the member states prepare business plans preparatory to loans. Income from all banking operations during 1996 was more than $3 million, with profit of $600,000. The Asian Development Bank has recently endorsed and provided more finance for this promising start. Individual businessmen in the Central Asian states understand the necessity of normal commercial relations, but statesmen who control major resources have other motives which often rank above profit. Particularly in Uzbekistan and Turkmenistan, they value order and stability above economic growth. Suppression of opposition parties and candidates notwithstanding, all the governments of the area appear to enjoy broad support for their main policies, especially when they can assure law and order and gradual economic improvement. More radical measures would, most feel, only encourage further corruption and inequality.

According to many observers, Uzbek president Karimov believes that Uzbekistan should be the hegemonic power in the area, owing to its greater size, central location, and cultural advantages. Naturally, his brother presidents do not agree, and such disagreements often break up their frequent meetings before real progress can be made. To an American visitor, there is also surprising degree of ethnocentrism towards other Central Asian nationalities. This may also dampen enthusiasm for regional cooperation. State trading in staples and energy, together with export globalize and very slow. privatization of medium-size or large enterprises, mean that the indigenous business class, those with a natural interest in trade with neighboring countries and the greatest need for liberalization of currency and banking practices, is growing only very slowly in Central Asia despite having lots of opportunities and potential in the. The state obtains most of its revenue from centralized sale of staples, such as cotton, gold, or petro-chemicals .or leases for exploration. Taxation of petty traders and craftsmen are pretty difficult and is complicated by a corruption-prone and backward bureaucracy. To encourage foreign-financed business, monopolies are created, which in turn discourage domestic competition from arising. Elaborate facilities would invite requests for bribes or jobs for relatives. Hence native entrepreneurs prefer to remain small and mobile, holding their assets in cash, precious metals and jewellry, or real estate. The major issues that are likely to influence the future course of events and thus have implications for stability and security include the opportunities for political participation, economic integration among Central Asian countries and their ability to sustain the legitimacy of their rule, socioeconomic issues, especially the distributive dimension, and

Table 3.9 Kazakhstan's Exports with central Asian Countries

	1990	*1991*	*1992*	*1993*	*1994*	*1995*	*1996*	*1997*
World Exports (DOTS)			315	247	281	483	494	609
Kazakhstan			54	72	95	113	113	87
Tajikistan			3	6	3	5	8	13
Turkmenistan			6	9	7	19	3	5
Uzbekistan			25	24	44	89	116	102
Total Central Asia			88	111	149	226	240	207
% Share of World:			27.94	44.94	53.02	46.79	48.58	33.99

(Contd)

(Contd Table 3.9)

	1998	*1999*	*2000*	*2001*	*2002*	*2003*	*2004*	*2005*
World Exports (DOTS)	508	454	503	476	485	581	703	710
Kazakhstan	86	44	34	39	37	57	79	90
Tajikistan	9	9	7	6	11	19	17	19
Turkmenistan	1	3	3	2	3	3	3	4
Uzbekistan	39	47	90	48	27	17	22	25
Total Central Asia	135	103	134	95	78	96	121	138
% Share of World:	26.57	22.69	26.64	19.96	16.08	16.52	17.21	19.44

Table 3.10 Kazakhstan's Imports with Central Asian Countries

	1990	*1991*	*1992*	*1993*	*1994*	*1995*	*1996*	*1997*
World Imports(DOTS)			460	1560	3709	4707	4261	4275
Krgz Republic						124	91	56
Tajikistan				18	11	8	18	6
Turkmenistan						140	176	33
Uzbekistan							89	66
Total Central Asia				18	11	272	374	161
% Share of World:				1.15	0.30	5.78	8.78	3.77

(Contd)

(Contd Table 3.10)

	1998	1999	2000	2001	2002	2003	2004	2005
World Imports(DOTS)	4373	3686	5048	6478	6584	8409	14776	20004
Krgz Republic	53	31	30	33	32	55	73	83
Tajikistan	4	2	5	2	3	7	4	22
Turkmenistan	24	20	43	77	75	49	64	74
Uzbekistan	96	87	71	81	87	90	118	135
Total Central Asia	177	140	149	193	197	201	259	314
% Share of World:	4.05	3.80	2.95	2.98	2.99	2.39	1.75	1.57

Table 3.11 Kyrgyz Republic's Exports with Central Asia

	1990	1991	1992	1993	1994	1995	1996	1997
World Exports (DOTS)			315	247	281	483	494	609
Kazakhstan			54	72	95	113	113	87
Tajikistan			3	6	3	5	8	13
Turkmenistan			6	9	7	19	3	5
Uzbekistan			25	24	44	89	116	102
Total Central Asia			88	111	149	226	240	207
% Share of World:			27.94	44.94	53.02	46.79	48.58	33.99

(Contd)

(Contd Table 3.11)

	1998	*1999*	*2000*	*2001*	*2002*	*2003*	*2004*	*2005*
World Exports (DOTS)	508	454	503	476	485	581	703	710
Kazakhstan	86	44	34	39	37	57	79	90
Tajikistan	9	9	7	6	11	19	17	19
Turkmenistan	1	3	3	2	3	3	3	4
Uzbekistan	39	47	90	48	27	17	22	25
Total Central Asia	135	103	134	95	78	96	121	138
% Share of World:	26.57	22.69	26.64	19.96	16.08	16.52	17.21	19.44

Table 3.12 Kyrgyz Republic's Imports with Central Asia

	1990	*1991*	*1992*	*1993*	*1994*	*1995*	*1996*	*1997*
World Imports(DOTS)			418	290	246	392	795	709
Kazakhstan			81	97	58	67	140	70
Tajikistan			2	2	1	8	6	10
Turkmenistan			21	7	10	2	14	15
Uzbekistan			32	58	64	70	132	129
Total Central Asia			136	164	133	147	292	224

(Contd)

(Contd Table 3.12)

	1998	*1999*	*2000*	*2001*	*2002*	*2003*	*2004*	*2005*
World Imports(DOTS)	841	610	555	464	587	711	1340	2205
Kazakhstan	76	73	58	81	124	171	230	263
Tajikistan	6	4	1	2	3	3	4	4
Turkmenistan	8	8	19	9	1	1	1	1
Uzbekistan	123	50	76	67	61	40	51	59
Total Central Asia	213	135	154	159	189	215	286	327

Table 3.13 Tajikstan 's Exports with Central Asia

	1990	*1991*	*1992*	*1993*	*1994*	*1995*	*1996*	*1997*
World Exports (DOTS)			29	350	492	749	770	803
Kazakhstan				16	10	7	24	10
Kyrgyz Republic				4	2	3	10	9
Turkmenistan				3	2	2	8	10
Uzbekistan				20	23	132	191	172
Total Central Asia				43	37	144	233	201
% Share of World:				12.29	7.52	19.23	30.26	25.03

(Contd)

(Contd Table 3.13)

	1998	*1999*	*2000*	*2001*	*2002*	*2003*	*2004*	*2005*
World Exports (DOTS)	596	688	770	651	737	790	914	908
Kazakhstan	10	4	3	2	2	4	4	19
Kyrgyz Republic	6	4	3	2	4	4	5	3
Turkmenistan	9	1	5	10	10	2	8	
Uzbekistan	126	180	98	88	73	68	66	67
Total Central Asia	151	189	109	102	89	78	83	89
% Share of World:	25.34	27.47	14.16	15.67	12.08	9.87	9.08	9.80

Table 3.14 Tajikstan Republic's Imports with Central Asia

	1990	*1991*	*1992*	*1993*	*1994*	*1995*	*1996*	*1997*
World Imports (DOTS)			73	532	547	810	668	750
Kazakhstan				65	33	27	52	42
Kyrgyz Republic				2	1	3	7	5
Turkmenistan				26	39	57	26	30
Uzbekistan				65	83	251	199	262
Total Central Asia				158	156	338	284	339
% Share of World:				29.7	28.5	41.7	42.5	45.2

(Contd)

(Contd Table 3.14)

	1998	*1999*	*2000*	*2001*	*2002*	*2003*	*2004*	*2005*
World Imports (DOTS)	711	663	670	680	710	880	1191	1330
Kazakhstan	52	79	82	89	72	95.8	153.65	168
Kyrgyz Republic	5	7	8	6	5	27.5	18	21
Turkmenistan	31	15	29	62	47	31.6	34	54
Uzbekistan	228	264	185	150	132	133	169	153
Total Central Asia	316	365	304	307	256	287.9	374.65	396
% Share of World:	44.4	55.1	45.4	45.1	36.1	32.7	31.5	29.8

Table 3.15 Turkmenistan 's Exports with Central Asia

	1990	*1991*	*1992*	*1993*	*1994*	*1995*	*1996*	*1997*
World Exports (DOTS)			64	416	673	1881	1693	751
Kazakhstan						127	54	31
Kyrgyz Republic						7	1	13
Tajikstan				24	36	5	10	30
Uzbekistan						21	4	5
Total Central Asia				**24**	**36**	**160**	**69**	**79**
% Share of World:				**5.77**	**5.35**	**8.51**	**4.08**	**10.52**

(Contd)

(Contd Table 3.15)

	1998	*1999*	*2000*	*2001*	*2002*	*2003*	*2004*	*2005*
World Exports (DOTS)	593	1187	2505	2555	2815	3449	3809	5597
Kazakhstan	25	12	5	13	2	3	4	5
Kyrgyz Republic	6	8	23	7	2	1	1	1
Tajikstan	27	12	29	50	33	26	30	49
Uzbekistan	7	7	6	15	13	12	16	16
Total Central Asia	**65**	**39**	**63**	**85**	**50**	**42**	**51**	**71**
% Share of World:	**10.96**	**3.29**	**2.51**	**3.33**	**1.78**	**1.22**	**1.34**	**1.27**

Table 3.16 Turkmenistan's Imports with Central Asia

	1990	*1991*	*1992*	*1993*	*1994*	*1995*	*1996*	*1997*
World Imports (DOTS)			141	497	774	1364	1313	1228
Kazakhstan						31	22	87
Kyrgyz Republic						4	1	2
Tajikstan				4	2	2	2	9
Uzbekistan						28	5	88
Total Central Asia				4	2	65	30	186
% Share of World:				0.80	0.26	4.77	2.28	15.15

(Contd)

(Contd Table 3.16)

	1998	*1999*	*2000*	*2001*	*2002*	*2003*	*2004*	*2005*
World Imports (DOTS)	1007	1478	1787	2210	2127	2510	2736	2770
Kazakhstan	29	19	20	15	27	77	100	69
Kyrgyz Republic	2	3	5	4	5	7	8	9
Tajikstan	7	3	7	19	15	4	8	
Uzbekistan	36	45	32	47	34	41	54	68
Total Central Asia	74	70	64	85	81	129	170	146
% Share of World:	7.35	4.74	3.58	3.85	3.81	5.14	6.21	5.27

Table 3.17 Uzbekistan 's Exports with Central Asia

	1990	*1991*	*1992*	*1993*	*1994*	*1995*	*1996*	*1997*
World Exports (DOTS)			162	636	1844	2457	2649	2890
Kazakhstan							81	60
Kyrgyz Republic						64	120	117
Tajikstan						229	181	238
Turkmenistan						26	5	80
Total Central Asia						319	387	495
% Share of World:						12.98	14.61	17.13

(Contd)

(Contd Table 3.17)

	1998	*1999*	*2000*	*2001*	*2002*	*2003*	*2004*	*2005*
World Exports (DOTS)	2310	1962	2180	2078	1561	1974	2523	3331
Kazakhstan	88	78	64	74	79	82	107	122
Kyrgyz Republic	111	46	68	60	55	36	46	52
Tajikstan	206	240	169	137	120	120	153	139
Turkmenistan	36	45	32	47	34	41	54	63
Total Central Asia	441	409	333	318	288	279	360	376
% Share of World:								

Table 3.18 Uzbekistan's Imports with Central Asia

	1990	*1991*	*1992*	*1993*	*1994*	*1995*	*1996*	*1997*
World Imports (DOTS)			300	813	1959	2783	4763	4538
Kazakhstan							225	163
Kyrgyz Republic						98	127	112
Tajikstan						145	210	190
Turkmenistan						23	4	5
Total Central Asia						266	566	470
% Share of World:								

(Contd)

(Contd Table 3.18)

	1998	*1999*	*2000*	*2001*	*2002*	*2003*	*2004*	*2005*
World Imports (DOTS)	2930	2481	2071	2293	2075	2487	3144	3540
Kazakhstan	131	73	146	165	111	151	199	227
Kyrgyz Republic	42	51	98	53	31	18	24	27
Tajikstan	138	199	107	96	80	73	72	73
Turkmenistan	8	7	7	15	13	12	16	165
Total Central Asia	319	330	358	329	235	254	311	492
% Share of World:								

Map 3: Central Asia Regional Economic Cooperation in Transport

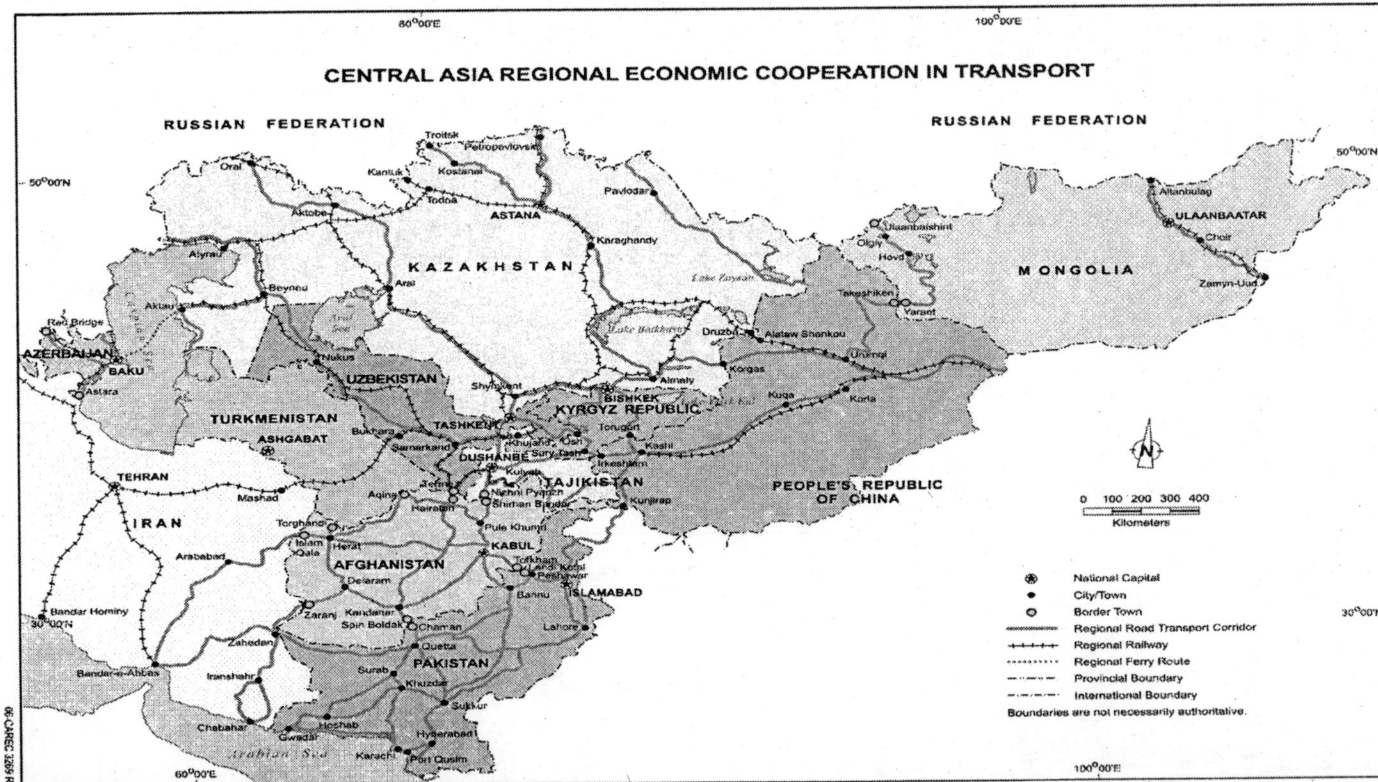

the role of the external actors, especially the neighboring states. On Feb 2007, at a joint session of the Parliament President Nursultan Nazarbayev had said that Kazakhstan has strengthened its position as a full fledged and responsible member of the world community contributing to geopolitical and international stability. Today they are cooperating with other countries in tackling an array of acute problems like ensuring energy security counter-terrorism and countering epidemic diseases and environmental disaster. He also said that Kazakhstan is also keen in economic integration of Central Asia and the establishment of dynamic market in the regions to explore all the opportunities of Caspian sea and black sea[43]. (Nursultan Nazarbayev, 2007)

Diversifying from oil and mining is a high government priority, though the prospects for developing business services around these industries should not be underestimated. The potential for maturing industries (mostly private but some state owned) to invest in neighboring countries is likely to continue. This will provide a natural incentive for improving competition and productivity of domestic companies. Regional cooperation is also important to promote cross-border business activities[44].

References

1. Islamov, Bakhtior, A. (2001), "The Central Asian States ten Year after: How To Overcome Traps of development, Transformation and Globalization" , Tokyo: Maruzen Com. Ltd., 2001, p.168.
2. *Ibid.*
3. *Ibid.*, p. 185.
4. Primbetove, M., (2004), "Globalization and Problems of Regional Integration" in *Central Asian Affairs,* Kazakhstan Institute of Strategic Studies, Kazakhstan Vol. No. 3 p. 25).
5. Andersen, W.,(2003), "Integration Based on the EU model: A Central Asian Union" in *Central Asian Affairs,* Kazakhstan Institute of Strategic Studies, Kazakhstan, Vol. No. 3 p. 22.
6. Chanachev, M., (2004), "The Central Asian Cooperation Organization and its Potential for the Development of Regional Integration Process, in *Central Asian Affairs,* Kazakhstan Institute of Strategic Studies, Kazakhstan., Vol. No. 3, p. 33.

7. www.adb.org/carec, Rebuilding the Silk Road, Strength through regional cooperation.
8. UNDP, (2005) " Bringing Down Barriers: Regional Cooperation for Human Development and Human Security" in *Central Asian Human Development Report*, Regional bureau for Europe and the CIS, Slovak Republic., p. 29.
9. *Ibid.*, p. 22.
10. *Ibid.*, p. (8-10).
11. Pomfret Richard,(2006), *The Central Asian Economies Since Independence,* Princeton University Press, New Jercy, p. 32.
12. Afzal Khan, U.N. Agency Highlights Economic Integration Need in Central Asia, by U.S. Agency for International Development aids Central Asian integration,By Washington File Special Correspondent) accessed on 07 April 2006.at www.un.org.
13. *Ibid.*
14. UNDP, (2005) " Bringing Down Barriers: Regional Cooperation for Human Development and Human Security" op.cit., p. 4.
15. ADB, (2006), "Central Asia; Gains from Trade Through Regional Cooperation in Trade Policy, Transport and Custom Transit", ADB, Philippines., p. 7.
16. UNDP, (2005) "Bringing Down Barriers: Regional Cooperation for Human Development and Human Security", op.cit., p. 50.
17. Pomfret Richard, (2006), op.cit., p. 212.
18. Compiled through many sources used as references
19. R Sampath Kumar, "Central Asian Economic Integration" in Economic and Political Weekly, May 2, 1998, p. 1013., Country Report on Kazakhstan In Europa Year Book 2003, p. 211.
20. Rumer, Boris, (2003) *Central Asia: The Challeanges of Independence,* AAKAR BOOKS, New Delhi., p. 21.
21. Andersen, W., (2003), "Integration Based on the EU model: A Central Asian Union", op.cit., p. 22.
22. Chanachev, M., (2004), "The Central Asian Cooperation Organization and its Potential for the Development of Regional Integration Process, op.cit., p. 33.
23. (President's address to the nation Kazakhstan weekly news Feb, 28, 2007. Vol. no. 4)
24. Chanachev, M., (2004), "The Central Asian Cooperation Organization and its Potential for the Development of Regional Integration Process, op.cit., p. 31.

25. Rumer Boris (ed.) 2003. *Central Asia in Transition: Dilemmas of Political and Economic Development* Aakar Books, New Delhi. p. 24.
26. Kojima, K., "The Pattern of International Trade among Advanced Countries", *Hitotsuboshi Journal of Economics*, Vol. 5, No.1, 1964.
27. ADB, (2006), "Central Asia; Gains from Trade Through Regional Cooperation in Trade Policy, Transport and Custom Transit",ADB, Philippines., p. 23.
25. Rumer, Boris, (2003) *Central Asia:The Challeanges of Independence*. op.cit., p. 106.
29. Emine Gurgen, et all (1999), "Economic Reforms in Kazakhstan, Kyrgyz Republic, Tajikistan, Turkmenistan and Uzbekistan" op.cit., p. 41.
30. UNDP, (2005) "Bringing Down Barriers: Regional Cooperation for Human Development and Human Security", op.cit., p. 50.
31. Islamov,Bakhtior, A. (2001), "The Central Asian States ten Year after: How To Overcome Traps of development, Transformation and Globalization", op.cit., p. 165.
32. Emine Gurgen, et all (1999), "Economic Reforms in Kazakhstan, Kyrgyz Republic, Tajikistan, Turkmenistan and Uzbekistan" op.cit., p. 40.
33. John Odlee-Smee, "Economic Performance and Trade of CIS", see the website www.imf.org.
34. UNDP, (2005) "Bringing Down Barriers: Regional Cooperation for Human Development and Human Security", op.cit., p. 50.
35. A speech by President Haruhiko Kuroda, Asian Development Bank, New York, September 13, 2005.
36. Asian Development Outlook, (2007), ADB, Manila., p. 106.
37. UNDP, (2005) "Bringing Down Barriers: Regional Cooperation for Human Development and Human Security", op.cit., p. 53.
38. Komilov, S., (2003), "Regional Economic Cooperation: Appraisal and Problem of Developmen" in *Central Asian Affairs,* Kazakhstan Institute of Strategic Studies, Kazakhstan., Vol. No. 2, p. 31.
39. Pomfret Richard, (2006), op.cit, p. 38.
40. UNDP, (2005) "Bringing Down Barriers: Regional Cooperation for Human Development and Human Security", op.cit., p. 45.
41. Regional cooperation strategy and program for central asia regional economic cooperation (CAREC) member countries: Regional

cooperation strategy, ADB 2005-2007, July 2004. www.adb.org/Documents/CSPs/CAREC/2004. Appendix 3. p.4.

42. Komilov, S., (2003), "Regional Economic Cooperation: Appraisal and Problem of Development", op.cit., p. 33.

43. Nursultan Nazarbayev, President's Address to Kazakhzstan Nation,(2007), in *Kazakhstan weekly News*.

44. Asian Development Outlook, (2007), ADB, Manila., p. 116.

4

Regional Economic Integration in South Asia

This chapter will describe and analyse all the regional/ bilateral and multilateral attempts towards regional integration in the South Asian region particularly since the 1980's. It will also assess challenges and opportunities of economic integration in the region and will describe all the bilateral and multilateral initiatives towards regional integration.

(1) Regional Economic Integration in South Asia

As the South Asian economies have been integrating into the world market, their export performance became highly dependent on global changes, this pattern gives rise to the question how can South Asian countries could achieve stability and prosperity? Regional economic cooperation, therefore, is pivotal for enhancing economic growth and development of individual countries. Even from the historical perspective, it is through regional arrangements that the countries of Europe, as well as those of South East Asia, secured additional benefits and eliminated the negative fallout of globalization. South Asia has great economic strength in terms of its market potential, rich natural resources and human capital. Considering the huge comparative advantage

Map 4: Political Map of South Asia

that these countries have in certain export sectors, the poorly managed events in recent years have brought South Asia into international limelight.

1.1. Motivation and Objectives of Economic Cooperation

A significant feature of the present day global trade scenario is the accelerated growth of regional economies coming closer to each other. It has been observed that this is the best way to utilize available resources and take full advantages of their commonalities as a regional partners for achieving higher level of economic growth. Though South Asia is geographically integrated region, the economic integration is still low despite a number of initiatives taken by the authorities. In the process of globalization and liberalization these countries need and require greater economic coordination among each other. The idea of regional co-operation in South Asia was first mooted in 1980. The foreign Secretaries of the seven countries met for the first time in Colombo in 1981 to discuss regional co-operation. South Asian Association for Regional

Box c

The main objectives of SAARC as stated in the charter are: (a) to promote the welfare of the peoples of South Asia and to improve their quality of life (b) to accelerate economic growth, social progress and cultural development in the region and to provide all individuals the opportunity to live in dignity and to realise their full potentials (c) to promote and strengthen collective self-reliance among the countries of South Asia; (d) to contribute to mutual trust, understanding and appreciation of one another's problem (e) to promote active and mutual assistance in the economic, social, cultural, technical and scientific fields(f) to strengthen cooperation with other developing countries (g) to strengthen cooperation among themselves in international forums on matters of common interests (h) to cooperate with international and regional organisations with similar aims and purposes. Source: http://www.saarc-sec.org.

cooperation (SAARC) was established in 1985. The main objective behind this was to promote the welfare of the people of member countries and improve their quality of life, accelerate economic growth, social progress, cultural development, peace and prosperity in the region. Although the first priority of economic co-operation is to bring stability in the region, SAARC has yet to emerge as a viable regional organization. Political instability and the souring relationship of Pakistan and India kept the region from coming together. The objectives of SAARC are acknowledged in the Box c.

1.2. Establishment of SAARC Status of Economic Cooperation

The South Asian Regional Trade Block (SAARC) was formed in 1985. SAARC Preferential Trading Arrangement (SAPTA) was finalized in 1993 and came into existence in 1995. It was regarded as the first achievement of SAARC. The agreement came into force on December 7, 1995. SAPTA has twin goals aiming to promote regional cooperation, and stimulating national economic growth and national employment levels and living standard of South Asian nations[1]. Although SAPTA has been a recent experiment in liberalizing intra-regional trade, the results have improved but not upto the mark. Recognizing the need to move quickly towards a South Asian Free Trade Area (SAFTA) the head of the state of government directed the council of ministers to finalize the text of the draft treaty Framework by the end of 2002 at the eleventh SAARC Summit held at Kathmandu, Nepal in January 2002. they also directed moving towards the goal of SAFTA[2]. The signing of agreement of South Asian Free Trade Area (SAFTA) in 2004 at Islamabad Summit has been regarded as another big success of the evolution of the SAARC. Achieving SAFTA by 2008, South Asian Custom Union (SACU) by 2015 and South Asian Economic Union (SAEU) in 2020 are the foreseeable prospects.[3] The objectives of SAFTA agreement are :

- to promote and enhance mutual trade and economic cooperation among these countries.
- Eliminating barriers to trade in, and facilitating the cross-order movement of goods between the territories of the contracting states,

- Promoting conditions of fair competition in the free trade area, and ensuring equitable benefits to all contracting states, taking into account their respective levels and pattern of economic development,
- Creating effective mechanism for the implementation and application of this Agreement, for its joint administration and for the resolution of disputes; and
- Establishing a framework for further regional cooperation to expand and enhance the mutual benefits of this agreement[4]

The Agreement on South Asia Free Trade Area (SAFTA), which was signed by Bhutan during the XII SAARC Summit in Islamabad, Pakistan is expected to open up new market for Bhutanese products as well as help in deeper economic integration with the other countries in the region[5]. This require a thorough understanding of the domestic political and economic dynamics of the South Asian countries. This will be helpful in discussing prospects of peace in South Asia through economic integration. An attempt has been made to identify major areas which have the potentials for cooperation in India and other South Asian Countries in trade, joint ventures and services. Thirteenth Summit meeting of the South Asian Association for Regional Cooperation (SAARC) was held in Dhaka, Bangladesh on 12 - 13 November 2005. The Heads of State or Government stressed that accelerating cooperation in the core economic areas which was vital for the realization of Charter objectives and also for making South Asia truly exciting, dynamic and secure in its healthy progress. They noted the progress in the negotiations on outstanding issues and directed early finalization of all the Annexes ensuring entry into force of the SAFTA Agreement as agreed, with effect from 1 January 2006.

The launching of SAFTA marked an important milestone on the road to a South Asian Economic Union. The Heads of State or Government agreed to undertake trade facilitation measures, including transit among SAARC countries, on the basis of understanding among concerned countries, for enhancing intra-regional trade and other economic activities. They reiterated the need to strengthen transportation and communication links across the region for accelerated and balanced economic growth. They directed further measures aimed at trade liberalization, as provided for in the SAFTA Agreement. They noted the Indian proposal in this regard and agreed to study the proposal put forward by India for daily air service facility by designated airlines, on a reciprocal basis and without discrimination to existing rights, to all the SAARC member states and also the proposal to extend fifth freedom rights to designated airlines from the member states, both intermediate and beyond, within the SAARC region on a reciprocal basis. The Heads of State or Government recognized the need to take the process of regional economic integration further by expanding the scope of SAFTA to include trade in services, enhanced investment and harmonized standards. The Heads of State or Government welcomed the signing of the following Agreements during the thirteenth SAARC Summit[6]:

- The Agreement on Mutual Administrative Assistance in Customs Matters
- The Agreement on the Establishment of SAARC Arbitration Council
- The Limited Agreement on Avoidance of Double Taxation and Mutual Administrative Assistance in Tax Matters

They emphasized the need for parallel initiatives for dismantling of non-tariff and para-tariff barriers. In this context, they called for expeditious action on conclusion of agreements on mutual recognition of standards, testing and measurements with a view to facilitating intra-regional trade. They recognized the potential of trade in services which have expanded rapidly at the informal level. They tryed to discuss that services could be integrated into the SAFTA process. The Heads of State or Government decided to encourage, where appropriate, trade-creating investment in the Member States. They stressed the need for closer regional cooperation in the field of Information and Communication Technologies (ICT), including Tele-Communications. They agreed to the recommendation to establish the SAARC energy centre in Islamabad; to promote development of energy resources, including hydropower; and energy trade in the region; to develop renewable and alternative energy resources and to promote energy efficiency and conservation in the region.

They underlined the need to comprise a South Asian Energy Dialogue process, involving officials, experts, academics, environmentalists and NGOs, to recommend measures to tap potentials of cooperation in energy sector to provide inputs to the Working Group on Energy

The key Summit decisions indicate a commitment towards deepening cooperation in South Asia. The SAFTA agreement is the first stage in deepening cooperation. However, if South Asia's trade is to be integrated, it will require integration of the infrastructure of the region. This would point to cooperation in the areas of energy as well as the strengthening of transportation, transit and communication links across the region. This would further require harmonization of standards and simplification of customs procedures. Trade cooperation would point to monetary cooperation thereby suggesting the need for greater coordination among Central Banks. Sustaining trading links would require investment cooperation involving public and private sector cooperation through joint ventures. Investment cooperation would need to be underwritten by financing through a prospective South Asia Development Bank. It would follow from such levels of cooperation that the governments would discuss, coordinate and exchange information with a view to adopting common positions, where appropriate, at multilateral forum.

In each of the above-mentioned areas, there would be scope for deepening cooperation. The Free Trade Area could evolve into a Customs Union with a common tariff barrier with the rest of the world. The Customs Union could lead to a common exchange rate policy and eventually a common currency underwritten by coordination of macro-economic policy across the region. Energy cooperation could evolve into a common energy grid across the region with integrated electricity and gas systems as is the case in Europe today. Transport cooperation would lead to an integrated transport infrastructure which permits uninterrupted travel from Peshawar to Chittagong and from Kathmandu to Colombo as in the European Union. Investment cooperation would culminate in regional corporations with production facilities located across the region within vertically and horizontally integrated production systems. Shares of both national and regional companies would be

Box d

Evolution of Economic Integration of South Asia

Evolution of Economic Integration of South Asia
First South Asia Foreign Secretaries's meeting, 1981
Technical Cooperation in five selected areas (agricultural, telecommunication, rural development, meteorology, and health and population)
First South Asia Foreign Ministers' Meeting, 1983
Launched the Integrated Programs of Actions through South Asian Regional Cooperation foreign ministers began to meet on a regular basis.
Establishment of SAARC, 1985
Objectives are defined on a wide range of issues, including: promoting welfare, accelerating economic growth, strengthening collective self-reliance, etc
A Secretariat was set up in Nepal A set of IPAs is discussed under SAARC
South Asian Preferential Trading Arrangement (SAPTA), 1995
Signed in 1993 by the Council of Ministers
Operational in December 1995; notified the WTO as a PTA
Three rounds of tariff cut under SAPTA
SAPTA-1 (226 6-digit HS items) concluded in 1995
SAPTA-2 (1800 6-digit HS items) concluded in 1997
SAPTA-3 (2700 6-digit HS items) concluded in 1998
SAPTA-4 initiated in 1999 but postponed

(Contd.)

(Contd. Box d)

Working toward a Free Trade Area (SAFTA) by 2001
Agreed in a summit in 1997 but seems to be difficult to implement by the deadline
The signing of agreement of South Asian Free Trade Area (SAFTA) in 2004 at Islamabad Summit has been regarded as another big success of the evolution
The Heads of State or Government welcomed the signing of the following Agreements during the thirteenth SAARC Summit 2005 in Dhaka: • The Agreement on Mutual Administrative Assistance in Customs Matters • The Agreement on the Establishment of SAARC Arbitration Council • The Limited Agreement on Avoidance of Double Taxation and Mutual Administrative Assistance in Tax Matters The Fourteenth SAARC Summit was held on 3-4th April 2007, in New Delhi Afghanistan a new member for the first time participated in this summit. Three of the observer countries, China, South Korea and Japan sent their foreign ministers to this Summit. EU and USA had sent their high level representatives and had observer status.

quoted in the stock exchanges across the region as capital flows without hindrance across national boundaries to underwrite investment in any part of the South Asia region. The evolution of economic integration can be seen in detail in the Box (d).

Table 4.1
Scope of Exports of Various Metal Products Exists from India to the other South Asian Countries

Metal Products	
Steels tubes, pipes, sanitary fitting etc.	Bangladesh, Nepal, Sri Lanka.
Seamless tubes	Bangladesh, Nepal, Sri Lanka, Pakistan
Sheets of iron and steel, billets, slabs, fabricated construction material	Bangladesh, Nepal, Sri Lanka, Bhutan Maldives
Industrial Fastners	Bangladesh, Sri Lanka.
Consumer durable and kitchenware, pressure cookers etc.	Bangladesh, Nepal, Sri Lanka, Pakistan
Tin plate and metal cans for packaging	Bangladesh, Nepal, Sri Lanka, Bhutan Maldives, Pakistan
Railway track material	Bangladesh, Pakistan, Sri Lanka
Transport Equipment	
Commercial Vehicles	Bangladesh, Nepal, Sri Lanka, Pakistan
Passenger Cars	Bangladesh, Nepal, Sri Lanka, Pakistan
Two/Three-wheeers (motorcycle,Scooters, mopeds)	Bangladesh, Sri Lanka, Pakistan
Automotive Component	Bangladesh, Nepal, Sri Lanka, Pakistan, and also imports from Pakistan and Srilanka
Railway locomotives, Coaches, Wagons, spares and signaling equipment etc.	Bangladesh, Pakistan
Bicycles and parts	Bangladesh, Nepal, Sri Lanka, Bhutan Maldives, Pakistan
Non-electrical Machinery	
Internal Combustion engines, and parts like pistons etc.	Bangladesh, Pakistan, Sri Lanka
Steam boilers and and auxiliary plants	Pakistan

(Contd.)

(Contd. Table 4.1)

Agricultural machinery tractors, tillers, harvestors, etc.and parts	Bangladesh, Nepal, Sri Lanka, Pakistan
Civil engineering and material handling equipment	Bangladesh, Nepal, Sri Lanka, Bhutan Maldives, Pakistan
Textiles, jute, and leather machinery	Bangladesh, Sri Lanka, Pakistan
Metal working machinery parts, machine tools, wire drawing machines	Bangladesh, Sri Lanka, Pakistan
Hand tools	Bangladesh, Nepal, Sri Lanka, Bhutan Maldives, Pakistan
Pumps, Centrifuges valves and compressors	Bangladesh, Sri Lanka, Pakistan
Chemical papers machinery	Bangladesh, Pakistan
Testing and scientific instruments and apparatus and medical instruments	Bangladesh, Sri Lanka, Pakistan
Oil prospecting instruments	Bangladesh, Pakistan
Fishing equipment such as mechanized fishing boats, FRP Beach Landing crafts, fishing nets, freezing plants etc.	Bangladesh, Sri Lanka, Maldives, Pakistan

Source: Economic cooperation in the SAARC Region by research team VR Panchmukhi, Nagesh Kumar, VL Rao, IN Mukherjee, SK Mohanty, MP Lama issued under Research and Information System. P,160-163. compiled from www.aric.adb.org.country profiles.

Despite having lots of potential and scope economically, South Asia is the poorest region in the world despite the largest population. Four of the seven member states are among the least developed countries. The common features of south Asia, among others, are the shared underdevelopment, manifested in many development indicators. South Asia's GDP growth was 7.0, 7.1 and 6.5 percent in 2003, 2004 and 2005 respectively. India, Pakistan, Sri Lanka and Bangladesh are the emerging economies in South Asia. Almost all the south Asian countries have abandoned the import substitution policy as a failed strategy. Orientation towards economic liberalization and greater reliance on private sector development is now more strongly rooted in these countries'

Table No.4.2
South Asian Countries's Trade Potential in Commodities

Country	*Major Export Items*	*Major Import Item*
Bangladesh	Jute and Jute Products, Tea, Readymade Garments, Frozen Fish and Shrimps, Seafood, ($ 5 billion or 75%) Leather and Leather Goods, Fertilizer, Spices, Vegetables, Manpower.	Petroleum (Crude), Official Equipments, Plant and Machinery, Automobile, Construction Materials, Dyestuffs Chemicals, Ferrous and Non-ferrous Metals, Minerals, Iron and Steel ($ 6 billion or 75%) Textile, Edible Oil, Milk Products, Raw Cotton, Cement, etc.
Bhutan	Timber, Dolomite, Spices, Calcium Carbide, Gypsum, Electricity, Cement, Fresh and Canned Fruits and Juices, Alcoholic Beverage, ($80 million or 75%) Cardamom, Timber Products, Minerals.	Petroleum Products, Machinery, Iron and Steel, Automobile, Textiles, Agriculture Equipments. Consumer Goods ($120 million or 75%), Sugar, Edible Oil, Rubber, Tyre, Wheat.

(Contd.)

(Contd.Table 4.2)

Country	Minerals. *Major Export Items*	*Major Import Item*
India	Software, Pearls, Jewellery and Precious Stones, Pharmaceuticals, Machinery, Vehicles, Metal Products, Tea Mate, Clothing, Iron Ore and Steel, Films $ 42 billion or 75%) Cotton Products, Petroleum, Handicrafts, Leather & Products	Crude Petroleum Products, Machinery, Pearls, Precious and Semi-Precious Stones, Chemical Products, Edible Oils, Vegetables and Fruits, food Stuff, ($43.5 billion, 75%) Vehicles, Fertilizers, Rock Salt, Cotton, Sugar, Ceramics and Melamine.
Maldives	Dried Skipjack, Canned Fish, Frozen Skipjack, Shark Liver Oil, Salted Dried Skipjack and Reef Fish, Apparel and Clothing Accessories ($ 67 million 0r 75%), Red Coral, Cowries Shells and Mica	Consumer Goods, Petroleum and Food Items, Manufactured Goods, Machinery, Vehicles, Chemicals, Steel, Rice, Cement ($ 292 million or 75%) Wheat, Sugar, Tobacco, Beverages, Paper.

(Contd.)

(Contd.Table 4.2)

Country	*Major Export Items*	*Major Import Item*
Nepal	Cotton Garments, Woolen Goods and Carpets, Oil Seeds, Pulses, Hides and Skin, Niger Seeds, Jute and Jute Products, Handicrafts, Tea, Leather Goods, Paper and Paper Products ($ 440 million or 75%), Silverware and Jewellery, Tooth Paste, Polyester Yarn, Toilet Soap, Pashmina Products, Vegetable Ghee.	Food and Live Animals, Chemicals and Drugs, Manufactured Articles, Construction Materials, Petroleum, Oil and Lubricants, Raw Wool, Automobiles and Transport Equipments, Machinery, Fertilizer, Textiles, Edible Oil ($ 1.07 billion or 75%) Cement, Electrical Goods, Industrial Raw Material
Pakistan	Raw Cotton, Textiles, Cotton Cloth, Cotton Yarn, Synthetic Textiles, Garments, Hosiery Rice ($7.1 billion 75%) Carpets and Rugs, Leather, Leather Products including Leather Garments and Footwear, Ceramic, and Fish & Fish Products.	Petroleum and its Products, Chemicals, Non-Electrical Equipments, Machinery, Transport Equipments, Iron and Steel Products, ($7.6 billion or 75%) Edible Oils, Electrical Goods, Fertilizers, Tea.
Sri Lanka	Tea, Rubber, Gems, Marine Foods, Semi Precious Stones, Coconut Oil and Coconut Products ($ 3.6 billion or 75%). Readymade Garments.	Machinery, Petroleum, Chemicals, Pharmaceuticals, Iron and Steel, Vehicles, Textiles, Dairy Products, Fertilizers ($ 4.7 billion or 75%), Pulp & Paper Products, Sugar.

Source; www.wto.org.wp.216191.on 29th Sept. 2004 at11.22am.

economic policies. As for intra-regional trade, the share is no more than 5 percent of the total extra-regional trade conducted by the seven countries.[7]

Intra-Regional Trade among South Asian Countries (5*5)

Intra-regional trade has increased significantly in the last decade, mostly through imports by all countries in the region, except Pakistan and India. While South Asia is a fast growing destination for Indian exports, it remains marginal as a source of India's imports. The principal export destination of all South Asian countries remains North America and the European Union (EU). Trade liberalization with South Asia has, thus, largely served to stimulate Indian exports within the region but with low levels of reciprocal export growth to India. This owes in some measure to India's relatively more restrictive import regime compared to its neighbors, but it also reflects the structural rigidities in the smaller economies who have relatively little to export to India. Thus a primary goal of trade cooperation in South Asia has been to encourage India to open up its import regime to imports from its

Table 4.3

Intra-Regional Trade Share of South Asia's Total Trade 1985-2004(%)

Country / Region	*1985*	*1990*	*1995*	*2000*	*2004*
Afghanistan	11.4	14.5	11.1	29.7	35.3
Bangladesh	4.7	6.0	12.8	7.9	10.5
Bhutan	-	-	-	-	-
India	1.7	1.6	2.7	2.5	3.0
Maldives	12.5	12.7	14.3	22.2	19.8
Nepal	34.3	11.9	14.8	22.3	47.2
Pakistan	3.1	2.7	2.3	3.6	5.0
Sri Lanka	5.5	5.6	7.8	7.4	15.1
South Asia	3.0	2.7	4.2	4.0	5.3

Source: ADO, various issues.

neighbors through significant trade concessions and to help the smaller countries to enhance as well as diversify their production and export capacity to exploit emerging market opportunities in India.

Table 4.4

Intra Regional Trade as Percentage of Total Exports: A Comparison of SAARC with other Southern RTAs

	1995	*2000*	*2002*	*2003*
Latin America				
ANDEAN	12.0	8.5	9.5	7.4
MERCOSUR	20.3	20.0	11.3	11.8
Africa				
COMESA	6.0	4.9	5.4	5.8
SADC	10.6	12.0	9.3	10.0
UEMOA	10.3	13.1	12.1	12.8
Asia				
ASEAN/AFTA	24.6	23.0	22.7	21.2
SAARC	4.4	4.1	4.2	4.5

Source: UNCTAD Handbook of Statistics, 2004.

Notes: COMESA — Common Market for Eastern and Southern Africa

SADC— Southern African Development Community

UEMOA —African Western union Economic and Monetary

ANDEAN —Andean Common Market

MERCOSUR — Common Market for Southern Cone

Unlike the other RTAs in Southern, the intra-regional trade is low. Intra-regional trade in South Asia is relatively low compared with other regions in Asia. Intraregional trade as a ratio of South Asia's total foreign trade was only 5.3 % in 2004, compared with 22.4% for Association of Southeast Asian Nations (ASEAN) member countries. For individual countries, the intra regional trade ratio varies from a low of 3.0% for India and 5.0% for Pakistan to a high of 47.2% for Nepal and 35.3% for Afghanistan.

In 2002, the official bilateral trade between India and Pakistan was about $212 million, less than 1% of their global trade.

Fig. 4.1 South Asia Lags behind in Regional Integration

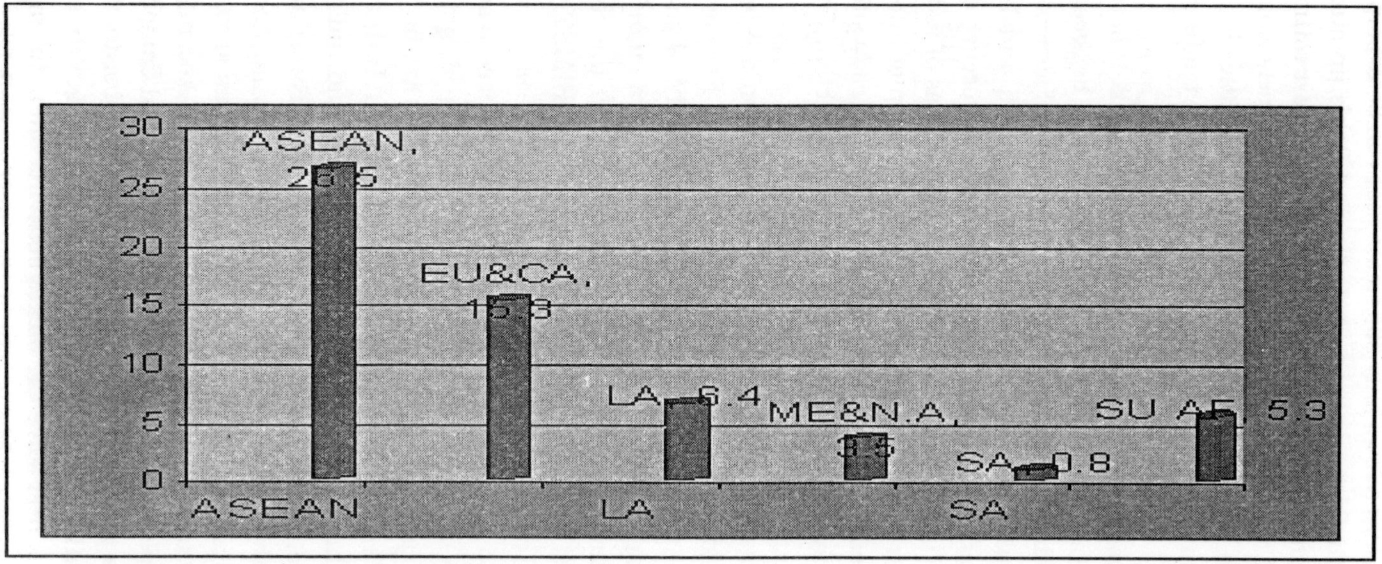

ASEAN; Association of Southeast Asian Nations.

EU&CA- European union and Central Asia

LA- Latin America

ME&N.A- Middle East and North America

SA- South Asia

SUAF- Sub-Saharan And Africa

At present, Pakistan allows only 596 items that can be exported to Pakistan. The official trade between India and Pakistan stood at barely US$262 mn in 2002-03, whereas unofficial trade is estimated at not less than US$1.5-2bn. A number of Indian products exported to Pakistan have been subject to not only customs duties but also para-tariff measures that must be reduced to enhance trade in this region[8].

Regional cooperation can help open up new markets between India and Pakistan, and substantially increase trade between the two countries. A thriving border trade in a wide range of agricultural and industrial products exists between Bangladesh and India. However, a significant percentage of this trade also occurs on an informal basis. Therefore, trade liberalization in terms of reduced tariff and non tariff barriers can lead to formalization of informal trade, thereby reducing associated costs of informal trade such as rent-seeking activities and increasing revenue collection for the governments.

Trade issues have primarily been dealt with on a bilateral rather than regional basis. In this regard, the Framework Agreement of the South Asian Free Trade Area (SAFTA) signed by the SAARC leaders at the Islamabad Summit was a significant step toward promoting free trade and investment in the region. Similarly, efforts have also been undertaken under BIMSTEC to establish a free trade area among its member countries.

In order to understand the preconditions for free trade in South Asia, it is necessary to analyze the factors impeding intra-regional trade expansion. For this purpose, reference can be made to bilateral trade agreements (BTAs) between India and Bangladesh, India and Nepal, India and Pakistan, and India and Sri Lanka. Taking account of the India and Bangladesh relationship, both possess a natural advantage in trading because of geographical contiguity. However, facts and figures show that this natural advantage is not fully utilized by either. According to a World Bank report, unofficial trade between India and Bangladesh and the volume and direction of unrecorded cross-border trade 'mirrored the pattern of official trade'. Hence, it is high time that the two countries first solve the illegal border trade problem. The India-Pakistan relationship is one of the most crucial issues for economic cooperation in South Asia. Fluctuations in two-way trade between India and Pakistan can be attributed mainly to trade policies adopted by them.

Even though South Asian economies have been bound in the South Asian Association for Regional cooperation for the last twenty two years, intraregional trade continues to be minimal as compare to other regional economic initiatives. This graph also represent that after liberalsation the exports and import has been on the increasing trend for this period. The Indian export is growing faster rate as compare to import from other south Asian Countries. Some bilateral initiatives are in place between India and Sri Lanka, India and Nepal, India and Bhutan and others are under negotiations like between Pakistan and Sri Lanka and India and Bangladesh. Major issues such as trade facilitation, investment, infrastructure, transit, hydroelectricity, natural gas exploitation, tourism, technology, water management have been discussed in regional co-operation since the negotiations started. Some common issues like lack of connectivity, geo-political issues, free movement of people and lack of information have also been discussed. Although some significant progress has been made in South Asia, regional cooperation has experienced several problems.

South Asia has a fast and growing trade in services. Large numbers of South Asians cross each other's borders as tourists, pilgrims, professionals, students and health care seekers as well as providers. Nepal, Maldives, Sri Lanka and India are major tourist destinations both globally and within the region. India is a major attraction for students and health care seekers while Indian nurses and doctors are much in evidence in a number of hospitals in Bangladesh, Nepal, Maldives and Bhutan. Managers and professionals from India are in service in Nepal and Bhutan just as Indian and Pakistani managers are running textile mills in Bangladesh while Bangladeshi cooks and waiters are ubiquitous in Maldivian tourist resorts. With the enhancement in the quality of service delivery across the region this trade in services will grow and may do so exponentially, since this is an area where South Asia has some comparative advantage.

There is, however, no reason why the market in services should be monopolized by India. Pakistan, Sri Lanka and

Bangladesh can invest in their education and health-care sector both directly and though collaboration with India, to attract service seekers from within the region as well as globally. Pakistan already has some excellent hospitals and institutions of educational excellence such as the Lahore University of Management Sciences which attracts clients from overseas. It has been observed that not much efforts has taken to upgrade such service sectors in these countries to serve a regional and even global market.

India is now emerging as one of the major exporters of IT services at the global level. There is an expectation that this could grow to US$ 50 billion. Here again Sri Lanka, because of its level of educational attainment, Pakistan, Bangladesh and even Maldives have the potential to share in the fast growing IT market. Here India, in particular, can play and indeed is beginning to play, a crucial role in enhancing capacity as well as investing in these sectors in all the countries of the region to enable them to connect with the global and regional IT market.

In an attempt to explore the potential of intra-SAARC trade expansion, this study computed trade intensities for a country verses other South Asian Countries as whole region.

Trade Intensity Index :

The Trade intensity Index is the measure of the extent to which one country's share in another country's Exports (Imports) differ from the former share in the world trade.

This index was first used by K. Kojima [9] (1964). It measures the share of one country's trade with other country. It can also measure a single country 's trade with other countries of the region or with region verses region as a proportion of the latter's share of world. Here the trade intensity has been measured for the one country with other South Asian countries, for ex India vs other South Asian countries.

The **Export Intensity Index** (EII) is defined as :

xij = **{(Xij)/(Xi)/(Mj)/(Mw-Mi)}** ..... [1]

where :

xij = EII of trade (Exports) of countryIndia(i) with other South Asian Countries (j)

Xij = Exports of India i to trading partner Other South Asian Countries (j)

Xi = Total exports of India (i)
Mj = Total imports of other South Asian Countries (j)
Mw = Total world imports
Mi = Total imports of India (i)

Similarly, **Import Intensity Index** (III) can be defined as:

mij = **{(Mij)/(Mi)/(Xj)/(Xw-Xi)}** .... **[2]**

where :

mij = EII of trade (Imports) of country **i** with country **(j)**
Mij = Imports of country **i** to trading partner **(j)**
Mi = Total Imports of country **(i)**
Xj = Total Exports of country **(j)**
Xw = Total world Exports
Xi = Total Exports of country **(i)**

v Here, i= India and j= other south Asian countries

Note: Here i is for India and j for South Asian region, in the same way other countries trade intensity has been calculated (eg. Pakistan with the whole region).

Agarwal and Panday (1992) have estimated the trade intensity by using Kojima's model for the period 1965-87.[10] In this chapter this study estimated the trade intensity for the period 1990-2005. According to Agarwal and Panday (1992), it was observed from estimated values that bilateral trade orientation is the highest between Maldives and SriLanka, India and Nepal, Bangladesh and Pakistan and Pakistan and Srilanka. In respect of other pairs of countries, the values of trade intensity was much less than unity reflecting low level of bilateral trade.[11] During 1990-2005 ,it would be more relevant to observe the trade intensity for this period because all the seven countries liberalize their economic policies. This would also show the impact of liberalization on trade.

The prospects and possibilities of trade expansion at any regional level can not be properly analyzed without first analyzing the role of foreign trade in national economies of the regional countries. It is necessary to examine the recent trends in Indian exports and imports to the other South Asian Countries. By exploring the statistical data from 1990-2005 period, this study try to attempt and explore the potential of intra- South Asian Countries

Table 4.5: South Asian Trade Intensity within the Region

		1990	1991	1992	1993	1994	1995	1996	1997
India	Export-intensity	2.49	3.58	3.70	3.84	3.94	4.42	4.39	3.81
	%age share of world	2.73	3.49	3.89	4.05	4.14	5.06	5.10	4.40
	Import- intensity	0.50	0.59	0.49	0.52	0.55	0.63	0.58	0.51
	%age share of world	0.40	0.49	0.40	0.46	0.50	0.57	0.55	0.46
Pakistan	Export-intensity	3.65	3.47	4.75	3.08	3.11	2.77	2.23	2.28
	%age share of world	3.99	3.37	4.97	3.24	3.26	3.45	2.58	2.62
	Import- intensity	2.03	1.75	1.83	1.79	1.75	1.62	2.57	2.13
	%age share of world	1.64	1.42	1.50	1.57	1.56	1.47	2.41	1.96
Bangladesh	Export-intensity	3.29	4.89	2.11	2.30	2.20	2.33	1.54	1.97
	%age share of world	3.59	4.74	2.21	2.42	2.30	2.65	1.79	2.26
	Import- intensity	8.73	9.19	12.5	13.6	14.5	19.5	17.0	14.0
	%age share of world	7.0	7.4	10.2	11.9	12.9	17.7	15.9	12.9
Nepal	Export-intensity	6.3	8.4	6.5	4.6	3.8	8.1	18.5	22.1
	%age share of world	6.9	8.1	6.8	4.9	3.9	9.2	21.3	25.4
	Import- intensity	14.3	24.4	21.2	19.7	20.6	18.3	35.8	29.8
	%age share of world	11.5	19.8	17.4	17.2	18.3	16.6	33.5	27.3
Srlanka	Export-intensity	3.3	3.1	2.1	2.3	25	2.3	2.3	2.2
	%age share of world	3.6	3.0	2.2	2.4	2.6	2.6	2.6	2.5
	Import- intensity	8.6	12.4	14.0	11.8	11.5	12.6	13.7	11.9
	%age share of world	6.9	10.6	11.4	10.3	10.2	11.4	12.8	10.9

(Contd.)

(Contd. Table 4.5)

		1998	*1999*	*2000*	*2001*	*2002*	*2003*	*2004*	*2005*
India	Export-intensity	4.12	3.15	3.53	3.37	4.35	4.53	3.79	2.94
	%age share of world	4.93	4.08	4.21	4.54	5.05	6.22	5.65	5.24
	Import- intensity	1.01	0.90	0.89	0.79	0.80	0.74	0.74	0.73
	%age share of world	0.98	0.87	0.89	0.85	0.89	0.85	0.85	0.92
Pakistan	Export-intensity	4.14	2.77	2.68	2.14	2.17	2.22	2.51	1.74
	%age share of world	4.92	3.57	3.18	2.87	2.32	3.03	3.72	3.07
	Import- intensity	2.54	2.03	2.36	2.71	1.80	2.11	2.73	2.43
	%age share of world	2.42	1.94	2.35	2.90	2.00	2.41	3.10	3.01
Bangladesh	Export-intensity	2.48	1.49	1.35	1.21	0.10	1.30	1.10	1.24
	%age share of world	2.96	1.92	1.61	1.62	1.36	1.77	1.63	2.19
	Import- intensity	18.2	14.1	11.8	13.4	14.0	14.6	14.3	12.3
	%age share of world	17.3	13.5	11.7	14.4	15.5	16.6	16.2	15.2
Nepal	Export-intensity	30.3	23.0	27.7	29.7	38.9	33.6	32.7	29
	%age share of world	36.0	29.7	32.8	39.6	50.1	45.6	48.3	52.3
	Import- intensity	33.3	14.6	15.5	18.3	31.0	40.9	41.4	39.7
	%age share of world	31.6	14.0	15.4	19.6	34.4	46.5	46.7	49.1
Srlanka	Export-intensity	1.9	2.4	2.9	2.5	0.4	4.3	5.9	4.9
	%age share of world	2.3	3.0	3.4	3.3	5.4	5.9	8.7	8.7
	Import- intensity	10.8	10.5	10.6	11.7	13.9	15.4	17.4	17.1
	%age share of world	10.3	10.0	10.5	12.5	15.4	17.6	19.6	21.1

(Contd.)

trade expansion. This graph shows the pace of growth of export from India to other South Asian Countries are on rising trend, after 1997-1998 growth rate is faster. Imports are also increasing but not as fast as fast as export has been increasing. The research study shows that during the period of 1965-87 (Agarwal and Panday), the values of trade intensity index were much less than unity reflecting the low levels of bilateral trade[12]. But it has observed that during the period 1990-2005, the export intensity between India and other South Asian countries is more than unity reflects that to some extent they are exploring these markets for trade. But the import intensity is less than unity reflects low level of import from these countries. Nepal's dependence on South Asia has increased substantially following the Indo-Nepal Trade and Transit Treaty in 1996. Between 1996 and 2005, Nepal's exports to India increased six times from an annual average of about $67 million to over $371 million. Exports from India to Nepal near about six times rising from $158 million to $830 million. India is the largest regional trading partner of Nepal, and other important trade partners are Bangladesh and Sri Lanka. Similarly, following a bilateral trade protocol between India and Nepal in 1996, access to the Indian market was improved and trade expanded drastically. At the same time, Indian investments in Nepal increased for a wide range of products, particularly light consumer goods such as toothpaste and ready-made garments where Indian entrepreneurs recognized the profitability of locating plants in Nepal for duty-free export to North India markets. Among other things these import restrictions hobbled SAPTA, especially in the first two negotiating rounds in 1995 and 1997, when the other South Asian countries complained that it was meaningless for India to grant tariff preferences when the same products were subject to import licensing. In response to these complaints, in 1998 India exempted the SAARC countries from its general system of import licensing. At about the same time (following pressure at the WTO) it started removing these controls the rest of the world, and the final 715 tariff lines were freed on April 1, 2001. Similar possibilities exist for other South Asian countries. Starting from a relatively low base, enormous opportunities are available to expand intraregional trade in South

Fig. 4.2 India VS other South Asian Countries (1*5)

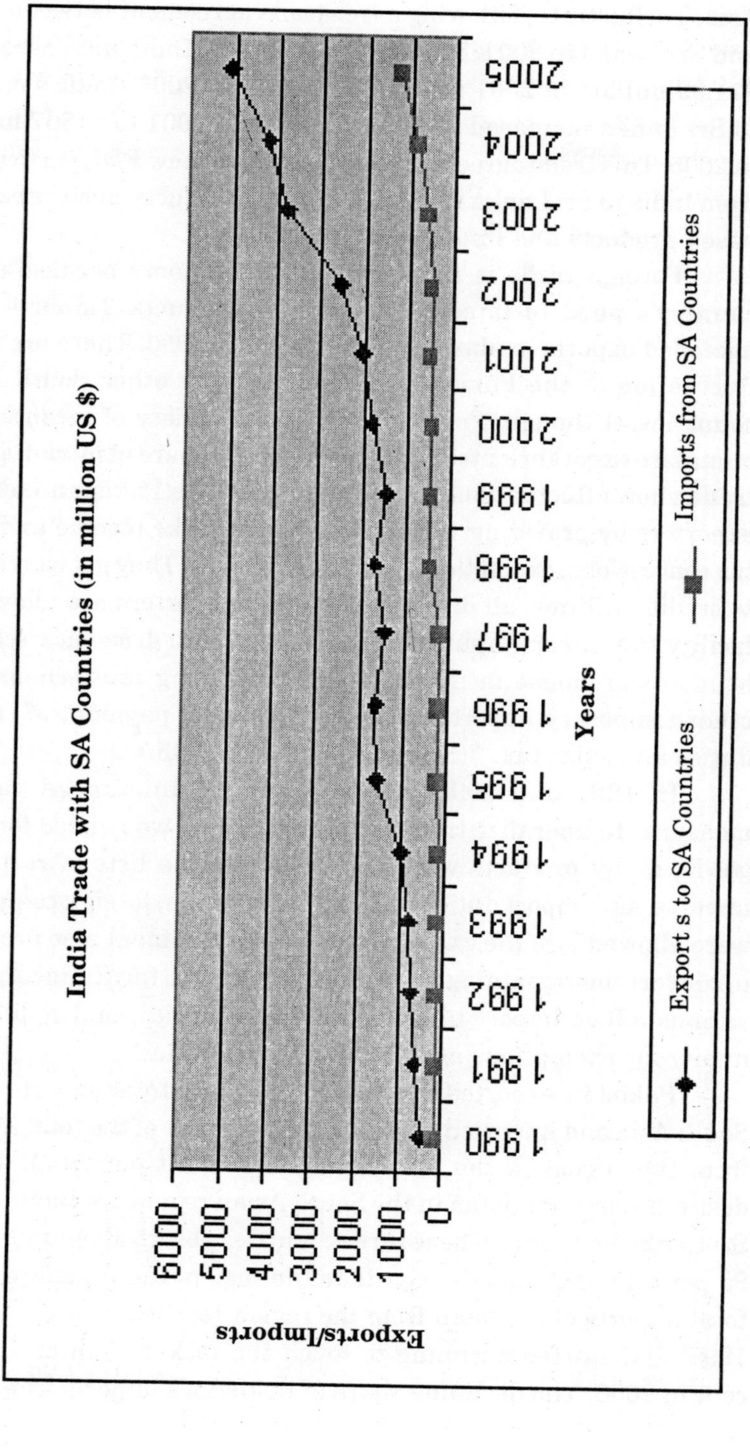

Asia. To illustrate, following a free trade agreement between India and Sri Lanka in 2001, Sri Lanka's exports to India increased from $71.99 million in 2001 to $475.79 million in 2005. India's exports to Sri Lanka increased from $547million in 2001 to $1867 million in 2005. This trade agreement also stimulated new FDI, particularly from India to Sri Lanka for a wide range of products, such as rubber-based products and information technology.

Foreign trade is important to the economy because of the country's need to import a variety of products. Imports have exceeded exports in almost every year since 1950. There are many fluctuation in the Pakistan 's trade with the other South Asian countries. Although, Pakistan provides a variety of incentives to stimulate export oriented industries, yet the share of intra-regional trade shows fluctuations within the region. As Pakistan facilitate exporters by providing variety of incentives like income and sales tax concessions, exemption from custom duties. They get easy access to credit facilities, all direct and indirect exporters are allowed to facility the import inputs through no duty, no drawback scheme, bonded warehouse facilities, export processing unit scheme and other temporary import schemes without the payment of custom duties and sales tax.[13] (Srinivasan, 2002, p, 245.)

In 1991 and 1992, the government announced various measures to liberalize trade. Import licensing was ended for most goods, many products were removed from the lists of restricted imports, and import duties were cut. In addition, foreign companies were allowed into the export trade. The government also promised to convert the remaining non tariff barriers into tariffs, incorporate various adhoc import taxes into customs duties, and reduce the numerous exemptions and concessions on duties.

Pakistan exported 3 to 5 per cent of its total exports to the South Asia and imported between 2 to 4 per cent of the total imports from the region in the last decade. The most important export destinations of Pakistan in the South Asian region are Bangladesh, Sri Lanka and India. These three countries absorb about more than 95 per cent of country's exports to the region. India's share in the total imports of Pakistan from the region reached 72.4 per cent in 1996, and started declining to touch the rock bottom of 42.8 per cent in 2000. The declining share of Pakistan's imports from India

Fig. 4.3 Pakistan vs other South Asian Countries (1*5)

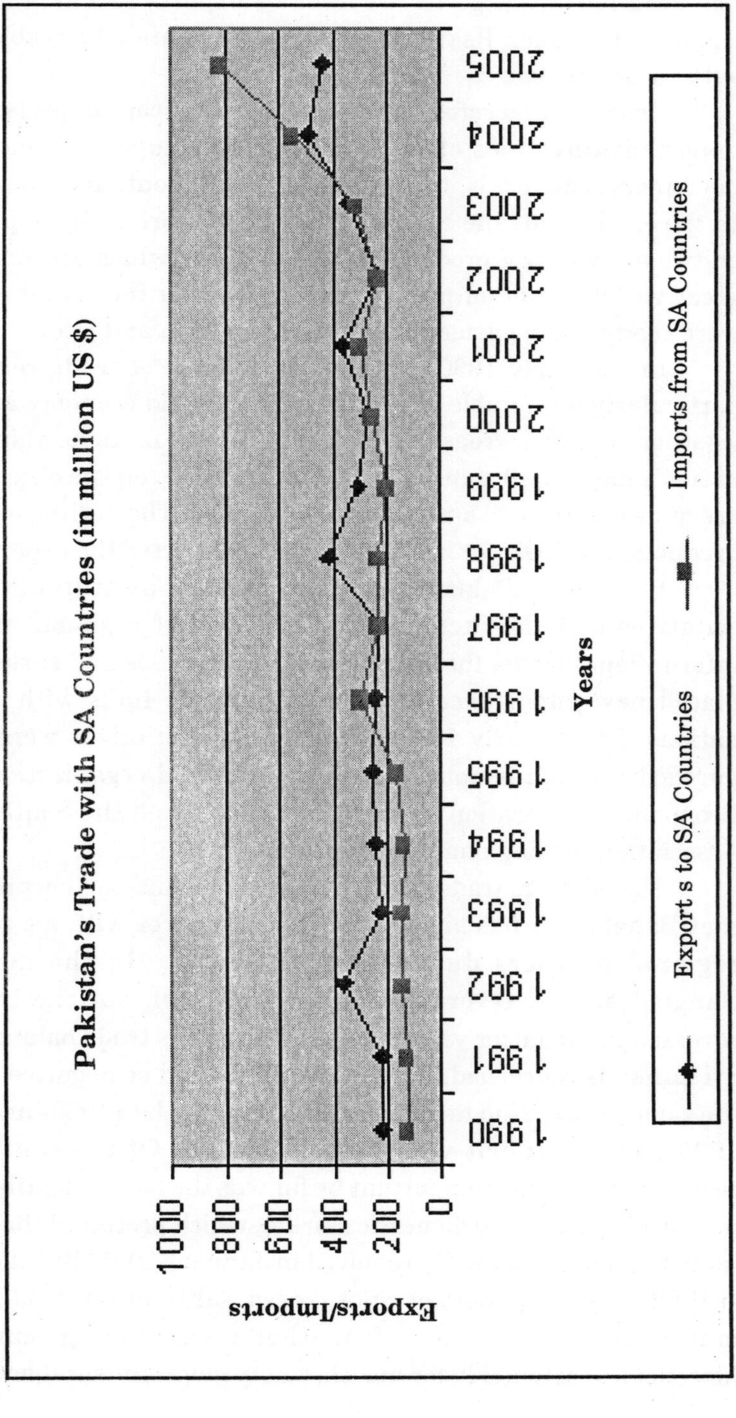

has resulted in surge in Sri Lanka's exports to Pakistan in a significant manner. Pakistan continued to maintain favorable trade with in the region.

Crude oil and refined products are significant imports. Other important categories of imports in 1992 included non-electrical machinery, chemicals, transportation equipment, and edible oils. In the early 1990s the export base remained primarily dependent on two agricultural products, cotton and rice, which are subject to great variations in output and demand. Other important exports were ready made garments. synthetic textiles, and rice.

In the early 1990s, Pakistan's balance of trade remained particularly vulnerable to changes in the world economy and bad weather. Sharp increases in crude oil prices in 1990, raised the nation's import bill significantly. Total exports, on the other hand, are more sensitive to agricultural production. The decline in cotton production in 1993, for instance, seriously affected the export level.

Because of Pakistani fears of protectionism in developed countries and the increasing importance of regional blocs in international trade, the government in the 1980s and early 1990s placed new importance on developing trade links with nearby nations. In the early 1990s, new trading initiatives were being pursued through membership in two regional organizations, the Economic Co-operation Organization (ECO) and the South Asian Association for Regional Cooperation.

The bilateral trade performances of regional partners indicate that Bangladesh has bilateral trade imbalances with most of the regional partners during the last decade. In the mid-90s, Bangladesh had favorable trade with Nepal, but the trend is reversed in the latter years. As far as country's trade balance with Sri Lanka is concerned, it was either balanced or negative during the same period. Non tariff barriers during the late 1980s and early 1990s, most explicit QRs were abolished. Of the continuing restrictions the most important by far was the ban on textile fabric imports for use in the domestic market, which protected the textile industry. This was finally removed in January 2005. But there are still QRs on the import of chicks, eggs, salt and some packaging materials, and also on a few other products (e.g. mosquito insecticides) ostensibly for health, safety environmental and other

Fig. 4.4 Bangladesh VS other South Asian Countries (1*5)

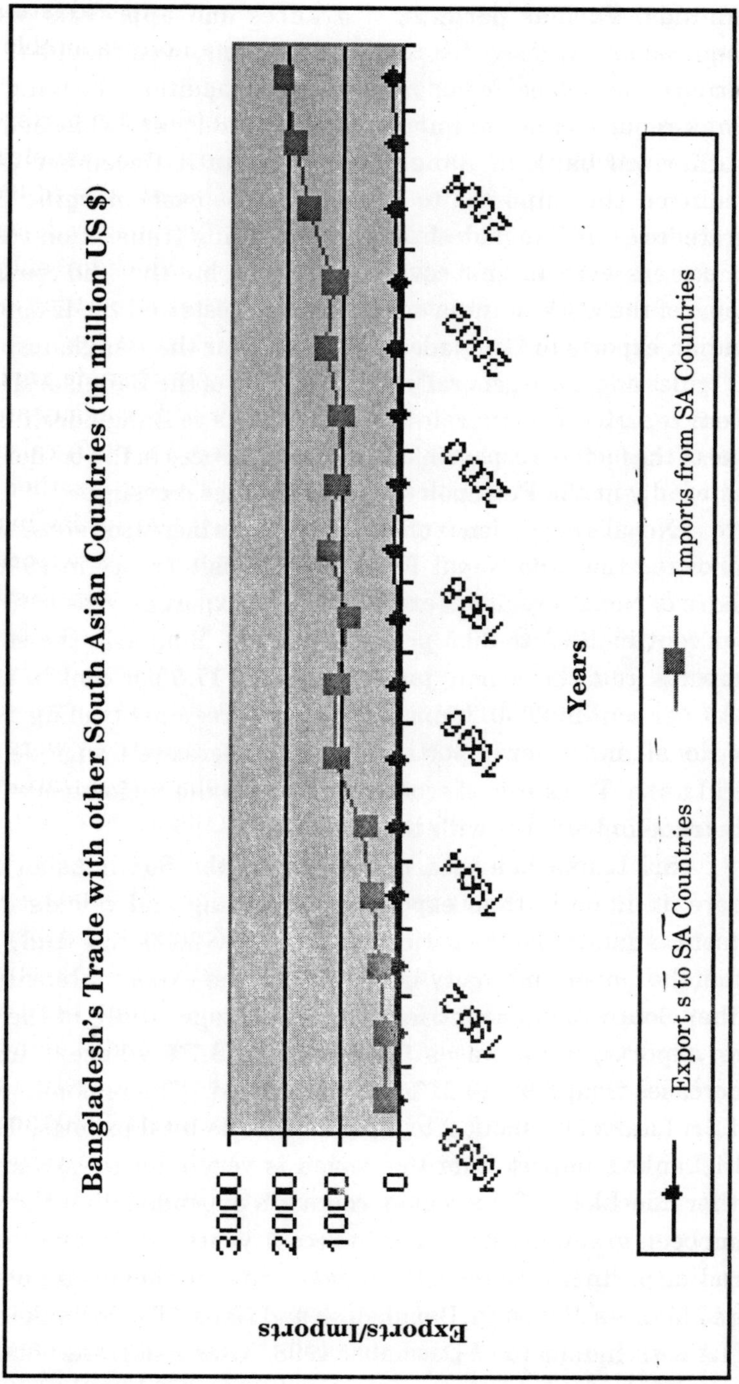

grounds. Various permits, clearances and approvals are also required for extensive lists of other products, even though they are not formally subject to import licensing. In addition, the Bangladesh Bank requires that all imports be financed by an LC issued by an authorized bank in Bangladesh, and until December 2003 it required the importer to deposit a 30% cash margin. Import procedures in Bangladesh and the resulting transaction costs for importers were also not covered explicitly, but they did come up in some of the work in India on transaction costs and the financing of Indian exports to Bangladesh. In particular the Bangladesh Bank LC rules and more generally the credibility of the Bangladesh banks were reported to constraint Indian exports to Bangladesh, and as one of the factors responsible for illegal practices in the border trade, especially at the Petrapole-Benapole border crossing.

Nepal's dependence on South Asia has increased substantially following the Indo-Nepal Trade and Transit Treaty in 1996. The share of Nepal's regional exports to total export increased from 9.3 per cent in 1995 to 36.5 per cent in 1998. Similarly the share of imports from the region jumped up from 17.5 per cent in 1995 to 33.1 per cent in 2000. India is the largest regional trading partner of Nepal, and other important trade partners are Bangladesh and Sri Lanka. The surge of economic ties with the region has widened its trade imbalances with the region.

Sri Lanka has been depending on the South Asian region more on imports than exports.By observing and calculating the stastical data, from the period between 1990-2005, this study shows that the import intensity is more than the export intensity with other South Asian countries. The percentage share of the world for exports, it increases from 3.8% to 8.7% whereas imports increases from 6.9% to 21% for this period. The regional exports of Sri Lanka are about 2 to 4 per cent of its total exports. Though Sri Lanka's import from the region is very high as compared to other non-LDCs of the region, country's dependence on the region has been gradually declining in recent years. Sri Lanka's largest trading partner is India in the region, and other important partners are Maldives, Pakistan, Bangladesh and Nepal. The Srilanka signed FTA with India on 28th December 1998. After that trade with India increases and it impacts on overall increase in trade with the region.

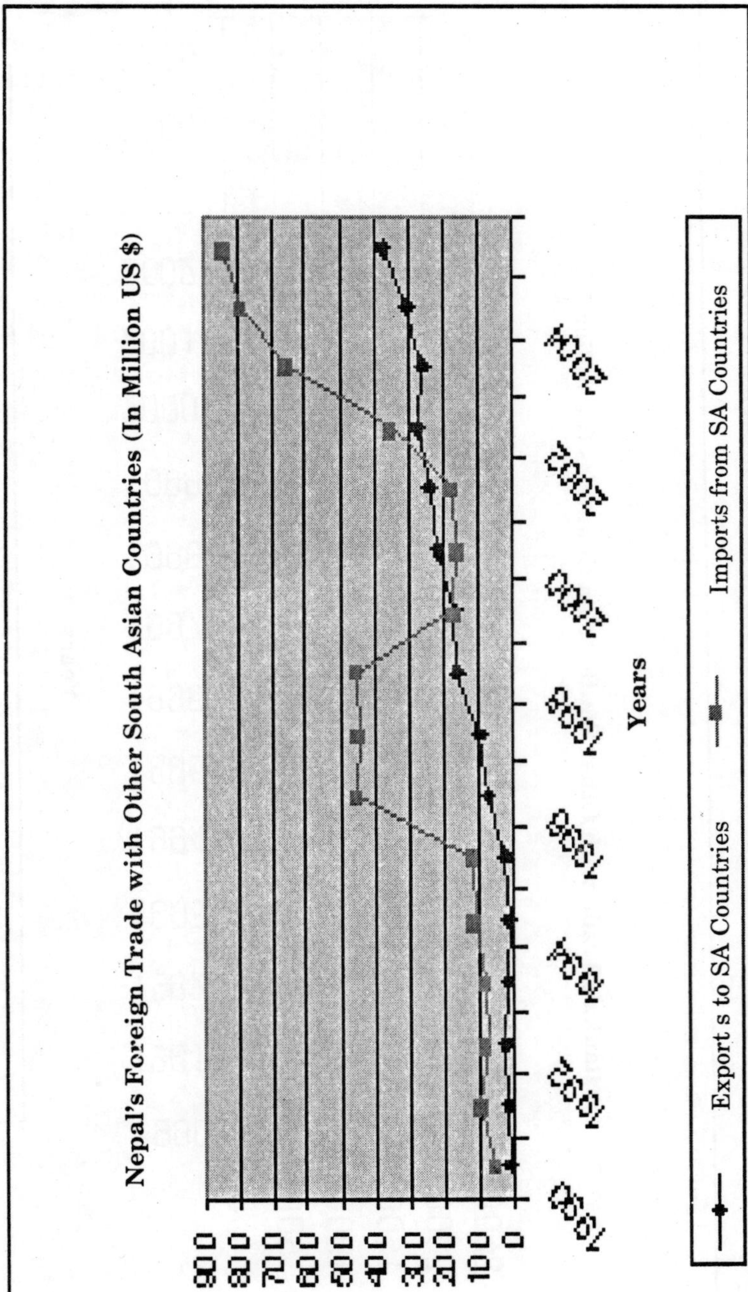

Fig. 4.5 Nepal vs other South Asian Countries (1*5)

Fig. 4.6 Sri Lanka vs other South Asian Countries (1*5)

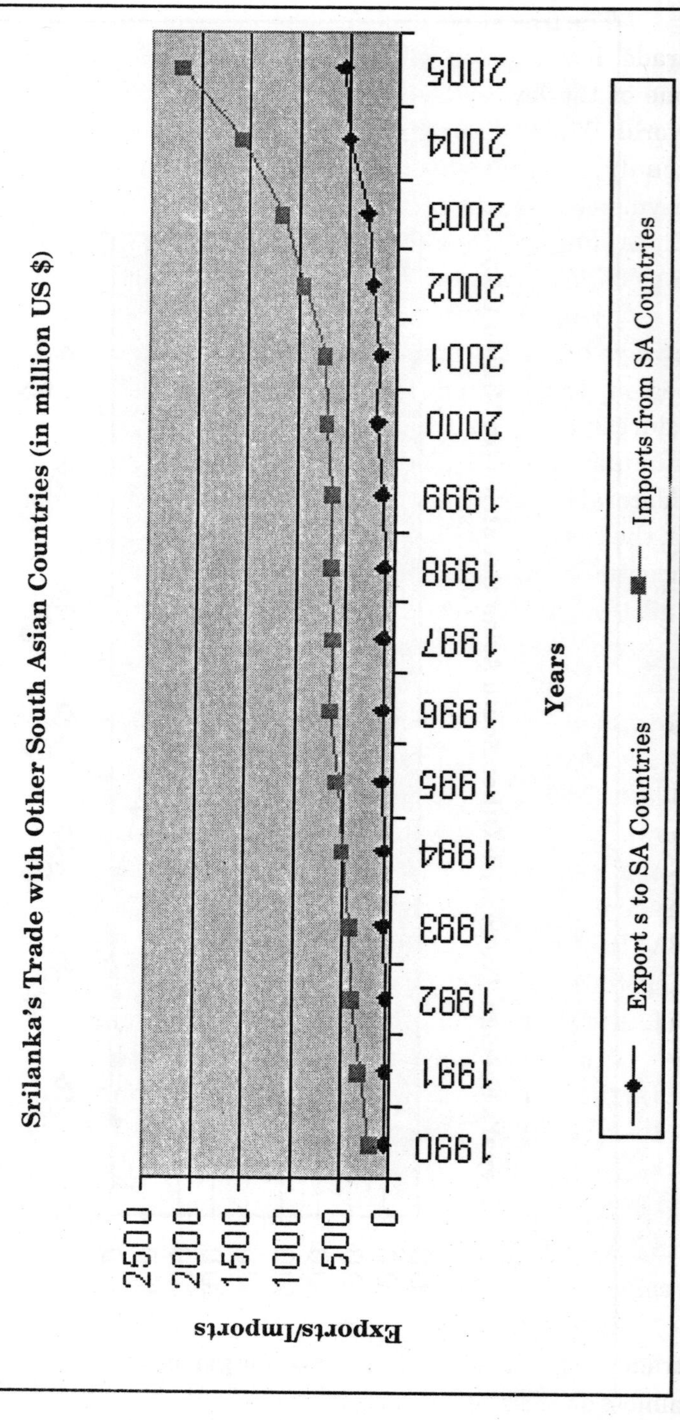

The first stage in deepening cooperation would be to enhance trade. For a region which aspires to an economic union, we have one of the lowest levels of intra-regional trade anywhere in the world. While this originates from prevailing trade barriers in each country, the more substantive constraint lies in the structural asymmetries in the national economies that limit the scope for trade. Since January 2004, the seven countries of South Asia have signed SAFTA agreement.

While SAFTA was seen as the route to opening up trade, it always needed to address the problem of trade asymmetry in the region. To the extent that the SAARC process moved too slowly to address these issues, bilateralism became a preferred option to stimulate intra-regional trade. As of today India has entered into bilateral free trade agreements with Nepal, Bhutan and Sri Lanka. In the case of Bangladesh a bilateral free trade agreement is under negotiation with India. It is expected from the negotiations that India would offer accelerated market access to Bangladeshi exports as has been permitted under the Indo-Lanka Free Trade Agreement (ILFTA). In return the smaller economies would be given more time to eliminate their trade barriers to Indian exports. There is some apprehension amongst economists in the region that the bilateral FTAs may compromise the move towards SAFTA. It could, however, be argued that these FTA's may facilitate the move to SAFTA since they have already opened up the doors for enhanced trade in the region. Negotiations have already begun through the SAARC Secretariat on working out the details of SAFTA. These negotiations will have to factor in the implications of the bilateral FTAs in place within the region or under negotiation.

The free trade pact among SAARC nations SAFTA has taken its flight toward implementation from July 1st. It promises to reduce import duties to 0-5 percent in three phases of decades. The Union Government of the department has issued the notification necessary to bring SAFTA into a true form. To discourage informal trade SAFTA's fully implementation is necessary condition in the SA regions.

It is worth noting some interesting features. Total informal trade in the South Asian region exceeds US$ 3 billion which is almost double the formal trade in the region for corresponding years

Table 4.6
Planned Phased Tariff cuts on Intra- SAFTATrade

SAARC Countries	*First Phase (Two Years) a 1/1/2006-1/1/2008*	*Second Phase 1/1/2008-1/1/2013*	*1/1/2008- 1/12016*
LDCs— Bangladesh, Nepal, Bhutan, Maldives	Reduce maximum trariff to 30%		Reduce tariffs to the 0.5% range in 8 years.
Non- LDCs—India Pakistan, Sri Lanka	Reduce maximum tariff rate to 20%	Reduce tariffs to the 0.5%range in 5 years(Sri Lanka in 6 years)Note: It is recommendation that reduction be done in equall installments at least 15 % reduction per year reduce tarrifs to 0-5% for products of the LDCs within a timeframe of 3 Years.	

Source: USAID, 2005, p. 23.

Table 4.7
India's Informal Trade with South Asia

	Exports (X)	*Imports (M)*	*Trade Balance (X-M)*	*Total Trade (X+M)*
Bangladesh 1	299.0	14.0	285.0	313.0
Sri Lanka 2	185.5	21.8	163.7	207.3
Pakistan 3	n.a.	n.a.	Positive	2000
Nepal 4	180.0	228.0	-48.0	408.0
Bhutan 5	31.3	1.2	30.1	32.6
Total South Asia	-	-	-	2960.9

Sources: Chaudhary (1995) for Bangladesh; Taneja et. al. (2002) for Sri Lanka and Nepal; Economist (1996) for Pakistan;
Rao et. al. (1997) for Bhutan.
Notes : X denotes exports while M denotes imports.
1. (1992-93), 2. (2000-01), 3. (1996), 4. (2000-01), 5. (1993-94)

see table 4.7 for which informal trade estimates are available. India's informal trade with Pakistan is almost ten times that of formal trade in the region, that with Nepal and Bangladesh is almost as large as formal trade, with Sri Lanka it is almost one-third of formal trade and that with Bhutan is three times as much as formal trade. (see Table 4.8)

Another noticeable feature is the fact that India has a trade surplus with Bangladesh, Pakistan, Sri Lanka and Bhutan on the unofficial trade account, while with Nepal it has a trade deficit. Interestingly, a similar pattern can be observed on the official trade account. (See Table 4.7)

Other Regional- Sub-Regional and Multilateral Economic Initiatives of South Asia

BIMST-EC (Bangladesh, India, Myanmar, Sri Lanka, Thailand-Economic Cooperation)

South Asian Growth Quadrangle was launched in 1997 among four countries (Bangladesh, Bhutan, Nepal and eleven contiguous

Table 4.8
India's Formal Trade with South Asia

	Exports (X)	*Imports (M)*	*Trade Balance (X-M)*	*Total Trade (X+M)*
Bangladesh1	349.1	7.8	341.2	356.9
Sri Lanka2	640.2	45.0	595.2	685.2
Pakistan3	157.2	36.1	121.1	193.3
Nepal4	141.0	255.0	-114.0	396.0
Bhutan5	7.0	3.0	4.0	10.0
Total South Asia	-	-	-	1641.4

Sources: Chaudhary (1995) for Bangladesh; Taneja et. al.(2002) for Sri Lanka and Nepal; Commodity Trade Statistics for Pakistan, Nepal and Bhutan.

Notes: X denotes exports while M denotes imports.

1. (1992-93), 2. (2000-01), 3. (1994), 4. (2000-01), 5. (1994).

eastern and north eastern states of India) BBIN quadrangle. Aiming at creating an enabling environment for rapid economic development and encourage co-operative projects in the Ganga-Brahmaputra- Meghna river basin. At the request of BBIN, Asian Development Bank launched assistance for sub-regional co-operation under the South Asian Sub-Regional Economic Co-operation program in 2001. With an objective to expand our economic relations with the SAARC and South East Asian countries, Bhutan joined the BIMST-EC in 2004. During the Sixth BIMST-EC Ministerial Meeting in Phuket, Thailand, in 2004, Bhutan and Nepal were formally admitted as new members. Bhutan also became a signatory to the BIMST-EC Free Trade Area[14]. Membership in this regional grouping will enable Bhutan to diversify its export markets and link transport infrastructure while harnessing other potential benefits of expanding economic relation beyond SAARC region.

Countries of the South Asian region are also enjoying the membership of other groups like, Indian Ocean Rim Association for Regional Cooperation (IOR-ARC), Bangladesh- India- Myanmar-Sri Lanka-Thailand Economic Co-operation (BIMST-EC). Etc.

BIMSTEC has been renamed recently as Bay Of Bengal Economic Community. Some of South Asian countries have also developed close relations with the ASEAN. RIS Studies on Regional Cooperation and Economic Integration in Asia BIMSTEC countries: characteristics and recent economic performance; economic cooperation for development and competitiveness; transport infrastructure and linkages; energy cooperation: towards a Bay of Bengal energy community; and other sectors of cooperation.

It recommends that the grouping should set its goal to form a Bay of Bengal Economic Community by the year 2020. To facilitate the flow of intra-regional investments, there is need for pursuing investment liberalization on a negative list basis and also incorporate provisions of double taxation avoidance in the Framework Agreement. A BIMSTEC Fund for Regional Projects should also be established for further strengthening of business links.

(5) Benefits, and Challenges of Regional Economic Integration

Benefits The one premise on which there is universal consensus amongst economists is that international trade is good for socio-economic development of all countries. South Asian countries will benefit significantly from greater economic integration and trade liberalization by taking advantage of the benefits of regionalism and globalization. Optimum economic benefit of regionalism and globalization can be reaped through the dynamic vehicle of the private business sector. South Asia is, in aggregate, an energy deficit area largely because India is emerging as one of the world's largest energy markets. In contrast, Nepal and Bhutan retain the potential to emerge as major sources of energy exports though harnessing the vast hydro power potential in their rivers. Indeed power is already Bhutan's largest source of export earnings directed to India which has helped to make it the only country in the region with a trade surplus with India. However, Nepal's export-oriented hydropower projects have been tied up in protracted negotiations with India, its principal prospective market for power. These negotiations have acquired political overtones which have strained bilateral relations and have also become a major issue in domestic politics in Nepal. Bangladesh has a potential for exporting natural gas to India but is reluctant to do so because of domestic political opposition to such exports on the grounds that its gas reserves are insufficient to justify such exports. Pakistan remains a potential transit point for connecting the vast energy reserves of West and Central Asia to South Asia but has not been able to benefit from its strategic location because of its political tensions with India. A stronger Indo-Pakistan relationship would realize multiple benefits for all the countries of the region, including reduced defense expenditure, enhanced economic growth from increased trade and the sharing of South Asia's water, oil and natural gas resources, and would increase the scope for further integration.

Challenges The main problems in promoting more trade within the South Asian region are:

Lack of complementarities

With the exception of India, and to some extent Pakistan, countries in the region do not have a diversified industrial structure. Regional exports largely consist of raw materials and traditional products such as textiles and garments, while regional imports consist mainly of capital goods and high-tech products. Some regional countries are direct competitors in the world export market for their products. Thus, the trade pattern of South Asian countries is quite similar and skewed towards developed countries.

Lack of transport and communication links

Transport and communication links between South Asian countries are poor. Some countries are cut off from other countries in the region. There are hardly any ships that call specifically for South Asia exports to other regional countries. For example, Bangladesh finds it easier to reach countries in Southeast Asia, West Asia or Africa than to reach Pakistan. This is also the case with Nepal, vis-à-vis Pakistan, as it uses mainly the Kolkata port for trade with countries other than India, Bangladesh and Bhutan. Although India shares borders with most countries, there has not been enough effort to develop transport and communication links. So much so that it often takes over a week to move goods between Amritsar (India) and Lahore (Pakistan), barely a distance of 30 km.

Restrictive trade policies

Restrictive trade policies also cause low levels of intra-regional trade within the region. The restrictions have been more severe on the export interests of South Asia. This is so because countries are generally more restrictive towards products that are considered non-essential, or those that are locally available. And products that their neighbours could possibly supply fall in this category. For example, while more than half the exports of manufactured goods from South Asia consist of textiles and leather products, they are subject to very high rates of import duties and/ or other restrictions in South Asia. This was reflected even in the SAPTA regime, as most products of export interest to regional countries were excluded from preferential treatment. Many believe that even under liberalization under SAFTA, countries could adopt similar tactics.

Political problems

Political differences have also been a major hurdle in fostering regional economic cooperation within South Asia. Political problems between India and Pakistan, the two largest economies in the region, have often put a question mark on the very existence of the regional bloc. Pakistan does not even offer MFN treatment to India, though they are both part of a regional Free Trade Agreement. Recently, however, Indo-Pak relations have improved significantly enhancing prospects for better trade cooperation. There are problems between other pairs of countries as well, though of a lesser degree. Furthermore, South Asia is an area of magnificent political complexities. States like Pakistan and Bangladesh have been largely ruled by authoritarian military rulers. India faces several unresolved issues that shoot from internal as well as external sources. These include ethnicity, border disputes, separatist demands, terrorism and revolutionary activities, communalism, religious problems and so on. All these issues break the basic ideals of nation building, the ideals of democracy, secularism, socialism and federalism. Moreover, the very fact that sub national interests are considered prior to the socio-economic and political well being of the country as a whole is harmful for the development of genuinely democratic policy. In Nepal, for example, the series of democratically elected government failed to produce any better result than the old royal regime due to widespread corruption and crisis of governance.[28] The political fundamentalists such as Maoists and mainstream political parties are posing major threat to democracy in Nepal. In addition to creating law and order problems, increased human rights violations and a heavy reliance on security forces have undermined the question of legitimacy of governance in Nepal. The recent political development of Nepal is that Mr. Prachanda a Maoist has become a Prime Minister now, the different situation can be expected.

The weak trade linkages in South Asian region can be attributed to several structural as well as policy induced factors. These includes identical comparative advantages, lack of exportable surpluses, lack of communication links, restrictive trade policies, lack of finances and adding to that Political problems. First, the asymmetry between India and the rest of South Asian countries has been a major problem. Due to these political problem, it has never taken off as a useful economic vehicle. SAARC has not been able to solve this. Secondly, adversarial relationship between India and Pakistan has affected adversely SAARC functioning. Finally, despite all the talk of regional cooperation, South Asian countries lack even minimal understanding on political and security issues.

This politicization of what would in most other regions have been viewed as economic or commercial decision derives from the political perspective guiding the development of the energy sector in every country. The idea that the supply and demand for energy must be balanced within a country is not very meaningful in a region where some countries are major importers of energy and others see it as their principal export. In such circumstances, it would make sense for South Asia to move away from conceiving of its energy security as a national project and will have to redefine its market in regional terms. If South Asia's energy scenario were to be redefined within a regional context its energy needs would expect to be served through a common distribution system integrated within a single energy grid of power and gas lines extending across the region. Such an integrated system would need to resolve quite complex problems of cross-border pricing, harmonisation of standards and equipments and the role of external players as sources of supply (Iran, Central Asia) or as corporate investors. The move towards SAFTA will be meaningless unless the issue of stimulating investment in the region, particularly in the less developed areas, including Sri Lanka, is accelerated. The substantive point of a Free Trade Area is for small economies with narrow markets, such as Bangladesh, Nepal and Sri Lanka, to be able to use the incentive of the larger South Asian and particularly Indian market to stimulate enhanced investment from within and without. In Bangladesh as in Sri Lanka, it is widely believed that the expectation of servicing a market of one billion people in India will open up new investment horizons. Domestic entrepreneurs seek to access global financing and foreign enterprises, particularly from East and South East Asia looking for entry into the large and growing Indian market, will be encouraged by SAFTA to rethink their investment plans. SAFTA's planning to allocate funds in the area are as follows: Any move towards an Economic Union cannot limit itself to a Free Trade Area. SAARC will sooner or later have to explore the scope for a Customs Union. This issue will not be as complex as it might have appeared some years ago. Under the pressure of the WTO in tariff levels across the world is the order of the day. Since all SAARC countries have been lowering their tariff rates, mostly under pressure from the World Bank/IMF structural adjustment reforms, the deep disparities in tariff levels which once characterised the region are less apparent today. It, therefore, makes sense to open up discussion on adopting a common tariff policy vis-à-vis the rest of the world. However, this task is also problematic. It is the smaller economies who have reduced their tariffs rather faster than India or Pakistan. However, this is not a problem which can persist over a long period of time due to the WTO rules of the game. It would therefore make sense to initiate work on the implications of a Customs Union within South Asia in order to see when, under what circumstance and at what pace such a Union can be put in place. Deepening integration will involve moving beyond trade to address the broader issue of harmonizing macro-economic policies.

Integrating the infrastructure

The proposal for a dedicated South Asian development fund may also be encouraged. The Fund's mission needs to be clarified and new life needs to be breathed into the organization. There is some confusion as to the scope of this fund and whether it will cover both financing of infrastructure projects as well as private investment. Here it is suggested that two funds may be developed. One fund should be dedicated to financing infrastructure development projects mostly located in the less developed countries. As in the case of the European Union, a special fund is needed to enhance the development capacity of weaker countries to enable them to enhance their competitiveness in an integrated market. Billions of Euros were invested through the EU in such funds, to finance investment in Spain, Portugal, Greece and Ireland when they entered the EU, to enable them to upgrade their infrastructure and enhance their competitive capacity. A similar fund, underwritten from within SAARC but supplemented by aid resources from outside the region should be established to enable Bangladesh, Bhutan, Maldives, Nepal and Sri Lanka to invest in infrastructure projects. Investment which modernizes and enhances capacity in transport and communications as well as energy, perhaps with a special focus on regional connectivity but not exclusive to it, will enhance the attractiveness of these economies to prospective investors.

A second fund should be established as an Investment Fund, serviced by both public and private capital, to finance private sector investment projects within the weaker economies, which involve cross border investment as well as projects for serving regional markets. This should attract prospective investors from India and Pakistan and could be used further private investment from outside the region which may even cover private investment in infrastructure projects.

The Islamabad Summit quite appropriately identified energy, transport and communications as important areas for cooperation. Of these, the need for transport integration is perhaps the most urgent since it is integral to the operationalization of a Free Trade Area. South Asia inherited an integrated transport infrastructure from the British Empire. This infrastructure was fractured not by the partition of India but by its political aftermath and now needs to be rebuilt within the context of greater political harmony in South Asia.

Across the mainland of South Asia the original transport infrastructure is already in place, but in many areas has been destroyed and needs upgrading. The main obstacle to improving connectivity is political. The barriers to cross-border movements make neither commercial or logistical sense and originate in the pathologies of inter-state as well as domestic politics. The political leaders of South Asia will therefore need to first dismantle the political barriers to transport integration. Once this is done, procedures for facilitating cross border movement of people and goods will need to be harmonized (visas, customs facilities) and system connectivity will have to be established (linking meter gauge rail systems with broad gauge systems). Infrastructure where fractured will have to be rebuilt or upgraded to sustain a heavier traffic load and capacity will need to be expanded to accommodate the enhanced traffic emanating from intra-regional movements. In some cases new investment would be needed to build transport links where none exit today.

So far SAARC has done very little to address the issue of transport integration. Some meetings have been convened by the SAARC Secretariat to look at the issue of standardizing the transport infrastructure but there is no strategic vision to guide the integration process largely because of the underlying political tensions which constrain issues of transport connectivity. Whatever dialogue on improving linkages has taken place owes largely either to the enterprise of multilateral bodies such as the World Bank, Asian Development Bank or UNESCAP or civil society initiatives. The mandate from the Islamabad Summit has inspired the SAARC Secretariat to place the issue of improving transport linkages on its work programme. However much work is needed to both design an underlying vision and then translate it into program and projects which free up movement of traffic across South Asia. The SAARC governments have already acknowledged the need for cooperation in the energy sector. But so far very little has been done to work out the economics or explore the political implications of such cooperation.

Indian external affairs minister Pranab Mukherji said that while South Asia made significant progress in integration in the world economy, but countries maintained higher level protection within the region. Our restricted policies have reduce the effect of the benefits of cultural similarity and geographical proximities. Restrictions on the free movement of people and goods have ensured that the trade remains the lowest for South Asia[15]

It makes little economic sense to talk of globalisation though integration of factor markets, in the form of commodities and capital, while omitting all discussion of labour which is a recognised factor of production. Freeing of the movement of labour across national boundaries is not discussed either at the WTO or the SAARC forum . In the WTO the SAARC countries come together to support the inclusion of the movement of natural persons in any discussion on trade in services. It is preposterous for the U.S. and the Europeans to include such issues as the liberalization of banking, insurance and consultancy services as part of the negotiations on the services sector at the WTO without any reference to labor services which are a major export from Bangladesh, India, Nepal, Pakistan and Sri Lanka. In contrast to South Asia's strong position on the subject in international forum it is verboten to discuss the issue of movement of natural or any other variety of persons in any SAARC forum. The truth is that the issue of labor flows across borders, whether at the WTO or in South Asia, is discussed as an issue of immigration, usually illegal, by ministries in-charge of internal security rather than those responsible for trade and economic affairs.

To the extent that SAARC governments may remain inhibited about discussing the problem of labor flows it is suggested that at the level of civil society serious discussion of the issue should take place. These dialogues would need to be backed by major research on the underlying economics, the social implications in the receiving and sending countries and the political fallout from this process. Such an exercise should recognize that important issues of human rights as well as national security are involved along with the criminal dimension associated with human trafficking of women and children. It is hoped that out of such research and consultation, a realistic and humanitarian policy will emerge which can serve to formalize the process of labor flows and integrate this into the process of economic cooperation in South Asia. Such an exercise will need to recognize that if a South Asian Economic Union is to emerge labor market integration will have to be a central component of the process.

SAARC initiatives in the service sector have not moved beyond some consultations related to the tourism sector. Much more work, again possibly at the level of civil society, needs to be done to estimate the extent and nature of this market as well as its underlying dynamics. Since much of this trade in services is informal and hence unrecorded, this trade will continue to expand through the play of market forces. It may be counter productive for SAARC to interfere with the market but the SAARC process should be used to explore ways to enhance the export capacity in services of the weaker SAARC member countries.

South Asia is united by its poverty. It contributes the largest share of the world's poor, illiterate, hungry and medically deprived, though Sri Lanka and Maldives contribute little to these numbers. Any move to integrate South Asia cannot, therefore, bypass this defining social reality. Citizens in the region do want to trade with each other, travel across borders as freely as do the citizens of the European Union or ASEAN and to live without the threat of war or fear of terrorism. The leaders of the SAARC countries need to respond to the needs of their citizens and demonstrate the statesmanship to resolve their short and long term conflicts. Such a perspective on South Asian cooperation appeared to have emerged out of the Islamabad summit but needs to be sustained by the commitment of the SAARC leaders and incorporated into the institutions governing inter-state relations. Due to the prejudiced nature of Pakistan Both the nation can not take the benefit of the trading potential. Both the countries should realize that if for economic benefits. They should take a lesson from the countries like France and Germany, which had problems on border for centuries, they solved their problem by cooperating economically and by opening border by free movements of people and goods and services. There is need to change mind set of politicians as well as of the people. Prof. Mahendra P. Lama, a renowned professor at the Jawaharlal Nehru University, India also presented his views on SAFTA from an Indian perspective. He emphasized the need to change the mindsets of the people in the region, which is also an obstacle to trade. He said that the role of the media is extremely crucial in changing the mindsets of people and a collective effort has to be made by the entire region including the private and public sector for SAFTA to be successful[16]. (18th December,2007, Islamabad conferences,)

Despite its potential benefits, socio-economic integration has been miserably slow in the South Asian region. The South Asian region is the least integrated economic region of the world in spite of having enormous physical resources and 22% of the global population. The regional trade of South Asia remains dismally low at 4% as compared to the regional trade of EU of 67%, NAFTA of 62%, ASEAN of 26%, COMESA of 22%, GCC of 8% and ECO of 6%. Regional trade between the seven SAARC countries in 2002 was $ 5 billion out of which the share of India was 76% ($3.8 billion) and Pakistan's share was 8% ($ 0.4 billion). The regional trade between the remaining five countries is limited to around 16% ($0.8 billion) of the total regional trade[17].The obstacles on the way to SAFTA are still ahead. Several things on ground are not ready. So SAFTA has to go through a tough phases. Trade in goods and services, a coommon currency and full fledged integration are distant dreams. There are many reasons. Pakistan and India's political skirmishes are the major challenge in front of SAFTA. Both have negative lists of items that can not be traded. Pakistan allowed only 773 items on its positive lists to be imported from India.[18] The State Bank of Pakistan recently estimated that the transaction costs are so high in the region due to the poor infrastructure facilities.

Opportunities and Potential in Regional Economic Cooperation

Expansion of Intra regional trade by trade diversion has been found to have a significant economic value for the regional countries. Broad Areas of potentials of Intra South Asian trade can be in primary commodities and minerals such as iron ore, natural rubber etc, manufactured goods such as cotton and textiles, silk, food products and beverages, metal products, steels product, rubber products including tiers and tubes, non-electrical machinery, dyes and dyes stuffs, pulp, papers and news print and cement, chemical fertilizers etc. These primary commodities and broad manufactured goods have potentials of increasing trade within the region. Given the opportunities for unrestricted access to an integrated South

Asian market, deep structural changes in their production capacities which can expand and diversify the basket of goods available for export are essential to transforming the fortunes of the smaller economies of South Asia. Business houses in India and outside investors could also be expected to adjust their production base by locating plants to serve South India in Sri Lanka or Northeast India and Eastern Bangladesh rather than servicing them from Mumbai or Haryana. New patterns of vertical and horizontal integration, with plants located across the region, could serve to restructure the manufacturing landscape of South Asia.

To realize such a transformation in the investment climate in each of these countries, preconditions will have to be created where perceptions of political hostility and the attendant security threats to investors, particularly from India, will have to be put to rest. It is the primary responsibility of the host governments, major political parties, the business community and the media of these countries, to create the preconditions whereby investors will feel secure. Allowing for improvements in the social environment for investment the major task will be to put in place the necessary financing facilities to service the emerging investment needs. Within India there is no shortage of private or public institutions which can underwrite investments across regional boundaries. But such facilities will need to be encouraged by changes in the laws governing capital market convertibility. While each South Asian country will take time to open up its capital account, India can take the initiative of moving to restricted convertibility by lifting all policy restrictions to capital flows within the region.

There could also be fruitful cooperation between the BIMSTEC countries in technology management and capability building, in dealing with the digital divide, among other areas. BIMST-EC needs an institutional structure to follow up the decisions taken by the Ministerial Conferences and the Summits and for preparing the agenda of different meetings. The energy demand-supply sectors in the countries of Bangladesh, India, Myanmar, Sri Lanka, Thailand, Nepal and Bhutan offer a potential for regional resource cooperation, which could go beyond export-import trade relations and link the region in a Bay of Bengal Energy Community and thus contribute to the process of regional integration. Cooperation should also be promoted in tourism, fisheries, auto and other sectors. To facilitate the exchange of development experiences, a BIMSTEC

Urgent Steps needed to improve trade relations so that It could develop faster pace :

- Improvement of infrastructure
- Communication gap
- Free mobility of people (especially Researchers politician, policy makers, business community) to understand the whole system demand preferences, lifestyle, culture of each other, for channelising trade.[19] (Dharamdasani, 2002)

In a declaration issued at the end of their 14th summit meeting, the leaders of the South Asian Association for Regional Cooperation (SAARC) stressed that SAFTA should be implemented in letter and spirit as successful implementation of the South Asia Free Trade Agreement (SAFTA) will catalyze other areas of regional cooperation. SAFTA entered into force from January 1, 2006. SAFTA came into force on July 1, 2005, and aims to establish free-trade areas by 2015. So far, tariffs have been reduced twice among the SAARC members, and a third cut in rates will take place on July 1. Where other countries apply across-the-board tariff cuts, Pakistan only reduces taxes on a list of 1,074 items from India, said the official. The official said India's efforts to bring Pakistan into a trading arrangement to blunt political issues would fail, but Pakistan had apparently no objections to easing travel restrictions. "An important agenda item of SAARC would be multi-model transportation across the region, which would facilitate road, air and rail links, and Pakistan has shown willingness to hold talks on it," the official said.[20] (dailyIndia.com/ANI, First April, 2007) In order to realize its full potential, SAFTA should integrate trade in services and the leaders called for a finalization of an agreement in the services sector at the earliest.

The leaders underlined the importance of implementing trade facilitation measures, especially standardization of basic customs documentation and clearing procedures. They also noted that harmonization of technical and phyto-sanitary standards and their implementation in a trade-friendly manner is important in boosting regional trade. The World Bank report analysed that there was potential for 20 billion dollars commerce by 2010 if barriers were reduced in the South Asian bloc, which groups Afghanistan, Bangladesh, Bhutan, India, the Maldives, Nepal, Sri Lanka and Pakistan[21].

Indian Prime Minister Manmohan Singh announced in his address at the inaugural session of the summit meeting that India will allow duty free access to India before the end of this year to its South Asian neighbors who are Least Developed Countries (LDC) and further reduce the sensitive list in respect of these countries[22].

The leaders also emphasized the need to develop, at an early date, a roadmap for a South Asian Customs Union and a South Asian Economic Union in a planned and phased manner. However, the combined gross domestic product of the SAARC countries is 932 billion U.S. dollars, which accounts for 2%of the World GDP[23] (Mu Xuequan,2007), Pakistan is unlikely to grant either the 'Most Favoured Nation (MFN)' status or other trade-related concessions to India under the South Asia Free Trade Agreement (SAFTA) during the 14th SAARC summit in India on April 3-4. Pakistani officials said although trade talks would be central to the summit, the "dream of a free-trade area would continue to remain hostage to the rivalry between Pakistan and India for the foreseeable future", as Pakistan believed that "trade depended on the resolution of outstanding issues" the cost of non-cooperation is highlighted to put forward the case for an RTA. CUTS (1996) showed that consumers in Pakistan paid extra costs of US $ 36.3 mn, US $ 48.9 mn. and US $ 33.7 mn. over the calendar years 1992, 1993, and 1994 respectively for their governments importing 82 to 83 per cent of their tea import requirements from outside the region, such as UK and Kenya29. Despite India being self-sufficient in sugar, it suffered an underproduction during 1992 and 1993 and had to import sugar. Though Pakistan had exportable surplus during that year, India chose to import sugar from outside the region, thus incurring additional costs to the ton of US $ 151 million in 1992 and US $ 215 mn. in 1993. Likewise, Pakistan is known to import steel from China at a price, which is twice that of exports from India. RIS (1999) used the unit value method in a comparative static framework to work out the cost of non-cooperation in the SAARC due to sourcing of imports from non-SAARC countries. Have they had good relations with each other they would have imported from each other, instead of paying more cost to the outside of the regions[24].

"But as a face saver, Pakistan will never say at the SAARC forum that progress on SAFTA should be linked to progress on the core issues, including Kashmir," the Daily Times quoted a Pakistani official as saying, adding that Pakistan had been "discreetly exploiting various technical issues to withhold the MFN status for India".

On being asked about Pakistan's obligations under SAFTA and its comparison with the signing of a free-trade agreement with China, an official said, "No SAFTA and MFN status for India, as Pakistan would suffer" As Pakistan showed concern with India and wants to improve trade within the region but unless it provides a MFN status to India, it will shows its unwillingness.

There is a strong desire at the public level to form South Asian Union (SAU) like the European Union, which may help enormously in bringing peace and prosperity in the region. The recent statement made by the former Indian Prime Minister Atal Bihari Vajpayee on introducing South Asian Union having an ultimate potential of introducing envisaged open borders, mutual security cooperation and even a single currency in the region is laudable. None is opposed to the concept of South Asian integration, and even Pakistan cautiously avers the ultimate hope expressed by Mr. Vajpayee for open border, free trade and common currency in South Asia[25]. European experience of integration has practically falsified the claim that such integration could be against the interests of smaller nations. It has also proved the fact that even historically rival countries can work together. The rivalry in South Asia compared to European Union is insignificant and very new. It is because more than half a century ago South Asians were living under one umbrella though there were petty principalities within the states where Hindus were ruled by Muslims and vice versa and never erupted War Between the States whereas same does not exist in the case of EU. Nevertheless, the existing challanges among South Asian nations can easily be sorted out if leaders of the region express genuine desire to bring about peace in the region.

Table 4.9 India's Exports with other South Asian Countries

(Million of US Dollars)

	1990	*1991*	*1992*	*1993*	*1994*	*1995*	*1996*
World Exports (DOTS):	17813	17872	18498	20258	24195	30537	32325
Bangladesh	297	325	353	430	521	960	832
Bhutan	nil	1	2	5	7	12	10
Nepal	40	77	73	75	85	107	158
Srilanka	102	175	231	247	334	383	458
Pakistan	43	40	52	58	59	70	141
Maldives	5	5	8	6	16	12	51
Toal South Asia:	**487**	**623**	**719**	**821**	**1022**	**1544**	**1650**
% Share of World:	**2.73**	**3.49**	**3.89**	**4.05**	**4.22**	**5.06**	**5.10**

(Contd.)

(Contd.Table 4.9)

	1997	1998	1999	2000	2001	2002	2003	2004	2005
World Exports (DOTS):	33248	33663	35920	42624	45224	50471	61043	75384	97918
Bangladesh	647	943	726	860	1087	1133	1600	1625	1632
Bhutan	9	11	8	3	3	31	77	85	96
Nepal	147	134	144	143	158	316	590	714	830
Srilanka	468	450	484	605	547	848	1220	1345	1867
Pakistan	186	115	96	163	219	191	267	451	642
Maldives	7	8	8	20	37	30	40	42	62
Toal South Asia:	**1464**	**1661**	**1466**	**1794**	**2051**	**2549**	**3794**	**4262**	**5129**
% Share of World:	**4.40**	**4.93**	**4.08**	**4.21**	**4.54**	**5.05**	**6.22**	**5.65**	**5.24**

Table 4.10 India's imports with other South Asian Countries

(Million of US Dollars)

	1990	*1991*	*1992*	*1993*	*1994*	*1995*	*1996*	*1997*
World Imports:	23990	19509	23227	21482	25981	34456	36055	39080
Bangladesh	15	6	10	13	34	79	58	39
Bhutan	nil	nil	1	3	3	16	17	11
Nepal	15	19	23	19	14	27	49	71
Srilanka	22	12	14	17	31	39	35	42
Pakistan	45	58	46	47	47	37	39	21
Maldives	nil	nil	nil	nil	nil	nil	nil	nil
Toal South Asia:	**97**	**95**	**94**	**99**	**129**	**198**	**198**	**184**
% Share of World:	0.40	0.49	0.40	0.46	0.50	0.57	0.55	0.47

(Contd.)

(Contd. Table 4.10)

	1998	*1999*	*2000*	*2001*	*2002*	*2003*	*2004*	*2005*
World Imports:	42162	47900	50336	58965	58912	73957	99833	134690
Bangladesh	60	74	80	67	61	74	61	104
Bhutan	8	15	20	22	30	47	51	84
Nepal	132	178	238	262	300	285	327	371
Srilanka	36	43	45	79	85	169	322	523
Pakistan	172	105	65	73	50	54	86	157
Maldives	nil	nil	nil	nil	nil	nil	nil	2
Toal South Asia:	**408**	**415**	**448**	**503**	**526**	**629**	**847**	**1241**
% Share of World:	0.97	0.87	0.89	0.85	0.89	0.85	0.85	0.92

Table 4.11 Pakistan's Exports with other South Asian Countries

	1990	*1991*	*1992*	*1993*	*1994*	*1995*	*1996*	*1997*
World Exports (DOTS)	5587	6494	7269	6701	7332	7991	9299	8632
Bangladesh	103	101	136	105	119	153	109	92
Bhutan	nil	1	1	1	1	1	1	1
Nepal	1	nil	1	nil	2	3	6	4
Srilanka	69	68	85	57	70	55	80	95
India	49	47	136	53	46	39	41	33
Maldies	1	2	2	1	1	1	3	1
Total South asia	223	219	361	217	239	252	240	226
% Share of World:	3.99	3.37	4.97	3.24	3.26	3.15	2.58	2.62

(Contd.)

(Contd. Table 4.11)

	1998	*1999*	*2000*	*2001*	*2002*	*2003*	*2004*	*2005*
World Exports (DOTS)	8433	8439	8870	9205	9883	11929	13284	14106
Bangladesh	107	106	139	119	104	166	197	131
Bhutan	nil	nil	nil	nil	nil	nil	nil	nil
Nepal	8	2	3	2	2	5	3	3
Srilanka	95	105	81	75	71	84	134	153
India	203	87	58	66	49	84	158	143
Maldies	2	1	1	2	3	3	2	3
Total South asia	415	301	282	264	229	342	494	433
% Share of World:	4.92	3.57	3.18	2.87	2.32	2.87	3.72	3.07

Table 4.12 Pakistan's Imports with other South Asian Countries

	1990	*1991*	*1992*	*1993*	*1994*	*1995*	*1996*	*1997*
World Imports(DOTS)	7383	8431	9375	9492	8884	11460	12150	11611
Bangladesh	38	37	50	38	24	35	36	44
Bhutan	nil	1	2	2	1	2	nil	nil
Nepal	nil	4	4	1	nil	1	nil	1
Srilanka	37	34	33	41	42	50	45	40
India	46	44	52	67	72	81	212	142
Maldies	nil	nil	nil	nil	nil	nil	nil	1
total with SA	121	120	141	149	139	169	293	228

(Contd.)

(Contd.Table 4.12)

	1998	*1999*	*2000*	*2001*	*2002*	*2003*	*2004*	*2005*
World Imports(DOTS)	9308	10297	10721	10165	11338	13049	17756	27333
Bangladesh	36	28	36	26	31	43	45	57
Bhutan	nil	nil	nil	nil	nil	nil	nil	nil
Nepal	1	1	3	1	1	2	4	4
Srilanka	34	37	35	27	32	43	46	53
India	154	134	178	241	163	226	455	706
Maldies	nil	nil	nil	nil	nil	nil	nil	3
total with SA	225	200	252	295	227	314	550	823

Table 4.13 Bangladesh's Exports with other South Asian Countries

	1990	*1991*	*1992*	*1993*	*1994*	*1995*	*1996*	*1997*
World Exports (DOTS)	1672	1687	2037	2277	2650	3129	3350	3628
Pakistan	23	39	30	26	19	26	37	40
Bhutan	nil	nil	nil	nil	nil	nil	nil	nil
Nepal	7	12	nil	7	14	10	nil	1
Srilanka	8	6	11	9	4	11	2	4
India	22	23	4	13	24	36	21	37
Maldies	nil	nil	nil	nil	nil	nil	nil	nil
Total South Asia	60	80	45	55	61	83	60	82
% Share of World:	3.59	4.74	2.21	2.42	2.30	2.65	1.79	2.26

(Contd.)

(Contd. Table 4.13)

	1998	1999	2000	2001	2002	2003	2004	2005
World Exports (DOTS)	3821	4520	5589	5735	5443	6229	7585	8495
Pakistan	38.76	24.87	34.52	25.6	27.18	42.7	40.46	52
Bhutan	0.4	0.69	0.9	1.48	1.41	2.38	3.64	3.3
Nepal	17.85	5.24	1.32	1.95	3.91	2.98	4.59	3.48
Srilanka	1.06	6.53	2.47	2.02	1.94	5.8	9.68	8.81
India	55.02	49.51	50.13	60.8	39.33	55.34	66.15	118.88
Maldies	nil	nil	nil	0.24	nil	nil	nil	nil
Total South Asia	113.09	86.84	89.34	92.09	73.77	109.2	124.52	186.47
% Share of World:	2.96	1.92	1.60	1.61	1.36	1.75	1.64	2.20

Table 4.14 Bangladesh's Imports with other South Asian Countries

	1990	*1991*	*1992*	*1993*	*1994*	*1995*	*1996*	*1997*
World Imports(DOTS)	3656	3421	3731	4015	4584	6496	7074	6863
Pakistan	70	57	88	90	110	138	90	69
Bhutan	7	4	4	3	8	4	5	4
Nepal	2	nil	Nil	nil	1	4	6	11
Srilanka	8	5	6	7	7	11	10	9
India	170	189	284	380	467	994	1018	796
Maldies	nil	nil	Nil	nil	nil	nil	nil	nil
Total South Asia	257	255	382	480	593	1151	1129	889
% Share of World:	7.03	7.45	10.24	11.96	12.94	17.72	15.96	12.95

(Contd.)

(Contd.Table 4.14)

	1998	*1999*	*2000*	*2001*	*2002*	*2003*	*2004*	*2005*
World Imports(DOTS)	7370	8352	9000	9010	7847	9673	11590	13850
Pakistan	73.37	85.38	93.17	85.63	59.78	95.49	121.19	143.88
Bhutan	4.81	4.35	4.53	5.07	3.3	3.84	6.05	10.44
Nepal	14.27	8.94	3.98	4.15	5.38	4.86	2.14	2.94
Srilanka	6.28	7.15	8.27	7.87	6.79	9.24	9.32	10.05
India	1178.83	1023.77	945.83	1195.49	1145.83	1494.22	1745.22	1951.24
Maldies	0.65	0.54	1.41	0.9		0.4		
Total South Asia	1278.21	1130.13	1057.19	1299.11	1221.08	1608.05	1883.92	2118.55
% Share of World:	17.34	13.53	11.75	14.42	15.56	16.62	16.25	15.30

Table 4.15 SriLanka's Exports with South Asian Countries

	1990	*1991*	*1992*	*1993*	*1994*	*1995*	*1996*	*1997*
World Exports (DOTS)	1895	1987	2488	2859	3210	3810	4097	4652
Bangladesh	10	5	7	7	9	12	12	11
India	20	13	12	20	24	32	43	44
Maldies	7	11	9	9	10	14	16	25
Nepal	nil	nil	nil	nil	nil	nil	1	2
Pakistan	32	32	29	35	43	43	37	38
Total South Asia	69	61	57	71	86	101	109	120
% Share of World:	3.64	3.07	2.29	2.48	2.68	2.65	2.66	2.58

(Contd.)

(Contd.Table 4.15)

	1998	*1999*	*2000*	*2001*	*2002*	*2003*	*2004*	*2005*
World Exports (DOTS)	4819	4621	5458	4722	4693	5298	5766	6513
Bangladesh	10.44	11.65	10.22	10.08	10.18	11.17	13.92	9.13
India	37.69	48.62	58.03	71.99	170.57	245.05	391.51	475.79
Maldies	37.39	50.02	90.94	50.45	45.91	55.46	61.43	38.7
Nepal	1.1	1.67	0.8	0.33	0.88	1.66	0.29	0.33
Pakistan	26.94	30.82	29.7	24.87	28.84	.36.73	39.45	45.08
Total South Asia	113.56	142.78	189.69	157.72	256.38	313.34	506.6	569.03
% Share of World:	2.36	3.09	3.48	3.34	5.46	5.91	8.79	8.74

Table 4.16 SriLanka's Imports with South Asian Countries

	1990	*1991*	*1992*	*1993*	*1994*	*1995*	*1996*	*1997*
World Imports(DOTS)	2636	3061	3473	4005	4767	4767	5028	5654
Bangladesh	9	4	15	7	8	6	2	2
India	118	220	307	343	404	469	562	560
Maldies	6	10	9	11	15	17	14	15
Nepal	nil	nil	nil	nil	1	1	nil	5
Pakistan	51	74	67	55	61	52	69	38
Total South Asia	184	308	398	416	489	545	647	620
% Share of World:	6.98	10.06	11.46	10.39	10.26	11.43	12.87	10.97

(Contd.)

(Contd.Table 4.16)

	1998	*1999*	*2000*	*2001*	*2002*	*2003*	*2004*	*2005*
World Imports(DOTS)	6263	6255	6688	5730	6021	6671	7999	10419
Bangladesh	1.08	4.54	3.56	2.05	3.89	5.64	7.7	9.69
India	539.33	511.6	600.14	610.48	832.07	1076.16	1439.15	2053.88
Maldies	15.48	17.85	31.37	35.11	31.12	22.65	19.84	17.77
Nepal	1.21	0.09	0.09	0.01	0.19	nil	0.08	0.09
Pakistan	90.63	94.71	72.17	73.82	65.69	70.98	107.92	123.3
Total South Asia	647.73	628.79	707.33	721.47	932.96	1175.43	1574.69	2204.73
% Share of World:	10.34	10.05	10.58	12.59	15.50	17.62	19.69	21.16

Table 4.17 Nepal's Exports with South Asian Countries

	1990	*1991*	*1992*	*1993*	*1994*	*1995*	*1996*	*1997*
World Exports (DOTS)	216	257	352	367	351	324	346	397
Bangladesh	1	Nil	nil	nil	nil	4	7	9
India	14	17	21	17	13	25	67	92
Maldies	nil	Nil	nil	nil	nil	nil	nil	nil
Pakistan	nil	4	3	1	nil	nil	nil	nil
Srilanka	nil	Nil	nil	nil	1	1	nil	nil
Total South Asia	15	21	24	18	14	30	74	101
% Share of World:	6.94	8.17	6.82	4.90	3.99	9.26	21.39	25.44

(Contd.)

(Contd.Table 4.17)

	1998	*1999*	*2000*	*2001*	*2002*	*2003*	*2004*	*2005*
World Exports (DOTS)	444	575	676	613	556	580	625	722
Bangladesh	9.6	8.12	3.62	3.77	4.89	4.42	1.94	2.94
India	145.5	161.52	216.8	239.34	273.01	259.06	296.84	371
Maldies	nil	nil	nil	nil	nil	nil	nil	nil
Pakistan	0.8	0.85	2.42	0.68	0.93	1.78	3.39	4
Srilanka	4.9	0.08	0.08	0.01	0.17		0.07	0.09
Total South Asia	160.8	170.57	222.92	243.8	279	265.26	302.24	378.03
% Share of World:	36.22	29.66	32.98	39.77	50.18	45.73	48.36	52.36

Table 4.18 Nepal's Imports with South Asian Countries

	1990	*1991*	*1992*	*1993*	*1994*	*1995*	*1996*	*1997*
World Imports(DOTS)	452	500	477	527	615	752	1348	1640
Bangladesh	8	13	nil	8	16	4	7	9
India	43	85	80	83	93	118	442	436
Maldies	nil	nil	nil	nil	nil	nil	nil	nil
Pakistan	1	1	2	nil	4	3	2	4
Srilanka	nil	nil	1	nil	nil	nil	1	
Total South Asia	52	99	83	91	113	125	452	449
% Share of World:	11.50	19.80	17.40	17.27	18.37	16.62	33.53	27.38

(Contd.)

(Contd.Table 4.18)

	1998	*1999*	*2000*	*2001*	*2002*	*2003*	*2004*	*2005*
World Imports(DOTS)	1433	1199	1058	908	1032	1414	1695	1702
Bangladesh	5.9	5.76	1.45	2.14	4.31	3.28	5.05	3.3
India	439.7	158.4	157.74	173.51	348.02	648.56	785.05	830
Maldies	nil	nil	nil	nil	nil	nil	nil	nil
Pakistan	6.2	2.05	3	2.51	2.48	5.3	3.35	3
Srilanka	2.2	1.83	0.88	0.37	0.97	1.83	0.31	0.33
Total South Asia	454	168.04	163.07	178.53	355.78	658.97	793.76	836.63
% Share of World:	31.68	14.02	15.41	19.66	34.47	46.60	46.83	49.16

References

1. Nepal Rashtra Bank, (2005), *Tne Economic Integration in South Asia* Nepal Rashtra Bank, Kathmandu, p. 7.
2. IN Mukherji, (2005), "Regional trade agreements in South Asia", in *South Asian Year Book of Trade and Development*,. p. 372.
3. The Hindu, 18/2/2007, New Delhi issue, p. 10.
4. Nepal Rashtra Bank, (2005), *The Economic Integration in South Asia, op.cit.*, p.7.
5. www.aric.adb.org.
6. DhakaDeclaration, Thirteenth SAARC Summit, 2005 Dhaka. www.aric.adb.org.
7. Nepal Rashtra Bank, 2005, *The Economic Integration in South Asia,* p. 6.
8. CUTS-CITEE briefing Paper, Economic cooperation in South Asia: Current state and prospects, No. 2, 2005. p. 3.
9. Kojima, K., "The Pattern of International Trade among Advanced Countries", *Hitotsuboshi Journal of Economics*, Vol. 5, No. 1, 1964.
10. Raghvan, S.N., (1996) *Regional Economic Cooperation among SAARC Countries,* Akash Publishers, New Delhi., p. 59.
11. *Ibid*, p. 59.
12. *Ibid*, p. 60.
13. Srinivasan, T.N., ed, (2002) *Trade Finance and Investment in South Asia,* Social Science Press, New Delhi., p. 245.
14. *Ibid.*, p. 246.
15. The Hindu, 18/2/2007, New Delhi issue, p. 10.
16. 18th December, 2005, Islamabad conferences, www.aric.adb.org)
17. "SAARC nations to work towards creating South Asian Eco Union", *Indiaexpress.com*, 6 January 2004, see at http://www. indiaexpress. com/news/business/20040106-0.html
18. The Hindustan Times 2nd July 2006. New Delhi., p. 10.
19. Dharamdasani, "Trade liberalization Among SAARC Countries" in *South Asia Politics,* Oct. 2002. p. 25.
20. (dailyIndia.com/ANI, First April, 2007)
21. S K Mohanty, Regional Trade liberalization under SAPTA and India's Trade linkages with South Asia, see in http://www.ris.org.in/dp48_pap.pdf
22. Forteenth SAARC summit, in New Delhi, 3-4th April 2007.
23. Mu Xuequan, 4-4-2007 on www.chinaview.ch.

24. Saman kelegama and Ratanakar adhikari,http://www.southasianmedia.net/Magazine/Journal/7_regionalism_debate.htm
25. Zia Iqbal Shahid 'Enlarged EU to support single currency, open borders in South Asia' at www.jang.com.pk/thenews visited on 15/06/04.

5

Comparison of Regional Economic Integration in Central Asia and South Asia

The chapter will compare objectives, significance, progress challanges and obstacles in the process of regional economic integration of both Central and South Asian regions.

The geo economic and geo strategic significance of Central Asian Region, its location between Europe and South Asia, between Middle East and Western Serbia- all this has many Centuries, made it attempting prize for various invaders. Those invaders brought different culture and more often a fusion of ethnic groups, languages. Economically these regions possesses extensive and still largely unexplored natural resources (including natural gas, petroleum gold uranium and ferrous and non-ferrous metals, primary products and IT industry and human capital) as well as the whole complex of nuclear facilities. A comparative look at both the regions shows some similarities in their process of regionalism and globalization. Central Asia was fully controlled by the Former Soviet Union and British ruled over the South Asia. The colonialism –imperialist vested interest craftily divided both the regions and sowed the seeds of confrontations, so that neither these regions could process peace in their region nor progress. Boarder issues are also the problem in both the regions. Both the regions have to face the "divide and rule" policy, and still struggling to overcome this challenge.

Moscow had decided in the 1920's and 1930's to maintain political control over Central Asia by creating five independent union-republics, with irregular and sometimes economically and ethnically irrational borders. The Soviet Union, though arbitrarily creating borders between Soviet Republics, brought a shared infrastructure to the region and allowed it to flourish as a single economic unit. The collapse of the USSR left the Central Asian states with nonsensical borders that cut through the central planned infrastructure. This interrupted trade and disrupted water and energy lines. The new borders separate farms from their water supplies and put trade and agriculture at the mercy of corrupt and inefficient border patrols.[1] (The Times of Central Asia, 2005). The economic integration of Uzbekistan, Kyrgyzstan, Tajikistan and Turkmenistan has at various time promoted and created by the Moscow. For example, Central Asian bureau of the CPSU (first established in 1924, then revived whatever their degree of in 1962-65), the State committee For Cotton cultivation, the Ministry of Construction in Central Asia and a no. of others. The concentration was to control over resources within the vast territory[2] (Rumer, 2003). Ethnic homogeneity - fairly high for Tajikistan, Turkmenistan, Kyrgyzstan, and even Uzbekistan - the former, now internationally recognized borders cut up natural economic areas. The Fergana Valley, fed by river systems rising in the mountains of Kyrgyzstan and Tajikistan, is divided among Kyrgyzstan, Uzbekistan, and Tajikistan. Moreover, the Leninabad region of Tajikistan and the Osh region of Kyrgyzstan are both separated by snow-covered mountains from their countries' respective capitals. Both of these areas have a high admixture of ethnic Uzbeks, a situation which has already led to violent confrontations over land and water rights in these border regions. These confrontations are the obstacle on the way of trade with in the region. Recently Uzbekistan has erected a barbed wire fence on its frontier with Kyrgyzstan; this has impeded, but apparently not altogether prevented, Uzbeks from crossing over and back to less trade with their relatives. That, combined with the region's isolation from the rest of the world, its poverty and remoteness, makes cooperation among the states and their neighbors crucial for their development.

The present political configuration of South Asia is the result of the process of de colonialisation that followed the end of Second World War 1945. The colonialism imperialist vested interest craftily divided India and Pakistan and sowed the seeds of confrontations.[3] In South Asia the Kashmir Valley is the source of confrontation. The tussle between Pakistan and India are obstacle in the way of flourishing trade among South Asian Countries. Despite the powers SAARC and CAREC initiative have, these initiatives are not much successful in the region like other Asian and European initiatives.

Both the regions are sailing in the same boat; they can understand each other well and help each other in improving trade facilitation, trade transit routes with each other. Kazakhstan can play an important role in bridging the gap between Europe and south Asia and India can play in bridging the gap between South East Asian Countries and Central Asia. Both the regions need to look at each other and undertake measures for regional economic co-operation for mutual benefit. They have shown great potentialities of higher economic growth. Central Asian countries are source of energy (oil, natural gas etc.) which are highly demanded in the South Asian countries especially by India and Pakistan. India fulfills its energy requirement mainly through imports from West Asia. Central Asia can explore Indian demands. South Asia could be a supplier of basic commodities, services etc for the Central Asian countries.

Central Asia has significant seasonal electricity surpluses and the potential to develop thousands of megawatts in new capacity. Its hydroelectric potential is particularly tempting. And gas and coal resources add to that capacity. For its part, South Asia needs energy to fuel its economic expansion. By 2015, Pakistan projects electricity demand to more than double. India's growing economy requires the addition of a nearly 50 percent increase in capacity by 2012. And while the Kyrgyz Republic currently earns about one U.S. cent per kilowatt hour on power sold northward, just think of the opportunities since Pakistan's power generation costs average about 5 cents while India's cost for generating power may be double even that. So the opportunities are great if and it remains an "if countries can cooperate to develop the right infrastructure and investment regime. That's why there are need to work closely with the countries of the region, including Tajikistan, as well with International Financial Institutions and the private sector, to bring such ideas into feasibility. Multilateral institutions are trying to help both the region in the areas of trade facilitation, transit, infrastructure etc. To link both the regions some initiatives are already underway. With the help of ADB in 2003, Pakistan, Afghanistan, Tajikistan and Uzbekistan signed an agreement called Central and South Asian Transport and Trade Forum (CSATTF)[4] (Chowdhary, Sachdeva, 2005, 2007) . The idea is to link north-south and east west trade and transport corridor linking Central Asia with the Indian Ocean.

Recently Iranian Foreign Minister also proposed the West Asian Economic Bloc comprising Iran, Pakistan, India and Central Asian Region. This would enhance the regional connectivity. Afghanistan has also become a member of SAARC[5]. Pakistan and Afghanistan are already members of the Economic Co-Operation Organization (ECO). ECO has signed FTA agreement with the ASEAN Other countries in the grouping are Azerbaijan, Iran Kazakhstan, Kyrgyz Republic, Tajikistan, Turkey, Turkmenistan and Uzbekistan. These links could be strengthened as many multilateral organizations are also trying to re-establish the old trade and other routes in Asia. The United Nations Asian Highway Project is already undergoing the process that will connect the South–East Asia with West Asia. Routes (rail, road, inter-modal) within the Asian Countries have been identified and agreements on the routes reached between the countries concerned. It has been revealed through the global experiences that improved transport integration leads to increased volume of trade at the regional as well as inter-regional trade. This would allow member countries to effectively exploit their comparative advantages and competitiveness. The price of non-cooperation could also be large. Lost economic opportunities and difficult access to markets would mean poor employment prospects, and slow progress in reducing poverty. These countries have already missed the bus to get maximum benefits from globalization and liberalsation. South East Asian countries and china gets maximum benefits by liberalsing their economic policies in 1970s.

Central Asia and neighboring countries are strategically located, rich in natural resources and at the cross-roads of commerce between some of the most dynamic of the world's economies. New avenues for trade and access to world markets and knowledge are opening up, reenergizing the enterprise of Silk Road legend. Regional organizations have been created and are gaining in strength, reflecting the shared conviction that borders that divide are borders lacking a human face[6]. There is a need to discuss ways to boost Central and South Asian economic activity with private businessmen, corporate multinational companies to explore maximum potential.

The success of European Union(EU) and North American Free Trade Area(NAFTA) compel these economies to think about the regional economic co-operations[7], as already explained in detail in second chapter of this book. Both the regions have taken step to cooperate within the regions Many regional initiative have been taken within the Central Asia and South Asia. Here this book will discus about all the regional initiatives in detail and compare the regions. First this book will compare the objectives of the regional economic initiatives in both the regions.

Comparison of Main Objectives of regional economic initiatives of both the Regions

Box. d

CAREC program is to promote economic growth and raise living standards by encouraging economic cooperation in the region. The program has focused on financing the infrastructure projects and improving the policy environment for promoting cross border activities in the areas of transport (especially road transport), energy (including the water energy nexus), trade policy and trade facilitation (especially customs cooperation)".

CACO's purpose is to increase regional cooperation; fight regional crime; create a unified economic space; harmonize customs and boarder policies; and expand water and environmental cooperation. Its aim is to expand cooperation in politics,

(Contd.)

(Contd.)

economics, transport and energy infrastructure, water and energy resources, agricultural trade, science, technology, environment, culture tourism, sports humanitarian issues and regional safety and stability.

CIS- -aim at serving for future development -strengthening the relationship of friendship, good neighborhood, inter ethinic harmony, trust, mutual understanding and mutually cooperation among members

ECO-These include sustainable development of member states, including progressive removal of trade barriers and promotion of intra-regional trade, a greater role of the ECO region in the growth of the world trade, and gradual integration of the economies of the member states with the world economy. Other objectives cover the development of transport and communication infrastructure linking the member states with each other and with the outside the world, economic liberalization and privatization and mobilization and utilization of ECO states, material statistics.

EEC-The primary goals are the establishment of common market for labour and capital, free intra community trade and trade policy harmonization. The 2004 summit in almaty declared that an important component is the coordination of WTO accession by the members states. One current EEC activity is to develop an agreement among Iran/Kazakstan ,Russia and Tajikstan to rehabilitate hydro-electric power plants in Tajikstan.

The SCO goals are ' to strengthen mutual trust, friendship and good –neighborliness between the member states to encourage effective cooperation between them in the political,trade and economic , scientific and technical , cultural , educational , energy , transport , environmental and other spheres , and to undertake joint efforts for the maintenance of peace ,security and stability in the region , the building of a new , democratic ,just and rational international political and economic order.'

SAARC-The main objective behind this was to promote the welfare of the peoples of the member countries and improve their quality of life, accelerate economic growth, social progress, cultural development and peace prosperity in the region. Although

(Contd.)

(Contd.)

economic co-operation should be first priority to bring stability in the region, SAFTA agreements signed by the SAARC countries the main objectives: To promote and enhance mutual trade among these countries. Try to eliminate barriers to trade in, and facilitating the cross-boarder movement of goods between the territories of the contracting states. Promote conditions of fair competition in Free trade areas and ensuring equitable benefits to all countries. To Create effective mechanism for implementation and application of this agreement. Under this the special provision has been given to the LDCs. BIMSTEC countries Implementation of transport linkages and physical connectivity among the member countries would generate huge benefits and made expedite the trading process.

If this study look into the regional economic initiatives in both the regions and compare, this will find that the objective behind all these efforts was to promote welfare of the people, to improve quality of life to bring stability in the regions. The efforts have been taken to improve infrastructure and transport linkages to reduce barriers to enhance trade for the last fifteen years. These regions are trying to control criminal activities and corruption. The question arises after taking so efforts both the regions lagging behind as compare to other regions.

Regional Economic Initiatives in Central Asia

. It has been observed that efforts to create greater regional economic cooperation are not only being imposed from the outside but they are willing to do so but due to some kind of insecurity towards their independent countries or the fear of hegemony of bigger countries stop them to implement the agreements signed by the authorities of the country. Kazakhstan, "recognized regional leader," is promoting greater economic cooperation not only within the former Soviet republics. Kazakhstan is pushing for more cooperation with Afghanistan as well, and also pledged that it was willing and able to make a meaningful contribution to the postwar reconstruction of Afghanistan, particularly assisting in oil field in northern Afghanistan[8]. Many agreements have been signed by the authorities of all the Central Asian countries so far.

"Ministers agreed that the way forward for Central Asia is 'development through cooperation'... Ministers called for sweeping measures to overcome trade and other impediments to development, and for the creation of transport corridors and the interconnection of energy markets. Ministers expressed interest in cooperative initiatives in a wide range of areas, including the environment, agriculture, tourism, human resource development, telecommunications, disaster management and avian flu preparedness... Ministers agreed that a strategic framework for regional cooperation is essential for charting the course ahead."[9] Joint Ministerial Statement, November 2005.

The Central Asia Regional Economic Co-operation Intitiatives (CAREC)

Building on the increasing trust and confidence among countries participating in the Central Asia Regional Economic Cooperation (CAREC) Program, Ministers called for a deepening of the program's agenda. "Through coordinated action Central Asia can build on its strengths and again become a vital trade route linking the countries of the famed Silk Road between Asia and Europe[10]"(The times of Central Asia, 2005)

Members: Azerbaijan, China, Kazakhstan, Kyrgyzstan, Mongolia Tajikstan and Uzbekistan.

History: The Asian Development established CAREC in 1997 to support increased economic cooperation among the Central Asian Countries. In 2003, CAREC expanded to include the EBRD, the IMF, the Islamic Development, UNDP and the World Bank. CAREC is the primary mechanism for multilateral donor coordination throughout the region.

Priorities: the objective in the transport sector is to rehabilitate transport networks to lesson geographic isolation and reduce transport costs. In the energy sector, the goal is to support efficient and rational use of energy and water through cooperation.

CAREC is a multi-institutional, multinational alliance, there are six multilateral institutions: the Asian Development Bank, the

European Bank for Reconstruction and Development, the Islamic Development Bank, the International Monetary Fund, the World Bank, as well as the United Nations Development Program 2006-07, the institutions in CAREC will provide more than $1.5 billion in the priority areas of transport, energy, and trade11 (Comprehensive Plan.) Asian Development Bank (ADB) Vice President Liqun Jin told the conference the Central Asian republics recently have registered a 10 percent average overall gross domestic product (GDP) growth, with Turkmenistan and Kazakhstan on the high end of the scale. He said the formation of the Central Asia Regional Economic Cooperation (CAREC) program in 1997 has provided benefits to the region by opening transport corridors to South Asia[12].

CAREC's overarching goal is development through cooperation, leading to accelerated economic growth and poverty reduction. CAREC's Long-term Vision: "Good Neighbours, Good Partners, and Good Prospects."

The Strategic Framework incorporates the following themes:

- Strategic direction and ownership, by the participating countries
- Connectivity, enabling business enterprises to access regional and global markets
- Knowledge and capacity-building, facilitating consensus and deal-making
- New approaches to development through cooperation, to include greater emphasis on policy initiatives, new sectors, and new concepts (e.g., economic corridors) As part of the emphasis on strategic direction, over the next year each of CAREC's transport, trade (facilitation and policy) and energy coordinating committees will develop medium-term sector strategies. Further, regional cooperation will be mainstreamed into country national development plans. Knowledge and capacity-building activities will be intensified in support of strategic direction, ownership and mainstreaming. Connectivity reflects the need of CAREC countries to turn their landlocked status into a land link for Eurasia, and to enable business enterprises to more readily access regional and global markets. CAREC must succeed in

helping to overcome barriers and impediments to trade in the region. New approaches to development through cooperation will contribute to momentum and gaining a wider appreciation of the benefits of regional cooperation.

The CAREC program also includes Afghanistan, Mongolia and the Xinjiang Uighur Autonomous Region of China, facilitating contacts of the Central Asian republics with their neighbors. However, Turkmenistan is not a member, and Russia is considering an invitation to participate. Central Asia's increased efforts to peddle its gas and oil abroad have highlighted that region's economic potential.

The Central Asian Cooperation Organisation (CACO)

Members: Kazakhstan, Kurgyzstan, Russia, Tajikstan and Uzbekistan

Observers: Afghanistan, Georgia, Turkey and Ukraine

History: Originally formed in 1994 as central Asian Economic Union (CAEU) by Kazakhstan, Kyrgyzstan, and Uzbekistan, it was expanded in 1998 to include Tajikstan and it was renamed Central Asia Economic Cooperation(CAEC). The attention behind CAEC was to create an integrated economic space and provide a mechanism for encouraging regional projects. In February 2002, CAEU established the interstate Central Asian Bank of cooperation and Development.

In 1995 Kazakhstan and Kyrgyzstan formed a customs union with Belarus and Russia, with Tajikistan joining in 1999. In October 2000, the customs union became the Eurasian Economic Community (EAEC). Ukraine, Moldova, and Armenia have also been granted observer status in the EAEC. As a result of the merger between EAEC and CACO, Uzbekistan gained membership in 2006. Its main objective is "to create the necessary conditions for cooperation between the member countries in the trade, economic, social, humanitarian and legal spheres with an optimal balance of national and common interests." Its stated long-term objective is to promote the creation of a customs union and the Common Economic Space, as well as to ensure the effective execution of other objectives defined in the Customs Union Agreement of January, 1995, and related agreements of 1996 and 1999. In 1994,

Kazakhstan, Kyrgyzstan, and Uzbekistan formed the Central Asian Union (CAU). The aim was to create a single economic space with improvements in payment arrangements and reduction in tariffs among member countries. In 1995, CAU members approved the principle of free trade. A Central Asian Bank for Cooperation and Development was also created. In 1998, Tajikistan joined the group. During the same year the organization was renamed the Central Asian Economic Community (CAEC). In 2001, the CAEC became the Central Asian Cooperation Organization (CACO) and Russia joined the organization in May 2004. Ukraine, Georgia, and Turkey were given observer status. In 2005, the member states of EAEC and CACO agreed to allow Uzbekistan to join the EAEC and to merge both organizations. This merger could lead to improved opportunities for meaningful regional cooperation. It also raises serious issues regarding harmonizing Uzbekistan's restrictive trade policies in line with other countries.

The Commonwealth of Independent States (CIS)

Nine CIS countries: Azerbaijan, Armenia, Belarus, Kazakhstan, Kyrgyzstan, Moldova, Russia, Tajikistan and Uzbekistan signed the CIS Economic Union Agreement. Ukraine joined the agreement as an Associate Member. Georgia and Turkmenistan did not sign it.

History: Belarus, Russia and Ukraine established in CIS in 1993 all of the former Soviet republics on principals of sovereign equality of all its members and aims at serving for the future development and strengthening of the relationship of friendship, good neighborhood inter ethnic harmony, trust, mutual understanding and mutually advantageous cooperation among the member states.

An official Economic Union Treaty was established in 1993 to manage and encourage economic interaction within the member states. The Treaty was based on the nessesity to formation of the common economic space on the principles of free movements of the goods, services, workers, capitals, elaboration of concentrated money and credit, tax, price, customs and economic policies, rapprochement of the methods of the management of economic activities, creation of favorable conditions for development of direct production links.

Four Central Asian countries are important members of the Commonwealth of the Independent States (CIS). This organization has not implemented a customs union or a free trade area covering all member states, but in September, 2003, the idea of Single Economic Space (SES) (sometimes called the "Common Economic Space" or "Common Economic Area") was introduced during a CIS Summit in Yalta. Among the states of a Greater Central Asia, only Kazakhstan is the member of the SES. The problem with the SES is that almost every member is pursuing a different goal. Russia and Belarus sought to create a customs union and a monetary union based on the ruble. Kazakhstan preferred a monetary union based on a new currency called the "Altyn." Ukraine feels that the Union conflicts with its European objective, and hence would like to see it as a free trade area. Despite these inherent problems, member states are trying hard to make it a meaningful organization. The parties have taken only very limited steps to fulfill their high sounding commitments.

Several regional organizations were created out of the CIS framework. These appear to have been more successful in their interventions. They include The Russia- Belarus Union State, the single economic space and the Eurasian Economic Community.

The Collective Security Treaty Organization:

In 1992, Armenia, Kazakhstan, Kyrgyzstan, Russia, Tajikistan and Uzbekistan signed the CIS collective Security Treaty. Azerbaijan, Belarus and Georgia signed in 1993. All signatories agreed to refuse the use of the threat of force. In 1999, Azerbaijan, Georgia and Uzbekistan choose not to renew their commitments to the treaty and official withdrew. In 2002, the six remaining members reaffirmed their commitment with a new charter and a New name- The collective Security Treaty Organization.

The Economic Cooperation Organization

Members: Afghanistan, Azerbaijan, Iran, Kazakhstan, Kyrgyzstan, Pakistan, Tajikistan, Turkey, Turkmenistan and Uzbekistan.

History: Iran, Pakistan and Treaty, created the ECO in 1985 "for the purpose of promoting economic technical and cultural cooperation among the member states" in 1992. It was enlarged with the addition of Afghanistan, Azerbaijan, Kazakhstan, Kyrgyzstan, Tajikistan, Turkmenistan and Uzbekistan. ECO was formed in 1985 with Pakistan, Iran, and Turkey as its only members, but Afghanistan, Azerbaijan, Kyrgyzstan, Tajikistan, Turkmenistan, and Uzbekistan joined in 1992. Some politicians in the member nations see the ECO as a potential Muslim common market, but political rivalries, especially between Iran and Turkey, limit its effectiveness. In 1994 most of the concrete measures being taken by the ECO concerned the improvement of transportation and communications among the member nations, including the construction of a highway from Turkey to Pakistan through Iran.

The organisation has signed a number of agreements with various multilateral agencies like the UNDP, ASEAN, and the Islamic Development Bank (IDB).However, the dozen agreements and MOUs signed by the ECO members, only four agreements have become operational. Immediately after the disintegration of the former Soviet Union, six new members (Afghanistan, Azerbaijan, Kazakhstan, Kyrgyzstan, Tajikistan, Turkmenistan and Uzbekistan) were admitted in the organization. All the Central Asian countries have joined the ECO. All CA countries have also joined the Organization of Islamic Conference (OIC), an intergovernmental organization with 56 members, established in 1971 in Saudi Arabia. Its aim is to promote Islamic solidarity by improving cooperation in the political, economic, social and cultural, and scientific fields.

The Shangahi Cooperation Organization (SCO)

Memebers: China, Kazakhstan, Kyrgyzstan, Russia, Tajikstan and Uzbekistan

Observers: India, Iran, Mongolia, Pakistan

History: The SCO emerged from the Shanghai five group created in 1996 by China, Kazakhstan, Kyrgyhtsan, Russia, and Tajikstan. The SCO was established in June 2001 in Shanghai, China, with the addition of Uzbeksitan. Iran and Pakistan both applied for membership 2005. The primary areas of focus for the

SCO have been in security and economic cooperation with security being the primary focus SCO security cooperation 'focuses on the fight against terrorism, separatism and extremism 'The SCOs secretariat is based in Beijing while the Regional Anti-Terrorism structure is based in Tashkent. China and Russia, Kazakhstan, Kyrgyzstan, Tajikistan and Uzbekistan are also members of the Shanghai Cooperation Organization (SCO). The SCO was founded in 2001 on the basis of its predecessor, the Shanghai Five grouping. It began as a forum for discussing border delineation issues, but as a result of the threat of terrorism in the region, it now focuses more on security issues. Economic cooperation among its members is also envisaged.

The Single Economic Space (SES)

Members: Belarus, Kazakhstan, Russia and Ukraine

History: Signed in an agreement in Yalta in September 2003,the SES is also called the Common Economic Space the United Economic Space Implementation of the agreement remains to be completed especially in view of Ukraine's uncertain commitment to the SES.

Objectives: The goal is to create a single economic space, preceded initially by a free trade zone and then a customs union, in conformity with WTO rules. Russia also has promoted the idea of a single currency, and advocated decreasing tariff and customs barriers.

The Special Programme for the Economies of Central Asia (SPECA)

Members: Afghanistan, Azerbaijan, Kazakhstan, Kyrgyzstan, Tajikistan, Turkmenistan and Uzbekistan.

History: SPECA was established in March 1998 by the presidents of Kazakhstan, Kyrgyzstan, Tajikistan and Uzbekistan. Turkmenistan joined the same year. Azerbaijan in 2002 and Afghanistan is expected to join in 2005. The programme is implemented with the support of UNECE and UNESCAP as well as other partners.

Coal and Metal Association

Azerbaijan, Armenia, Belarus, Georgia, Kazakhstan, Kyrgyzstan, Moldova, Russia, Tajikistan, Ukraine and Uzbekistan established the "Eurasian Association of Coal and Metal". The primary purpose of the Association was to create favorable conditions for the development of coal and metal industries, including promotion of rational use of raw materials, coordination of scientific-technical and investment policies, and promotion of terms of supply and sale that are mutually beneficial to the parties involved in sale/purchase transactions. The Association aimed to takes into consideration interests of all member countries in a manner that would prevent unfair competition and creation of monopolies.[13] (Sanaullah, 2003)

Regional Economic initiatives in South Asia

SAFTA

SAARC was founded in the mid-1980s primarily as a vehicle to increase trade within South Asia by declining the region's political conflicts from economic cooperation. Its seven member states—Bangladesh, Bhutan, India, Maldives, Nepal, Pakistan, and Sri Lanka adopted the principle of unanimity in selecting multilateral questions for debate. Despite frequent consultative committee meetings, progress toward increased trade remained limited in 1994. Pakistan's trade with India, for instance, is extremely limited. At the annual SAARC summit in April 1993, members agreed to negotiate a South Asian Preferential Trade Agreement by 1996 that would lower or abolish tariffs among members. The conclusion of the Summit meeting of the South Asian Association for Regional Cooperation (SAARC) on 6 January 2004 has instilled hope across the ESCAP region. Major outcomes of the Summit include the conclusion of a long-awaited regional free trade agreement between the seven SAARC members, the signing of the SAARC Social Charter and of an Additional Protocol to the SAARC Regional Convention on Suppression of Terrorism. The Summit furthermore declared that poverty alleviation should be the overarching goal of all SAARC activities, and approved a report by the Independent Commission on Poverty Alleviation, which sets out a road map for poverty alleviation in the subregion. A decision towards the establishment of a South Asian development bank was taken, and the establishment of a food bank and a South Asian fund on poverty alleviation were proposed. Decisions were also taken to initiate studies on the feasibility of a common currency for the subregion and eventually the setting up of a South Asian economic union, as well as on creating South Asian energy cooperation. However, equally important for the development of the subregion is the announcement, on the sidelines of the meeting, of the start of bilateral talks between India and Pakistan.

SAFTA Agreements

A major outcome of the Summit is the long-awaited agreement to set up a free trade area among the SAARC members. The South Asia Free-Trade Area (SAFTA) will come into force on 1 January 2006, upon completion of the formalities including ratification by all contracting States, and will reduce intraregional tariffs to a level of 0- 5 per cent within 10 years from the date of entering into force. Within two years, i.e. by 1 January 2008, tariffs will be reduced to a maximum level of 20 per cent (30 per cent for LDCs). (If actual tariff rates after the coming into force of the agreement were below these percentages, then there shall be an annual reduction on a margin of preference basis of 10 per cent (5 per cent for LDCs) on actual tariff rates for each of the two years.) The subsequent tariff reduction to 0-5 per cent for all SAARC countries will be done within a second time frame of 5 years (6 years for Sri Lanka and 8 years for LDCs), beginning from the third year from the date of coming into force of the agreement. Thus, the final date of implementation is 1 January 2013 for India and Pakistan, 2014 for Sri Lanka, and 2016 for Bangladesh, Bhutan, the Maldives and Nepal. These schedules will not, however, prevent contracting States from immediately reducing their tariffs to 0-5 per cent or from following an accelerated schedule of tariff reduction. For the import and export of products of least developed contracting States (Bangladesh, Bhutan, Maldives and Nepal), the non-least developed contracting States (India, Pakistan and Sri Lanka) commit to reducing their tariff to 0-5 per cent within a time frame of three years beginning from 1 January 2006. See Table 4.6 in chapter 4.

Special treatment to LDC.

The agreement sets up a sensitive list where products exempted from the Trade Liberalization Programme will be listed.

This list will be negotiated by the contracting States and incorporated in the agreement as an integral part. However, the number of products in the sensitive lists will be subject to maximum ceiling, which will be mutually agreed among the contracting States, with flexibility to least developed contracting States to seek derogation in respect of the products of their export interest. Furthermore, the agreement stipulates that the sensitive list shall be reviewed every four years or sooner, as may be decided by SAFTA Ministerial Council, with a view to reducing the number of items in the sensitive list.

They also agree to consider the adoption of trade facilitation and other measures to support and complement the Trade Liberalization Programme. These may include, among others, the following: harmonization of standards the reciprocal recognition of tests and accreditation of testing laboratories of contracting states and certification of products; simplification and harmonization of customs clearance procedures; harmonization of national customs classification based on HS coding system; customs cooperation to resolve dispute at customs entry points; simplification and harmonization of import licensing and registration procedures; simplification of banking procedures for import financing; transit facilities for efficient intra-SAARC trade, especially for the land-locked contracting states; removal or barriers to intra-SAARC investments; macroeconomic consultations; rules for fair competition and the promotion of venture capital; development of communication systems and transport infrastructure; making exceptions to foreign exchange restrictions and repatriation of such payments, and; simplification of procedures for business visas.

They also agree to give special regard to the situation of LDCs when considering the application of anti-dumping and/or countervailing measures, to consider greater flexibility for LDCs in continuation of quantitative restrictions as well as to take direct trade measures (such as buy-back arrangements, state trading operations and public procurement) with a view to sustainable exports from LDCs, as well as to establish an appropriate mechanism to compensate LDCs for their loss of customs revenue until alternative domestic arrangements are formulated to address the situation. Rules of Origin will be negotiated by the contracting

States and will be incorporated into the SAFTA agreement as an integral part.

Although some analysts have found that countries in South Asia compete with similar products and would therefore not have much to gain from a regional trade agreement, others have contradicted this position and estimated there to be a large potential for intra-regional trade and thus for gains from a regional free trade agreement. For one, bigger countries like India and Pakistan are said to have a lot to gain, especially as currently a lot of trade between the two countries is routed through third countries. Trade between the two neighbors amounted officially to US$ 200 million in 2003, but many analysts put the real figure at around US$ 1-2 billion if the trade that is routed through third countries is counted. Secondly, it is generally known that the main gains from trade liberalization actually accrue to the liberalizing country itself. Thus, since a large part of the gain from regional trade agreements come from resources for production being allocated in a more efficient way, it is important that the number of products on the sensitive list is kept to a minimum, and that industrial restructuring is allowed to take place. Furthermore, appropriate measures need to be taken to address the problems in the protected sectors with a view to removing the products from the list as soon as possible. Thirdly, a regional trade agreement also has many other beneficial implications. With properly constructed trade agreements, growing interdependence in trade can have politically beneficial consequences. This in turn can improve the investment climate and further stimulate economic growth and trade. Improved political relations in the region could also help in rationalizing the subcontinent's energy resources, thus further increasing the potential for trade and growth. Moreover, with several countries in the region now taking part in many regional, plurilateral and bilateral trade agreements, besides from being members of WTO, efforts should be made to assure that these agreements are mutually compatible. The ultimate objective would be to devise a framework of common principles, practices and procedures that would coalesce and rationalize these initiatives. Its main focus is to put people at the centre of development and to direct the economies to meet human needs more effectively. Furthermore, it states that access to basic education, adequate housing, safe drinking water and sanitation and primary healthcare should be guaranteed in legislation, executive and administrative provisions, in addition to ensuring adequate standard of living, including adequate shelter, food and clothing. The member states also pledge to provide universal education to children between six to fourteen years, to provide the youth access to education, and job opportunities, to promote the status of women and facilitate their participation in the local, regional and national development process as well as reduce the gender gap in literacy and education, and to promote the rights and well-being of children. The member states will integrate the provisions into their national plans of action and other processes for policy-making. National co-ordination committees, or a similar mechanism as may be decided in each country, shall look after and facilitate the implementation for these opportunities.

BIMSTEC

In addition to SAFTA, there are a number of sub-regional initiatives for trade liberalization. The Bangladesh-Bhutan-India-Nepal Growth Quadrilateral Initiative (BBIN-GQ) is being pursued under the SAARC framework. Its prime objective is to promote rapid economic development through the identification and implementation of specific projects. The Bangladesh-India-Myanmar-Sri Lanka-Thailand Economic Cooperation (BIMST-EC) is outside the SAARC process and includes two countries that belong to the Association of South East Asian Nations (ASEAN). Later, Bhutan and Nepal also joined this initiative BIMSTEC covers a population of approximately 1.3 billion and combined GDP of about $1.3 trillion. The forum is the first formal link between South Asia and South East Asia, bridging India's look East Policy with Thailand's Look West Policy. Broad sectors for cooperation identified at the First Summit level meeting held in July 2004 covered trade and investment, technology, tourism, transport and communication, energy, and fisheries. For India, BIMSTEC resolves the problem of slow movement in South Asian cooperation by eliminating Pakistan and including Myanmar and Thailand. So far, Thailand has been the real thrust giver to this regional grouping. Besides providing a link between South East Asia and South Asia, BIMSTEC can serve Indian interests through the exploitation of its massive potential in hydroelectricity and hydrocarbons. Issues of hydroelectricity and natural gas supply from Nepal and Bangladesh have to be addressed. BIMSTEC offers to open vast markets to Indian interests (that are already open to it through other trade agreements), and yet the low levels of trade and investment suggest that these opportunities have not been fully utilized. In 2003, India's trade with BIMSTEC was $6 billion, about 3.5-4 % of India's global trade. Apart from Nepal and to an extent Myanmar, the trade of the other countries with BIMSTEC is miniscule and offers opportunities for greater expansion. Member countries for example, should work towards greater air transport liberalization, short-sea shipping, and trilateral highway linkages among India, Myanmar and Thailand and between Bangladesh, Myanmar and Thailand, including linkages with other BIMSTEC countries implementation of transport linkages and physical connectivity among the member countries would generate huge benefits and made expedite the trading process.

Bilateral trade agreements are also very common among SAARC member countries. Indo-Bhutan economic cooperation stems from a 1949 treaty that creates free trade and commerce between the two countries. India has been the principal donor of foreign aid to Bhutan. Indo-Nepal economic relations are governed by the Treaty of Trade, Treaty of Transit and Agreement for Cooperation to Control Unauthorized Trade. These agreements state that, with few exceptions, India will import goods from Nepal without import duty or other restrictions.

The Indo-Sri Lanka Free Trade Agreement (ISFTA) was signed in 1998 and became effective in March 2000. Similarly, a free trade agreement has been signed between Pakistan and Sri Lanka. Other bilateral agreements are in various stages of negotiation.

By comparing both the regions, this study concludes that the economic cooperation within the regions is slow as compare to other regions. Even the trade among the Central Asian countries is on the decreasing trend in percentage but in South Asia it has been increasing trend since their liberalization.

Their efforts focused on ways to position Central Asia and Afghanistan as a regional crossroads for trade. Research Studies suggested that global conditions are ripe for economic gains in Central Asia, and stressed the need for regional cooperation and the participation of international financial institutions. Brent Dark, deputy resident director of the Asian Development Bank's (ADB) office in Washington, described the business climate in Central Asia as "improved" but "far from perfect." Truckers and traders faced closed roads on a daily basis," Dark said. "Small business owners are struggling to stay competitive in new market economies. Something as simple as obtaining a tourist visa is time-consuming and expensive." He suggested, however, the potential for economic growth in the region remains strong. Its key advantage, he said, is its location." With proximity to rapidly growing markets like China, India, and Russia, all of which have huge demands for energy and with the greater transit access to the sea through Afghanistan, the region is well poised to reap the benefits of its strategic location,". Dark said the ADB believes that if the global economic environment remains favorable and if Central Asian countries continue to press ahead with necessary economic reforms — per capita incomes could double by 2015[14]. (Dark, 2006) The ADB predicts that commodity exports, especially oil and gas, will be the primary driver of growth in the region. To encourage regional cooperation, the ADB initiated a program called Central Asia Regional Economic Cooperation (CAREC). The operational strategy of CAREC is to finance infrastructural projects and improve the policy environment for promoting cross-border activities in the areas of trade, energy, and transportation. The United Nations also started a Special Program for the Economies of Central Asia (SPECA) in 1997. The objective of the program is to strengthen regional cooperation in order to stimulate economic development and facilitate integration into Europe and Asia. Another international initiative, known as the CIS 7 Initiative, promotes poverty reduction, growth, and debt sustainability in the following seven low-income CIS countries: Armenia, Azerbaijan, Georgia, the Kyrgyz Republic, Moldova, Uzbekistan and Tajikistan. The initiative is sponsored by the following organizations: ADB, EBRD, IMF and IDA (part of the World Bank), and a group of bilateral creditors and donors. Currently 24 countries participate in the CIS 7 Initiative and an additional six organizations and countries act as observers. These include Canada, China, the European Union, the Organization for Economic Cooperation and Development (OECD), the IDB, France, Germany, Italy, Japan, Russia, Turkey, the United Kingdom, and the United States.

Other regional initiatives, including the Inter-governmental Commission on Central Asian Sustainable Development, the Inter-State Water Commission, the Central Asian Energy Advisory Group, and Regional Electricity Grid, focus on technical issues .Afghanistan's membership into the South Asian Association for Regional Cooperation (SAARC) in late 2005 created a new dimension in the economic integration of Greater Central Asia. Afghanistan's membership to SAARC has the potential to fundamentally change and rejuvenate regional economic linkages between the South and Central Asian regions. Central Asia also includes a significant scientific technical intelligentsia and a level of higher education than found elsewhere in the Muslim world.

During the first month of independence theses states aimed an intensive search for new ties with Muslim countries. In May 1992, they held a summit in Ashgabat in the capital of the Turkmenistan. Central Asian region joined the organization for economic co-operation (OEC) which has previously consisted of the Muslim States of Iran, Turkey and

In Dushanbe last October, Afghanistan, Kyrgyzstan, Pakistan and Tajikistan signed a memorandum of understanding for a model project to trade 1,000 megawatts of electricity, if feasibility studies demonstrate economic viability. The World and Asian Development Banks (ADB) are financing these studies, which should allow concrete decisions to move forward by mid-2007 and electricity trade to begin in 2010. If the international community can help build these power lines and if they can supply reliable electricity on a sustained basis more investors will be looking to develop Central Asia's hydropower to help meet consumer need as it explained in detail in 3rd chapter of this book.

The difference in economic potential of the various Central and South Asian countries are enormous. As mentioned earlier, progress in South Asia is slow because of political problems between India and Pakistan. In Central Asia, Kazakhstan and Uzbekistan have competed for regional leadership. And Turkmenistan is least interested in regional economic integration.

There are several factors which have been responsible for poor expansion of Intra regional Trade between both the regions but common are :

Differ in Terms of Size

Central Asia: There are different geographic, demographic, natural resources endowments, social environmental conditions among all the Central Asian countries. Kazakhstan has enormous fossil fuel reserves and significant supplies of minerals and metals. Kyrgyzstan is predominantly an agricultural economy and Kyrgyzstan and Tajikistan are more dependent on other countries of the region. Tajikistan is mountainous country with little oil and natural gas and significant underdeveloped and hydropower potential. Turkmenistan is desert country and largest producer of cotton. Uzbekistan is a dry and double land locked country with sixty percent of the population is living in the rural areas.

South Asia: There are different geographic, demographic, natural resources endowments, social, environmental conditions among the South Asian countries. South Asian economies differ significantly in size, For example India accounts for more than three-fourth of the regions GDP while Srilanka and Nepal have only 3 percent and 0.9 percent of the regional GDP, respectively. Pakistan and Bangladesh with medium sized economies account for 12.5 percent and 8.4 percent, respectively of the regional GDP. There are also sharp variations in per capita income among all the countries of the region[15].

Common Legacies of Russian Empire and British Empire

Central Asia : Another reason why regional integration remains limited at the moment could also be attributed to history. Having been dominated by the the Soviet Union for decades, the Central Asian States are working to assert their own national independence, autonomy and identity[16]. The presence of a "dependent" feeling in Central Asia is important to note when examining the region. Since its inclusion in the Russian Empire, Central Asia has been a subsidized region. Analysis by experts of the European community on the distribution processes in the Soviet economy (based on data from 1988) showed that every Central Asian republic had a trade deficit with the Russia Federation. This deficit was covered by subsidies totaling 18.86 billion dollars. According to the data from the International Monetary Fund, subsidies in 1991 made up 44 percent of the budget of Tajikistan, 43 percent of the budget of Uzbekistan, 34 percent of Kyrgyzstan's budget, 23 percent of Kazakhstan's budget, and 22 percent of Turkmenistan's budget. Reduction of subsidies had truly detrimental effects in the social and economic spheres, and led to a general growth in dissatisfaction with Russia. Furthermore, Central Asian leaders have not yet been able to modernize the economy. For example, Uzbekistan is demanding that Russia should pay world prices for its cotton, but that they continue to receive energy resources from Russia at less than market prices. Russia exploited Central Asia for its own interest. Whatever infrastructure developed in Central Asia have not been linked with each other within the Central Asia till today even. Walk of connectivity is also a major problem in Central Asia region. Each country in Central Asia has a relatively small population. Only in sum total are these states able to maintain populations comparable to their neighbor countries. None of the Central Asian states has a single nationality population. During the last few years of the Soviet Union, only in Turkmenistan and in Uzbekistan did the titular nationality make up about 70 percent of the population: in Tajikistan, 60 percent of the population were Tajik; 50 percent of Kyrgyzstan's population were Kyrgyz; and 40 percent of Kazakhstan's population were Kazakh. Emigration of Russian-speaking people has increased these percentages, but even if the entire Russian population of these countries was to leave, the Uzbek population would be preserved and even be slightly increased in each of the states except for Kazakhstan.

South Asia: The present political scenario of South Asia is the result of the process of decolonialization. The colonolist imperialist vested interests craftly devided the region sowed the seeds of instability. That's why this region has been lagging behind in regional cooperation than the other regional cooperation initiatives. All the countries are possessive for their independence and afraid of bigger countries hegemony in the regions. India has foreign policy goals similar to those of the Central Asian states. If Islamic fundamentalism is opposed by the world community, South Asia will become a major region of struggle. Indian leaders, taking into account fundamental differences with Pakistan, and the presence of over 100 million Muslims in their country, greatly fear that Central Asia will become an ally of fundamentalists. Thus, during any negotiations, India always attempts to secure promises that the Central Asian regimes will oppose the growth of Islamic fundamentalism. Through diplomatic and economic methods India tries to prevent the appearance of an extensive block of fundamentalist Islamic nations on its borders. However, the relative weakness of Pakistan will prevent it from becoming the main partner in the region. In addition, Central Asia and the rest of the world find the Pakistani-Afghan narcotics cooperation threatening and could pose threat to South Asia also.

Different Political Regime

Central Asia: The authoritarian natures of the Central Asian Regimes also affect the regional integration process because of their tendency to impose control over society. Thus boarders have a propensity to be tightly controlled and information restricted. Kazakhstan is a constitutional republic with a strong presidency. Kyrgyzstan has presidential form of government. Tajikistan has a strong presidential form of government with all powers concentrated in the office of the president. In Turkmenistan, the president is both the chief of the state and head of the government. President Sapramurat Niyazov has held both office since 27th October 1990. Niyazov's term extended indefinitely on 28th Dec. 1999 by the assembly(Majlis)[17] (Banerjie, 2004). In Uzbekistan President heads a strong form of government and all powers are concentrated in the office of the President.

South Asia: South Asia is an area of tremendous political complexities. States like Pakistan and Bangladesh have been largely ruled by authoritarian military rulers. India, per se faces several unresolved issues that stem from internal as well as external sources. These include ethnicity, border disputes, separatist demands, terrorism and subversive activities, communalism, religious problems and so on. All these issues flout the basic ideals of nation building in India, that is, the ideals of democracy, secularism, socialism and federalism.

Competitive Structure of Production

Central Asia; Central Asian Region's exports comprises Gas, oil and oil products, cotton oil, steel products, copper, non- ferrous metallurgy, electric energy and machine building, Aluminum and gold. Intra-regional trade among the CARs has remained relatively small. One reason for this is that the degree of their trade complementarities is low. Some countries of the region are direct competitor in the world market. In contrast, the degree of trade complementarities between the CARs and the PRC South Asia and is high.

South Asia : With the exception of India, and to some extent Pakistan, countries in the region do not have a diversified industrial structure. Regional exports largely consist of raw materials and traditional products such as textiles and garments, while regional imports consist mainly of capital goods and high-tech products. Some regional countries are direct competitors in the world export market for their products. Thus, the trade pattern of South Asian countries is quite similar and skewed towards developed countries.

Lack of *Transport and Communication Links*

Central Asia : Central Asia , the world's largest land locked region, due to lack of effective transport routes and relative isolation made it difficult for all the five countries to access within the region as well as with the world market. Complete dependence on running through the foreign countries's pipelines made it difficult for these countries to access to the hard currency market, define volumes and negotiated prices on the basis of existing international practices and rules(this is especially true for gas from Turkmenistan and oil from Kazakhstan)[18]. Due to lack of information and regulations it restricted the cross boarder trade and cooperation. Data also proves that the percentage of trade among the region decrease over the past years.

South Asia: Transport and communication links between South Asian countries are poor. Some countries are cut off from other countries in the region. There are hardly any ships that call specifically for South Asia exports to other regional countries. For example, Bangladesh finds it easier to reach countries in Southeast Asia, West Asia or Africa than to reach Pakistan. This is also the case with Nepal, vis-à-vis Pakistan, as it uses mainly the Kolkata port for trade with countries other than India, Bangladesh and Bhutan. Although India shares borders with most countries, there has not been enough effort to develop transport and communication links. So much so that it often takes over a week to move goods between Amritsar (India) and Lahore (Pakistan), barely a distance of 30 km.

Absence of Common Approach to Trade Policies

Central Asia: One of the basic challenges is that these countries are pursuing different development strategies in their countries. From the very beginning Kazakhzstan opened up its economy and undertook drastic reforms as a means to stimulate its economy. Uzbekistan adopted stepped reforms and continue to carry on the state management techniques of the former Soviet Union[19]. Turkmenistan has adopted the mixed policies at the pace rate of law reforms. Kyrgyzstan mean while able to got a membership from the WTO but due to less cooperation from neighboring countries are not able to get maximum benefits. Tajikstan is a very small economy and more dependent on other countries of the region. It has no alternate rather than integrating with the region.

South Asia: Restrictive trade policies also cause low levels of intra-regional trade within the region. The restrictions have been more severe on the export interests of South Asia. This is so because countries are generally more restrictive towards products that are considered non-essential, or those that are locally available. And products that their neighbors could possibly supply fall in this category. For example, while more than half the exports of manufactured goods from South Asia consist of textiles and leather products, they are subject to very high rates of import duties and/ or other restrictions in South Asia. This was reflected even in the SAPTA regime, as most products of export interest to regional countries were excluded from preferential treatment. Many believe that even under liberalization under SAFTA, countries could adopt similar tactics.

Political Uncertainty in the Regions

Central Asia: The Islamic movements of Uzbekistan, (IMU) a militant group based in Afghanistan, has been carrying out the terror acts in all the Central Asian countries in order to overthrow the government and established Islamic regime. Turkmenistan faces a major threat from Islamic groups suspected of links with the Taliban. Several acts of violence have been committed by IMU. Simmering ethinic tension , particularly amongst the large Russian group, is another source of internal conflicts. There is tension between the Kyrgyz and Uzbek communities over access to land and housing. The Civil war in Tajikistan was also another cause of conflict. Whether this civil war ended in 1997 but this has led to migration of thousands of refugees to Afghanistan. The disintegration of the regional economy of Russia and the disappearance of an economically united Russia was another cause of tension. Cooperation could ease some of these problems, all of these scenarios are possible, for this, it is necessary that the situation be constantly monitored in order to determine in which direction the region seems to be developing.

South Asia: Political differences have also been a major hurdle in fostering regional economic cooperation within South Asia. Political problems between India and Pakistan, the two largest economies in the region, have often put a question mark on the very existence of the regional bloc. Pakistan does not even offer MFN treatment to India, though they are both part of a regional free trade agreement. Recently, however, Indo-Pak relations have improved significantly enhancing prospects for better trade cooperation. There are problems between other pairs of countries as well, though of a lesser degree. Furthermore, South Asia is an area of tremendous political complexities. States like Pakistan and Bangladesh have been largely ruled by authoritarian military rulers. India, per se faces several unresolved issues that stem from internal as well as external sources. These include ethnicity, border disputes, separatist demands, terrorism and subversive activities, communalism, religious problems and so on. In Nepal, for example, the series of democratically elected government failed to produce any better result than the old royal regime due to widespread corruption and crisis of governance. The political fundamentalists such as Maoists and mainstream political parties are posing major threat to democracy in Nepal. In addition to creating law and order problems, increased human rights violations and a heavy reliance on security forces have undermined the question of legitimacy of governance in Nepal. The recent political development in Nepal is that the royal regime become to an end and maoist leader Mr. Premchanda become a Prime Minister of Nepal.

Comparison of the process of Regional economic initiatives in both the regions

The region comprising India, Pakistan and others in the South Asian Association for regional Cooperation (SAARC) and the Central Asian Republics (CARs) presents a depressing spectacle. Beset with problems of economic underdevelopment, the countries are mired in ethnic, religious, territorial and other disputes and problems. Culturally, linguistically, ethnically and spiritually no other regions and people have so much in common. the economic and strategic interests of South Asia and Central Asia that will subsume political and other differences. The first step is to try cutting through the past 150 years of British and Russian colonial fog separating South and Central Asia, which share millennia of history, culture and civilization. During the past five decades developing countries in Asia have provided the most persuasive and credible story as to how poor countries can progress and bring about prosperity for their downtrodden people. Beginning with Japan, followed by NICs particularly Korea, ASEAN countries and now China, these countries have not only doubled or quadrupled per capita incomes in a record time but also significantly reduced the incidence of poverty. There are several different interpretations of the East Asian miracle and every school of thought has taken the credit for the unprecedented success of more than 1.5 billion people inhabiting this region. Those who believe in the supremacy of state led industrialization have attributed the turn around to the selective interventions by the Government through directed credit, subsidized foreign exchange, tax concessions, tariff exemptions and picking the winners. Those whose faith in pure market mechanism remains unblemished argue that unilateral trade liberalization, integration with the global economy, attracting foreign investment and technology and generally pursuing market friendly economic policies were responsible for these spectacular results.[20] Both the regions all sailing in the same boat and they should take the lessons from the South East Asian countries. As both wanted to pursue market friendly economic policies and also some countries in the region already pursuing. They should get maximum benefit in this globalization era and help to reduce the incidence of poverity.

The contribution of the private sector to GDP is hindered by a poor business environment, reflecting the continued presence of large state enterprises, the lack of necessary support services, and a generally poor policy, legal, and regulatory framework for private sector development. This view, however, is conditional on continued buoyancy from natural resources, adequate infrastructure investment, a climate conducive to private enterprise development, and greater regional integration to overcome impediments to trade, investment, and development. Political stability, or at least the avoidance of civil strife in the transition to more democratic and transparent policies and regulations, will be critical. Private sector development in the region continues to be of concern, for in most cases the reforms that have spurred such growth in the PRC (and in Mongolia) have lagged behind in the CARs. The policy is designed to create conditions supportive of a wide range of competitive economic activities. Investments in transport infrastructure, logistics, and utilities feature prominently in the strategy, as do protection of the natural environment, investment in education and health, and promotion of private investment. However, several common elements of strategy that have also been practiced outside East Asia and have also generated similar results. There is now a wide consensus that participation in international, inter-regional and intra-regional trade enhances the market size for sale of goods and services substantially relative to those who remain confined to the domestic markets. This added purchasing power accelerates the pace of economic growth and shortens the period required for doubling incomes. Second, as the poor countries have low domestic savings in relation of their investment needs they have to draw on foreign savings either in form of official flows, commercial loans or foreign direct investment to supplement this inadequate pool of domestic savings. Third, even if the countries have large pool of domestic savings they cannot transform this pool into productive and remunerative investment over sustained period unless they acquire, assimilate and disseminate the latest technology in production, process and marketing. Embodied in foreign investment is the transfer of technology that can be adapted and internalized to suit the local conditions. Fourth, the state has a major role to play and cannot retreat to the sidelines as a disinterested bystander. Maintenance of macroeconomic stability, pursuit of sound economic policies, provision of physical infrastructure, assuring security of property and person, adjudicating disputes, respecting property rights and enforcing contracts, investing in research and development and more generally in public goods are some of the elements of the enabling environment that Governments create for private businesses to flourish. Fifth, no country in the world can aspire to achieve sustainable improvement in the living standards of its people unless it has invested in education health, nutrition, drinking water, in other words, in human development. This is going to be even more pressing in the 21st century as the world becomes a knowledge-based economy. A literate, healthy, educated and continuously learning and adapting labor force will make the difference between the success and failure of countries. It is against this background that we should examine the future course of Economic Cooperation in Asia. There is no way that increased cooperation can be wished.. South Asia and Central Asia, on the other hand, have neither benefited from integration within their respective regions nor with the ASEAN + 3 region. The market size, the increased purchasing power, the nature of economic reforms and pursuit of liberal and open door policies, a large pool of trained manpower and the emergence of India as the reservoir of scientific and technological manpower do create a win-win situation for all the participants. Pakistan has completely turned its economy around during the last five years and is now experiencing 7 percent plus growth rate with a fast emerging middle class of 15 million people. Similarly, the other countries of South Asia are also making considerable progress economically. Thus together the South Asia and Central Asia offer an expanding and floating market and also provide source of supplies to the value chain for the more advanced countries of the region. Japan and Korea are already using ASEAN Countries and China as the platform for production of goods in a cost effective way while providing design, technology and specifications and taking care of marketing and sales. Singapore and Malaysia are capital surplus countries with high foreign trade-GDP ratios and limited domestic markets. They are now looking towards the middle classes of South Asia whose incomes are rising fast and whose appetite for goods and services is voracious. India alone is adding about 2 million cellular phone subscribers every month while Pakistan has increased the size of cellular phone market from 3 million to 8 million within just one year. This example can be multiplied for fast moving consumer goods, energy, infrastructure, services of all kinds. Thus investment in these countries can be beneficial for both the capital surplus and large market size countries.

Central Asia has huge energy resources but is geographically disadvantaged as it is landlocked. Infrastructure development providing access to seaports as well as gas pipelines, hydroelectric power transmission lines can make their economies more competitive and at the same time ease the energy shortages in India and Pakistan. India's proven prowess in information technology, Internet-related services, Biotechnology and other intellectual fields can be used to enhance the productivity across the board in all the countries of Asia. Given the growing demand of skills among the Asian economies the inter operability of skilled manpower across the territorial boundaries of each individual country will help meet this demand. This above scenario can be doubled in this study's view but it requires a shared vision, a long term strategy, political will and commitment, a time bound action plan, an institutional mechanism for implementation and monitoring, and a machinery for follow up, dispute resolution, and problem solving attitude. Historians will then rightly describe 21st Century as the Asian Century just like the past three centuries were the American and European centuries.

The difference in economic potential of the various Central and South Asian countries are enormous. The presence of huge economic and cultural potential and vast human resources make South Asia one of the most preferable Partners for the countries of Central Asia and one of the corner stones in the potential system of international security[21]. Trade and political relations between both the regions still not fully developed because of geographical, economic and geopolitical factors. Despite that the mutual interest between both the regions has been growing due to number of related problems of economy and security. However, trade between the CARs and South Asian countries remained quite small despite their geographical proximity. An analysis based on the Trade Intensity model suggests that the CARs fully realized their bilateral trade potential most other CIS countries in 2004. At the same time, their actual bilateral trade with most East and South Asian and Western European countries as well as the US was below the estimated potential trade. Whether the CARs fully realized their bilateral trade potential vis-à-vis the PRC, Iran, and Turkey depends on the assumptions underlying the estimates of the potential bilateral trade[22]. (Regional economic integration, gains, 2006) Pakistan and Afghanistan are already members of the Economic Co-Operation Organization (ECO). Other countries in the grouping are Azerbaijan, Iran Kazakhstan, Kyrgyz Republic, Tajikistan, Turkey, Turkmenistan and Uzbekistan. Both the regions need to look at each other and undertake measures for regional economic co-operation for mutual benefit. They have shown great potentialities of higher economic growth. Central Asian countries are source of energy (oil, natural gas etc.) which are highly demanded in the South Asian countries especially by India and Pakistan. India fulfills its energy requirement mainly through imports from West Asia. Central Asia can explore Indian demands. South Asia could be a supplier of basic commodities, services etc. for the Central Asian countries. These links could be strengthened as many multilateral organizations are also trying to re-establish the old trade and other routes in Asia. The United Nations Asian Highway Project is already undergoing the process that will connect the South–East Asia with West Asia. Routes (rail, road, inter-modal) within the Asian Countries have been identified and agreements on the routes reached between the countries concerned. It has been revealed through the global experiences that improved transport integration leads to increased volume of trade at the regional as well as inter-regional trade. This would allow member countries to effectively exploit their comparative advantages and competitiveness.

By comparing both the regions, the process of economic integration within the region is very slow. Progress in South Asia is slow because of political problems between India and Pakistan. In Central Asia, Kazakhstan and Uzbekistan have competed for regional leadership. And Turkmenistan is least interested in regional economic integration. Pakistan is least interested in implementing FTA with India[23]. Pakistan has substantial potential to cooperate with Afghanistan, India, and the Central Asian republics given its strategic location and complementarily in resources and markets with its neighbors. Cooperation could proceed in such areas as energy – including oil, gas, coal, and electricity. Instability in Pakistan would lead to intensified regional instability and help create an environment in which terrorism could flourish. India and Pakistan can play a major role in cooperating and integrating the region economically and can help in bringing the stability in the region.

Regional Economic initiatives in Central Asia
FTAs/FAs in Central Asia (as of March 2006)

A. Summary of WTO Status

Table 5.1

	WTO notified	*Not notified*	*Total*
Total	18	21	39
Central Asia only	5	7	12
Cross regional	13	14	27
Central Asia and others	12	13	25
Multi regional	1	1	2

B. Individual FTAs in Central Asia Agreements Central Asia 1 (Central Asia 5)

	Date	*Status*	*WTO notification*
Tajikistan-Kyrgyz FTA	1996	FTA signed	
Tajikistan –Uzbekistan FTA	1996	FTA signed	

(Contd.)

(Contd. Table 5.1)

	Date	*Status*	*WTO notification*
Uzbekistan- Kazakhstan FTA	1996	FTA signed	
Kyrgyzstan- Kazakhstan FTA	1995	FTA under implementation	Yes
Kyrgyzstan- Uzbekistan FTA	1996	FTA under implementation	Yes

Cross Regional Agreements

	Date	*Status*	*WTO notification*
Tajikistan- Armenia FTA	1994	FTA signed	
Azerbaijan – Uzbekistan FTA	1996	FTA signed	
Turkmenistan FTA			
Pakistan-Kazakhstan PTA	2003	PTA proposed	
Pakistan - Tajikistan PTA	2004	PTA proposed	
Azerbaijan – Russia FTA	1992	FTA signed	
Uzbekistan – Russia FTA	1992	FTA signed	
CIS FTA	1994	FTA signed	Yes
Tajikistan – Russia FTA	1994	FTA signed	
Azerbaijan – Moldova FTA	1995	FTA signed	
Azerbaijan – Ukraine FTA	1995	FTA signed	
Uzbekistan – Georgia FTA	1995	FTA signed	
Uzbekistan – Moldova FTA	1995	FTA signed	
Tajikistan – Belarus FTA	1998	FTA signed	
Tajikistan – Ukraine FTA	2001	FTA signed	
GAUM FTA	2002	FTA signed	
Common economic space	2003	FTA signed	
Armenia – Russia FTA	1992	FTA Under Implementation	Yes
Kyrgyz – Russia FTA	1993	FTA Under Implementation	Yes

(Contd.)

(Contd. Table 5.1)

	Date	*Status*	*WTO notification*
Armenia – Moldova FTA	1995	FTA Under Implementation	Yes
Armenia – Ukraine FTA	1996	FTA Under Implementation	Yes
Azerbaijan – Georgia FTA	1996	FTA Under Implementation	Yes
Kyrgyz – Moldova FTA	1996	FTA Under Implementation	Yes
Armenia – Georgia FTA	1998	FTA Under Implementation	Yes
Kyrgyz – Ukraine FTA	1998	FTA Under Implementation	Yes
Kazakhstan – Georgia FTA	1999	FTA Under Implementation	Yes
Turkmenistan – Georgia FTA	2000	FTA Under Implementation	Yes
EurAsEC Customs union	2001	FTA Under Implementation	Yes
Multi – Regional			
SCO FTA	2003	FTA proposed	
ECOTA	2003	FTA signed	Yes

Regional Economic Initiatives in South Asian Countries

Table 5.2

INDIA'S REGIONAL INITIATIVES15

STAGE	*FTAs / PTAs / RTAs*	*YEAR*
SIGNED	• FTA with Sri Lanka	28th Dec 1998
	• SAPTA	11th April 1993

(Contd.)

(Contd. Table 5.2)

STAGE	*FTAs/PTAs/RTAs*	*YEAR*
	• SAFTA (to be implemented by 1st Jan 2006)	6th Jan 2004
	• BIMST-EC Free Trade Area	8th Feb 2004, Protocol agreement signed in June 2004
	• FTA with Thailand	29th Aug 2004
	• PTA with Afghanistan	6th March 2003
	• Framework Agreement for FTA with Gulf Cooperation Council [GCC]	25th Aug 2004
	• Framework Economic Cooperation Agreement with Chile	20th Jan 2005
	• Framework Agreement for CEPA and PTA with MERCOSUR [to evolve into an FTA]	25th Jan 2004
	• Framework Agreements for Economic Cooperation with the Andean Community, Caricom [Caribbean Nations] and Central America	Date unknown"16
	• Framework Agreement for Economic Cooperation with SACU	10th Sep 2004
	• MoU for Economic, Commercial and Technical Cooperation with TEAM 9 [Burkina Faso, Chad, Equatorial Guinea, Ghana, Guinea Bissau, Ivory Coast, Mali and Senegal]	1st March 2004
IMPLEMENTED		
	• Early Harvest Scheme under	1st March 2000

(Contd.)

(Contd. Table 5.2)

STAGE	*FTAs/PTAs/RTAs*	*YEAR*
	FTA with Sri Lanka	
	• Early Harvest Scheme under FTA with Thailand	1st Sep 2004
	• SAPTA	1st Jan 1998
ONGOING		
	• Framework Agreement for Comprehensive Economic Cooperation with ASEAN	8th Oct 2003
NEGOTIATIONS		
	◦ CEPA with Sri Lanka	March 2004
	• FTA with MERCOSUR	17th June 2003
	• Framework Agreement for FTA between India SACU finalized	6th-7th Sep 2004
	• PTA with South Africa	To be concluded by Dec 2005
	• Draft Text for a PTA with Egypt finalized	Dec 2003
	• India Mauritius FTA	1st April 2005
	• PTA with Chile	To be concluded by 2005
	• FTA with SACU	March 2004
CONCLUDED AWAITING TO BE SIGNED TALKS		
	• CECA with Singapore	Sometime past mid-June 2005
	• CECA with Malaysia	By Dec 2005
FTAs/RTA/sPTAs		
	• Joint Study Group Report proposes feasibility study of An FTA with China	11th April 2005 (Under Negotiation till 2008)
IN THE PIPELINE		
	• Trade and Economic Framework Agreement leading to An FTA with Australia	May 2005

(Contd.)

(Contd. Table 5.2)

STAGE	*FTAs/PTAs/RTAs*	*YEAR*
	• Comprehensive Economic Partnership including FTA with Malaysia	20th Dec 2004
	• Comprehensive Economic Partnership Agreement (CEPA) with Sri Lanka	March 2004
	• PTA with South Africa	January 2000
	• India Chile PTA	March 2004
	• Framework Cooperation Agreement with COMESA [Common Market for Easterr and Southern Africa]	May 2004
	• India Brazil South Africa [IBSA] Partnership	Date unknown; post Cancun
	• PTA with Iran	Date unknown
	• India Egypt PTA	30th April 2001
	• India Mauritius FTA [Joint Study Group launched]	6th-7th Sep 2004
	PAKISTAN'S REGIONAL INTIATIVES18	
	• FTA with Sri Lanka to be operation from 12th June 2005	10th Feb 2005
	• SAPTA	11th April 1993
	• SAFTA to be implemented by 1st Jan 2006	6th Jan 2004
	• Trade and Investment Framework Agreement [TIFA] with USA	25th June 2003
	• PTA b/w Pakistan, Turkey and Iran under the auspices of Economic Cooperation Organization (ECO). Other members of ECO: Azerbaijan, Kyrgyz Republic, Afghanistan, Kazakhstan, Tajikistan,	1992

(Contd.)

(Contd. Table 5.2)

STAGE	*FTAs/PTAs/RTAs*	*YEAR*
	Turkmenistan, Uzbekistan	
	• ECO Trade Agreement realized by 2011 for all countries except Afghanistan)	July 2003 (to be
	• (OIC-TPS) Trade Preferential System under the auspices of the Organization of Islamic Conference (OIC). The OIC comprises: Bangladesh, Pakistan, Cameroon, Egypt, Guinea, Iran, Jordan, Lebanon, Libya, Malaysia, Pakistan, Senegal, Tunisia, Turkey and Uganda	30th June 2004
	• PTA with China	3rd Nov 2003
	• PTA with Iran	25th Feb 2005
IMPLEMENTED		
	• PTA with China	1st Jan 2004
	• SAPTA	1st Jan 1998
ONGOING NEGOTIATIONS		
	• Comprehensive FTA with Singapore	June 2005 till 2008 under Negotiation.
	• FTA with Mexico	3rd Dec 2004
	• PTA with Developing Eight (D-8) countries that include: Bangladesh, Indonesia, Egypt, Nigeria, Pakistan, Iran and Turkey	15th Feb 2004
	FTA with Bangladesh	Jan 2002
	PTA with Kenya	2003-4
	(to sign protocol for PTA by this	2004
	(recently launched proposal for	2004
	TIFA with USA Bilateral	Since 25th June 2003

(Contd.)

(Contd. Table 5.2)

STAGE	*FTAs/PTAs/RTAs*	*YEAR*
	Investment Treaty Agreement	28th Sept 2004
	(BITA) with USA (to be signed	July 2004
	after implementation of	Feb 2005
	Comprehensive FTA with Nepal	
CONCLUDED TALKS		
	PTA with Turkey	April 2005
FTA SIGNED		
	FTA with China	24th Nov 2008
FTAs/PTAs/RTAs IN THE PIEPLINE		
	PTA with Japan	2003
	PTA with Vietnam	2003
	FTA with Malaysia	2004
	Comprehensive Economic Partnership agreement (CEPA) with Sri Lanka	10th Feb 2005
	PTA with EU	2003/4
	Recently granted Full Dialogue partner us in ASEAN	May 2005
SRI LANKA'S REGIONAL INITIAITVES19		
	BIMST-EC Free Trade Area	8th Feb 2004, Protocol Agreement signed in June 2004
	SAPTA	11th April 1993
	SAFTA to be implemented by 1st Jan 2006	6th Jan 2004
	FTA with India	28th Dec 1998
	EU Sri Lanka Cooperation	1995
	Agreement Trade and Investment Framework (TIFA) with Agreement USA	25th July 2002
	US-Sri Lanka IPR Agreement	20th Sep 1991
	PTA with Iran	25th Nov 2004

(Contd.)

(Contd. Table 5.2)

STAGE	*FTAs/PTAs/RTAs*	*YEAR*
IMPLEMENTED		
	FTA with India	1st March 2000
	SAPTA	1st Jan 1998
ONGOING		
	• FTA with USA	June 2004
NEGOTIATIONS		
	• FTA with Egypt (though Egypt has reported that it's trade with Sri Lanka has been falling rapidly over the past 3 years)	Started 2003
	• FTA with Bangladesh	Nov-Dec 2003
	• FTA with The Maldives	Oct 2003
FTAs/PTAs/RTAs IN THE PIPELINE		
	• Comprehensive Economic Partnership Agreement with Pakistan (CEPA)	10th Feb 2005
	• FTA with Italy	See footnote20
	• FTA with France	See footnote21
	• CEPA with India	10th Feb 2005
	• FTA with Nepal	Dec 2003
BANGLADESH'S REGIONAL INITIATIVES22		
	• Trade Agreement and Protocol for Trade Agreement with	May 2003 (B'desh Bhutan does not want an FTA with Bhutan and has chosen to only renew the Trade Agreement that was signed in 1988)
	• SAPTA	11th April 1993
	• SAFTA to be implemented by 1st Jan 2006	6th Jan 2004
IMPLEMENTED		
	• SAPTA	1st Jan 1998

(Contd.)

(Contd. Table 5.2)

STAGE	*FTAs/PTAs/RTAs*	*YEAR*
ONGOING		
	• FTA with Pakistan (talks stalled after 2 rounds and have been Recently resumed)**	Jan 2002
NEGOTIATIONS		
	• FTA with Sri Lanka (talks moving slowly)**	Nov-Dec 2003
	• TIFA with USA talks resumed but 2 countries failed to sign agreement in March 2004	On 25th Feb 2005
	• FTA with India	March 2004 (modalities were decided upon and agreement should be signed soon. Bangladesh has attached maximum priority to this agreement for fear of India's access to LDCs in ASEAN and its proposed FTA with Nepal)
	• BIMST-EC Free Trade Area Bangladesh joined the agreement on 25th June 2004	8th Feb 2004,
	• (OIC-TPS) Trade Preferential System under the auspices of the Organization of Islamic Conference (OIC). The OIC comprises: Bangladesh, Pakistan, Cameroon, Egypt, Guinea, Iran, Jordan,	30th June 2004 (Bangladesh is negotiating special and differential treatment)

(Contd.)

(Contd. Table 5.2)

STAGE	FTAs/PTAs/RTAs	YEAR
	Lebanon, Libya, Malaysia, Pakistan, Senegal, Tunisia, Turkey and Uganda	
FTAs/PTAs/RTAs		
	• FTA with Malayasia	Dec 2004
IN THE PIEPLINE		
	• FTA with Morocco (was set to sign in Dec 2004, despite reservations from domestic research wings like the Tariff Commission)	2004
	• PTA with Egypt	2004
	• PTA with Iran (new trade deal as Iran had suspended the previous one)	2004
	• FTA with Nepal	2003-4
	NEPAL'S REGIONAL INITIATIVES23	
SIGNED	• India-Nepal Treaty of Trade 1951	Protocol renewed in Feb 2002
	• SAPTA	11th April 1993
	• SAFTA to be implemented by 1st Jan 2006	6th Jan 2004
IMPLEMENTED		
	• SAPTA	1st Jan 1998
ONGOING		
	• Comprehensive FTA with Pakistan, so far has been granted duty Free access to export of tea to Pakistan	Feb 2005
NEGOTIATIONS		
	• FTA with Sri Lanka	(talks moving slowly) Nov-Dec 2003
	• Bilateral Investment Protection Agreement (BIPA) with India	26th Aug 2003 (proposal forwarded in 1998 from India.

(Contd.)

(Contd. Table 5.2)

STAGE	*FTAs/PTAs/RTAs*	*YEAR*
		Negotiations should have begun in 2001 but focused on trade Issues instead)
FTAs/PTAs/RTAs IN THE PIPELINE		
	• BIMST-EC	Though a trade agreement exists between the other member countries, Nepal only joined in March 2004 and isn't a co-signee
	• FTA with Bangladesh (no progress has been made so far)	2003-04
	BHUTAN'S REGIONAL INITIATIVES24	
FTAs/PTAs/RTAs		
	• Trade Agreement and Protocol for Trade Agreement with Bangladesh	May 2003 (B'desh does not want an FTA with Bhutan and has chosen to only renew the Trade Agreement that was signed in 1988)
	• Framework Agreement for FTA with Thailand	July 2004
	• Treaty of Trade and Commerce with India	Signed in 1972 and due to expire in March 2005. I am unsure whether and how it has been renewed.
	• SAPTA	11th April 1998
	• SAFTA to be implemented by 1st Jan 2006	6th Jan 2004

(Contd.)

(Contd. Table 5.2)

STAGE	FTAs/PTAs/RTAs	YEAR
IMPLEMENTED		
	• SAPTA	1st Jan 1998
	• Treaty of Trade and Commerce with India	1972
FTAs/PTAs/RTAs IN THE PIPELINE		
	• BIMST-EC FTA	Though a trade agreement exists between the other member countries, Bhutan only joined in March 2004 and isn't a co-signee

References

1. Central Asian Regional Economic Cooperation in *The times of Central Asia, Independent weekly*, Nov.11,2005. Vol.7 No.30 (333)p.9. see at www.timesca.com.
2. Borris Rumer, 2003,Central Asia in Transition: dilemmas of political and economic developments. p. 42.
3. K.Gopal, et all (2003), *Globalization, Democracy and Governence in South Asia: Issues and Alternatives,* in ed and Regional cooperation, KALINGA Publications, New Delhi., p. 44.
4. www.adb.org.
5. www.saarc.org.
6. CAREC, Central Asia Regional Economic Cooperation Comprehensive Action plan, Fifth Ministerial Conference on Central Asian Regional Economic Cooperation, 18-20 Oct. 2006 at Urumqi, XUAR, People 's Republic Of China., 2007. p. 1.
7. with economic co-operation, nobody losses each country can be benefited. As economists refers to " zero Sum Game" and " non zero sum gains". Precisely aim of EC is to provide benefits to both countries. See in detailJohn Magill, Economic Co-operation in Central Asia, Manilla, Phillipines: Asian Development Bank, 1999. p. 41.

8. Komilov, S, (2003), "Regional Economic Cooperation: Appraisal and Problems of Development, in *Central Asian Affairs*, Kazakhstan Institute of Strategic Studies, Kazakhstan.
9. CAREC, Central Asia Regional Economic Cooperation Comprehensive Action plan, Fifth Ministerial Conference on Central Asian Regional Economic Cooperation, 18-20 Oct. 2006 at Urumqi, XUAR, People's Republic Of China., p. 2.
10. Central Asian Regional Economic Cooperation , in The Times of Central Asia, 11th Nov.2005, Vol.7 No.3(333). Sighted on .www. timessca.com.
11. CAREC, Central Asia Regional Economic Cooperation Comprehensive Action plan. op.cit, p.3
12. www.aric.adb.org
13. Sanaullah, (2003), *Improvement of Transit System in Central Asia,* UNCTAD/ LDC/2003/5, paper presented on 23-27 June2003. in New York. p.6. (pdf).
14. Brent Dark, 2006. p.
15. Srinivasan,T.N., (2002), *Trade Finance Investment in South Asia,* Social Sciences Press, New Delhi., p. 240.
16. Christopher Len, (2004), "Regional cooperation in Central Asia and Japan's Belated Regional Initiative" in *Contemporary Central Asia*, Vol. 8, No. 3. p.
17. *Ibid,* p. 24.
18. Indranil Banerjee, ed., (2004), *India and Central Asia*, Brunel Academic Publishers Ltd. UK., p. 36.
19. Islamov, Bakhtior, A., (2001), *The Central Asian States Ten Years After: How to overcome Traps of Development, Transformation and Globalization?* Maruzen Co., Ltd, Tokyo., p. 185.
20. Christopher Len, (2004), "Regional cooperation in Central Asia and Japan's Belated Regional Initiative" in *Contemporary Central Asia,* Vol. 8, No. 3. p. 23.
21. Islamabad conference, 2005.
22. Sanat Kushkumbayev, (2006) "International and Regional Organisationsand their role in Ensuring security in Central Asia and South Asia" Central Asia's Affairs, Vol. 3., p. 5.
23. ADB, (2006), "Central Asia; Gains from Trade Through Regional Cooperation in Trade Policy, Transport and Custom Transit", ADB, Philippines. REI, Gains from trade policy, 2006. p. 32.
24. SAFTA, www.aric.org.

6

Possible Linkages Between the Central Asian and South Asian Regions

This chapter will deal with the possibilities and obstacles of the expansion of South Asian economic co-operation to the Central Asian region. Importance of other countries like Iran and Afghanistan might also be discussed in this context. It is well known that in the historical period the regions of Central Asia and South Asia were closely interrelated. But after the World War II these linkages disrupted. In this globalization era, economy of any country will never flourish in isolation from its neighbors and from the larger region of which it is a part. As South Asia and Central Asia large no. of inhabitants engage mainly in subsistence agriculture. With help, they would engage in manufacturing, which will boost GDP but will require investment in equipment and the development of skills. For the foreseeable future, the chief driver of economic growth in countries would be trade: trade from town to town, province to province, between countries to countries or countries to region or region to the world. Afghanistan can play a positive role in linking the South Asia and Central Asia. Because Afghanistan's geographical position places it at the crossroads between the Middle East and Asia, Europe and India, and between Northern Europe, Russia, and the Indian Ocean. Asia and Europe are linked by roads and railroads passing through Afghanistan. Trade along these routes existed for 2,500 years until it was blocked after 1917, when the Soviet Union's southern border sliced through the region, and then by the breakdown of continental trade across Afghanistan after 1979. American action in 2001 had the unanticipated consequence of paving the way for reopening trade channels that had enriched Afghans and other Central Asians over the millennia[1] (Fredric, Starr, 2005,)

The success of regional blocs like the EU, ASEAN and NAFTA in promoting trade among member nations and boosting their economic growth has influenced both the regions to go in for regional economic integration. Both the regions have taken many initiatives to form regional groupings within the regions as well as with the rest of the world, which are discussed in detail in the earlier chapters.

Geographical Contiguity, Shared History and Culture

The vast area of Central Asia and Kazakhstan which spread from the Urals to Pamirs from the shores of the Caspian Sea to the Altai mountains has been historically, geographically and economically a distinct regional identity with specific features. The region has also had several names such as Turan, Maverannahr , Deshtikipchek and Turkstan, before the incorporation in the tsarist Rusian Empire period. South Asia was also an Indian subcontinenent, which has now fragmented into seven countries. Both the regions are somehow trying to create lost economic linkages. For centuries, Central Asia thrived as the meeting place of East and West, as the bridge between great civilizations, the region evolved as a centre of trade, ideas and prosperity. The literature of the medieval times shows that the Himalaya's were the Part of India and people were familiar with it. In too many ways, the Central Asia region is not an easy territory. Great ideas may have connected Eastern and Western civilizations by way of the Silk Road, which is actually a network of routes rather than a single by way, but the multicolored terrain of Central Asia is as physically daunting as its history is legendary. From east to west, the region stretches nearly 4,500 kilometers and occupies a land area about the size of Europe. Central Asia is a vast landlocked region of Asia. Central Asia has historically been closely tied to its nomadic peoples and the Silk Road. As a result, it has acted as a crossroads for the movement of people, goods, and ideas between Europe, the Middle East, South Asia, and East Asia. It is also sometimes known as Middle Asia or Inner Asia, and is within the scope of the wider Eurasian continent.

Aryan tribes from India migrated from north of the Black Sea and the Caspian and Kazakh steppes during the second and first millennium BC. Later, Turkish tribes marched from the eastern Asian steppes to the Indian sub-continent, Iran and Turkey, then known as Asia Minor, where earlier Greek, Roman and Hellenic thought, culture and polity, which forms the basis of Western civilization, had already evolved. This was the result of the interaction of incoming Greeks with the existing higher Asian civilizations of Asia Minor, Mesopotamia, Persia, Egypt and India. Home to over 40 civilizations, Turkey has more Greek sites than Greece and more Roman monuments than Italy.

Both the regions are somehow trying to create lost economic linkages. Multilateral institutions are trying to help both the region in the areas of trade facilitation, transit, infrastructure etc. Central Asians will be able to choose whether to export their cotton, oil, gas, and manufactured goods through Russia or through the South, and will choose the cheapest alternative or mix of alternatives. Firms like Russia's state-controlled Gazprom may still play a role, but they will do so as competitors and not as monopolists. New routes to the South will also open vast new prospects for trade and contact with South and Southeast Asia, and open the countries of Greater Central Asia to investment from India and beyond on Iran Pipeline and Iran has the monopoly that's why trying to do it own terms and condition. To reduce the region's dependence on Russia, a few massive projects like the Caspian Pipeline Consortium Project (CPC), the Baku-Tiblisi-Ceyhan oil pipeline (BTC), and the South Caucasus Pipeline (SCP) have been outlined. These will redirect the region's energy flows from the existing northern routes toward

Russia, to western, eastern and southern routes toward Europe and Asia. In recent years, Asian demand (particularly in China and India) has been expected to grow much faster than European demand, and eastward routes towards China and southern routes (through Iran) or southwest routes via Afghanistan were looked upon as economically lucrative options[2]. In the latest developments The Chinese delegations who visited India they are also in favor of economic cooperation. The Chinese Ambassador to India, explained this reversal of procedure by saying that now the ' B' of Business is more important than the 'B' of Boundary[3]. During perestroika, India had begun to create an economic partnership with this region. India led several construction projects, increased training for local workers, and began selling Indian goods in the region. Pakistan began its activities in Central Asia during the Soviet period, trying to gain influence most through its religious leaders. As soon as the Central Asian states declared independence, Pakistan began providing economic assistance. To reduce the importance of Russia and other CIS countries, Central Asia looked towards the other countries for their Trade. This region's outlook changed for India also. Many high level meetings have been set up to encourage economic cooperation since their independence.

South Asia's Foreign Trade with Central Asian Countries

During the past decade it has been observed that the Central Asian trade has been diverted. It has started trade with South Asia, especially with India and Pakistan. The pace of growth of Indian export to central Asia was steady in the initial years but after 1999 the growth is faster. Still imports are low. Pakistan's growth of export is on the decreasing trend. In the initial years it increased but later on despite there is a great potential, it has witnessed decreasing trend in export and import. Fig. 6.1 shows that the Indian trade growth rate with the Central Asian region is higher than Pakistan's trade growth. It might be due to the restrictive policies of the Pakistan. Despite having a great potential among both the regions the trade level is very low. Due to the restrictive policies of the Central Asian countries, especially Turkmenistan's the trade level is very low.

Fig. 6.1

South Asian Economic Linkages with Central Asia (in million dollar)

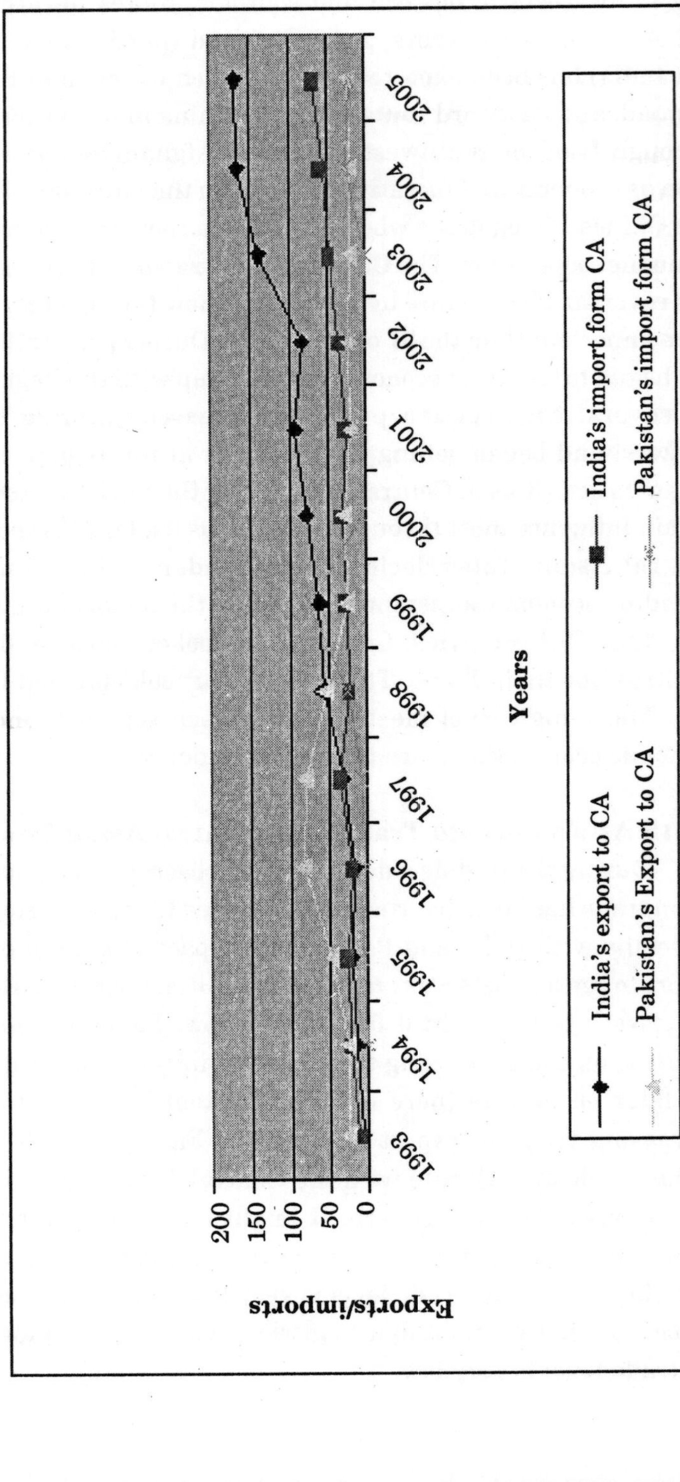

Table 6.1 India's Export to Central Asia (in million US $)

	2000-01	*2001-02*	*2002-03*	*2003-04*	*2004-05*
Kazakhstan	50.08	45.70	46.88	74.81	79.40
Kyrgyzstan	17.59	10.95	14.67	38.20	49.10
Tajikistan	3.55	1.22	8.65	4.47	6.25
Turkmenistan	2.71	4.35	10.29	19.21	14.63
Uzbekistan	9.39	6.53	5.08	15.14	19.66
Total Central Asia	109.19	93.15	146.34	297.30	326.77

Source: Directorate of General Foreign Trade of Government of India.

Table 6.2 Indian Import from Central Asia (in million US $)

	2000– 01	*2001– 02*	*2002–03*	*2003– 04*	*2004– 05*
Kazakhstan	14.04	7.39	12.73	9.26	15.35
Kyrgyzstan	4.43	0.56	0.47	0.54	0.62
Tajikistan	0.54	1.34	0.08	3.95	3.98
Turkmenistan	1.12	1.95	5.40	9.34	10.69
Uzbekistan	10.58	17.27	20.54	27.70	29.43
Total Central Asia	56.91	46.02	57.68	91.30	106.39

Source: Directorate of General Foreign Trade of Government of India.

Traditionaly, India,s warm and cordial relations with Kazakhzstan and Uzbekistan progressed smoothly. Their outlook toward India has changed significantly in the last few years. The visit of former Prime Minister of India Atal Bihari Vajpayee to Almaty on June 2002 provided an opportunities for consolidation and concretization of the relationship in the areas of cooperation that were identifying during the visit of president Nursultan Nazarbayev to India[4]. The relations with Uzbekistan were also marked by traditional warmth and based on shared historical and cultural ties. Over the past few years there has been a steady

Table 6.3 Commodity wise India's Export to Central Asian Countries

Kazakhstan	*Kyrgyzstan*	*Tajikistan*	*Uzbekistan*	*Turkmenistan*
Coffee, tea, mate, and spices	Pharmaceutical products	Inorganic chemicals	Meat and edible meat offal	Pharmaceutical products
Tobacco and manufactured tobacco substitutes	Soap, crocheted preparations etc.	Pharmaceutical products	Ores, slag, and ash	Perfumery and cosmetic ingredients
Organic chemicals	Articles of leather, tack; travel goods, handbags and similar articles of animal gut(other than silk-worm)	Articles of apparel and clothing	Pharmaceutical products	Articles of apparel and clothing accessories knitted or crocheted.
Pharmaceutical products	Articles of apparel and clothing	Accessories, knitted or crocheted	Machinery and mechanical appliances	Articles of apparel and clothing accessories not
Perfumery and cosmetic ingredients		Articles of apparel and clothing		
Articles of leather, travel goods, handbags and similar articles of animal gut (other than silk-worm).		Accessories, not knitted or crocheted		

(Contd.)

(Contd. Table 6.3)

Kazakhstan	*Kyrgyzstan*	*Tajikistan*	*Uzbekistan*	*Turkmenistan*
Articles of apparel and clothing accessories, knitted or crocheted	accessories knitted or crocheted.	Machinery and mechanical appliances; parts		knitted or crocheted.
Articles of apparel and clothing accessories, not knitted or crocheted	Articles of apparel and clothing accessories not knitted or crocheted.			Machinery and mechanical appliances; parts
Iron and steel				Electrical machinery and equipments
Articles of iron or steel				
Nuclear reactors, boilers, machinery and Mechanical appliances and parts thereof				

Table 6.4 Commodity wise India's Import from Central Asian Countries

Kazakhstan	*Kyrgyzstan*	*Tajikistan*	*Turkmenistan*	*Uzbekistan*
Salt, sulphur, earths and stone;		Cotton	Cotton	Cotton
Plastering materials, lime and cement		Aluminum And Articles Thereof.	Inorganic chemicals	Edible vegetables and certain roots and tubers
Iron and steel				
Machinery and mechanical appliances				Natural or cultured pearls, precious or
Natural or cultured pearls, precious or				Semiprecious stones, precious metals, clad
Semiprecious stones, precious metals, clad				with precious metal and articles thereof,
with precious metal and articles thereof ;				imitated jewelry, coin
imitated jewelry, coin				Zinc and articles thereof
Zinc and articles thereof				Aircraft, spacecraft, and parts thereof

Source: Directorate of General Foreign Trade of Government of India.

exchange of high level visits between two countries. The president of Uzbekistan H.E. Islam Karimov visited India from 17-19th August. Agreements on Economic, Commercial, Scientific and Technical cooperation in the Spheres of culture Art and education Tourism, Sports and mass media were signed. The former Prime Minister paid an official visit to Uzbekistan in May 1993.Trade relations between India and Uzbekistan are governed by the agreements on trade economic cooperation were signed in May 1993. It can be observed through the data that India has good trade with these two countries. This study has compared the distances of Pakistan and Russia with Central Asian countries. The table 6.5 shows that some distances of Russia are very far than Pakistan. If Pakistan is too close to Central Asia and it's very easy to access to India. The concentration should be paid on the development of Infrastructure of rail road linkages to explore the potential between the two regions.

Although the Karakuram Highway and Pakistan's national highway system already constitute an important North-South transit corridor, new internal bypasses, motorways and expressways that will facilitate Central Asian trade are now under construction or have been completed. It has been believed by Pakistani officials that the addressing of underdevelopment, poverty and instability within Pakistan and nearby regions requires a formal network of commercial communication; official Pakistani investments in the transit sector reflect this concern. This reliance has made the development of road infrastructure a top priority. N-5, the main national highway, connects Karachi in the south with Torkham at the Afghan border in the north; an additional Torkham-Jalalabad link with Afghanistan is nearing completion. Central and South Asia's complex ethno-political situation complicates matters. Regional state-building processes must include means of fostering interethnic communication, in addition to measures to establish rule of law, civil society, and constitutionalism. This is also true about Pakistan. New transit routes via Pakistan and subsequent economic developments will help stabilize political processes throughout Central and South Asia; but for the time being balance between economic and political development has yet to be achieved. In Pakistan, a democratic federal administration would greatly

Table 6.5 The distances of destination of Pakistan, Russia and Central Asia[5]

From	*To*	*Distance*	*From*	*To*	*Distance*
Islamabad	Tashkent	800 km	Karachi	Dushanbe	2720 km
Islamabad	Dushanbe	640 km	Abadan	Dushanbe	3200 km
Islamabad	Alma Ata	1040 km	Bandar Abbas	Dushanbe	3440 km
Islamabad	Bishkek	960 km	Odessa	Dushanbe	3400 km
Tashkent	Chaman	1292 km	Vladivostok	Dushanbe	9500 km
Karachi	Lahore	1292 km	Gwadar	Karachi	489 km

advance this cause. The essential administrative structures are already in place. Central Asia is a relatively stable region, thanks mainly to the efforts of Central Asian countries themselves. They have solved the vast majority of boundary issues through bi-lateral negotiations.

Pakistan and Central Asia are major cotton producers and it has been suggested that both regions would benefit by initiating joint projects in cotton and textiles. Facilitating transportation inside Pakistan and footwear and headgear, articles of stone, plaster, cement, and asbestos, pearls, precious or semi-precious stones, and metals, base metals and articles thereof, machinery, mechanical appliances, and electrical equipment, transportation equipment, instruments (both measuring and musical), arms and ammunition, miscellaneous manufactured articles, works of art and other materials (list drawn from the ADB report). Afghanistan may eventually encourage Pakistan, Kazakhstan, the Kyrgyz Republic, Tajikistan, Turkmenistan and Uzbekistan to establish a world cotton cartel, either bilaterally or under ECO or all other frameworks. The cartel would be based in the port city of Karachi with satellite offices in regional capitals, and would likely increase regional and cross-continental trade volumes. It can provide Central Asia regions to access to the port also. India could also join the cartel at a later stage, after the India- Pakistan détente leads to agreements on transit. A cotton and textile cartel could expand regional trade by billions of dollars, generating economic cooperation in other mutually beneficial areas, such as natural gas and oil, minerals, jewelry, hydroelectric power, education and institutional cooperation, software technology, regional agriculture, and tourism. Indeed a cotton cartel and related developments could become a cornerstone of the Central Asian prosperity.

Recreating Historical linkages to Explore Potential

To link both the regions, this chapter will put stress on the economic potentials and geo-physical realities. This places Central Asia within both an analytical category and a geographical context. Economically, the region's future development is tied directly to the exploitation of its rich natural resources, which requires the political as well as economic cooperation of the Central Asian states with their immediate neighbors to the north, south, east, and west. The exploitation of vast oil and gas reserves is also rapidly becoming the main integrating force both within this region and between these regions and the global economy. Geographically, beginning with the main water basins in the region the Aral Sea and the Caspian Sea, both of which contain substantial oil reserves[6]. Considering the region's mountain ranges, it also includes Afghanistan and Xinjiang. Most importantly, there are several natural trade routes between Central Asia, broadly conceived, and China, Europe, Russia, South Asia, and the Middle East. In the context of South Asia and Central Asia Afghanistan plays crucial role. This has become more significant because it has become a member of SAARC as well as a member of CAREC. The systematic development of regional and continental transport will enable Afghanistan and its neighbors to move from the economic periphery to the very center of a new but at the same time ancient world economic region, that of Greater Central Asia[7]. This in turn encourages modern market-oriented forces in Russia, at the expense of those who still dream of old-fashioned political hegemonies. These links will go far towards balancing the complex political pressures to which Afghanistan and the countries of Greater Central Asia are currently subjected, and thus further strengthen their fragile sovereignties. And with respect to both Pakistan and Iran, it will open promising visas to the pragmatic men and women who comprise the modern commercial sector in those countries, and will undercut the appeal of religious extremists. Moreover Afghanistan, like all countries in the region, will benefit from the payment of transit fees and duties. Its neighbor Iran will be able to reclaim its traditional vocation as a moderate trading state looking eastward as opposed to its present role as a militant Shii'a state fighting for influence in the Arab lands to its West. And the reopening of ancient east-west trade corridors across Pakistan and the expansion of new ones coming south from China will break the isolation that has been Pakistan's fate since its founding and return the Indus valley to its ancient status as an entrepot for trade in all directions. Trade and economic development must be the centerpiece of any pro-active U.S. strategy for Afghanistan and its neighbors, but other components must be equally important. Security, institutional development, the expansion of elections, and cultural and educational programs must all be transformed from issues pursued on a purely national basis to region-wide concerns. To acknowledge the centrality of trade in no way diminishes the importance of these other areas: it is simply the end result for their long-term success[8]. The Silk Road, or Silk Route, is an interconnected series of ancient trade routes through various regions of the Asian continent mainly connecting Chang'an (today's Xi'an) in China, with Asia Minor and the Mediterranean. It extends over 8,000 km (5,000 miles) on land and sea. Trade on the Silk Route was a significant factor in the development of the great civilizations, and helped to lay the foundations for the modern world. Apart from restricted contacts since 1947 between India and the CARs, then part of the USSR, and except for a century and a half when the Indian sub-continent was ruled by the British and Central Asia by the Russians, there has always been natural interaction through travel, trade, migration and conquest between the sub-continent and Central Asia, Iran and Turkey.

Regional Economic Initiatives in Central Asia and South Asia

Many steps have been taken to initiate to economic cooperation in Central Asia and South Asia. Many high level meeting took place between both the regions, due to a lots of potential in both the regions. The country's Dauletabad gas field in the south has gross reserves of 1.4 trillion cubic meters (TCM) of gas. Some analysts said that it can meet the proposed target of piping 30 billion cubic meters (BCM) of gas a year to South Asia via Afghanistan. A $3.3 billion scheme for Turkmenistan to feed growing demand for gas in India and Pakistan took a step nearer reality with the recent release of additional information on natural gas reserves and production forecasts, the next step is for the project's steering committee to meet and discuss inviting an international consortium of investors to build the pipeline. Turkmenistan's growing trade with Turkey builds on deep historical, linguistic, and cultural foundations. The ruined palaces and mosques of the southern city of Merv, also known as Mary, testify to its former glory as a capital of the Seljuk Empire.

Descendants of the Seljuk Turks helped found the Ottoman Empire. Trade flows along two main routes, either along the southern road through Iran or via the northern road through Turkmenbashi and across the Caspian Sea by ferry to Baku and Georgia. Although largely a desert country, Turkmenistan has plenty to trade, with large reserves of oil and natural gas. It is also one of the world's top cotton producers[9] Region-wide transport will enable Afghan farmers to get their dried fruits and produce to world markets, creating an alternative to opium poppies. It will knit the country's various regions with one another, create millions of jobs, and provide major revenues to the central government in the form of tariffs and taxes. Internationally, Afghanistan will open a "window to the sea" for all the rest of Central Asia, for vast and economically struggling parts of Siberia and the Urals, and also for China's wealthy Xinjiang Uyghur Autonomous Region. The expansion of region-wide commerce across Afghanistan will have major geopolitical consequences. First, by fostering economic progress and social stability within Afghanistan and Greater Central Asia it will help remove once and for all but both China and Russia perceive as a major security threat. It has already been noted that the resulting new patterns of trade will benefit China's "Develop the West" program and will equally benefit development in western Siberia and the southern Urals. This will effectively open a "window to the south" for both countries, but one based on local sovereignties rather than conquest or domination. This in turn will discourage whatever neo-imperial aspirations may exist, notably in Moscow[10].

The South Asian countries are also trying to make integration process at slow rate. The Asian Development Bank is committed to helping these nations create a better future for their people and the region. The CAREC Program has an urgent need to broaden its geographical scope. Given recent developments relating to Afghanistan and the joining of new members, concrete ways of cooperation need to be explored and developed to assist the countries in Central Asia to seize this historic window of opportunities. Afganistan has become a member of SAARC also. CARs could make significant contributions to the reconstruction and development of Afghanistan by using available human and natural resources. In turn, Afghanistan could provide a route for exporting natural resources of CARs to South Asia. The CARs and Afghanistan have expressed their strong interests in close cooperation in the reconstruction of Afghanistan. The building of trust, mutual understanding, and consensus has been a key to past progress of the CAREC Program and continues to be critical for its future success. Experience demonstrates that effective institutional support could contribute much to this end, and, in this regard, the overall institutional framework established in 2002 between ADB and the participating countries will play a crucial role. ADB, as CAREC Program's secretariat, is committed to ensuring the effective functioning of the framework. At the same time, closer coordination with development partners will be sought as other agencies are also increasing their assistance to address regional challenges. The Greater Silk Road Initiative will be launched in support of regional economic cooperation, aimed at achieving concrete progress toward stability and prosperity in Central Asia.[11] (ADB, Technical Assistance for the Greater Silk Road Initiative, 2002)

Central Asia–South Asia Regional Electricity Market (CASAREM)

The Asian Development Bank (ADB) has been requested to provide technical assistance (TA) for a techno-economic assessment to help prepare the Central Asia–South Asia Regional Electricity Market (CASAREM) power transmission project. The World Bank was requested to support the countries through an institutional, financial, risk mitigation, and legal framework study (commercial assessment). The Kyrgyz Republic and Tajikistan in Central Asia, and Afghanistan and Pakistan in South Asia have been pursuing the development of a regional electricity market. To examine the possibilities for regional electricity trade, the countries, together with international financial institutions and private sector met in Islamabad (May 2006), Istanbul (June 2006), Manila (October 2006), and Dushanbe (October 2006). Significant progress was made during the Multi-Country Working Group (MCWG) meeting, which was hosted by ADB and held in Manila on 5 and 6 October 2006. Concept clearance was given on24 October 2006. A memorandum of understanding on project development was signed between the countries on 29 October 2006 at the Second CASAREM Conference. fact-finding was undertaken through consultations during the conferences and the MCWG meeting[12] (ADB's Technical Assistance Report, 2006). The governments agreed on the impact, outcome, outputs, implementation arrangements, and outline terms of reference of the consultants, because they know that Afghanistan and Pakistan have significant electricity shortages and need to meet increasing demand. Importing electricity is becoming more important in their strategies for energy supply security, in addition to building power generation plants. Neighboring Central Asian countries the Kyrgyz Republic and Tajikistan have electricity surpluses available for export and are actively looking for export markets. They also have the potential to increase supply by developing additional low-cost hydropower generation facilities. Some electricity interconnections already exist between Afghanistan and Central Asian countries, notably Tajikistan, Turkmenistan, and Uzbekistan, but there is scope for expansion. Construction of a 220-kilovolt line between Uzbekistan and Afghanistan is already under way (with financial assistance from ADB, the Government of India, and the World Bank), and a similar project is under consideration for an Afghanistan Tajikistan connection with potential ADB financing. The Kyrgyz Republic and Tajikistan, with their large hydropower resources, have been seeking opportunities to expand electricity exports to Afghanistan and beyond to South Asia.

Afghanistan, the Kyrgyz Republic, Pakistan, and Tajikistan have been pursuing the development of electricity trading arrangements and the establishment of CASAREM, together with international financial institutions and the private sector. The initial plan is to export a minimum of 1,000 megawatts (MW) from the Kyrgyz Republic and Tajikistan to Afghanistan and Pakistan. Although the preference for Pakistan would be year-round supply of 1,000 MW, agreement has been reached on seasonal supply for the initial period. Pakistan expressed interest in increasing imports over the medium term beyond the initial 1,000 MW.

Any electricity trade project has some risk, and CASAREM has some specific ones. General risks include: governments basing their decisions more on political than economic rationales. This has delayed or and impeded other projects. Electricity trade projects have financial risks as off-take risk of the importers and compensation risk of the transmission providers and exporters when they fail to meet their contracted obligations. Legal and regulatory risks include inability to enforce contracts and changes in laws or regulations, which makes projects economically unsustainable. Projects can likewise face political violence or sabotage. CASAREM also faces technical risks in crossing high mountains and rugged terrain, and technical losses. These risks must be mitigated if the project is to be economically attractive for the countries and to attract financing from commercial partners. Active partnership to address all risks and clear decision points before progressing with the Project will be necessary to start the electricity trade by 2010. The first decision point was the memorandum of understanding (MOU) for CASAREM signed at the Dushanbe conference. The second will be the intergovernmental agreement scheduled for mid 2007 when the final decision to proceed with the Project is made. ADB has been active in CASAREM meetings and conferences. At the first MCWG meeting in Manila, the countries reconfirmed their keen interest in going forward with the Project and agreed to accelerate its processing and implementation to start the electricity trade by 2010. The MCWG requested ADB support for the techno-economic feasibility study. Through the MOU, the countries endorsed the terms of reference for the two studies to be undertaken by ADB and World Bank The signing of the MOU in Dushanbe also commits the countries to pursue the feasibility of the transmission and trading system with the concomitant institutional and legal framework for the 1,000 MW power transfer and confirms that private sector participation will be given preference. Once its feasibility is established, the MOU commit the countries to pursue it until financial closure[13]. Once this trade will start between countries, Tajikstan will get extra incentives through trade will produce more electricity and the in future it might be the possibility that not only Afganistan, Pakistan's demand fulfilled but India's also can be. Let us hope for the better start.

The Central-South Asian Transport and Trade Forum (CSATTF)

The Central-South Asian Transport and Trade Forum (CSATTF) is an initiative to establish transport corridors in Central and South Asian. It began with ADB assistance in 2003 with the aim of promoting economic growth and social development and reducing poverty in the six participating countries Afghanistan, Iran, Pakistan, Tajikistan, Turkmenistan, and Uzbekistan. This will be done by strengthening regional transport and trade links and by opening up alternative routes for third country trade. The corridor initiative is expected to cost about US$5.7 billion. Iran also participates in its meetings as an observer and uses its own resources for infrastructural and customs improvement. China, India, Kazakhstan, and Kyrgyz Republic participated in its second meeting in March, 2005[14] (Fredrick, Starr, 2007). It is expected that funding will be a joint effort of the countries concerned and assistance will be provided by multilateral institutions and the international community.

Asian Highway Network

During the Sixtieth Session of UNESCAP at Shanghai, China in April 2004, Bhutan along with 22 other countries signed the Intergovernmental Agreement on the Asian Highway Network[15]. (IMF Report, 2004) With 140,000 kms in span, the Asian highway Network will extend to 32 Asian countries, linking the capital cities and other major commercial centers. It is expected to open opportunities, especially for landlocked central Asian countries, to reach the European markets.

UNDP and UNESCAP initiated Silk Route Area Program formally in the autumn of 2000. The project focused on reviving the traditional Silk Route connecting Asia with Europe. China, Kazakhstan, Uzbekistan, Kyrgyzstan and Tajikistan are its members. For the moment Turkmenistan is not participating in the project. The program not only related to the development of the corridor but also looks after transport and border crossing facilitation. It aims at activating a specific transport corridor and to link the economic resources of this region to international markets. Transportation and Railway Ministers of 17 Asian countries signed an agreement on 10th November 2006 in Bussan, South Korea on a continental railway net work in Asia. Ministers of Armenia, Azerbaijan, Combodia, China, Indonesia, Iran Kazakhstan, Laos, Mongolia, Nepal, South Korea, Russia, Sri lanka, Tajikistan, Thailand, Turkey, Uzbekistan and Vietnam is regarded as a major breakthrough in accelerating the establishment of an international transport system in the Asia pacific region. The Trans – Asian Railway Network Starts on the Pacific Seaboard of Asia and ends on the door step of Europe. It comprises 81000 km of railway lines passing through 28 countries[16] (The Hindu, 2006).

North-South Transport Corridor

India, Iran and Russia have established this corridor to restore the historical trade between South Asia and Europe. The corridor stretches from ports in India and cross the Arabian Sea towards the southern Iranian ports of Bandar Abbas and onward to Caspian. From there, it moves on to Moscow and onward to northern Europe. It has been believed that the delivery time can be reduced by 10 to 20 days and the cost of container by US$ 400 to US$ 500. Many regional countries like Kazakhstan, Kyrgyzstan, Uzbekistan and Azerbaijan are interested in the project.

(From chinese point of view) Sharing the efforts to promote regional integration, Toru Shibuchi, China country Director of the Asian Development Bank (ADB), said the ADB has been devoted to promote regional integration in Asia through some trade-facilitation measures. Henry Wang, corporate planning director of Shell China, said he totally agreed with the importance of regional co-operation. The Chinese Ambassador to India Giving the chemical industry as an example, Wang said the promotion of the use of clean energy such as natural gas and LNG (liquefied natural gas) in Asian countries, including China, would help achieve win-win integration and benefit the countries and the companies involved. "When it comes to regional integration, China could be a major pool of talent in Asia," (Nathula trade pass) With the opening of the Nathua Pass Trade between India and China, Even People here in Ladakh hope that traditional trade routes would reopen soon They are recalling Leh as a flourishing base for traders from as far as Central Asia who came here to sell their products and which

Map 5: International North South Transport Corridor

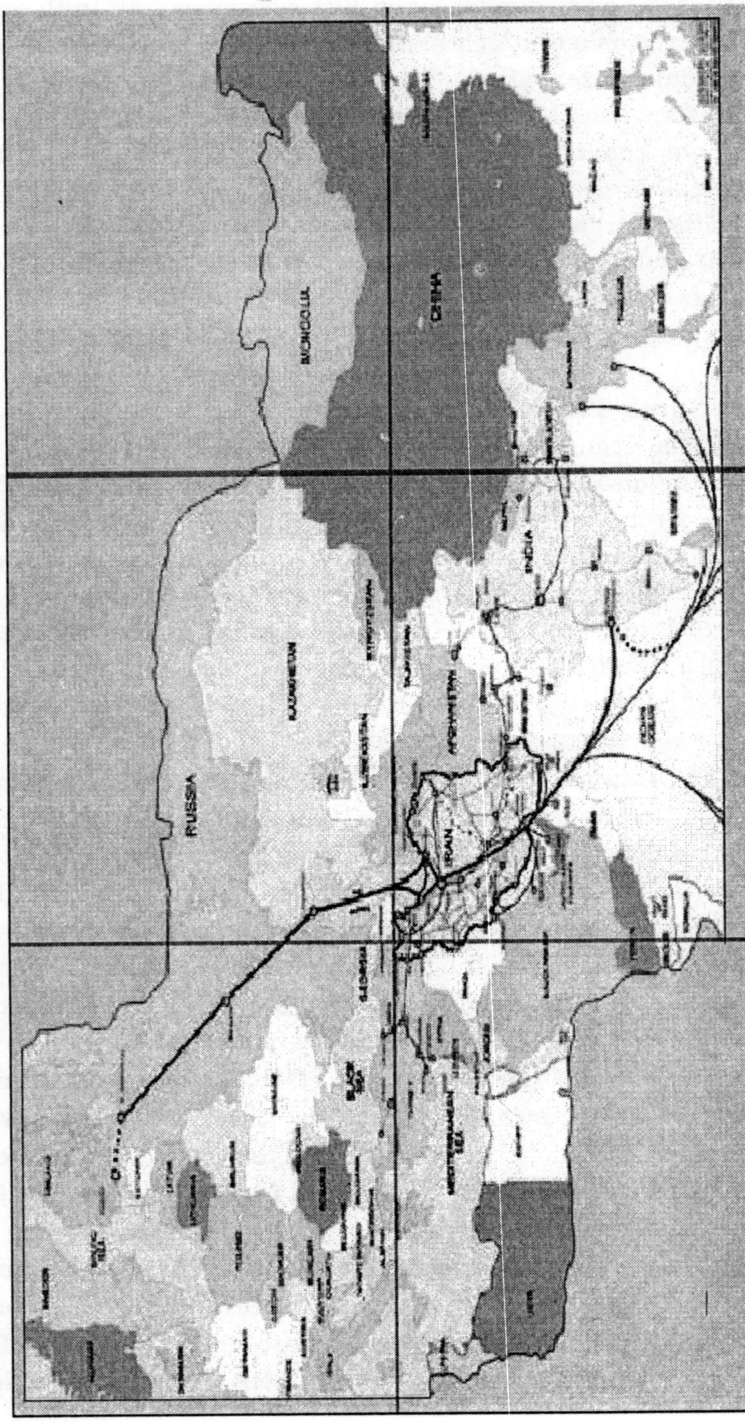

Source: International North South Transport Corridor Secretariat website www.instc.org

they made their way to the Indian plains or we can say to all South Asian Countries. Similarly caravan from Ladakh used to go to Central Asia. This would also help in a way that Ladakh is cut off from the rest of the countries for more than six months, during which all economic activities came to standstill [17]. (The Hindu, 2006)

India, Pakistan and Afghanistan as a bridge to South, West and Central Asia for East Asia

With its excellent trading and transport links and emerging preferential trading arrangements with South Asian countries, GCC and West Asian countries India could act as a bridge for East Asia for the markets in South, West and Central Asian countries.[18] (Kumar, 2005) It can be argued that India's participation in the grouping will make it more balanced and less susceptible to domination by any particular large country. As Hon'ble Keizo Takemi, Member, National Diet, Japan has argued, India is needed for maintaining a balance in East Asia given the huge influence of China. Noted Singapore diplomat Mr K. Kesavapany has observed that any such group without India in it will seem unbalanced, as though one leg of the table is missing. The first rail connection between the Central Asian republics and China only opened in 1990, and no rail link to their southern neighbors existed before the 1990s[19]. (Richard, 2003)

Kyrgyzstan has become a member of the WTO and the other regional states have also shown interest in becoming members. The European Union (EU) has granted Central Asian countries access to the Generalized System of Preferences (GSP). It allows tariff reductions on manufactured products and certain agricultural goods.

Indian policy makers and analysts believe that the region is important because of its strategic location, proximity – Tajikistan is just 20 kilometers from Greater Kashmir - and of its energy resources. Therefore, restoring traditional linkages with its extended neighborhood in Central Asia and beyond has been one of the primary strategic priorities of the government. Despite the intentions and rhetoric, India was never really part of any competition there. With no direct road or transportation access plus difficult market conditions, the region never became attractive to

Indian private companies. In the post-socialist period, economic relations with the region have declined considerably. In the last few years, the annual official trade between India and the whole of Central Asian region is about US$200 million. Kazakhstan itself accounts for half of this trade. Still, opportunities are enormous as shown by London based Indian steel tycoon Laxmi Mittal who owns a 5.5 million ton capacity steel plant in Kazakhstan. His company employs 50,000 people in Kazakhstan alone from where it supplies the Chinese market. In May 2006, the Indian government also officially approved its participation in the US$5 billion Turkmenistan-Afghanistan-Pakistan- India (TAPI) gas pipeline project. In another development, there are also reports that India has established an airbase in Tajikistan. The Indian Air Force is going to deploy a fleet of MiG-29 fighter-bombers at the Ayni airbase near Dushanbe. The airbase follows the establishment of India's first military "outpost" in Tajikistan at Farkhor, adjoining the Tajik-Afghan border. The location is important as it is close to the bases of anti-Indian terrorist groups as well as near the territory where Pakistan and China are engaged in military cooperation. Indian policy makers have been more or less comfortable in dealing with Central Asian authoritarian leaders. They were part of the former Soviet elite, with whom India was dealing with for decades. They have provided stability and are committed to fight religious terrorism. Moreover, many analysts believed that Russia will continue to have a decisive role in Central Asia because of its advantage of history and geography. Although many Indian analysts still believe in the reemergence of Russia, a sober assessment is also made of a scenario in which over time China becomes a dominant player in Central Asia while maintaining very friendly relations with Russia[20].

However, the proposition of linking Central and South Asian regions could only be attractive to Central Asians if they have direct access to the rapidly growing Indian market. This can happen only if Afghanistan stabilizes and Pakistan provides direct access of Central Asian goods to India and vice versa. Afghanistan's on-going transformation from a failed into a viable democratic state with a market economy could facilitate this linkage[21] (Sachdeva, 2006). (From the commitments of the international community and multilateral institutions, it is clear that a massive effort to rebuild Afghanistan's transport network and economy is underway. Already, the Asian Development Bank is working on many plans to improve institutional as well as infrastructural development in the region. Pakistan has also still not extended MFN status to India and has refused to implement the South Asian Free Trade Area (SAFTA) with India, which became operational on 1 July 2006. (Iran and China for transit of Caspian oil to international markets (like the Baku- Tbilisi-Ceyhan pipeline) could jeopardize the energy security of India and China. Therefore, they argue that India, China and Iran "need to evolve multiple strategies for security and economic cooperation in Central Asia, including trilateral framework involving the three"[22] (Patnaik, 2005).

The studies show that there is demand of energy in South Asia and Central Asia has the capabilities to fulfill that. But there are other school of thought also they worry that one should explore the potential that for how long Central Asia can provide the supply. Are there sufficient resources to fulfill the requirements? A senior ADB energy specialist has given his views

"The reserves information shows that Turkmenistan could supply enough gas for the first few years but then production is predicted to decline instead of increase," says Dan Millison, a senior Asian Development Bank (ADB) energy specialist. "They will need to find gas from other fields to meet pipeline design targets." In the meantime, a $7 billion scheme to pipe natural gas to India and Pakistan from offshore Iran is also gaining momentum. "If the Iran pipeline is green lighted first, the Turkmenistan project might be put on the back burner for a while. However, with long-term gas demand from India and Pakistan estimated at 50 BCM a year, there is a need for more than one pipeline,"[23] notes Mr. Millison. ADB has brokered the 1,700-kilometer (km) pipeline project from Turkmenistan since 2002, promoting it as a win-win example of regional cooperationa pioneering effort to link gas-rich Central Asia with energy-deficient South Asia through Afghanistan[24]. (the Hindu, 2005)

Meaanwhile, Bowie said China should focus more on establishing a sound financial system and free flow of services in the country to help propel the process of regional integration.

Furthermore, William Lo, Executive Director and Vice-President of China Unicom Ltd, said he was familiar with integration as it happened a lot in the telecom industry, and he had a distinctive view on the issue. "Integration is a matter of time. It does not come from the government's initiatives but from the contribution of the private sector," said Lo. Ying Yeh, chairman of Eastman Kodak Greater China Region, pointed out that governments in Asia should consider more for the multinational companies when formulating regional trade and economic policies. "The business sector should be the primary force of the process of regional integration, and integration would turn into empty talk, without a contribution from the private sector," Long said.

"Multinationals should play an active role here by providing information and incentives, as well as policy advice to governments," Long concluded.[25] (China, 2005)

Challenges of Expansion of Central Asian to South Asia

Due to the land locked location, this has become a challenge for this region to achieve steady growth and integration into global economy. Some other factors such as Ideological rivalry, Islamic fundamentalism, Russian's unwillingness to part away with the resource rich region are obstacle on the way of economic growth and integration into world economic system. As these economies are naturally rich in resources, the western sectors' interest is there in the region. United States' moves in the region, China's interest in this region and Pakistan and Saudi Arabia have shown their own narrow sectarian dominance in the region. India has also shown traditional friendly relations by helping them in nation building process. But question arises that whether the domestic economic policies are favorable or not.

The two largest countries Uzbekistan and Kazakhstan compete for regional hegemony.[26] They have avoided any significant commitment to regional trading arrangements may be due to Turkmenistan's with its fierce neutrality and Tajikistan's civil war. Kyrgyzstan has also become a member of World Trade Organisation (WTO).

Even then the Central Asia has reached the forefront of international attention. The Central Asia, the world's land locked region is resource rich and offers considerable trade and investment opportunities. But due to lack of effective transport routes and relative isolation made it difficult for all countries to access international markets immediately after the independence. So creating attention transit transport routes has become an important pre-condition for the promotion of trade and development.[27] (Islamov, 2001)

ECO was initially involved in the conceptualization of this project. However, later UNDP adopted the program and in collaboration with China and UNESCAP has been spearheading the program. The program enjoyed recognition and support of western countries. It holds some prospects for success in integrating Central Asian Transport corridors with global corridors.

As a result of these initiatives, the countries in the region have made some modest gains in regional cooperation. Although a limited amount of regional trade has developed in Central Asia, its growth has been uneven at best. These countries started with roughly similar trade policies, but trade policy regimes today vary from very liberal in the Kyrgyz Republic to quite restrictive in Uzbekistan and Turkmenistan. Despite the common interest of increasing trade, all the countries in the region have trade-restricting policies and practices such as tariffs, restrictive procedures and regulations, and weak financial systems. Other policy-related constraints to trade include import quotas, export licensing requirements, and transport restrictions. Arbitrary and often corrupt bureaucracies throughout the region administer regulations that are archaic and frequently conflicting. Slow and difficult border procedures, multiple cargo inspections within a single country, and prohibitions that prevent vehicles from transporting goods between countries also hinder further gains in cooperation. Other barriers to trade include high transit fees and the costs of dealing with corrupt border officials and local police in both the regions. Trade is also restricted by such practices as requiring importers to register contracts and restrictions on currency conversion. Due to the lack of a healthy financial system, a large part of trade is still conducted through inefficient cash transfers or barter.

Similar initiatives are underway in South Asia and in Central Asia, with exciting prospects for future development. The two sub-regions have joined together in an effort to connect landlocked

Central Asia and seaports in South Asia via Afghanistan. Based on this partnership, we can envisage Afghanistan as a regional hub, and a critical link between the South and Central Asian markets[28] (Kurodo, 2005).

Tashkent, Dushanbe and Bishkek, the capitals of Uzbekistan, Tajikistan and Kyrgyzstan, are as close to Delhi by air as Chennai. Now independent and sovereign, they look elsewhere, despite their almost umbilical past connections with Russia. The republic of Kazakhstan is as large as India, and the CARs are extremely rich in energy resources and other raw materials, such as gold, uranium, iron and non-ferrous metals. Central Asia became a separate geopolitical region after the breakup of the USSR, which had united ethnic groups who had long shared a historical period of truly difficult relations. The disintegration of the Soviet state led to a situation in which historical conflicts between ethnic groups and former Soviet republics (or their sub-regions) began to manifest themselves in an open form. The breakup of the USSR initiated the process of ethnic state-formation on the territory of Central Asia. Nation-states had never before in history existed in Central Asia, and their establishment was completely new. The Soviets arbitrarily redrew borders between republics in the 1920s which created the present situation. Today one finds that the natural borders between settlements of various groups of people were replaced by administrative ones, thus these non-historical divisions have received the status of state borders. The new state borders of the republics do not correspond with their ethnic borders. This, in the future, could serve as a reason for interstate conflicts. This could occur in the south of Kazakhstan between Kazakhs and Uzbeks; in Osh and Uzgen between Kyrgyz and Uzbeks; in Samarqand, Bukhara and in the Khujand oblast of Tajikistan between Uzbeks and Tajiks; in Karakalpakstan between Uzbeks and Karakalpaki; in the oasis of the Amu Darya river, between Uzbeks and Turkmen; or in northern Kazakhstan between Kazakhs and Russians, who are the native residents of the area. In these regions, greatly differing national, religious and cultural groups find them selves united in one state.

The state borders in Central Asia are, for the most part, very long and difficult to protect. In the western regions of Central Asia, almost all run through the desert and are "real" only on maps. The opposite situation exists in the Fergana valley, where the fertile land is divided between Uzbekistan, Tajikistan and Kyrgyzstan. The high population density in this region, and lack of natural borders, make this area potentially volatile as far as ethnic conflicts are concerned. As part of the Soviet Union, Central Asia was a united economic region, with a focus on the delivery of raw materials. Russia served as the supplier of many crucial resources and products to the region, which allowed for the creation of a modern transportation network. Administrative borders were not taken into account in economic relations. Thus, the unity of the regional economy during the Soviet period has been eliminated with the introduction of the modern status of independent states.

Kyrgyzstan is the only country in which there are no restrictions on the activities of opposition parties. Thus, it seems quite logical for the Central Asian states to be included in numerous organizations and institutions, namely the United Nations, the Organization of Security and Cooperation in Europe, The Community of Central Asian States (Uzbekistan, Kazakhstan and Kyrgyzstan), and the Organization for Economic Cooperation, whose main objective is to strengthen economic cooperation with the region and to render political support to Central Asia and Azerbaijan. Security risks for Central Asia come from within, as well as from their neighbors. Concern over preserving the status quo in Central Asia demonstrated by Russia, China, the US, Western Europe and Turkey serves as a stabilizing force itself. Nevertheless, the overall situation may change as a result of geopolitical shifts and internal regrouping of forces. Afghanistan is probably the only real source of instability, as it actively supports Central Asian fundamentalism.

However, the Islamification of society has taken place in groups of society who object to the rule of the local elite established during the Soviet period. The realization of the threat to personal interests forced the local elite to carry out selective policies, supporting moderate Islamists and suppressing extremist forces. Therefore, during the end of 1993 politics, began to change: multi-party and two-party agreements were made which would provide for the restoration of destroyed relations, the financing of Central

Asian states by Russia was reestablished, and the emigration of native Russians was discouraged. However, the unclear political definition of Russia itself gave this policy a rather contradictory and illogical character. From an objective point of view, Central Asia is "doomed" to have close relations with Russia in the short-term. The Central Asian countries are trying to distance themselves from Russia, as many see its actions as recurrences of imperialism and do not approve of the increase in Russia's influence. For example, the attempts by Tajik President Imomali Rahmonov to concentrate exclusively on Russia led to changes by Uzbekistan, Kazakhstan and Kyrgyzstan in their positions regarding the current regime in Tajikistan. However, the Central Asian countries do admit that Russia, more or less, guarantees political stability in the region. Even representatives of Tajikistan's unrecognized opposition (located in Afghanistan) recognize this, and the 100-year anniversary of Gorno Badakshan's union with Russia was celebrated in Pamir. Russia is the guarantor of stable external borders of the CIS states. The republics are dependant on Russia for military and defense purposes as well. This does not just mean military supplies and Russian border guards, but also the training of military troops and the short-term necessity of retaining the overwhelmingly Slavic officer corps. Central Asian elites also need to pay attention to the position of Slavs and Tatars in the economy of their republics. Nationalism flourishes in this regard; clear discrimination exists against non-Central Asian natives in higher education, promotions at work, cultural autonomy and obtaining property during privatization (everywhere except Kyrgyzstan). However, the leaders recognize that it is precisely these non-Central Asian natives who embody the modern sector of the economy, and their mass exodus would put the region decades behind in development and modernization. Russia's cultural and ideological relations are also quite significant. Practically all non-Central Asian natives (not just Russians) perceive Russia as their center. Representatives of local ethnic groups are oriented toward Russia, as they probably were educated in Russia, have Slavic relatives or were raised in the spirit of Russian culture. This group is highly opposed to Islamic fundamentalism, knowing that they will have no place in their own country in case of an Islamification of the government. To conclude, we can say that Russia povided boarder issue to Central Asia and British Empire Provided boarder issues to South Asia. So that both the region should fight on the issues of boarder Islamic fundamentalism. They can not be able to think about the peace and prosperity.

Successful regional cooperation will be a crucial element in the future peace and prosperity of Central Asia as well as of South Asia, according to a recent Asian Development Bank (ADB) survey The time is right, then to seriously promote the concept of a free trade zone, and later even an economic community, for the countries of the two regions, shifting the emphasis from the current agenda of ethnic, linguistic and border strife to one of close economic cooperation and integration, as in the Europe Union, or nearer home, ASEAN, and its alliance with China, which should make the leadership in South and Central Asia sit up and take note. If the Europeans could overcome their vast differences, having constantly fought wars against each other, why can't the South and Central Asians? Meanwhile, they are the only ones unprepared for the world as a new global bazaar and the economic challenges of this century. It is worth noting that the proliferation of free trade agreements poses challenges, as well as opportunities. Now is the time, as so many deals are being struck, to ensure consistency within the web of free trade agreements that is emerging in Asia. To promote this approach, ADB has recently initiated a study of free trade agreements in Asia, which will provide recommendations for harmonizing these agreements. Doing so will ensure that Asian regionalism remains an open regionalism open to trade and investment within the region, and with the global economy. (President Haruhiko hurdo, ADB), New York, 13th Sep. 2005) strongly believe that regional cooperation and integration provides a key to unlocking Asia's vast economic potential and help raise the living standards of its people. This, in turn, will bring greater stability to the region, improve the business climate and provide growing opportunities for the business sector, both in Asia and abroad. These debates have played a significant role in creating an intellectual environment for introducing and advancing economic changes. During the first two millennium upto 1820 Asia (including Japan) accounted for 68% of the world population and

60% of the world income going back further around the year 1500 Asia accounted for the global GDP. During 1820 to 1950 Asia Including Japan still accounted for the bulk of world population 55% and share of world income declined dramatically to about 18%.[29] A Statement made by John Samy, Director General of South Asian Development Bank that Regional co-operation and deep economic integration are key to ensuring that Asia reemerges and regains its position as the Centre of gravity of the world economy. So for economic integration these countries have to take step towards liberalising economic policies.

Asia is a region of great diversity. It is also a region blessed with diligent and capable human resources as well as with a vast pool of savings. It is essential to maximize these advantages in strengthening regional cooperation. The policy efforts on regional cooperation have been active in East Asia. Similar momentum for regional cooperation has been starting in South Asia for few years actively. The potential for regional cooperation in Central Asia and Afghanistan can not even under estimated.

Japan has been actively promoting monetary and financial cooperation in East Asia under the framework of ASEAN+3 Finance Ministers' Meeting and hopes that such regional cooperation will expand all over Asia in the future. Regional cooperation and integration should contribute to the growth of the global economy and should not be exclusive of other regions.

The economy of scale can be drive by the expansion of the market. Since the Asian region contains more than half the world's population, it could make up a truly mega-market beyond national boundaries. Notably, the ratio of intra-regional trade in East Asia has dramatically increased in recent years. This is a sign that the potential of a regional integrated market has turned into reality. In Asia, comparative advantages vary from country to country. Some are industrial, while others are agricultural. Some excel in sophisticated manufactured goods, others in versatile products. Some have knowledge-intensive industries, others a labor force that is inexpensive and plentiful. Thus, regional integration in Asia can generate an even greater synergy effect than by simply adding up the strength of each country. There have also been initiatives to strengthen linkages of policy-making in the region in order to create a regional economic structure that is resilient to global economic changes. While referring to the case of EU integration, A step towards economic integration has already been taken in Asia. This would be helpful in exploring the possibility of future regional integration of Asia. Regional Initiative such like JICAK (Japan, India, China, ASEAN, Korea), if work actively, it would be helpful for the whole Asia. As Japan, India and China are committed to promoting economic cooperation and integration for the future prosperity of the region[30] (Kumar, 2005). Now, time has come to think about the Asia's prosperity. All Asian govt. authorities, intellectual, think tank community, business community should work together to make Asian continent as a single rich continent so that it could help to break the hegemony of west especially us.

References

1. Starr, Fredric, (2005) *A Greater Central Asia Parternership for Afganistan and its Neighbors,* Caucaus Institute and Silk Road Studies Program, Washington DC., p. 14.
2. Starr, Fredric, ed., (2007), *the New Silk Roads Transport and trade in greater Central Asia,* Central Asia- Caucaus Institute and Silk Road Studies Program, Washington DC, p. 348. avialble on www.silkroadstudies.org/new/inside/publications/GCA.html.
3. The Hindu, "Myths and Borders" 17th Ausust, 2008, Magazine, New Delhi, p. 3.
4. Ibrokhim R. Mavionov, "India- Central Asia: Moderen economic Diplomacy Trends" in *Central Asia's Affairs*, No. 2, 2006. p
5. Starr, Fredric, ed., (2007), *the New Silk Roads Transport and trade in greater Central Asia,* op.cit, p. 89.
6. UNDP, Central Asia: Increasing Gains from Trade Through Regional Cooperation in Trade Policy, Transport and Customs Transit (Manila: Asian Development Bank, 2006), p. 97.
7. Fradric Starr, has developed the concept of greater Central asia in which these countries are involved, All the central Asian countries Plus India, Pakistan, China, Iran and Afganistan.

8. Fredric Starr, (2007), *the New Silk Roads Transport and trade in greater Central Asia,* op.cit p. 9)
9. ADB review, Central Asia strongest together, October 2005, on www.adb.org/review. p.10.
10. www.adb.org/carec, Rebuilding the Silk Road, Strength through regional cooperation.
11. ADB, (2002), "Technical Assistance for the Greater Silk Road Initiative, TAR:REG 36064, ADB, Manila.
12. ADB 's Technical Assistance Report, (2006), "Preparing the Central Asia–South Asia Regional Electricity Market Project" Project Number: 40537, ADB, Manilla p. 1.
13. ADB technical assistance report, project no. 40537, Dec. 2006, Preparing the Central Asia- South Asia Regional Electricity project) p. 2.
14. Fredrick Starr, ed., (2007), *the New Silk Roads Transport and trade in greater Central Asia,* Central Asia- Caucaus Institute and Silk Road Studies Program, Washington DC, p. 353. avialble on www.silkroadstudies.org/new/inside/publications/GCA.html.
15. Bhutan: Poverty reduction Strategy Paper, IMF Country Report no. 04/246. August, 2004. p. 14.
16. The Hindu, 11.11.2006, New Delhi edition, p. 18.
17. The Hindu, 31st July 2006, N D, p. 13.
18. Nagesh Kumar, 2005, Regional economic cooperation in Asia, RIS, New Delhi. p. 14.
19. Richard Pomfret, 2003, "Central Asia Since 1991: The Experience of new Independent states" paper presented in OECD seminar on 19th Feb. 2003. p. 4.
20. (Gulshan Sachdeva, (2006) India's attitude towards China's growing influence in Central Asia", in *China and Eurasian Forum Quartly* Volume 4 No. 3, 2006 p. 24.) (23-34)
21. Gulshan Sachdeva, (2006)" India's attitude towards China's growing influence in Central Asia", op.cit., p. 28.)
22. (Ajay Patnaik, "Central Asia's Security: the Asian Dimension" in R. R. Sharma, Ed., *India and Emerging Asia* (New Delhi: Sage Publications, 2005), p. 228.)
23. www.adb.org.
24. The Hindu, 2005, p.
25. (China Daily March 30, 2005)

26. Bakhtior A., Islamov, "The Central Asian States ten Year after: How To Overcome Traps of development, Transformation and Globalization", Tokyo: Maruzen Com. Ltd., 2001, p. 185.
27. *Ibid,* p. 186.
28. A speech by President Haruhiko Kuroda, Asian Development Bank,New York, September 13, 2005) 29 (5th April Islamabad, Pakistan).
30. Kumar, Nagesh, (2005), "Regional Economic Cooperation in Asia" in paper presented in 4th High level Conference on Asian Economic Unity by RIS and ISEAS in New Delhi on 18-19 November 2005.

7

Conclusion

In this chapter, major findings of this research work will be summarized.

Major Findings of Central Asia

Regional cooperation in Central Asia is necessary condition to break the land locked situation. While neighboring the world's largest and fastest-growing markets (PRC, India, and Russia), Central Asia's landlocked status means regional transport costs are a serious impediment to development. Cooperation in transport, trade, and transit will yield important benefits. Central Asian countries share vital resources, notably energy and water. Harnessing these resources in a sustainable manner and managing their shared use in support of agriculture, industry, and livelihoods require a high degree of regional cooperation and third party assistance. Regional trade agreements have been, and will likely remain, an important tool for trade liberalization. Most empirical studies find that trade creation dominates trade diversion. In practice several factors increase the benefits of RTAs including large and diverse membership, low external most-favored-nation tariffs, liberal rules of origin and trade facilitation measures. There remains significant scope for trade liberalization in Central Asia. Regional and bilateral preference schemes can play a useful role in promoting regional trade, which remains underdeveloped in Central

Asia. Closer regional cooperation through increased market integration needs to extend beyond trade. Regional transportation networks need to be developed to facilitate access to world markets. Kazakhstan, which accounts for a significant share of Central Asian transit trade, should bears a particular responsibility in this area. Certain aspects of the transit systems currently in place in the CARs impose constraints on cross-border movements of goods by rail and by road. These are, however, not crucial for cross-border movements of goods by rail, for which transport-related factors are a binding constraint. By contrast, inadequacies of the road transit systems impose a binding constraint on trade in Central Asia.

All countries in the region need to ensure that arbitrary restrictions and corruption do not interfere with the flow of goods and services. Moreover, a handful of primary commodities, such as crude oil, metals, and cotton fiber, continued to dominate the CARs' exports. Indeed, the rise in world prices for these commodities was a major factor that contributed to rapid growth of their exports. At the same time, participation of the CARs in GPNs and related international trade in manufactured products remained very limited. Furthermore, the CARs' exports and, to a lesser extent, imports remained concentrated in a small number of countries.

There is another debate going on among scholars, Are the natural resources being proved a curse rather than a blessing? Collectively, these countries can use these rich resources in an efficient manner. Emphasizing cooperation in the areas of water and energy will be crucial for the development of the region. Sound and sustained economic growth requires transparency and good governance. Experience, as well as recent research studies at the IMF, ADB and EBRD shows that transparency is correlated with better investment and growth performance.

Recent developments demonstrate that regional cooperation has not increased in Central Asia despite a number of factors favoring it. Insofar as the Central Asian states are retaining influence over trade and production, their actions so far do not for the most part conform with their many verbal commitments to regional cooperation. Financing for truly cooperative projects is small, and petty interferences at the border do occur. Recognizing that their trade performance depends not only on their trade policy, transport sector, and transit systems but also on the trade policy, transport sector, and transit systems of neighboring countries, the CARs have actively pursued regional cooperation in these areas. In particular, they have joined several regional organizations that involve or seek to reach a multilateral RTA. The two most promising regional institutions, the Intergovernmental Commission and the Central Asian Bank, are still finding their place and influence. Economic policy in these countries discourages mid-sized businesses that would most benefit from a free regional market. Political frictions among the states of the region and their preference for dealing with outsiders, perceived to be more capable and less dangerous, are responsible for the failure to put speech-making into practice. If regional cooperation is to increase, with all its benefits, it will require leadership from the inside or determined and patient assistance from the outside. This region has to face because of the lack of the diversification and the network of economic ties, the infrastructure for export specialization. To overcome from Land locked status, this region continues to suffer from inadequate infrastructure, poor utilization of assets with weak managerial procedural, regularity and institutional system.

There have been a number of regional cooperation initiatives aimed at removing the deficiencies of transport infrastructure and services and facilitating cross-border and transit traffic in the CARs and in neighboring countries. Notably, the CAREC member countries have recently agreed on the Regional Transport Sector Road Map, which formulates the strategic priorities for regional cooperation in the transport sector and addresses most of the deficiencies of rail and road transport in Central Asia. These agreements have, however, had very limited effects on the custom transit in Central Asia due to many reasons. Some of them have not been entered into force, while those that have entered into force not have not been implemented.

This is mainly due to unfinished reforms, especially in establishment of strong institutions to support market economy through the transparent, predictable and well-enforced rules and regulations.

Major findings of South Asia

South Asia has recently witnessed some dynamism in economic growth. India is regarded as a major global player, especially in services. Pakistan and India achieved a growth favourable growth rate in the last fiscal year and is on its way to becoming a significant global player. Recent growth performance is impressive also in Sri Lanka and Bangladesh. Regional cooperation in South Asia cannot be said to have evolved into a complete bloc in terms of 'regionalism and economic integration' due mainly to the prevalence of conflict over the desire of peace and stability. Given the historical legacy and contemporary reality of endemic conflicts and mistrust in the region, the fact that the formal cooperation process in the region has survived recurrent setbacks is testimony of resilience of the organization. The antagonistic nature of relations with large sets of outstanding issues, low levels of intra-SAARC trade and joint economic ventures, inadequate information and infrastructure facilities. Independent and largely uncoordinated economic policies pursued by each country of the region are all indicators of lack of 'region-ness' and indication a unwelcoming future for any type of sustainable economic integration.

However, South Asian countries are also fast reducing barriers to trade to the rest of the world under the auspices of the WTO, thereby opening themselves to trade with many other countries, Yet the trade within the region is very low as compare to other region. Low external tariffs can reduce the possibility of trade diversion, and non-restrictive rules of origin result in expanded trade possibilities. But compared to the successful South East Asian countries, South Asia has been unable as yet to integrate within the region as well as with the global economy in terms of its potential. The South Asian countries are keen to move towards a stronger regional groupings and bilateral trade arrangements. Though the signing of bilateral FTAs has resulted in a spaghetti bowl of FTAs, these can lead to benefits in terms of an increase in exports from the lesser-developed countries in the region, as well as an expansion in investment flows. India should take the lead in this regard and play the role of an anchor economy, especially for the successful implementation of SAFTA.

There is now a growing opinion that the process of economic integration in south Asia will remain held up unless there is a change in the mindset of the political establishment in these countries. There is an urgent need to redefine our strategy for the development of this region. Needless to say there is a need to put more emphasis on the security of the state and on human security in these countries. So in this context it is hard to over emphasize the need for closer economic ties among all the countries of South Asia as economic cooperation and economic integration has been observed to have played a positive role in providing political stability in many regions earlier suffering from political strive. European Union has set an example of stability and also proves the poor countries can also get the benefits of regional economic cooperation. The countries like German and France, which fought for many years, could cooperate by opening their boarders. This is an example of stability and progress. Moreover, under the impact of globalization and liberalization the states in South Asia have lost much of the space available to them earlier for the exercise of policy options and for making macroeconomic policy decisions. This has serious implications for ensuring peace, justice and sustainability of development in their own countries and for their ability to cooperate with each other. Therefore, a major task in the south Asian countries should cooperate with each other so that they could get the maximum benefits of this globalization process in order to have better space in this world. The South Asian countries missed the tide that carried many of their East and Southeast Asian neighbors to record rates of growth and poverty reduction during the 1960s and 1970s, but their later trade policy and other liberalizing reforms came in time to for them to benefit from the expansion of production and trade in the world economy. Now both the region should not miss the bus again. They should work collectively and help each other to overcome the challenges. The countries like Turkmenistan and Pakistan should realize that in this globalization era and interdependent on each other, it is difficult to survive in isolalism. So for the betterment of living standard of people they should cooperate with each other.

Recommendations

The first and a major measure to undertake is support for cross border infrastructure development. In order to capitalize on the benefits from scale of regional integration, it is essential to improve key infrastructure such as cross-border transport, telecommunications and power transmission. It is also important to unify the rules for power interchange to ensure its effective use.

Liberalize trade policy in a more coordinated manner to avoid a situation in which trade liberalization by one country prompts its neighbors with a more restrictive trade policy to tighten restrictions on cross-border movements of people and transport equipment in an effort to counter the aversion of their trade with other countries through the country, liberalizing trade policy more rapidly;

The second point is provision of assistance for strengthening regional financial markets. In order to channel regional savings for regional infrastructure, the ADB's regional departments can facilitate financial sector reform. The Private Sector Operations Department provides supports to catalyze private capital flows and to strengthen private financial institutions. The Treasury Department is expected to contribute to the development of regional bond markets by issuing local currency bonds. It is essential for the ADB to establish systematic linkage between the roles of these departments, so that the ADB can increase its effectiveness as a whole. The third point is promotion of intra-regional cooperation on trade. Remove the infrastructure bottlenecks constraining movements of goods across borders by rail, Enhance competition in rail, air, and international road transport—in particular, by restructuring state -owned railways and airlines, separating regulatory and commercial functions in the transport sector, and creating a level playing field for domestic and foreign transport operators.

The final point is the encouragement of policy dialogues on regional economy to help exchanges of views on economic policies of each country. Multilateral and bilateral development agencies will help the both the regions closely integrate within the region as well as into the international trading system, increase the gains from trade, and achieve sustainable development if they integrate technical and financial assistance in the areas of trade policy, transport, and trade facilitation, for example, by tying funding for transport infrastructure projects to requirements aimed at facilitating cross-border movements of goods and transport equipment. These institutions will assist them, if they increase technical and financial assistance in improving the quality of transport and logistics services in both the regions. They can support them to get maximum benefits of improved regional economic cooperation and helps build supportive constituencies

The ADB has played a key role in promoting dialogue among countries of the Greater Mekong Subregion (GMS) and Central Asia to facilitate intra-regional trade, for example, by harmonizing customs procedures. It is also important for the ADB to supplement private financial institutions by trade finance facilitation. ADB has already been playing a significant role to improve economic cooperation within the regions. These countries should also cooperate in implementing the trade policies to enhance trade among their countries.

Many Institutions and economic initiatives set up for the regional economic cooperation in Central Asia and South Asia should be active and they should keep eye on :

- establish and maintain, through regular, day-to-day contact and consultation,
- long-term working relationships with key government agencies responsible for regional economic cooperation;
- help identify the government's needs and implementing capacity building for Regional economic cooperation;
- ensure the implementation of the regional work program in the country;
- help identify and develop potential new areas of the initiative;
- monitor programs and initiatives of the government and regional organizations on regional economic cooperation; identify, evaluate, and recommend potential areas.
- monitor programs of other stakeholders, especially of external funding agencies
- operating in the country; identify, evaluate, and recommend potential areas of Cooperation;
- report on all activities, monthly; and yearly.

Empirical findings of this research shows there is lot of potential for growth for both the regions since both are complementary to each other. This study also highlighted the feasibility aspects to reach to the potential level.

I personally feel that Asia is a rich continent. There is compresive need to preserve is rich resources, culture values, customs by cooperiting with each other. With unity of strategy, thought and action we can fight out terrorism and could establish peace in the regions. Apart from boarder issues there is need to concentrate on economic mutual benefits and enhance the prosperity and welfare of the people. There is utmost need to change the mind set of the people involved thereof and make them understood that fighting with each other would yield no substantial results.

Bibliography

Primary Sources

Asian Development Outlook, Manila: Asian Development Bank, 1985-2004.

Regional Economic Co-operation in Central Asia, Manila: Asian Development Bank, July 1998.

Global Economic Prospects 2005: Trade, Regionalism and Development, Washington DC: World Bank, 2005.

Government Finance Statistics Yearbook, IMF Publication Services, 1991,1995.

IMF Balance of Payments Statistics Yearbook, Washington DC: IMF Publication Services, 1991-2003.

IMF Directions of Trades Statistics Year Book, Washington DC: IMF Publication Services, 1991-2003.

International Financial Statistics, Washington DC: IMF Publications, 1985-2004.

Key Indicators of Developing Asian Pacific Countries, Manila: Asian Development Bank, 1993-2003.

UN CATAD Report, Central Asia, Vol I, 2002.

UN CATAD Report, Central Asia, Vol II, 2002

UN Economic Bulletin of Europe, Geneva: United Nations Economic Commission of Europe (UNECE), 1992-1997.

UN Economic Survey of Europe, Geneva: UNECE, 1992-2004.

UN *Foreign Trade Statistics of Asia and Pacific'*, UN Publications.

World Development Report, Washington DC: the World Bank, 1991-2004.

World Development Indicators, Washington DC: the World Bank, *(various years)*

World Trade Organization, Regional Trade Agreements Gateway http://www.wto.org/english/tratop_e/region_e/region_e.htm

Important Web Sites

www.adb.org
www.alca-ftaa.org
www.apecsec.org.
www.aric.adb.org.
www.cer.org.uk.
www.recep.org
www.ebrd.com
www.eurasianet.org
www.europa.eu.int
www.hw.ac.uk/ecoWWW/cert
www.icrier.res.in/south Asia
www.imf.org
www.oecd.org
www.ris.org.in.
www.saarc-sec.org
www.southasia.net
www.unece.org
www.worldbank.org
www.wto.org

Secondary Sources

Books

Akiner, Shirin, (1994), *Political and Economic Trends in Central Asia,* British Academy Press, London.

Anand R P, (1991), *South Asian Search of Regional Identity*, Bagan Publications, New Delhi.

Athukorala, Prema-Chandra, (1998), *Trade policy Issues in Asian Development,* London: Routeledge,

Battacharya,B.& S.Mukhopadhyay, (1996) *Duty Free Access to India with in SAPTA Frame Work,*: Indian Institute of Foreign Trade, New Delhi.

Bhagwati,Jagdish, (1991), *The World Trading System at Risk* ,Princeton University Press, New Jercy.

Bhagwati, Jagdish, (1993) *India in Transition: Freeing the Economy,* Clarendon Press, Oxford.

Bhagwati, Jagdish.,(1999), *A Stream of Windows,* Oxford University Press, New Delhi.

Bhargava, K.K, I.N Mukherjee,. & et al,(1994), *South Asia: Towards Dynamism and Co-operation* ,Popular Prakashan, Bombay.

Bhargava K.K et. al,(1995) *Shaping South Asian Future: Role of Regional Cooperative,* CGSSAO / FES, Colombo.

Bhargava K.K et. al,(2001), *South Asia 2010, Challenges and Opportunities,* Konark Publications, New Delhi.

Blarel Blenoit, Pursell Garry and Albert Valdes, (eds).,(1999) *Implications of the Uruguay Round Agreement for South Asia: The Case Study of Agriculture,* The World Bank, Washington DC.

Brun- Despange, C, (1998), *Central Asian Economies in Transition: A Comparative Review of Economic Reforms in Uzbekistan,* French Institute of Central Asian Studies, Tokyo, Japan.

Chen, B., (ed.), (1997), *International Trade and Finance: New Frontiers for Research Essays,* Cambridge University Press, New York.

Ferdinand, Peter (1994) *The New Central Asia and its Neighbors,* Royal Institute of International Affairs, London.

Gidadhubli,R.G.,(ed), (1987), *Socio-economic transformation of Soviet Central Asia,* Patriot publishers, New Delhi.

Gonsalves, E.and Jetley, N., (eds), (1999), *The Dynamics of South Asia: Regional Cooperation and SAARC,* Sage Publications, New Delhi.

John Baylis and Steve Smith (2006), *The Globalisation of The World Politics,Oxford* University Press; New Delhi.

Kanai, M., Titapieatanakum,B. & Stolz, D.(2000), *Effects of Trade Liberalization onAgriculture in Asia,* CGPRT, Indonesia.

Kesar, Michael and Santosh Mehrotra.(1992), *The Central Asian Economies after Independence,*Royal Institute of International Affairs, London.

Lawerance,R.,(1996), *Regionalism,Multilaterism and Deep Integration,*Washington: Booking Institution,1996.

Linn, J.F.(2004), *Economic (DIS) Integration Matters: The Soviet Collapse Revisited* Brooking Institutions, Washington DC.

Lubin, Nancy, (1995) *Central Asian Take Stock:Reforms, Coruuption and Identety,* National Council for Soviet and East European Research, Washington DC.

Mandelbaum, Michael,(2000) *Central Asia and the World: Kazakhstan, Uzbekistan, Tajikstan, Kyrgyzstan and Turkmenistan* Council on Foreign Relations Press, New York.

Meade, J.E, (1995), *The Theory of Customs Unions,* Amsterdam, North Holland.

Mirosolav, N.Jovanovic, (2007), *The Economics of International Integration,*UN Economic Commission for Europe, Switzerland.

Mogilavisky, R.(2004) *Role of Multilateral and Regional Trade Dicipline: KyrgyzExperience,* Center For Social Sciences, Warsaw.

Nepal Rashtra Bank, (2005), *Economic Integration in South Asia,* Nepal Rashtra Bank, Kathmandu.

Olcott, Martha, B, (1995) *Central Asia New States: Independence, Foreign Policy, and Regional Security,* United States Institutes of Peace process, Washington DC.

Organization for Economic Cooperation and Development (OECD), (1995), *Regional Integration and the Multilateral Trading System: Synergy and Divergence*, OECD, Paris.

Panagariya.A and J. de Melo (eds.), (1993). *New Dimensions in Regional Integration*, World Bank, Washington DC.

Pomfret, Richard, (1995), *The Economies of Central Asia,* Princeton University Press, Princeton NJ.

Pomfret, Richard, (1996a), *Asian Economies in Transition: Reforming Centrally Planned Economies*, Clarendon Press, UK..

Pomfret, Richard, (1999), *Central Asia Turns South? Trade Relation in Transition,* The Brooking Institution, Washington DC.

Pomfret, Richard,(1997), *The Economics of Regional Trading Arrangements,* Clarendon Press, Oxford.

Pomfret, Richard, (2003), *An Assessment of Regional Organization in Central Asia,* Asian Development Bank, Manila.

Rostai, D.(1998) *Transition Countries in the First Qouter 1998: Widening Gap between fast and slow reformers,* The Vienna Institute for Comparative Economic Studies, Vienna.

Rumer Boris (ed.),(2000), *Central Asiaand the New Global Economy*, M.E. Sharpe, New York.

Rumer Boris and Stanislav Zhukov, (2003), *Central Asia: The Challenges of independence*, Aakar Books, New Delhi.

Rumer Boris (ed.) 2003. *Central Asia in Transition: Dilemmas of Political and Economic Development* Aakar Books, New Delhi.

Salvatore, Dominick, (2001), *International Economics*, John Wiley & Sons, New York.

Sampson, G.& Woolcock, S. (2003), *Regionalism, Multilateralism and Economic Integration,* United Nation University Press, Tokyo.

Schiff, M.& A. Winters, (2003), *Regional Integration and Developments,* Oxford University Press, Washington D.C.

Scollay, R.& J.P. Gilbert, (2001), *New Regional Trading Arrangements in Asia Pacific,* Institute for International Economics, Washington DC.

Schiff, Maurice, and Alan Winters, (2003), *Regional Economic Integration and Development* World Bank and Oxford University Press, Washington DC.

Sharp, M. Ansel, Charles, A. Register & Paul W. Grimes, (2002), *Economic of Social Issues,* McGraw- Hill Irwin, New York.

Spoor, Max, (1993) *Transition to Market Economies in Former Soviet Central Asia: Dependency, Cotton, and Water,* Institute of Social Studies, The Hague.

Shand, Ric. (ed). (1999), *Economic Liberalization in South Asia,* Macmillan, New Delhi.

Srinivasan, T.N. (2002), *Trade, Finance and Investment in South Asia,* Social Science Press, New Delhi.

Tran Van Hoa, Charles Harvie, ed. (2007) *Regional Trade Agreements in Asia,* University of Wollongong, Australia.

Viner. J (1950)., *The Custom Union Issue*, Carnegie Endowment press, New York.

Waqif A. Arif, (ed). (1987), *South Asian Co-operation in Industry, Energy and Technology,* Sage Publications, New Delhi.

Warikoo,K,(ed),(1995), *Central Asia, Emerging New Order*, Har-Anand Publication, New Delhi.

Articles

Agarwal, Manmohan (2004), "Regional trading Arrangements in the Era of Globalisation: An Indian Perspective" in *International Studies*, 41(4): pp. 411-425.

Baier, S. L., and Bergstrand, J.H., (2001) "International Trade in Services, Free Trade Agreements, and the WTO", in R. M. Stern (ed.), *Services in the International Economy*, Michigan. University of Michigan Press.

Bandara, J.S.,& Smith, C. (2002), "Trade Policy Reforms in South Asia and Australia- South Asia Trade: Intensities and Complementries", in *South Asia Economic Journal* 3 (2): 177-199.

Baldwin, R. E. and A. J. Venables, (1995) "Regional Economic Integration", in, G. M. Grossman and K. Rogoff (eds), in *Handbook of International Economics,* Vol. 3, North-Holland: Amsterdam.

Baldwin, R.E., (1997) "The Causes of Regionalism", in *The World Economy*, Vol. 20, No.7, pp. 865-888.

Bergsten, C., (1997) "Open Regionalism", *The World Economy*, Vol. 20, No. 5, p. 545.

Bhagwati, Jagdish., "Regionalism versus Multilateralism", in *The World Economy*, Vol. 15, No. 5, 1992. pp. 535-555.

Bhagwati, Jagdish.(1993) "Regionalism and Multilateralism: An Overview", in A. Panagariya and J. de Melo (eds.), *New Dimensions in Regional Integration*, Washington D.C: World Bank.

Bhagwati, Panagriya, (1996), "Preferential Trade Areas and Multilateralism: Strangers, Freiends or Foes?" in *The Economics of Preferential Trade Agreements*, ed., AEI Press, Washington DC (2001).

Bhattacharya, S.K., (2001) "Regional-Trading Arrangements among SAARC Countries: Do They Increase India's Imports? in *South Asia Economic Journal,* Vol. 2, No. 2, pp. 281-312.

Brown, D.K., A. V. Deardorff and R. M. Stern (1992) "A North American Free Trade Agreement: Analytical Issues and Computational Assessment", in *The World Economy*, Vol. 15, 1992. pp. 11-29.

Brown, D. K., A. V. Deardorff and R. M. Stern (2003), "Multilateral, Regional and Bilateral Trade: Policy Options for the United States and Japan", in *The World Economy* ,Vol. 26, pp. 803-828.

Dharamasani, M.D., (2002) "Trade Liberalization Among SAARC Countries" in *South AsiaPolitics,* October. pp. 23-25.

Dieter, Heribert (1996) "Regional Integration in Central Asia: Current Economic Position and Prospects" in *Central Asian Survey,* Vol. 15 No. 3-4, pp. 369-386.

Estevadeordal, A., (2002) "Traditional Market Access Issues in RTAs: An Unfinished Agenda in the Americas?", paper presented to the WTO Seminar on Regionalism and the WTO, Geneva, http://www.wto.org.

Ethier, W., (2002) "The New Regionalism", in *The Economic Journa*l, Vol. 108, pp. 1149-1161.

Fernandez, R.&J.Portes (1998) "Return to Regionalism: An analysis of Non Traditional Gains From The Regional Trade Agreement", in *The World Bank Economic Review,* Vol. 12, No.2, pp. 197-220.

Frankel, J., E. Stein and S. Wei. (1995) "Trading Blocs and the Americas: The Natural, the Unnatural and the Supernatural", *Journal of Development Economics*, Vol. 47, pp. 61-96.

Garnaut, R., (1994) "Open Regionalism: Its Analitic Basis and Relevance to the International system"*Journal of Asian Economics*, Vol. 5, No. 2, pp. 273-90.

Grinols, E., (1981) "An Extension of the Kemp-Wan Theorem on the Formation of Customs Unions", *Journal of International Economics,* Vol. 11, pp. 259-266.

Gurgen, Emine, et.al., (1999) "Economic Reforms in Kazakhstan; Kyrgyz Republic, Tajiksitan, Turkmenistan and Uzbekistan", *IMF Occasional Paper, 183*, Washington D.C., IMF.

Hossain, M. Manhir " South Asian Economies in the Global Trading System" in http: // dsnet. anu. edu. au/ publications/online.

Kohlar. Horst, "Opportunities and Challenges for Central Asia" speech at the conference for the tenth Anniversary of the introduction the Tenge, Almaty, on 14th Nov. 2003.

Kohlar. Horst, "Strengthening Growth Through Regional and Global Economic Co-operation" speech on 4th September 2003.

Krugman, P. (1993), "Regionalism, Multilateralism and deep integration" in J De Melo and A panagriya(eds), in *New Dimensions in Regional Integration,*Cambridge University press, Cambridge. pp. 58-79.

Kumar Nagesh, (2002) "Towards an Asian Economic Community: The Relevance of India" RIS-DP # 34/in www.ris.org.in.

Islamove Bakhtior, (1999) "Central Asian States: on the way from Autarchic Dependence to Regional and Global Interdependence", in *Hitotsubashi Journal of Economics,* Vol. 40, pp.75-96.

Johnson. H. G., (1960) "The Economic Theory of Customs Unions", in *Pakistan Economic Review*, Vol. 10, pp. 14-30.

Julie Mckay, at all.ed., (2005) *Regional Economic Integration in the global Framework,* G-20 Workshop, 23-24 September, 2004, Germany : European central Bank.

Kalegama, Saman, (2002) "A Need for a New Direction for SAARC : An Economic Perspective" in *South Asian Survey*, Vol. 9, No. 2, pp. 171-185.

Kemp, M. C. and H. Y. Wan, (1976) "An Elementary Proposition Concerning the Formation of Customs Unions", *Journal of International Economics,* 6, February, pp. 95-98.

Kishore Kumar Guru -Gharana,(2003) " Macro economic modeling of South Asian Economies with Intra-SAARC Trade Link" A report submitted to South Asian Network of Economic institutes.

Kolodoko, Grzegorz (1999), "Ten Years of Post-Socialist Transition: The Lessons for Policy Reforms" in *Policy Research Working Paper* No. 2095, The World Bank, Washington DC.

Kornai, Janos, (1994), "Transformation Recession: The Main Causes" in *Journal of Comparative Economics,* Vol. 19, No.1, pp. 33-63.

Kornai Janos, (2001) "Ten Years After the Road to a Free Economy: The Authors Self-Evaluation", *Annual World Bank Conference on Development Economics 2000,* World Bank, pp. 53-54.

Krishna, P. (1998) "Regionalism and Multilateralism a Political Economy Approach" in *Quarterly Journal of Economics,* February, pp. 227-51.

Krueger, A. (1995), "Free Trade Agreements versus Customs Unions", NBER WorkingPaper no. 5084, Cambridge, Mass.

Lawrence, R.Z. "Regionalism, Multilateralism and Deeper Integration: Changing Paradigms for Developing Countries" in *Trade Rules in the Making* in eds,. M. Rodríguez

Levy, P. I., (1994) "A Political-Economic Analysis of Free Trade Agreements." in *American Economic Review* Vol. 87, pp. 506-19.

Lloyd, P. J. and A. G. Schweinberger, (1998) "Trade Expenditure Functions and the Gains from Trade", in *Journal of International Economics*, Vol. 24, pp. 275-97.

Loyed, P.J., (2002) "New Bilateralism in the Asia Pecific", in *The World Economy* Vol. 25, pp. 1279-1296.

Lloyd, P. J. and D. MacLaren, (2002) "Measures of Trade Openness Using CGE analysis", in *Journal of Policy Modeling*, Vol. 24, pp. 67-81.

Lloyd, P.J.& Donald, " The Case for Free Trade and Role of RTAS" Paper presented in seminar on regionalism and the WTO, Geneva, 14, Nov. 2003.

Lipsey, R. G. and K. Lancaster (1957) "The General Theory of the Second Best", in *Review of Economic Studies*, pp. 11-32.

Lumenga Neso, Olivier, Marcelo Olarreaga and Maurice Schiff, ((2001) "On Indirect Trade-Related Research and Development Spillovers, " in *Policy Research Working Paper* no. 2580. Washington DC: The World Bank.

Martyn, Tim, "A complete Guide of Regional Trade Agreements of the Asia-Pacific" in www.asia.com and www.apecsec.org.

Mattoo, A. & Carsten Fink, (2002) "Regional Agreements and Trade in Services: Policy Issues" in *World Bank Policy Research Working Papers* no. 2852.

Matveeva Anna, (1999) "Democratization, Legitimacy and Political Change in Central Asia", in *International Affairs,* Vol. 75, No. 1, pp. 23-44.

Max, Sapoor, "Central Asian Transition: Dual Economies and Growth Inequality", www. Iss.nl/cest rad.

Mendoza, B. Kotschwar and P. Low, Washington D.C: Brookings Institution and Organization of American States, 1999.

Michely, M, (1965) "On Customs Unions and Gains from Trade", in *Economic Journal*, Vol. 75, pp. 577-583.

Michlopous Constastine (1999), "The integration of transition economies in the World Trading System", world Bank working paper 2182, The World Bank, Washington DC.

Mukherjee, I.N., (2004) "Towards a Free Trade Area in South Asia" Charting a Feasible Course for Trade Liberalisation with reference to India" RIS-DP # 86/ in www.ris.org.in.

Murrel, P. (1992) "Evolutionary and Radical Approaches to Economic Reform", *Economic of Planning,* 25, p. 81.

NEA- Transport Research and Training, (2003a) *Central Asia Trade and Transport Facilitation* Kazakhstan National Report.

NEA- (2003b,) *Central Asia Trade and Transport Facilitation Audit* Kyrgyzstan National Report.

NEA- (2003c,) *Central Asia Trade and Transport Facilitation Audit* Uzbekistan National Report.

Panagariya, A.(1999) "The Regionalism Debate: An Overview", in *The World Economy*, Vol. 22, pp. 477-511.

Panagariya, A., (2000) "Preferential Trade Liberalization: The Traditional Theory and New Developments", in *Journal of Economic Literature,* Vol.38, No.2, pp. 287-331.

Panagariya, A. and P. Krishna, (2002) "On Necessarily Welfare-enhancing Free Trade Areas", in *Journal of International Economics*, Vol.57, pp.353-67.

Panagariya, A., (1997) "The Meade Model of Preferential Trading: History, Analytics and Policy Implications", in B. Chen(ed.), *International Trade and Finance: New Frontiers for Research, Essays,* Cambridge University Press, New York.

Panchamukhi, V.R.& Das Ram Upendra, (2001) "Economic Reforms, Regional Integration and Labor Markets in South Asian Region", in *South Asia Economic Journal*, Vol. 2, No. 1, pp. 3-30.

Pomfret, Richard, "Regionalism in Asia and its Impacts on Sino-European Trade" in Rogar Strange, Jim Slater and Liminwang, eds, *Trade and Investment in China: The European Perspective,* London: Routledge, 1998.

Poon, J., (1995), "Global Regionalization Tendencies: spatial structure and Linkages" South East Asian Studies working paper, National University of Singapore, Singapore., pp. 5-7.

Sachdeva, (2006), "India's attitude towards China's growing influence in Central Asia", in *China and Eurasian Forum quartly* Vol. 4, No.3, p. 23-34.

Sapir, A., (2000) "GATS 1994-2000", in *Journal of World Trade,* Vol. 33, pp. 51-66.

Srinivasan, T., (1997) "The common External Tariff of a Customs Union: Alternative Approaches" *Japan and World Economy,* Vol. 9, pp. 447-465.

Stiglitz, E. Joesph, (2000) "Wither Reform? Ten Years of the Transitioin", *Annual World Bank Conference on Development Economics 1999*, World Bank.

Sugisaki Shigemitsu, "Central Asia Regional Economic Co-operation" speech at Tashkent, Uzbekistan on 13th Nov. 2003.

Tokarick, Stephen, (2006) "Does Import Protection Discourage Exports?" IMF Working Paper 06/20, Washington DC: International Monetary Fund.

UNDP, (2005) "Bringing Down Barriers: Regional Cooperation for Human Development and Human Security" in *Central Asian Human Development Report*, Regional bureau for Europe and the CIS, Slovak Republic.

Vamvakidis, Athanasios, (1999) "Regional Trade Agreements or Broad Liberalization" which Path Leads to Faster Growth? In *IMF staff papers*, Vol. 46, No. 1, in www.imf.org.

Weerakoon, D., (1999) "SAPTA/SAFTA: Implications for Sri Lanka" in *Upanath: Journal of the Sri Lanka Association of Economists,* Vol. 9, no. 1 & 2, pp.63-98.

—————, (2001) "Indo Sri Lanka Free Trade Agreement": How Free is it?, in *Economic and Political Weekly*, Vol. 34, No. 8, pp.627-629.

Weerakoon, D.& Wijayasiri, (2002) "Regionalism In South Asia: The Relevance of SAPTA for Sri Lanka", in *South Asia Economic Journal,* Vol. 3, No. 1, pp. 95-107.

Winters, L.A., (1996) "Regionalism versus Multilateralism", *World Bank Policy Research Working Paper*, no. 1687, Washington DC :World Bank.

World Bank,(1996) "Understanding Transition" in *World Development Report 1996*, Washington DC World Bank.

International Sources

S K Mohanty, Regional Trade liberalisation under SAPTA and India's Trade linkages with South Asia, see in http://www.ris.org.in/dp48_pap.pdf

"SAARC nations to work towards creating South Asian Eco Union", *Indiaexpress.com*, 6 January 2004, see in http://www.indiaexpress.com/news/business/20040106-0.html

Asimina Caminis, (2006) Integrating poor countries into the world trading system, economic issues no.37, www.imf.org/pub.

Director-General Pascal Lamy, welcomes WTO agreement on regional trade agreements at www.wto.org/english/traptop_e/region_e/region_ehtm., visited on 10th July 2

(USSFTA, the ASEAN FTA (AFTA), 2 the Republic of Korea-Chile FTA, the JSEPA, the ASEAN- 1 Information taken from the WTO web site as of October 12, 2004. http://www.wto.org/english/tratop_e/region_e/region_e.htm, and from WTO (2003a).

M.E. Tusneem, A speech by Director General of ADB's East and Central Asia Department at www.adb.org/.

Asad Aslam and Arup Banerji, "Uzbekistan and Kazakhstan: A Tale of Two Transition Path". See on www.imf.org.

Ellman, M. "The Socialistic Costs and Consequences of the TransformationProcess", 2000, see on the website ww.unese.org.

Max, Sapoor, (2000) "Central Asian Transition: Dual Economies and Growth and equality", see on website, www Iss.nl/cest rad.

Index

F

J

K

L

M

O

P

R